The Audubon
Society
Field Guide
to the
Natural Places
of the
Northeast:
Inland

Other titles in this series include:

**The Audubon Society
Field Guide
to the Natural Places
of the Mid-Atlantic States:
Coastal**

**The Audubon Society
Field Guide
to the Natural Places
of the Mid-Atlantic States:
Inland**

**The Audubon Society
Field Guide
to the Natural Places
of the Northeast: Coastal**

The Audubon Society Field Guide to the Natural Places of the Northeast: Inland

Stephen Kulik
Pete Salmansohn
Matthew Schmidt
Heidi Welch

A Hilltown Book
Pantheon Books, New York

Staff for this volume

Editor:	Caroline Sutton
Reporters:	Lisa Crosby
	Diane DeLuca
	Stephen Kulik
	Pete Salmansohn
	Matthew Schmidt
	Jerry Stelmok
	Wendy Tilghman
	Susan R. Warner
	Heidi Welch
	Ronald B. Woodland
Cartography:	Rebecca Lazear Okrent
	Gene Gort
Essays:	Edward Ricciuti
Consultants:	Edward Ricciuti
	Tudor Richards

Copyright © 1984 by The Hilltown Press, Inc.

All rights reserved under International and Pan-American Copyright Conventions. Published in the United States by Pantheon Books, a division of Random House, Inc., New York, and simultaneously in Canada by Random House of Canada Limited, Toronto.

Library of Congress Cataloging in Publication Data

Main entry under title:
The Audubon Society field guide to the natural places of the Northeast.

    Bibliography: v. 1, p.
    Includes index.
    Contents: Coastal—Inland.
    1. Natural areas—Northeastern States—Guide-books.
I. Kulik, Stephen. II. National Audubon Society.
QH76.5.N96A93 1984 917.4′0443 83-23629
ISBN 0-394-72281-7 (v. 1)
ISBN 0-394-72282-5 (v. 2)

Text design: Clint Anglin

Manufactured in the United States of America
First Edition

The National Audubon Society

For more than three-quarters of a century, the National Audubon Society has provided leadership in scientific research, conservation education, and citizen-action programs to save birds and other wildlife and the habitat necessary for their survival.

To accomplish these goals, the society has formally adopted the Audubon Cause: TO CARRY OUT RESEARCH, EDUCATION, AND ACTION TO CONSERVE WILD BIRDS AND OTHER ANIMALS, TREES AND OTHER PLANTS, SOIL, AIR, AND WATER, AND ALSO TO PROMOTE A BETTER UNDERSTANDING OF THE INTERDEPENDENCE OF THESE NATURAL RESOURCES. To carry out the Audubon Cause, the society's programs are structured around five specific missions that encompass the tremendous scope of the organization:

—Conserve native plants and animals and their habitats
—Further the wise use of land and water
—Promote rational strategies for energy development and use
—Protect life from pollution, radiation, and toxic substances
—Seek solutions for global problems involving the interaction of population, resources, the environment, and sustainable development.

Our underlying belief is that all forms of life are interdependent and that the diversity of nature is essential to both our economic and our environmental well-being.

Audubon, through its nationwide system of sanctuaries, protects more than 250,000 acres of essential habitat and unique natural areas for birds and other wild animals and rare plant life. The sanctuaries range in size from 9 acres around Theodore Roosevelt's grave in New York State to 26,000 acres of coastal marsh in Louisiana. Most of the sanctuaries are staffed by resident wardens who also patrol adjacent natural areas not owned by Audubon.

Audubon's 500,000 members provide the underpinning for all the society's programs and activities. Two-thirds of our members also belong to local Audubon chapters, now numbering more than 480, which serve in their communities as focal points for conservation, nature education, and citizen action on environmental issues.

We also maintain ten regional offices, each staffed by two or more full-time professional conservationists who advance Audubon programs throughout the fifty states.

Our staff conducts wildlife research to aid such endangered species as the bald eagle, whooping crane, eastern timber wolf, and bog turtle and to provide knowledge of the ecologically sound management of our sanctuaries. The society also publishes the award-winning *Audubon* magazine and *American Birds* magazine.

For further information about the society, write or call:

National Audubon Society
950 Third Avenue
New York, N.Y. 10022
(212) 832-3200

Contents

**The Taconics, the Berkshires,
and the Green Mountains: Inland Empire   1**

The Connecticut River Valley:
Land of Dinosaurs   129

The White Mountains, Monadnocks, and Eastern Connecticut Highlands: Above the Timberline   179

Interior Maine: Northern Wilderness   277

Baxter State Park   350

Acknowledgments

A project as ambitious and as comprehensive as these *Audubon Society Field Guides to the Natural Places of the Northeast* has required the expertise and assistance of dozens of people throughout New York and New England. Foremost thanks must go to Dan Okrent, who conceived and developed the idea for this series, and to the National Audubon Society for recognizing the need for the series and sponsoring its publication.

I cannot say enough about the dedication, enthusiasm, and knowledge that the contributors to the Northeast volumes brought to their work. Pete Salmansohn, Matt Schmidt, and Heidi Welch spent many months traveling through the Northeast, hiking, researching, and writing major portions of the books. Significant contributions were also made by Lisa Crosby, Diane DeLuca, Gerry Stelmak, Wendy Tilghman, Susan Warner, and Ronald Woodland. I am very grateful to them all.

Many naturalists, both amateur and professional, served as advisors at various stages of this project. Foremost among them is Ed Ricciuti of Connecticut, who wrote the four regional essays in each volume. Tudor Richards, of the Audubon Society of New Hampshire, was a great help in the latter stages of the research. Their thorough knowledge of natural history served not only as a valuable resource but as an inspiration.

Many other individuals and organizations provided help in identifying and evaluating natural areas for inclusion, providing guided tours and special knowledge of specific sites, reviewing manuscripts, and checking site descriptions for accuracy. I want to thank all of the following people: Gary Van Wart, Anthony Boutard, Steven Bassett, Philip Truesdell, Doug Cross, and James Dodge of the Trustees of Reservations in Massachusetts, a private, nonprofit organization that serves as a national model for land conservation efforts; Walter Ellison and Nancy Martin of the Vermont Institute of Natural Science; Richard Enser of the Rhode Island Natural Heritage Program; Charles Johnson, Vermont State Naturalist; Jan McLure of the Society for the Protection of New Hampshire Forests; Erik Kiviat of the Hudsonia Institute; Bob Moeller; Marshall and Jean Case of the Northeast Audubon Center; James Gibb, Clifford Emanuelson, Tom Carrolan, and Whitney Beals of The Nature Conservancy; Art and Sue Gingert; Dave Rosgen; Bill Kolodnicki; Larry Penny; Les Mehroff; Scott Sutcliffe; Joanne Chandler; Susan Cooley; Gordon Loery; Allison Beall; Elsa Bumstead; Thelma Haight; Steve Maslansky; Phil Schaeffer; Ted Gilman; Rick Ryder; Margo Myles; Bill Paterson; Allan Lindberg; Lois Lindberg; Carol Ryder; Paul Stoutenburgh; Steve Englebright; Gil Bergen; Russell Hoeflich; Schuyler Horton; Frank Burzynski; Roger Spaulding; Terry Schreiner; Jim Rod; Dave Beglin; Bob Devine; Ann Pesiri; Nick Shoumatoff; Michael Pochan; Bernard Kane; Dean Bouton; Bob Brandt; Ted Fink; Tom French; Sid Quarrier; Ed Kirby; Hobson Calhoun; Don Ritter; Lois Kelley; Robert Craig; Dianne Mayerfield; Michael Bell; Carl Helms; Mary Lamont; Marty Strong; Louise Harrison; Herb Mills; Ed Zero; Ed Rufleth; Steve Resler; Bill Norton; Ed Reilly; Kate Dunham; Fred Johnson; Lauren Brown; Chip David; Ron Rosza; Heinz Meng; Hans Weber; Jim Stapleton; Rob Smith; Neil Jorgensen; Lincoln Page; Margaret Watkins; Fred Steele; Sarah Fried; Dr. Peter Rosen; Dr. Hubert Vogelmann; Rod MacDonald; Jonathan Tucker; and Steve Johnson.

In a state as large and diverse as Maine, whose natural areas constitute a large portion of these volumes, special thanks are due from Heidi Welch to a number of people: Joyce Harms, for making the original connection; Hank Tyler of the Maine Critical Areas Project for helping to ferret out information; and Bill Drury of the College of the Atlantic for being there to answer questions. The following people were wonderfully helpful in many ways: Doug Miller of Moosehorn National Wildlife Refuge; Jean Hockwater Gordon; Gerald Merry of Baxter State Park; Karen Gustafson of the Maine Chapter of The Nature Conservancy; Pam Truesdale of Wolf Neck Woods State Park; Leslie Van Cott of Maine Audubon; Pat Welch for being the first editor and a captive audience; Diana Cohen for invaluable advice and encouragement; Than James for a typewriter; and the Maine Geologic Survey for providing maps. In addition, many thanks are due to: Jerry Bley of the Main Natural Resources Council; Lois

Winter and Bob Rothe of Acadia National Park; Ron Davis and Sally Stockwell of the University of Maine; Nora Davis; Steve Kress of the Audubon Ecology Camp in Maine; Craig Greene and Janet Andrews of the College of the Atlantic; and Howard Richard, Bill Towsend, and Paul Favour.

My thanks and appreciation goes out to the editors and staff at Pantheon Books, and especially to David Frederickson for his pains-taking work with the directions for the entries. I am grateful to Becky Okrent and Gene Gort for their practical and artistic maps, which add so much to the site descriptions.

In a project such as this, there is usually one person without whom it just would not have happened, and these guidebooks are no exception. Caroline Sutton served in the invaluable role of editor, liaison, and coach throughout the two-year process of producing these volumes. Her sensitive, direct, and incisive editing improved both the content and style of the entries, and I believe that all of us are better writers today for having worked with her. I cannot thank her enough.

Finally, I want to thank my wife, Suzanne, and my son, Sam, who was born in the middle of this project, for their patience and support during the long months spent traveling and writing. The books are for them, and I now look forward to revisiting many of these natural places of the Northeast together.

—Stephen Kulik
Worthington, Massachusetts
January 1984

How to Use
This Book

The aim of the Audubon Society Field Guides is to enable
the reader to explore and enjoy the natural history and
ecology of selected natural areas in the United States.
Unlike any other guide to the outdoors, this series describes the interaction of plants, animals, topography, and
climate so that the hiker, birder, or amateur naturalist
will be able to understand and more fully appreciate what
he sees. Today almost all the sites presented in these
guides, whether in public or private ownership, are maintained for public education and enrichment. All offer geological, botanical, or biological points of interest, as well
as the beauty, excitement, and tremendous variety of the
outdoors.

This guide is one of an initial set also including a
Northeast coastal volume, a Mid-Atlantic inland volume,
and a Mid-Atlantic coastal volume. The areas covered in
each guide have been determined, as often as possible,
according to geological rather than governmental boundaries. The separation of coastal and inland volumes in the
Mid-Atlantic series, for example, is clearly indicated by
the *fall line*. This roughly north–south demarcation, running from New York City into Georgia, occurs where the
flat Coastal Plain rises to meet the rolling hills of the
Piedmont. In the Northeast, there is no such distinct dividing line between coast and interior, but rather a gradual blending of one into the other. Here, the coastal region has been determined by both ecological and social
factors, a region where the landscape and outlook of the
people reflect the proximity of the sea.

Each guide contains descriptions of over a hundred natural areas, and each site description pinpoints what is most significant, intriguing, or unusual about that area. More important, it explains *how* the site came to look as it does and *why* certain species of vegetation and wildlife can be found there. Thus, while one narrative unravels the geological history of a region as it is revealed in the rock outcrops along a trail, another centers on a rare and ancient stand of Atlantic white-cedar, and still another highlights the waterfowl that gather in an area, explaining their feeding, breeding, and migratory habits. Indeed, if the diverse entries about a particular area such as Baxter State Park are read as a group, the visitor can reach a fuller, more in-depth understanding of both the existing biotic climate and the workings of human and natural history. Furthermore, the sites have been organized by geological and ecological regions, each prefaced by an introductory essay providing a general look at the geology, vegetation, and wildlife in that region and the human influence on it.

The interior of the Northeast readily lends itself to being divided into physiographic sections. Splitting the middle of the region is the Connecticut River, with its valley that broadens increasingly toward the south. East of the river are the great White Mountains, which grade south into the highlands of eastern Connecticut and Massachusetts. To the north and east of the White Mountains lies interior Maine, a world unto itself. West of the river lies another mountain complex, the Green Mountains of Vermont, the Berkshires of western Massachusetts and northwestern Connecticut, and the Taconic Mountains that range the border with New York State.

All sites in this guide are numbered, and a system of cross-referencing throughout enables the reader to locate the most thorough discussion of a particular species or geological formation. For example, ospreys may be mentioned briefly in one description, but there will also be a reference to a fuller discussion elsewhere in the book. Each site opens with precise directions to the area and ends with a section called "Remarks." Here is included such practical information as the length and difficulty of a recommended walk; what equipment to bring; possible activities such as swimming, fishing, and skiing; the availability of boat rentals; nearby places to camp; and best times of the year to visit.

Most site descriptions include a map, keyed by letter to the narrative, which leads the visitor along a suggested walk or boat trip. A sample map follows, along with a key to the various symbols that appear throughout the book.

The back of each guide includes a brief glossary, a bibliography of works on related subjects, and an extensive index. The Index is

Wooded area

Paved road

Dirt road

Brook or stream

Secondary trail

Tidal flat

Shore line

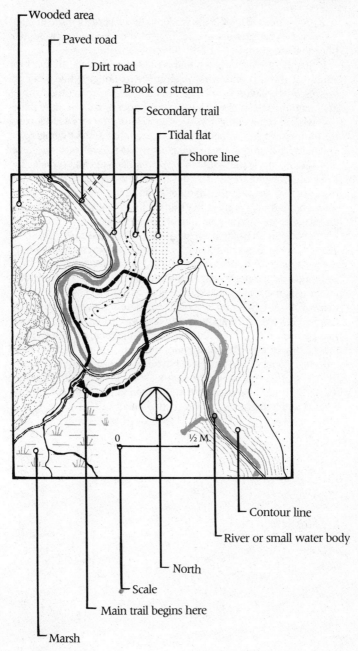

Contour line

River or small water body

North

Scale

Main trail begins here

Marsh

cross-referenced to enable the reader to find a particular site of interest, whether because of a species or geological formation or because of certain sports and other activities.

It may be useful to read about a site before visiting, to learn the length of the trip and what equipment to bring. While principal species of vegetation or wildlife are identified in the entries, others are mentioned in passing. The amateur birder or botanist may therefore wish to bring along a field guide to birds, trees, or wildflowers. Recommended supplementary guides are listed in the Bibliography.

Finally, it is important to remember that natural sites are never unchanging places, but rather always in flux. Wind and wave action alter the profile of the coast; bogs fill in with vegetation; some animals learn to adapt to the influx of civilization, while others vanish. Many natural areas reflect the human impact of the past two centuries, be it the draining of marshes or the reseeding of forests. No such change is an isolated event. As an old field returns to forest, for example, pioneer seedlings give way to mature forest, and the birds of prey that once hunted the open field are replaced by their forest counterparts. Similarly, our knowledge about such phenomena is interdisciplinary, and forever changing as further observations are made and past theories uprooted. In these volumes we have attempted to present the most widely accepted geological and ecological theories. We do not presume to be comprehensive, nor to judge the validity of other recent theories and conclusions. Our aim is to introduce some of the processes botanists, biologists, and geologists believe to be at work in the natural world, thereby offering the reader a deeper appreciation and understanding of the complexity, beauty, and vulnerability of our natural areas.

The Taconics,
the Berkshires,
and the Green
Mountains:
Inland Empire

For all their vaunted greenery, the hilly northern fringes of Fairfield County, Conn., and adjacent Westchester County, N.Y., have increasingly become suburban reflections of New York City rather than "the country" still touted by the real estate agents. Highly developed as it is, the region still looks superficially rural—its shopping malls, corporate headquarters, and sprawling housing developments spread over a pleasantly uneven topography that here and there still has a touch of craggy wildness. These hills within the expanding boundaries of the megalopolis form the beginnings of a mountain realm that in its heartland, from western Massachusetts into northern Vermont, contains some of the most picturesque (and truly rural) countryside in New England.

The mountainous interior of western New England, from northwestern Connecticut to Vermont's border with Canada, contains two closely associated ranges, the Taconics and the Green Mountains, which in the south tail off into the Berkshire Hills. The Taconic Mountains span the border between New York on the one hand and Massachusetts and Vermont on the other, and wall the eastern banks of the Hudson River. Less than 20 miles to the east of the Taconics is the western flank of the Berkshires and, to the north, the Green Mountains, both of which in turn are bounded on the east by the Connecticut River country.

These western mountains and hills constitute a unique part of New England. Geologically they can claim links closer to the mountain chains farther south than, say, to

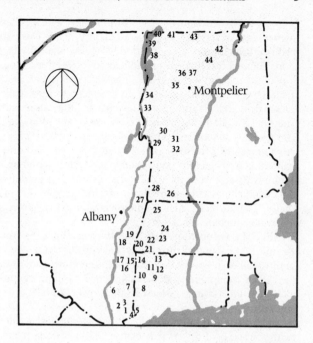

the nearby White Mountains. Unlike the disorganized jumble of the White Mountains, the Green Mountains and their associated ranges are organized in an orderly north–south fashion, like other Appalachian chains running through the Mid-Atlantic states and culminating in the Blue Ridge of Virginia and North Carolina. Their neat arrangement results from enormous folding of the earth's crust on a north–south axis about 450 million years ago.

There is for many visitors a strong feeling that the Green Mountain country and associated highlands are a land apart from the rest of New England. Perhaps the feeling stems from the fact that almost all the rest of New England is bound ultimately to the sea, while these mountains seem to look inland, to the west and south, for their influences. In this sense, the western mountains are the heart of New England's inland empire.

The tallest peaks of the inland empire belong to the Green Mountains, which surpass 4,000 feet in altitude at their highest, near Lincoln and Warren, Vt. The highest of the Berkshires are about half that, grading to rolling hills in Connecticut. The greatest of the Taconics are Big Equinox, near Manchester, Vt., at 3,186 feet, and Mount Greylock, a 3,491-foot mountain near Adams, Mass.

Some of the rock in the Green Mountains and the Berkshires, particularly, is very old, perhaps a billion years. It was part of the bedrock brought to the surface during folding and subsequent erosion. There is considerable scientific debate over the geological history of the rocks in western New England and adjacent areas of New York. One reason is that the record is difficult to read. Tumultuous events deep in the earth have vastly changed the nature of the rock. The gneiss underlying much of New York City, Westchester, and Fairfield County, for instance, was so stressed by heat, pressure, and other forces of a colossal nature that it flowed plastically before hardening to its present state, obliterating all fossils and obstructing attempts to determine its age. Be that as it may, the mountains of the inland empire contain myriad rocks, including masses of ancient shales, granite, slate, gneiss, limestone, and, where limestone has undergone metamorphosis, marble.

While the Green Mountains and the Berkshires, as well as the Taconics, are founded on ancient folds in the crust, their overall outlines differ in appearance. Except in the northernmost portions, the Green Mountains and Berkshires have a more gentle, rolling look than the Taconics, which even at lower altitudes seem rough and jagged.

Perhaps it is best to think of the Green Mountains and Berkshires as the remains of an ancient plateau, uplifted long after original folding, then gentled by erosion. Here and there, especially in the northern Green Mountains, rise higher peaks of granite shoved upward by primal vulcanism. For the most part, however, this great highland region has been rounded in outline by erosion. Throughout much of the area, the feeling of being "in the mountains" comes not at the top but while ascending or descending one of the valleys that lace the uplands, or the approaches from the east or west.

The Taconics, on the other hand, look every inch "mountainous." They are sharp and severe, cut with gorges and steep-sided valleys. It makes them seem larger than life. Under the surface, rocks are topsy-turvy, with older strata often resting upon younger.

Mostly shale, once formed below the sea, the Taconics owe their contorted outline to an event that occurred during the folding that formed the roots of all the western mountains. Great blocks of rock from the east, perhaps atop the Green Mountain folds, or even to the east of that, were thrust westward, riding over the rest of the landscape. Deformed, broken, and scattered about, these eastern rocks, now considerably worn, created the crest of the Taconics.

The monumental forces that made mountains move played havoc with the rock over which the Taconics-to-be rode. Much of the rock was limestone that was metamorphosed into marble—the marble that makes Vermont one of the world's major producers of this stone. It is largely found in a narrow strip of lowland between the Taconics and the Green Mountains.

To the north of the marble-producing region, which lies in central Vermont, the lowland broadens into the valley that cradles Lake Champlain. The site of a vast glacial lake at the end of the ice ages, and flooded temporarily by the sea pouring down from the Saint Lawrence valley after that, Champlain today is impressive enough to be known as the "sixth Great Lake." Only the five proper Great Lakes, in fact, are larger among the freshwater lakes of the continental United States.

Lake Champlain stretches north from Whitehall, N.Y., for 100 miles to become Quebec's Richelieu River. The deep-water channel down the middle of the lake—in places more than 400 feet deep—constitutes the boundary between Vermont and New York.

West of the lake, the Adirondack Mountains of New York State replace the Taconics, which peter out farther south. The Adirondacks and the Green Mountains together provide Champlain with a drainage of more than 8,000 square miles.

Northern hardwoods such as sugar maple, birch, and beech cover the entire inland empire, sometimes mixing liberally with spruce and balsam. Given the coolness of the fall weather in the region, these trees boast unusually striking fall colors, turning hillsides and mountain slopes into a dazzle of vivid reds, yellows, oranges, and a host of hues in between.

In the portion of the Berkshires that reaches into northwestern Connecticut, the northern hardwoods edge farther south than anywhere else in New England. Rising amidst the oak-hickory forest of the surrounding lowlands, the northern hardwoods at Campbell Falls State Park in Norfolk, Conn., are an outstanding example. The park has great stands of sugar maples, yellow birch, and beech, together with conifers, a mixture totally different from that growing in woodlands just a dozen or so miles south or east.

Immediately south of the Berkshires, the countryside remains thickly forested, with a different mix of trees, still fairly hilly. This region is called the Housatonic Highlands, after the river that cuts through them toward Long Island Sound. At the margins of Fairfield County the highlands begin to dwindle, and the land flattens toward the sea. Similarly, the Hudson Highlands stretch south of the Taconics, edging into the northern portions of Westchester County.

In northern Westchester and Fairfield, the highlands abut the limits of the greater New York City area, the antithesis of wilderness. Especially in the dusk, when they seem to loom lonelier and higher, they are reminders that not terribly far away wilderness—a gentle sort, but wilderness nonetheless—persists.

—Edward Ricciuti

1.

Mianus
River Gorge

Directions: Bedford, N.Y. From New York City, take the
Hutchinson River Parkway and Merritt Parkway to Exit
34, about 20 miles. Go north 7.5 miles on Route 104. Turn
west (left) on Miller's Mill Rd.; go 0.1 mile and over a bridge.
Turn left on Mianus Rd.; go 0.6 mile to a parking area on
the left.

Ownership: The Nature Conservancy.

This gorge was the first acquisition of The Nature Conservancy 30
years ago, and the first area recognized as a National Natural Landmark. It is undoubtedly one of the most significant and beautiful
natural areas in the Northeast, especially considering its proximity to
New York City. A virtual laboratory for students of natural history,
Mianus's 375 acres include over 100 varieties of trees and shrubs,
150 species of birds, and 250 varieties of plants and wildflowers. The
rugged topography and cool, moist conditions of the gorge have
created a microclimate that supports diverse vegetation. Its most
prominent botanical features are the clusters of wildflowers that
bloom from early spring to midsummer and the stand of huge, 350-
year-old hemlocks that grow on the ledge high above the river. The
deep ravine itself was carved by the Wisconsin glacier as it moved
over the area 10,000 to 15,000 years ago.

Mianus has 5 miles of well-marked trails that offer a choice of
several walks, varying in length and difficulty. There is one entrance
to the trails, which begins at the parking area, where trail maps are
available at the registration-information station. The flowers, shrubs,
and trees throughout the first part of the trail (**A**) are labeled for
identification, including the time of year they are in bloom. Lady's
slippers are common in this area, under a canopy of American hophornbeam trees. These are commonly known as blue-beech, although they are actually members of the birch, not beech, family.
The misnomer will probably be kept alive by usage, especially since
the tree is easily identified by its distinctive blue-gray bark. It is
usually found growing in areas of wet soil, and its buds are favored
by many types of birds, especially ruffed grouse. Saplings of

American chestnut attempt to grow despite blight infestation (see **#67**). Several of the thirty-eight varieties of ferns (see **#100**) in the gorge are found here: Christmas, bracken, and maidenhair ferns all grow within a short distance of each other. The presence of these ferns indicates an alkaline soil, probably due to the existence of limestone deposits in the bedrock, which leach into the soil in this wet area. Several American cedar trees grow along the trail, as well as the European buckthorn and the shrub dogwood, whose small white flowers appear in early summer. All of these plants and trees thrive in the moist, shaded conditions found on the west side of the gorge.

The trail continues through an old field in a middle stage of succession to woodland—now dominated by young hardwoods as older conifers die off. At **B** is an area rich in wildflowers. To the left are several summer-blooming varieties, including wood lily, aster, Canada lily, and saxifrage. On the right are patches of columbine and hepatica, which flower in the spring. Passing over a footbridge, the trail goes through a moist area along the bank of the stream, where many types of mosses and lichens grow on the rocks and trees. Reindeer lichen (see **#43**) is the most abundant among them (**C**). Walking among the ferns along the river, one can often see trout, particularly in late summer and early fall as they swim upstream to spawn. This broad, shallow area of the river is where animals such

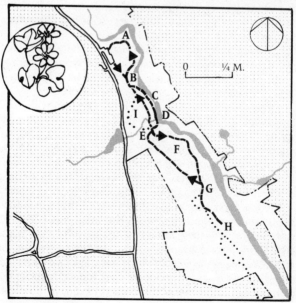

Inset: Hepatica

as deer and raccoon come to drink. The closed gentian, which blooms in late August, is found here.

At **D** the trail rises to a rocky cascade coming off the high western ridge. On the right side of the trail (**E**) is a large American chestnut tree, leaning upright, that was killed by the blight over 70 years ago. Since it did not rot on the ground, its wood is still solid, and it stands as a remarkable example of this once-common tree. The trail now enters the narrowest part of the river gorge, an area populated by the oldest and largest hemlocks. The river picks up speed as it flows past this glacial cut. The trail proceeds to climb steeply past a fallen hemlock that has been cut through; miterwort, a snowflake-like flower that blooms in May, is prevalent here. In the dense hemlock grove (**F**) the largest of these 100- to 400-foot-tall trees is over 325 years old; circumferences reach 12 feet. Because of their inaccessibility on the steep slope, these trees were left undisturbed when this area was cut. They have since been nurtured to these great sizes by the cool, moist climate and have been protected by the high ridges to the east and west. Because these trees so effectively block sunlight from the forest floor, there is no understory here, although mushrooms and fungi can be found in the shade. (For more on hemlocks, see **#23** and **#65**.)

The trail now passes through an example of succession (see **#67**) from a coniferous to a deciduous forest. As the hemlocks fall, the fast-growing black birch is taking over. Some red oaks are present here, including a very large specimen on the left. This community of hemlock, oak, beech, and black birch is an example of a climax-forest type usually found only farther north. The moist, cool microclimate of the gorge is responsible for its occurrence here. When the giant hemlocks eventually fall, the oak and black birch will quickly seed themselves, and a deciduous forest will develop.

As the trail turns uphill, the hillside is covered with a dense undergrowth of wild ginger and trillium, both of which bloom in the spring (**G**). Beech grows almost exclusively through here, with some unusually large specimens approximately 200 years old. The boulders scattered around are glacial erratics (see **#78**). Studies have shown that they are very similar in composition to rocks found in southeastern Canada and were probably carried here by the ice.

The trail forks here in two directions. To the right is Havemeyer Falls, 1 mile away, which is particularly impressive in the spring and early summer. To the left the trail descends to an old mica quarry (**H**). This is a good example of a diverse mineral deposit with pink and white quartz mixed with silvery mica and dark tourmaline. Here one sees how pockets of minerals were formed in the granite bedrock during the metamorphic process of heating and cooling, under great pressure, deep within the earth about 400 million years ago. Rock of this composition is known as pegmatite, and differs from granite primarily in the size of the individual crystallized grains of minerals. In granite the mineral grains are very small, usually only a fraction of an inch in diameter. In pegmatite, the individual minerals may occur in pockets up to several feet or more in diameter. Thus they are able to be mined commercially, as both mica and tourmaline were at this location. Rock polypody ferns grow on the high face of the quarry.

Returning to the main trail, go back to where the ginger and trillium grow. Take the left fork. At **I** is a fern glen in a low, swampy area. The wide variety of ferns growing here includes the New York, cinnamon, and interruptus. At times the ferns in this glen reach heights of 6 feet. From here the trail continues on to the parking area, leaving behind a different and very special natural world.

Remarks: *The walk is approximately 1 to 1½ hours over easy-to-moderate terrain. Trout fishing is permitted in the river, which is stocked. A complete trail map is available at the trail entrance. A warden-naturalist is on duty weekends and holidays from April through November. Guided walks are also available to groups by prior arrangement. For more information contact the chief warden or the preserve committee at Bartlett Arboretum, 157 Brookdale Rd., Stamford, Conn. 06902. Camping in the lower Hudson valley is available at two state parks. The 7,000-acre Clarence Fahenstock Memorial State Park is located in Carmel, north of Peekskill. For information write to the headquarters at R.D. 2, Carmel, N.Y. 10512, or call (914) 225-7207. The 52,000-acre Bear Mountain and Harriman State Park has over 200 tent and trailer sites. For information contact the headquarters at Palisade Interstate Park Commission, Bear Mountain, N.Y. 10911; (914) 786-2701.*

2.

Butler
Sanctuary

Directions: Mount Kisco, N.Y. From New York City, take I-684 north about 25 miles to Exit 4. Go west on Route 172 toward Mount Kisco for 0.3 mile; turn left onto Chestnut

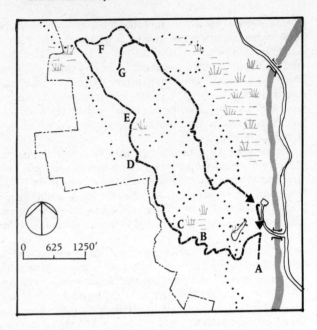

Ridge Rd. Go 1.5 miles south; turn right over the bridge. Park on the left near the entrance sign.

Ownership: **The Nature Conservancy.**

This preserve and the adjacent Meyer Preserve, only about 1 hour from Manhattan, include over 20 miles of trails through a variety of habitats, including swamps, ravines, open fields, and ledges. They are a good example of what the lower Hudson valley countryside was like before the land was so intensively developed.

This region was once very active geologically, as seen in the swirls of metamorphic rock, which forms high ledges at the sanctuary's entrance. These ledges provide an excellent vantage point for hawk-watching in late summer and early fall. On September days up to a thousand hawks may pass overhead, comprising a dozen different species. Most common are the broad-winged and sharp-shinned hawks. Hawks migrate north in the spring to their breeding grounds and return south in the early fall. Their long journey is made easier by their ability to ride the air currents and thermals, where they can glide for miles with very little effort. Temperature inversions at different altitudes create thermals, and this site where warm air over land meets colder air from Long Island Sound provides the ideal conditions they seek. In other seasons the hawk-watch platform is a good place from which to admire the view south and east to Long Island Sound.

Take the Basin Ravine Trail from the parking lot and continue past the trail junction to the hawk-watch platform (**A**) at the top of the ledge. These rocks are Fordham gneiss and schist, formed by a heating, melting, and cooling process about 3 billion years ago. The different layers, which are clearly visible, show the various minerals contained within the rock, which settled and hardened at different stages of the metamorphic process.

Return to the junction of the Basin Trail and turn left, continuing through a mature hemlock grove with an understory of American chestnut. The chestnuts will not grow any bigger than these saplings owing to the blight that attacked the species early in this century. It was once the dominant species in this region, and stumps can still be seen where trees were cut after being stricken with blight. It was a remarkably resilient tree and is resistant to decay, which is why the stumps still stand.

At **B** is a red-maple swamp in a depression between two ridges. The very wet conditions here have attracted sphagnum moss (see **#76** and **#103**) and polygonum weed, as well as red maple, a fast-growing species that thrives when its roots are saturated.

As the trail climbs, there is a large red oak (**C**) about 30 inches in diameter and probably 150 to 200 years old. It was also a dominant species, along with chestnut, in this region, but mature trees such as this are unusual. This one escaped being cut because of its inaccessibility.

The trail descends a steep ravine and climbs again. At **D** are some rock outcroppings that contain a large percentage of white and gray marble. This was formed when heat and pressure deep within the earth transformed limestone into a hard, crystalline substance, which was later brought to the surface by geological upheavals (see **Taconics, Berkshires, and Green Mountains** and **#5**).

The trail descends again and continues along the bottom of the high ridge on the right. At **E** is a large boulder that is a glacial erratic. It was plucked off the ridge above by the ice and deposited here when the ice melted. Unlike some erratics, it was not carried far, because it was already near the terminal moraine—the stopping point of the glacier—which is Long Island.

The trail now climbs steeply up a field of boulders (**F**), which were pulled off the ridge above as the glacier moved down the side. Notice the dark to light gray color variations in the rock, which indicate that some may have been carried here from some distance away where the composition of the rock is different. The leafy plants growing on the boulders are rock polypody ferns.

At the top of the ridge is a side trail that leads to Sunset Ledge (**G**), a good place to rest and enjoy the view west. In the distance are the Hudson Highlands, and the other side of the river can sometimes be seen about 5 miles away.

The strenuous part of the hike is now over, and the trail gradually descends through mixed forest and open fields, bordered by a white pine and Norway spruce plantation, back to the entrance and parking area. Remember to look for birds throughout the hike. Warblers are a highlight from late May to mid-June.

Remarks: *The hike is moderate, steep in places. It covers about 3 miles, requiring 2 hours. There are other trails, and a complete map is available at the registration point near the parking area. There is a warden-naturalist in residence. The preserve is open to cross-country skiing in winter. For camping in the lower Hudson valley region, see* **#1**.

3.

Meyer

Preserve

Directions: **Mount Kisco, N.Y. Follow directions for #2. Follow Chestnut Ridge Rd. to the end (less than 3 miles) and turn right onto Route 22. Take the first right onto Baldwin Rd.; go 0.3 mile; turn left onto Byram Lake Rd. Follow the road for 0.9 mile; turn right onto Oregon Rd. The preserve is on both sides of the road; go 0.1 mile to the first trailhead on the right. Park in the designated area.**

Ownership: **The Nature Conservancy.**

The Meyer Preserve is more remote and is visited less frequently than the neighboring Butler Sanctuary. It also has several trails through typical hemlock-laurel-beech forest that offer hikes of varying difficulty. Its prominent features are a rocky ravine and small gorge, abundant and varied wildflowers, and good bird-watching. The red-tailed hawk, pileated woodpecker and screech owl are both seen and heard here, and the red-breasted nuthatch is a year-round resident.

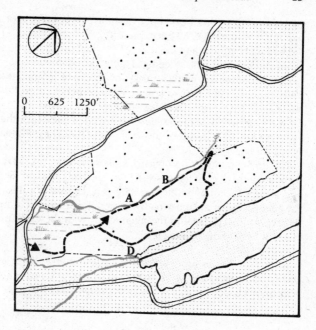

The Ravine Trail begins at the parking area and follows the edge of a marsh dominated by grasslike tussock sedge until it rises and continues along the ridge above the stream. Hemlock (see **#23** and **#65**) and mountain laurel (see **#69**), which like the shade and cool moisture found here, are the dominant species. The small gorge below (**A**) is filled with rocks that have fallen from the ledge on the other side of the ravine. In the springtime, meltwater forms several falls and pools here, although the gorge is quiet in other seasons.

Near the intersection with the Oregon Trail (**B**) are several varieties of orchids, including pink lady's slippers and showy orchids, which also thrive in the cool, wet climate. There are several large old hemlocks and beech on the steep slopes of the ravine. Their remote location has preserved them from cutting and allowed them to reach great sizes of up to 3 feet in diameter. These trees are a climax forest, indicated by the existence of the same species thriving in the understory. Hemlock-beech and chestnut-oak associations were the climax forests in this area before they were disturbed. The chestnuts and oaks, which were of more commercial value, were cut down, leaving the faster-growing hemlocks and beech to take over. Chestnut blight, which appeared in 1910, further prevented these trees from becoming established again (see **#67**). Some of the dead and dying trees bear large holes made by the pileated woodpecker, a bird that is unusual in this region but that survives here because of abundant food on the large, 604-acre preserve.

The trail continues and loops around to join the Cliff Trail, which returns along the same ridge but higher up. More large hemlocks and beech dominate, with a thick understory of mountain laurel. Early June is a good time to visit to see them in bloom. At **C** is a big stone ledge that shows the marks of stonecutters who made stones for walls bordering private estates. It is anyone's guess how the huge "cap" stones on the top of the walls were brought out along the steep, narrow trail.

The trail continues to an overlook above Byram Lake (**D**). Here there are a number of ferns (see **#100**) and club mosses (see **#107** and **#110**), including spotted wintergreen. Throughout this area is the goodyeara, an upland-woodland orchid that blooms in August. Retrace your steps back to the intersection with the Cliff Trail and follow it back to the parking area.

Remarks: *This is an easy hike of about 1 hour over moderate terrain. Other trails are more difficult and remote. A complete trail map is available at the entrance. For camping in the lower Hudson valley region, see* **#1.**

4.

Ward Pound Ridge
Reservation

Directions: **Cross River, N.Y. From New York City, take I-684 north about 30 miles to Exit 6. Go east on Route 35 about 4 miles. Turn south (right) on Route 121; go 0.1 mile to the entrance road. Drive to the tollbooth, then another 0.1 mile to Michigan Rd. Turn right and go 0.5 mile to a parking lot at a ski-touring area.**

Ownership: **Westchester County Parks System.**

One of the last remaining places in Westchester County where you might see a bobcat, Ward Pound Ridge Reservation is a vast 4,750-acre parkland on the edge of rural suburbia. Here lie huge open fields, bordered by second-growth deciduous forest and thick evergreen groves planted in the 1930s by the Civilian Conservation Corps.

A complex system of trails and dirt roads guides one not only to these areas but also to high ridgetops, river shorelines, and wooded swamps. The reservation is an important archaeological location where Indian artifacts and a petroglyph have been discovered.

The unusual terrain along the left side of the trail can be described as somewhere between a wet meadow, a shrub swamp, and a bog (**A**). Tussock sedges rise about 6 inches above the water in their characteristic hummocky shape, while several acid-tolerant plants, including highbush blueberry (see **#74**), sphagnum moss (see **#103**), and bog orchids, are also present. Maleberry, pepperbush, viburnums, and willows grow along the wet edges. One might expect the area to undergo a gradual succession (see **#74** and **#76**), eventually becoming a wooded swamp where trees such as red maples will slowly replace the shrubs. However, this might not occur. The shade cast by the shrubs may be dense enough to keep the tree seedlings from germinating, and the acidity levels of the soil may be too great. On the other hand, if the water supply fails owing to drought conditions, some of the wetland plants may not be able to survive, and the area may be colonized by nearby forest trees, such as redcedar, black birch, gray birch, and cherry.

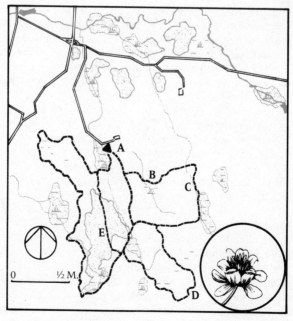

Inset: Tuliptree

As one gets deeper into the woods, the signs of former agricultural uses of the property begin to stand out. Notice the many stone walls, the occasional redcedars, which probably began life in old fields (see **#7**), and a row of ancient sugar maples, most likely planted by settlers in the last century.

Here, too, are several naturally occurring tuliptrees (**B**) that are thoroughly riddled with thousands of holes made by yellow-bellied sapsuckers. The holes are drilled by this 8- to 9-inch member of the woodpecker family in order to obtain both sap and insects that are attracted to the sweet liquid. Sapsuckers make their holes in lines, usually horizontal but often vertical, a fact ornithologists cannot explain.

Sapsuckers and other woodpeckers have many special adaptations for a life spent on tree trunks and branches. Each foot has four toes (rather than the usual three of common songbirds) arranged in a way that maximizes gripping and control: two point straight ahead, one usually to the side, though it may be toward the back if so desired, and a fourth always toward the back. Additionally, their long pointed tailfeathers act as a prop against the tree surface.

The trail skirts a series of dramatic 50-foot-high cliffs and piles of large broken boulders (**C**). This outcropping is composed of pink granitic gneiss, also referred to by geologists as Pound Ridge gneiss. Gneiss is a product of metamorphism, or the processes of heat and pressure within the earth's crust (see **Taconics, Berkshires, and Green Mountains**). In this case it probably originated as granite, but for one reason or another did not undergo total metamorphism. Its age is generally given as 600 million years old, or Precambrian.

What is particularly fascinating here is that the maze of boulders one sees below the cliffs occurs mainly because of frost action. Great chunks of gneiss split off from the main body when the repeated expansion of frozen water within the joints and fractures built up enough pressure to break the rock apart. This may seem hard to believe, but one must remember that the volume of water increases a full 9 percent when frozen.

An opening atop some high bluffs looks out to the southeast over woods, fields reverting to forest, and several houses (**D**). The high-and-dry conditions here are tolerated by chestnut and white oaks and a shrub layer that includes lowbush blueberry. Notice the thin soil and exposed bedrock. Excess rainwater has a tendency to run downhill rather than to collect. The plants growing in this environment must therefore be able to withstand low-moisture conditions.

The name Wildcat Hollow strikes a vivid chord in the hearts and minds of those people who have long hoped to see a bobcat (**E**). Because they are so elusive and are mainly nocturnal, bobcats are rarely seen. More often than not, one knows they are in the area by finding tracks and droppings. This section of the reservation, with its hilly and irregular topography and secluded location, is known to be attractive to bobcats.

Bobcats prey on mammals such as rabbits, squirrels, and chipmunks. They rarely grow to more than 35 pounds, but may live for 15 years or more in the wild. They are found in many parts of New York and much of New England, making their dens in rocky crevices, large hollow logs, and other hiding places. Bobcats have an average feeding range of about 2 miles, but wander over greater distances.

The trail cuts through a small wooded swamp where skunk cabbage is abundant and then back to the parking lot.

Remarks: *Walking time is about 3 hours. Follow the red plastic ski-trail tags for most of the walk until you meet the green-tagged trail. Use the map carefully, since there are many intersecting trails and obscure turnoffs throughout. Eastern bluebirds are common in the fields that line the main entrance road. Look for them near the wooden nesting boxes or on electric power lines, especially during the warmer months. A trailside museum has many interesting exhibits, a good collection of stuffed hawks, and a detailed map showing how you can find the petroglyph and other park features. For camping in the lower Hudson valley region, see #1.*

5.
Halle Ravine

Directions: **Pound Ridge, N.Y. From New York City, take I-684 north about 25 miles to Exit 4. Go east (right) on Route 172 for 1.8 miles, then northeast (left) on Route 22 for 1.2 miles, then east (right) on Pound Ridge Rd. for 4 miles. Go north (left) on Route 124 about 0.5 mile; turn northeast (right) onto Trinity Pass. Go 0.7 mile; the preserve is on the right, just before the intersection with Donbrook Rd. Look for a white fence and gate.**

Ownership: **The Nature Conservancy.**

Although small in size (38 acres), Halle Ravine is a lovely hemlock gorge, which surrounds the hiker with woodland beauty. The trail follows a narrow stream that winds its way down from two ponds

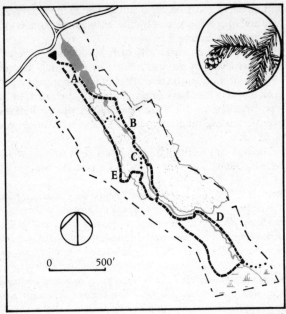

Inset: Hemlock

through towering hemlock trees to the edge of a wetland. Barred, screech, and great horned owls are known to have nested on the preserve.

At the turn of the century the property was part of the Scofield Farm, but in 1928 it was bought by Hiram Halle, a local conservationist. These two ponds were built in the 1930s, presumably for enhancing wildlife use of the area (**A**). The unnamed stream that flows through the grounds descends about 100 feet from here through the winding ⅓-mile-long gorge. The trail crosses and recrosses the stream several times.

As you head into the deepest part of the gorge, the hillside to your left rises sharply to a height of about 60 feet (**B**). This ridge is composed of monocline granite, one of the two main rock types forming the ravine. The other type that you can see throughout is Inwood marble, which is less resistant to weathering than the granite and has eroded significantly over millions of years. Marble is metamorphosed limestone and is made up primarily of recrystallized calcium and magnesium carbonates. These carbonates came from seashells long ago. Since they slowly dissolve in slightly acidic rainfall (caused by airborne carbon dioxide mixing with precipitation to form weak carbonic acid), they have eroded rather seriously and quite visibly.

Differential erosion, or weathering, of granite and marble has, in fact, helped create the dramatic setting of Halle Ravine.

Steep slopes are perfect areas for the growth and perpetuation of hemlock forests (**C**). The cool microclimate here, the inaccessibility of the area to loggers in the earlier centuries, and the fact that hemlock saplings can grow under the shade of a dense canopy all account for the presence of these 125-foot-high giants. Notice the sparse understory. Christmas fern and common polypody, along with mosses (see **#107**), lichens (see **#7**), and liverworts (see **#101**), grow here because they can adapt to the shaded, moist environment. Partridgeberry, rattlesnake plantain (see **#59**), Indian pipe (see **#90**), and spotted wintergreen are among the only flowering plants in the area. Look for them scattered throughout the needle-covered forest floor.

After the fourth footbridge, the ravine opens up and the vegetation changes. Aspen, cherry, ash, beech, maple, and oak share the flat bottomland to the right of the stream. As you cross the fifth bridge, notice two large tuliptrees on the left and a big sycamore on the right. The sunnier conditions are immediately evident.

A patch of rough horsetails (*Equisetum hyemale*) is growing to the left of the trail (**D**). The Latin name *hyemale* means "of winter" and refers to the fact that this species is evergreen. Note the thin, green, bamboolike stalks about 5 inches high in an area approximately 10 by 50 feet. Horsetails are among the most primitive of all living plants, being closely allied to vegetation that lived 300 million years ago. Because of its tough, fibrous body and high silica content, this species was used by early settlers for cleaning dishes and pots. Thus the nickname—scouring rush.

Cross the last, or sixth, bridge and walk back through the hardwood bottomland that was probably once used as a timber lot. Proceed along the streambed and bear left to the upper trail and left again up a small hill.

At the top of the hill to the left is a large, tilted rock outcropping (**E**). If you take a closer look, you'll see the layered, wavy-and-undulating appearance characteristic of schist, a metamorphic rock. There are several surface pock holes, probably caused by differential weathering—the same process that created the ravine. This schist is an extension of the formation that underlies Manhattan Island (see **#7**).

Remarks: *Walking time is 1 hour. The ravine is shaded and cool, so dress accordingly. There are a number of other Nature Conservancy properties in this region. Check elsewhere in this guidebook or with their office at RFD 2, Chestnut Ridge Rd., Mount Kisco, N.Y. 10549; (914) 666-5365. For camping in the lower Hudson valley region, see* **#1**.

6.

Constitution Island
Marsh Sanctuary

Directions: Garrison, N.Y. From New York City, take the Taconic State Parkway north about 45 miles. Take Route 301 west about 8 miles into Cold Spring Harbor; turn south (left) onto Route 9D. Go 1.4 miles to Indian Brook Rd. (unmarked), the first right past the well-marked Boscobel restoration. Turn right; go 0.5 mile until the road splits off to the left. Park along the roadside at this quiet intersection; the entrance to the sanctuary is 60 yards west by a locked wire gate.

Ownership: New York State; leased and managed by the National Audubon Society.

Amidst the towering mountains and rocky cliffs of the historic Hudson Highlands is a 270-acre freshwater tidal marsh that can be explored either by foot or by canoe. Numerous inlets and channels wind their way through the thick cattail stands and pickerelweed, past muskrat dens and turtles basking in the sun. Birdlife is especially abundant, and long-billed marsh wrens commonly nest here. A marked trail leads to a new boardwalk that crosses a portion of the marsh and ends at a bird-observation deck.

Walk down the dirt entrance road, with Indian Brook gorge to your left. Begin the trail on the north side of the remains of an old building. This hillside, which dips down to the edge of the marsh, is a popular site in early June for snapping turtles seeking a dry, earthen place in which to lay and bury their eggs (**A**). Although most of the females leave the water after dusk, it is not unusual to see one during daylight hours. Upon finding a suitable site, the turtle will deposit between ten and forty hickory-nut-size eggs in a small hole she has dug with her back claws. She will then cover the eggs with dirt and crawl back to the marsh. Despite this protection, many of the eggs are eaten by raccoons, skunks, and foxes. Those that do survive incubate in the heat of the sun and hatch during late August and early September, the baby turtles eventually finding their way to the safety of the water.

Male long-billed marsh wrens can usually be heard singing throughout the days during May and June, when their mates are

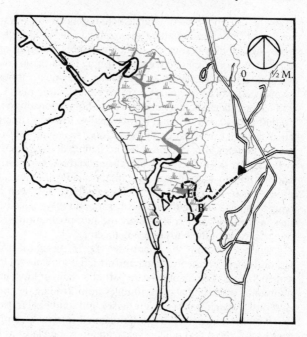

sitting on eggs (**B**). Listen for a reedy, guttural song similar to the sound of a treadle sewing machine being operated. The nests are amazing constructions of dead cattail leaves woven together to form a baseball-size capsule located on a cattail stalk, hidden from view. Marsh wrens have an interesting habit of making several "dummy" nests, which serve as territorial boundaries to keep away other wrens. The real nest can be determined by the presence of a small woven lip at the bottom of the entrance hole. If this marsh were more disturbed than it is, as most along the Hudson are, and invading phragmites and purple loosestrife were to replace the extensive cattails, the number of marsh wrens here would fall dramatically.

According to unconfirmed local reports, both the south and north ends of the marsh were diked (**C**) during the early 1800s, and several straight channels were dug to facilitate the culture of wild rice (see **#18**). Today, both the channels and dikes persist. The marsh receives water from the Hudson through openings beneath the railroad trestles, on the western edge. The construction of the railroad in 1851 further served to isolate the marsh from the main body of the river and also allowed the buildup of sediments and the continued growth of associated plant communities.

As the tide goes out—the range here is about 4 feet—watch for a variety of birds feeding along the exposed mudflats. Gulls, shore-birds, egrets, and herons are frequent visitors. In April and May ospreys can sometimes be seen here fishing for carp and goldfish.

An unusual and spectacular phenomenon involving thousands of swallows has been a regular occurrence here during mid-August to early September. About 45 minutes to an hour before dusk, between 10,000 and 40,000 tree and barn swallows begin to congregate in great cloudlike masses, flying about and swooping low over the marsh, perhaps for a last insect before settling down to roost for the night. As the sky darkens, the birds begin to roost, almost in unison, and within 3 to 4 minutes all have disappeared within the safety and protection of the cattails. Local observers have also seen cliff and bank swallows among the huge swarms, and they suggest that this massing behavior takes place before the autumnal southward migra-tion as a way for the birds to group together.

A good view from the boardwalk (**D**) to the north allows the visitor to focus on the imposing and ancient mountains of the Hud-son Highlands. The highlands are part of a chain of low but rugged mountains extending about 140 miles from Reading, Penn., north-eastward through northern New Jersey and southeastern New York into western Connecticut. Their formation is extremely complex and goes back at least 800 million years, and in some places as far back as 1.2 billion years. The rock is mostly metamorphic, with some igneous phases, and has been folded and faulted during several mountain-building periods. Storm King, on the west shore of the river to the north, rises to over 1,000 feet.

Look over the marsh for the cattail lodges and feeding platforms of the ever-present muskrat (**E**). The lodges are small domed or teepee-shaped affairs, while the feeding platforms are flattened areas at the edge of the water where the muskrat will sit and eat cattail tubers. If you happen to be canoeing, you may also see a second type of lodge: a tunnel burrowed into the mudbank right below the high-water mark. Muskrats use their lodges for several purposes, including the raising of young. A prolific female may have as many as four litters a year, averaging five babies per litter. They begin nesting in March, and their season peaks at the end of May to the beginning of June. Unwary young muskrats sometimes wind up as dinner for snapping turtles, foxes, and great horned owls. (See **#70** for more on muskrats.)

Remarks: *Walking time is about 1 hour. Serious birders should bring spotting scopes for viewing birds of the mudflat and open water. Canoeists should call the warden-biologist at (914) 265-3119 for information on tides and launching procedures. There are no canoe-rental facilities in the im-mediate area. The Boscobel restoration is directly above the marsh and offers a tour of an outstanding nineteenth-century colonial mansion and grounds. One can also see the marsh from a different perspective here, as well as the entire Hudson Highlands area. Camping facilities are available at Clarence Fahenstock Memorial State Park, about 9 miles east of Cold Spring Harbor on Route 301. For information contact park headquarters at R.D. 2, Carmel, N.Y. 10512; (914) 225-7207.*

7.

Pawling
Nature Reserve

Directions: **Pawling, N.Y. From New York City, go north on I-684 to the end, then on Route 22, to Pawling, about 55 miles. Continue another 2.5 miles north; turn east (right) on North Quaker Hill Rd. (Route 68). Bear right and con-tinue for 1.4 miles, then make a left onto Quaker Lake Rd. Go 1.5 miles to a small parking lot on the left. The north parking area is 1.4 miles farther, also on the left.**

Ownership: **The Nature Conservancy.**

The Pawling Nature Reserve is a large and delightfully unspoiled parcel of land in eastern New York State, noted for an impressive hemlock gorge, small woodland swamps, and different stages of forest succession (see **#67**). Its 1,014 acres are surrounded by an additional 2,000 acres of privately owned land, creating an extensive tract of undisturbed countryside. A number of plant and bird species that reach their northern or southern limits are known to occur here. For example, the hermit thrush and the winter wren (see **#61**), both usually found farther north, nest on the reserve.

Take the yellow-blazed trail, which heads generally westward from the south or main parking lot. As the trail begins a moderate climb toward the top of Hammersley Ridge, you will encounter a narrow but rugged hemlock gorge (**A**) where the cascading waters of Duell Brook drop 50 feet in a series of waterfalls. The eastern hemlocks are very tolerant of shade and thrive on this cool, moist slope, which faces northeast and receives little direct sunlight.

Across the stream and up into an open hemlock stand is a cavelike overhang (**B**), which is a good place to observe the exposed bedrock of the 2½-mile-long Hammersley Ridge. The dark layered rock is known as *mica schist*, a metamorphosed material composed of micas, quartz, and feldspars. If you look closely, you'll see light-colored veins of quartz running throughout the schist. This is the result of igneous activity within the earth, which occurred late in the Paleozoic era. The quartz was squeezed up through weak folds in the schist as in an underground volcano. The formations that occur here in Pawling are part of the long Manhattan schist formation, stretching from Manhattan northwest for many miles. Thus the schist found here is the same as that on Manhattan Island, 70 miles to the south.

As the trail climbs through a mixed-oak forest (**C**), you can see Quaker Lake just to the south. Small woodland swamps occur here, situated in shallow bedrock basins that trap seepage and rainwater. Here also are found the first few examples of mountain laurel, a member of the same plant family as rhododendrons and azaleas. In June, these hardy 5- to 6-foot-high shrubs display their delicate pink flowers, bathing the woods in color. During the rest of the year their shiny evergreen leaves stand out against the muted tones of the

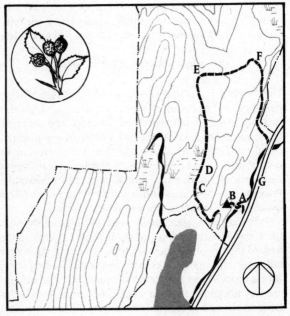

Inset: Hawthorn

upland oak forest. Mountain laurels require acidic soil, a quality that the underlying bedrock and the decaying oak leaves amply provide (see **#69**).

Along the flattened ridgetop itself, the yellow-blazed trail joins the famous Appalachian Trail and continues through areas that show signs of having been farmed many years ago. The Quakers settled here in the late 1700s, clearing the land for farming and grazing and building several homesteads along the ridge.

An old stone wall (**D**) on the right once served as a boundary for open pasture or crop land. Notice that the rocks are covered with two types of lichen: crustose and foliose. Lichens arc hardy pioneers that grow on bare rock surfaces and start the slow process of turning these rocks into soil. A lichen is actually two plants, an alga and a fungus, living together in a symbiotic, or mutually beneficial, relationship. Food manufactured by the alga is shared with the fungus, which furnishes a protective, moisture-retaining environment for the alga. The alga's chlorophyll gives the lichen its greenish tinge. Crustose lichens grow like a close-clinging crust, their color varying with the moisture content. The foliose lichens are greener here and grow in leafier, more papery arrangements.

Other clues to the past agricultural uses of this land include barberry bushes, redcedars, and hawthorn trees. The barberry shrub, a European native introduced to the United States, was often planted along fence and hedgerows but now grows wild. Redcedars almost always germinate in turf, indicating that the land on which they now stand was once a grassy pasture. They are sun-loving trees that thrive in open fields but eventually die if overshadowed. Mice and birds unwittingly aid in seed dispersal by eating the blue berries of the cedar; the vital seeds survive the animals' digestive tracts and are deposited in the droppings. Thus, redcedars are often found scattered across fields and along fencerows, where these animals live and search for food.

In the European tradition, hawthorn trees were used for centuries as hedges between fields. Like the redcedar, they tend to grow along fences where birds void their seed. The hawthorns were known to farmers as ubiquitous pasture "weeds," and a constant battle was necessary to keep them from encroaching on grazing tracts. Their long thorns can deliver a nasty wound.

The red-blazed trail (**E**), which eventually returns to the parking lot, is found along the ridgetop as the trail begins to descend. The Appalachian and yellow-blazed trails continue, with the yellow-blazed ending at the north parking lot, at least a mile away. Red maple, black cherry, gray birch, and black birch dominate the forest here. These are all relatively young trees of a second-growth forest, for the area remained cleared up until the early 1900s. Maple, cherry, and birch indicate a rich *mesic* (medium moisture) soil here, in contrast to the dry, rocky ridgetops dominated by oak. An old logging road and bridle trail serves as the route here for the descending red-blazed trail.

As the slope steepens (**F**), the hemlock trees, which have been noticeably absent since the other side of the ridge, begin to reappear and soon predominate. Cross a wooden footbridge and turn right onto Quaker Lake Rd. through the evergreen forest.

A large yellow-birch snag, or dead tree (**G**), along this quiet and relatively untraveled road has been thoroughly excavated by pileated woodpeckers and other members of the woodpecker family searching for insects. The pileated woodpeckers usually dig narrow, rectangular-shaped holes. The birch is also covered with horsehoof fungus *(Fomes fomentarius)*, a firm, hard, woody growth that attacks dead trees. Note the semicircular shape, or horsehoof appearance, of the invading plant.

Remarks: *The trail loop takes about 2 hours. The top of the ridge is likely to be wet, so wear appropriate footwear. (The small footbridge near the north parking lot where the yellow-blazed trail crosses the brook was out at the time of this writing.) An adult bald eagle was sighted here in 1982. Camping is available about 15 miles northeast of Pawling at Macedonia Brook State Park in Kent, Conn. For information contact the Parks and Recreation Unit, Department of Environmental Protection, Hartford, Conn. 06115; (203) 566-2304.*

8.

Mine Hill Preserve

Directions: **Roxbury, Conn. From Hartford, go southwest on I-84 about 40 miles to Exit 15. Take U.S. 6 north 1 mile, then turn northwest (left) onto Route 67. Go about 8 miles through Roxbury; at the junction with Route 199, turn west (left), still on Route 67. Continue 1.5 miles to Mine Hill Rd. Turn right and continue 0.4 mile along this rustic road to a parking area with preserve sign on the right.**

Ownership: **Roxbury Land Trust.**

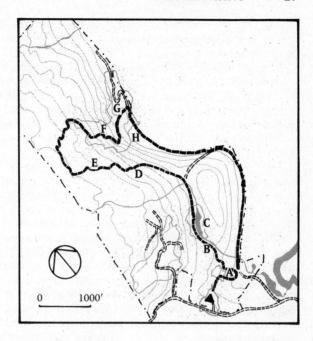

The 360 acres of the Mine Hill Preserve lie along the western edge of the picturesque, free-flowing Shepaug River and rise sharply above it as a thickly wooded ridge. This property is part of one of the largest protected natural areas in Connecticut, stretching for 1,400 acres from Roxbury Station to the Steep Rock Preserve in Washington, Conn. Rich in habitat diversity, Mine Hill and the surrounding land support numerous wildlife species, including fox (see **#98**) and bobcat (see **#4**). In addition, the area is significant as a historical testimony to Connecticut's iron industry, which tapped the unusual mineral deposits here in the nineteenth century. A few structural remains of the early mining operations still stand, adding to the distinction of this preservation. The abandoned mining tunnels have created a unique and important spot for hibernating bats that frequent the area.

Enter the trail from the parking lot and walk a short and gradual descent to the site of several furnaces set along a series of flattened terraces (**A**). The furnaces are evidence of western Connecticut's once-prosperous iron industry. This complex of structures was built by the Shepaug Spathic Iron and Steel Company in 1865 to produce pig iron from the mined iron ore. Yet their success was short-lived, and in 1872 the small mine operations all but ceased due to plummeting steel prices and the opening of huge pit furnaces elsewhere in the United States.

Scattered remnants of the once-impressive complex of chimneys, roasting ovens, puddling furnaces, and a large blast furnace are seen along here. During prime production years, these structures and various other support systems were enclosed in one huge building. Perhaps the large blast furnace is most imposing, still standing strong with its red brick exterior and lining of heat-resistent yellow firebrick.

Take the blue-blazed trail west and upward to join the yellow-blazed donkey trail. This 8-foot-wide raised-bed trail was once lined with tracks over which donkeys hauled empty iron-ore carts to the mines. Imagine the flurry of activity that must have existed then—a sharp contrast to the quiet, tree-lined hiking trail of today.

After leaving the mixed-oak hardwoods that surround the furnace sites, the trail winds through thick but relatively young hemlocks, with scattered stands of mountain laurel (see **#7** and **#69**) where openings have allowed light to penetrate (**B**). According to authorities, the stands of almost pure, regenerating hemlocks probably became established as a result of forest-fire protection during the last three or four decades. With continued protection, hemlock will eventually shade out many of the hardwood species now growing on these formerly clear-cut slopes (see **#65**).

Soon a small hemlock-lined pond (**C**) comes into view along the eastern edge of the trail—a good place to surprise a resting mallard, black duck, or heron. If you go quietly, you may get a good look at one of these birds under the protective camouflage of the trees. Originally created as a reservoir for protection against fires, this pond was formed by damming Mineral Spring Brook in the mid-1800s.

Continue on as the path begins to narrow and climb. The thick, moist stands of hemlock thin out, and you begin to see more and more hardwoods, mainly red oak, chestnut oak, and scattered red maple and black birch. The soil is noticeably more rocky and shallow here as you climb steeply along loose rock deposits to the entrance of an abandoned mine tunnel (**D**). The loose rocks that line the hillside here are left over from the mining and contain beautiful mineral specimens. Look for the mineral siderite, which ranges in color from cream to copper brown, an iron carbonate rarely found in the United States. This mineral was the object of the mid-19th-century iron-ore mining efforts here. The tunnel entrance ahead is one of three that were cut across intruded quartz-siderite veins found in Mine Hill. The origin and formation of these veins is uncertain, but it is known that because they are an intrusion, they are younger than the surrounding Mine Hill granite-gneiss. The tunnels have now fallen into disrepair and are both off-limits and extremely dangerous for human exploration.

The uphill climb continues to a series of vertical shafts (**E**) built to allow air circulation within the tunnels. They are now all covered over with heavy steel grating as a protective measure, but you can look through to see the moist, moss-lined faces that cut through the thick bedrock. The openings in these grates are large enough to allow numerous species of bats to enter and make their way to the abandoned tunnels to hibernate, and possibly to breed. The deep tunnels provide a consistently cool, moist environment and quiet, subdued light or darkness—perfect for the requirements of hibernating bats. The eastern pipistrelle, little brown bat, Keen's bat, and big brown bat have all recently been found wintering here at Mine Hill.

Although certain species, such as the red and hoary bats, migrate to warmer climates during the winter, the majority of bats seek refuge in northern caves, where they spend the cold months in hibernation. Movement for these species of bats can be in any direction, often westward in New England, but always toward accessible caves. While hibernating, bats ordinarily hang by their hind claws, head down, with their wings folded close to their sides and their bodies often wedged in some protective corner. They eat little or nothing for months, relying entirely on their supply of body fat. Yet they seem to sleep unevenly, with several days of torpor followed by a day when they move about briefly.

Bats are widely distributed, and nearly all North American species are insectivorous. One of the more numerous species here at the Mine Hill Preserve is the Keen's bat *(Myotis keenii)*, similar in appearance to the uniformly colored little brown bat but distinguished by noticeably longer ears. The Keen's bat is strictly insectivorous; an individual may devour hundreds of mosquitoes, gnats, or other flying insects in a single night. Like other bats, it has a finely developed system of sonar, or echolocation, which allows it to find its way around in the dark as well as locate food by sending out high-frequency cries. The cries bounce off the object and are received by the bat, which is prevented from hearing its own cries by means of a tiny contracting muscle within its ear. Zoologist Alfred Grodin states that "for an object six inches from the bat's mouth, the time delay for the echo is about a thousandth of a second, and a bat can detect a mosquito that quickly from the echo." The Keen's bat mates during July or August and gives birth to a single young in August of the following year. It generally roosts singly or in small colonies and usually does not fly or feed until late at night. Thus, it is much less visible than the little brown bat in this area.

As the trail climbs, the vegetation continues to open up and you will soon come to a fork in the trail. Take the right fork that descends through the rock-covered slopes. Although this route takes you down the steep sides of Mine Hill, the upper trail here allows you to make a much more gentle and gradual descent and winds through more-open hardwoods where numerous wildflowers grow, including lady's slipper.

Along the downward portions of the blue-blazed trail, hemlocks again begin to dominate. Steep cliffs of layered granite-gneiss are sandwiched along the hill, revealing the dominant 360-million-year-old rock that underlies most of the Mine Hill Preserve (**F**). Hemlocks perch tenaciously upon the rocks with their roots exposed to the elements as they fight to survive. The thick conifers provide protection for birds such as golden-crowned kinglets and chickadees, and also serve as suitable nesting sites for hawks and owls.

Continue along a series of rock jumbles; proceed carefully, as the rocks can be treacherous and require agile navigation. You will arrive at a portion of trail that appears to be the flattened top of a rock cliff. There are a lot of blue markers here, which may be confusing, but proceed straight across, then head down to your left and back under the cliff overhang.

The trail brings you to the top of an abandoned granite quarry (**G**). Mine Hill served as a successful quarry in the nineteenth century, and certain areas are still worked today. Big, angled chunks of granite (see **#93**) are heaped throughout the site, and the steep, flat sides of the quarry rise to your west. Big blocks from this source were used as façades for local buildings, and additional ones were hauled to New Milford by oxcart and then shipped to New York for use in construction of both the Brooklyn Bridge and Grand Central Station.

Join the old dirt road that parallels the Shepaug River flowing across the eastern boundary. True to its Mohegan Indian name, which means "rocky waters," the Shepaug River rises out of the Bantam Lakes and bears southward into the Housatonic. The bottomland here is wet all year round and supports more water-tolerant species of plants and animals. Bur reeds, arrowhead, and highbush blueberry are prevalent, serving as protective cover for the many amphibian species that converge on these areas in spring (**H**). During April and May at just about dusk, the mating calls of the spring peeper, gray treefrog, and American toad can be intensely penetrating. Try to distinguish the different calls of these species. If you are lucky, you may catch a glimpse of the tiny individuals capable of such volume.

The road will eventually take you back to the parking area. Wildflowers are abundant along most of the borders, as the moist soil and additional sunlight combine to nourish wild leek, trout lily, false hellebore, mints, and cinquefoil, among others.

Remarks: *The entire walk takes at least 3 hours, so allow plenty of time. A map can be found on the welcome board at the parking area, but if you want additional information you should contact the Roxbury Land Trust. The trail that we highlighted is steep and requires rather agile hikers; others should use the upper trail. Camping is available about 12 miles away to the southeast at Kettletown State Park, in Southbury, Conn. For information contact park headquarters at Southbury, Conn. 06488; (203) 264-5678.*

9.
White Memorial
Foundation

Directions: **Litchfield, Conn. From Hartford, take U.S. 202 west about 35 miles to Litchfield. Continue southwest on U.S. 202 about 2 miles to the intersection with Bissell Rd. Turn east (left) here into a marked driveway; go 0.5 mile to the parking lot.**

Ownership: **White Memorial Foundation, Inc.**

Catlin Woods, a forest of old-growth hemlock and white pine estimated to be close to 190 years old, is perhaps the most unique part of the 4,000-acre holdings here on the outskirts of Litchfield. The woods are one of four designated natural areas on the grounds, which also include a red maple swamp and bog, an oak–mountain laurel cliffside, and the marshy shoreline of Bantam Lake. Though not a wilderness area, White Memorial offers a mosaic of plant communities, 10 miles of walking trails, 25 miles of woodland roads, a lakefront beach, and a distinguished natural history museum.

Begin walking on a gravel road, past the museum and a large field on the right, until you cross the Bantam River via a small bridge.

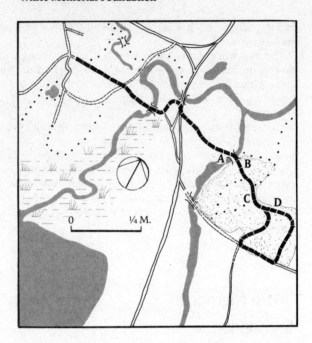

(This is a good spot to put in a canoe for a leisurely paddle south to Bantam Lake.) Bear left on the other side of the river, past a farm field, and right until you reach Alain White Rd. Bear right and walk about 100 yards, cross the road, and pick up the blue-blazed J trail, which leads into Catlin Woods.

A change in the vegetation here at the edge of Miry Brook has occurred as the result of flooding, due to beaver dams constructed about 15 years ago (**A**). Before that time, red maples grew along the wet shores, with white pines farther back in the wetland area, but both species, along with all woody plants, have since died due to the rising of the water level. The trunks of many of those trees are visible now as bare snags standing within the enlarged brook itself. Cattails, arrow arum, duckweed, and other water-loving vegetation have moved in as a new miniature ecosystem takes form. If the beavers leave and the dams fall apart, varying water levels may again bring great changes within the plant communities.

White pines dominate the western and southwestern part of the 30-acre Catlin Woods, whereas hemlocks are in great abundance to the east and northeast (**B** and **C**). The existence of these giants on a relatively level piece of ground is highly unusual in New England, as most trees this size are confined to isolated ravines and rocky slopes where human access is, and has been, limited (see **#5, #23,** and **#12**). Scientists studying the property have proposed a general theory about how and why Catlin Woods grew and survived.

Early white settlers in the seventeenth and eighteenth centuries cut local forests for fuel and timber and used the cutover areas as pastures for their sheep and cattle. Catlin Woods was probably lumbered and cleared during this time. Over the decades, however, as farming became less and less profitable due to poor and overworked soils, many acreages were slowly allowed to revert to woodland. This plot of land may have eventually become some farmer's "back forty," a place off the beaten track where lumbering was eventually curtailed.

Pines and hemlocks came to predominate over hardwoods in Catlin Woods largely because grazing cattle do not like conifer sprouts but do eat young hardwoods. Also, it is theorized that deer herds, which are known to enjoy hemlocks, were low in population during the time the present forest was growing up (early 1800s), probably because of frequent hunting.

Pines colonized the areas near Miry Brook, possibly because of the presence of glacially deposited sandy soils, which they thrive in. The hemlocks grew a bit farther to the east, where the underlying soils were of a more stony nature. A number of "mother" trees, which most likely served as shade for domestic animals in this once-cleared land, provided the seed source for the additional members of the present forest.

Another factor in the story concerns the presence of American chestnut trees and the subsequent blight that reached central Connecticut in the years 1910 to 1925 (see **#67**). Chestnuts made up approximately 80 percent of the forest in areas of Catlin Woods before that time. (Old stumps and downed logs provide evidence.) When the blight struck, the trees died, and the hemlocks and pines spread their crowns and increased their hold in the area, thus assuring their survival. The entire property was saved from any outside disturbance in 1913 when local residents Alain and May White consolidated their recent land purchases into a preserve-oriented foundation.

Notice that there is a greater abundance of hardwood species among the white pines than among the mature hemlocks. Oaks, maples, and birches have been able to grow in these sunnier locations, while the dense shade between the hemlocks has reduced the competition considerably.

One of the most unusual features of Catlin Woods, and of the hemlock area in particular, is the existence of small mounds and depressions on the forest floor, which indicate blowdowns from ancient ancestors (**C**). The blowdowns eventually became assimilated into the soil, but a mound or a dip remained where the stump either decayed or pulled up roots and earth. These so-called pillows and cradles are believed to be remnants of a pre-1700 forest that occupied the area for several generations, at least. If the land had ever been plowed, and it is believed not to have been, the pillows and cradles would have disappeared. It is believed, however, that the area was pastured, or cut over, during the 1700s and early 1800s, for otherwise the pillows and cradles would be larger and more apparent than they are today. Because the blowdowns happened so long ago, they now appear as a somewhat leveled surface, covered almost uniformly with duff and forest litter. This type of topography is extremely rare in southern New England, and for those who observe it with a keen eye, it is a genuine glimpse into the past.*

A huge hemlock has recently blown down across the trail (**D**). If the marshy area between the path and the base of the tree is not too wet, take a close look at the exposed and massive root system. The root base is approximately 15 feet high and 20 feet across. Why the tree blew down will probably remain a mystery, although it was growing in a somewhat open spot, which may have made it more vulnerable to windstorms. If the fallen tree is not cut up or disturbed, it too will become a pillow and cradle of the future.

Once the trail comes out of the woods onto Webster Rd., turn right, walk a few hundred yards back to the blue-blazed trail, and go right, into the forest again. This will loop back to the heart of Catlin Woods, over the bridge at Miry Brook, and return toward the parking lot.

Remarks: *Walking time is approximately 1 hour and 45 minutes. Campgrounds are available and may be reserved by calling (203) 567-0089. For the museum and bookstore hours, call (203) 567-0015. For a fuller explanation of the area, see Frank Egler and William Niering's* The Natural Areas of the White Memorial Foundation, *which is available at the bookstore.*

*The author is much indebted to Frank Egler and William Niering's *The Natural Areas of the White Memorial Foundation* for this information.

10.

Saint John's Ledges

Directions: Kent, Conn. From Hartford, take U.S. 202 west about 30 miles to Torrington; continue west on Route 4 about 15 miles, then go southwest on U.S. 7 about 9 miles to Kent. Turn west (right) onto Route 341; go about 0.7 mile. Turn right on Skiff Mountain Rd.; go along the river for about 1 mile and bear right where the road forks. Continue for 1.7 miles along this dirt road to the trailhead, marked with white blazes.

Ownership: The Nature Conservancy.

Rising steeply for 500 feet above the rural Housatonic River valley, Saint John's Ledges offer an exciting view and a short but challenging climb. Situated along the Appalachian Trail and in the midst of a dry oak forest, the ledges are bordered on one side by sheer rockfaces of gneiss, which extend almost 80 feet high in one smooth plane. At the base of the ridgetop lies River Rd., an unusually good birding area during spring migration.

The familiar white blazes of the 2,100-mile-long Appalachian Trail head up into the woods from the road, through red oaks, American hornbeam, dogwood, witch-hazel, honeysuckle, and maple-leaved viburnum (**A**). As the soil here at the bottom of the ledges is richer, moister, and deeper than that higher up, the woody plants are greater in size and variety.

There is also a wider variety of nesting birds in this lowland section and along the other side of River Rd., due to the more varied habitat, greater number of seeds and fruits, and closer proximity to the river and its store of insect life. Breeding here are black-throated blue, and blue-winged warblers. Golden-winged warblers nest in open spots along the roadway, and phoebes, least flycatchers, and various members of the swallow family nearby. As the slope increases, the trees and shrubs thin out, as does the degree of cover, and fewer breeding birds are found. Yet, worm-eating warblers and redstarts like hillsides, and turkey vultures nest high up in the cliffs. Birds, like all living creatures, have evolved to take advantage of different habitats.

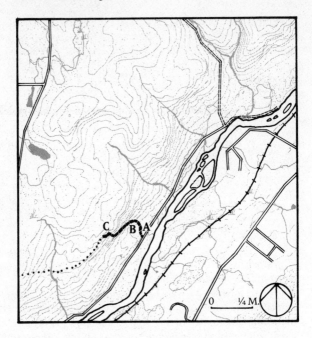

One soon feels rather small and humble as the trail skirts the bottom edge of towering rockfaces (**B**). These granitic gneiss walls may actually continue below the ground for as much as another 800 feet. They are part of the very old Precambrian complex of rocks that runs up the sides of the Housatonic Highlands. Though their definite origins are unknown, it is believed that they started as volcanic material that was deposited on top of layers of sediments and later recrystallized during regional metamorphism (see **Taconics, Berkshires, and Green Mountains**).

Use your hands to climb over boulders along a break in the wall followed by a series of small rock platforms or ledges, most likely placed here by a trail crew as an aid to hikers and as a means of lessening erosion on this popular route.

A viewpoint awaits you at the top of the ledges and an even better one about 50 yards to the west (**C**). The narrow Housatonic River snakes its way through a steep and narrow valley, and farm fields, houses, and an old cemetery stand out along the rising western slope. Notice the large sycamore trees down along the waterway—their characteristic light, mottled bark can be seen from quite a distance.

Here at the top of the valley, note the many soot-blackened tree trunks and the openings in the modest forest canopy. A low-intensity ground fire probably burned the fire-sensitive varieties such as black and yellow birch, but left the thick-barked oaks and pitch pines. Look for lowbush blueberry and huckleberry, which are common pioneers after a fire.

It is here on the exposed cliffs that turkey vultures establish nesting sites. These birds also nest in small caves, on rock outcroppings, in hollow stumps, or in other secluded places. They do not use nesting materials such as grasses or mosses, but lay their average of two eggs on the bare ground. The eggs are incubated by both sexes for about 6 weeks, and the chicks will fly, or fledge, after about 2 months. You may catch a glimpse of these graceful soaring birds as they search the countryside for dead animals, road kills, and other "natural garbage." A turkey vulture can be identified from hundreds of yards away because of the unique flattened V-shape of its wings in flight.

Remarks: *The walk up takes about 30 minutes, while the walk down takes about 20 minutes. Wear sturdy shoes. Camping is available nearby at either Macedonia Brook State Park in Macedonia or Housatonic Meadows State Park in Cornwall Bridge. Canoes may be rented for running the Housatonic along Route 7, just south of West Cornwall.*

11.

Black Spruce Bog

Directions: **Cornwall, Conn. From Hartford, take U.S. 202 west about 30 miles to Torrington; continue west on Route 4 to the intersection with Route 63 in Goshen. Stay on Route 4 another 2.8 miles, then turn south (left) onto Allyn Rd. Go 1.6 miles to the parking lot and ranger headquarters. The trail to the bog is to the right of the entrance road, about 75 yards from the parking lot.**

Ownership: **Parks and Recreation Unit, Connecticut Department of Environmental Protection.**

Tucked away on top of Mohawk Mountain at an elevation of 1,500 feet is a 2-acre black spruce bog, common in northern New England (see **#74** and **#79**) but quite rare in Connecticut and southern locations. A sturdy, newly constructed boardwalk allows the visitor to venture into the heart of this captivating wetland. Black spruce trees of varied heights grow through a thick luxuriant mat of sphagnum moss—the ubiquitous plant of the bog. Here and there, stunted white pines struggle to survive, and the stark remains of those that have died stand silhouetted against the sky. Specially adapted woody shrubs and herbaceous plants can be found along the sphagnum floor where openings in the tree canopy have allowed them to prosper. It is an enchanting community, full of unusual and fascinating life forms.

The entrance to the bog is along a footpath that winds through a knoll of impressive red pine trees and mountain laurel. The red pine (see **#108**) is a tall forest tree with an open crown supported by a long, well-formed trunk usually clear of branches. Notice the flaky red bark, which gives the tree its name. These particular red pines are the result of reforestation plantings, as suggested by their similar ages and equal spacing. Look for red-breasted nuthatches, which like cool conifer forests.

The vegetation changes abruptly as you reach the outer fringes of the bog. The tall clean trunks of pine, patches of mountain laurel (see **#69**), and rocky soil are replaced by thick black spruce growth, low ericaceous (heath family) shrubs (see **#74**), and a base of sphagnum moss (see **#76** and **#103**). Bog communities are often of special interest to naturalists in this area, because they are one of the least common of all wetland types in the region. The boardwalk allows you to glimpse an otherwise inaccessible area, since bog vegetation grows in wet places and is easily destroyed by trampling.

The bog probably arose from a kettle hole, created about 12,000 to 15,000 years ago, when a chunk of glacial ice that was insulated by a covering of soil and debris did not melt as fast as the surrounding glacier. When the ice finally did melt, it left a depression about 40 feet deep that filled with water. Over the years, the bog developed. As plant succession evolved and vegetation grew outward from the shores to create a floating mat, the present black spruce community took form.

Generally speaking, a bog is a poorly drained, acidic quagmire. Its formation rests on certain key conditions, one of the most important being a cool, moist climate. A second condition is the composition of the underlying bedrock, which is commonly granite and therefore low in important plant minerals and nutrients. The shortage of nutrients is exaggerated by a lack of oxygen due to little or no inflow of water. Highly acidic conditions thus result. Specially adapted plants, the most abundant being sphagnum moss, grow out over the water as a floating mat. As materials on the bottom portion of the mat die, they fall to the depths and accumulate. Because little oxygen is present, the dead organic materials do not decay but form a solid organic deposit in the bottom of the bog. This mass of undecayed vegetation is the peat moss commonly used as garden fertilizer.

Some of our most unusual plants occur in habitats such as this. High acidity makes water absorption difficult, and many of the bog shrubs compensate by having small leathery or woolly leaves to retard water loss. Sheep laurel and leatherleaf can both be seen along the boardwalk and are good examples of bog adaptation. Take a close look at each of these plants. Sheep laurel (see **#100**) is a low shrub whose evergreen leaves are pale green above but lined beneath with a whitish wool. Its small, cuplike flowers of purple or pink bloom from the leaf axils in late spring. Leatherleaf is another small shrub with thick brownish-green leaves that are oblong in shape. Before the snow melts, this common bog plant often blooms with delicate white, bell-like flowers borne in clusters at the upper leaf axils.

Black spruce is a small conifer, growing here to about 30 feet tall. Its normal range is farther north, in Canada to Hudson Bay, but it is found in these cool isolated pockets along the ridges of the Appalachians all the way south to Tennessee. Early settlers made spruce beer from its young twigs and needles by boiling them with molasses, honey, or maple sugar. Once fermented, it was ready to be used as a cure for scurvy.

The boardwalk ends at a small viewing platform, and the visitor must then return the same way he or she entered. The end of the trail, however, is a very good place to enjoy the peace and tranquillity of this uncommon site.

Remarks: *Walking time from the parking lot to the end of the boardwalk is about 10 minutes. Please stay on the trail and boardwalk, as the vegetation here is fragile. Mohawk State Forest has many other attractions, including hiking trails, lookout towers, and a ski area. Camping is available at nearby Housatonic Meadows State Park. For information contact park headquarters at Cornwall Bridge, Conn. 06754; (203) 672-6139.*

12.

Cathedral Pines

Preserve

Directions: Cornwall, Conn. From Hartford, take U.S. 202
west about 30 miles to Torrington; continue west on Route
4 about 12 miles to Cornwall. Turn south (left) onto Pine
St., go to the end, and turn left onto Valley Rd. Go 0.2 mile
and turn left onto Essex Hill Rd. In 0.2 mile there is a large
boulder on the left, with parking just beyond it.

Ownership: The Nature Conservancy.

Of the several stands of old-age white pine in New England (see
#28 and **#71**), this one in the Litchfield Hills of northwestern Connecticut is the largest and best preserved. Since the 1880s, no healthy
trees have been felled here, except for those that have succumbed to
the infrequent but intense southwesterly winds that sweep through
the area. Few "cathedral" stands of white pine survived the charcoal
cutting and agricultural land clearing of the nineteenth century. Of
those that did, many were obliterated by the 1938 hurricane that
ravaged the New England landscape (see **#53**). These pines in Cornwall, managed and preserved by The Nature Conservancy and its
predecessors since the early 1900s, exist today primarily because
they were protected from the destructive hurricane by the southwesterly slope that rises above them.

The effects of the chestnut blight (see **#9** and **#67**), which cleared
out much of the deciduous undergrowth, combined with the growth
characteristics of pine stands, have left this stand as a rare study in
botanical exclusivity. The enormous, dense canopy created by these
200-year-old pines prevents sunlight from reaching the forest floor
and has left the preserve with fewer plant species than would be
found in an average city lot. All told, there are fewer than twenty-
five different species here.

A segment of the Appalachian Trail, marked by white blazes on
adjacent trees, passes through the preserve and is the best route to
follow. Begin at the large boulder (**A**) and walk northward up the
trail. The bramble thicket at **B** is a classic example of the evolution
of a pine stand and of the process of forest succession. The bramble
seeds, which are able to remain dormant for as many as 50 years,

began to germinate only when adequate sunlight reached the forest floor after storm-felled trees opened a sun-hole in the canopy above. A dozen pines were felled at this spot by an intense storm in 1973, and the thicket has since burst into life. Eventually, some shade-tolerant hardwood species such as maple and beech may become established here where they can get the proper mixture of shade from the brambles, sunlight, and water to grow. They may become the dominant species in this area after the pines disappear due to old age, disease, and storm damage.

As you move up the trail, the canopy begins to thicken. These white pines, competing avidly for sun, are able to reach as high as 150 to 160 feet for their life-giving sunlight. There is no in-between size among white pines in a mature stand; those that do not reach at least 120 feet are inevitably seedlings less than 3 feet tall. Newly germinated plants cannot hope to compete with the established ones, and soon give up. The absence of bush-habit and ground-cover plants derives not only from the perpetual shade but also from the extreme acidity of fallen pine needles. The only animal life present here with any frequency is red squirrels, which feed on pine seeds, and woodpeckers and flickers, which nest in fallen, decaying tree

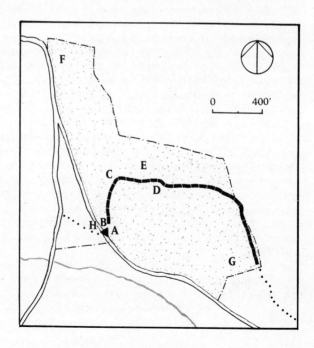

trunks and feed on insects in those trees. Because of the thick canopy, there is insufficient forage for other species.

Passing the rivulet on the trail at **C**, you encounter an enormous pine, likely more than 200 years old, surrounded by a clutch of smaller evergreens. These, and all the other evergreens within the preserve except for the pines themselves, are hemlocks, shade- and humidity-loving trees. (The rivulet itself may be dry at certain times of the year; however, the relative thickness of the ground cover—wood ferns and mosses in particular—indicates the presence of water even in late autumn.) At **D** a fallen tree, marked by a white blaze, has been cut clear through to make way for the trail. About 20 feet ahead, large rocks reveal clues to the geological history of the area. These rocks are covered with phenocrysts, small, pimplelike protrusions that identify the rocks' glacial origins. The slope itself is a ground moraine—the gouged-out remnant of the glacier that scooped up rocks and soil as it moved southwest.

Several feet to the left of these rocks and slightly back down the trail (**E**) stands a small, solitary black-birch sapling; this is the direct consequence of the hole in the canopy directly above. Black-birch seeds germinate aboveground and are thus suited to such a spot, not just because of the sun that is able to break through here but also because of the shallowness of the soil layer above the glacial bedrock, which would not easily accommodate the more extensive root systems of many other deciduous trees. From this point, examine as well the visible tops of the pines that tower above the surrounding hemlock; many have bent, twisted so-called stagheads, indicating that they have reached their uppermost limit of growth. The inability of these trees to draw water and ground nutrients, up such a great height has left them misshapen at the top.

As you reach the plateau at the top of the trail, where two gigantic pines have fallen across each other, hemlocks become dominant over pines, and occasional red oaks and other deciduous species appear as well. Unprotected by the slope below, more trees of all varieties have been felled by severe weather; only here might you find the occasional white pine of mature size that is less than 100 years old. The white-pine cycle has begun again in this spot, but because of the exposed location, will never reach the position of utter dominance and majesty that characterizes the stand immediately below.

It is difficult to measure tree size in such an enclosed space, but a massive fallen trunk near the road at **F** measures 165 feet. A short distance off the trail to the right at **G** is a boulder pile that was deposited by the Wisconsin glacier as it melted about 15,000 years ago. These rocks were picked up by the ice and carried here from anywhere between 100 feet and 100 miles away.

Back at **A**, follow the trail on the other side of the road; the preserve stretches about 300 feet in this direction. At **H** is a rock known as a glacial erratic (see **#78**). One rock, perhaps carried from 3 or 4 miles distant, is perched on top of another and can only have been put in that position by the ice when it melted. Both rocks boast a population of polypody or rockcap ferns. Beyond the rocks, to the north, is an outstanding example of a lightning-struck oak in the process of healing.

Remarks: *Allow about 1 hour to explore the preserve. You may visit at any time of the year, although the preserve is impassable much of winter without snowshoes. There is camping on the Appalachian Trail, and camping and other facilities and activities at nearby Housatonic Meadows State Park (see #11 for details).*

13.
Campbell Falls
State Park

Directions: **Norfolk, Conn. From Hartford, take U.S. 44 northwest about 35 miles to Norfolk. Turn north (right) onto Route 272; go about 4 miles. Turn left onto Spaulding Rd; go 0.2 mile to a parking and picnic area on the right. For only a brief visit to the falls, stay on Route 272 for 0.1 mile past Spaulding Rd.; turn left on the next dirt road and go 0.4 mile to a parking area.**

Ownership: **Parks and Recreation Unit, Connecticut Department of Environmental Protection.**

The southern extension of the Berkshire Hills reaches down into the northwest corner of Connecticut, creating some of the highest and most rugged terrain in the state (see **Taconics, Berkshires, and Green Mountains**). Within this arm of the Berkshires is Campbell Falls State Park, a relatively isolated parcel of 102 acres that supports hemlock, white pine, and northern hardwoods. The park is named

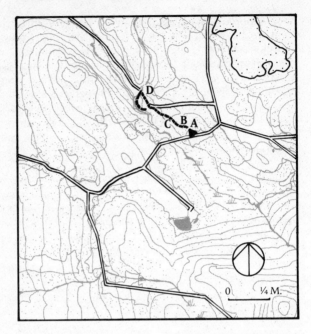

for the dramatic 50-foot falls that thunder down through a narrow, rocky ravine. Campbell Falls is a taste of the Far North and brings to Connecticut a host of northern species, particularly birds, normally not found in southern New England.

The yellow-blazed trail begins at the northwest corner of the picnic area, marked by a white wooden post, and proceeds directly over a sturdy Youth Conservation Corps bridge, which spans this gentle stretch of Ginger Creek. Sun-loving white pines dominate this edge of woodland, but are quickly replaced by hemlocks and hardwoods, which include beech, sugar maple, and yellow birch (**A**). These three hardwood species in combination form the so-called northern beech–birch–maple forest, which covers wide areas in the Northeast and Great Lakes states (see **Taconics, Berkshires, and Green Mountains**). All are trees of cool, moist habitats and can grow under heavier forest cover than other associated hardwoods. Thus they are well situated for the deep shade and chill provided by the dominant hemlock population of these woods.

Yet another indicator of this northern vegetation is the presence of striped maple as a common understory tree (**B**). This small species, normally less than 25 feet in height, grows best in shady ravines and cool, moist sites. More prominent farther north, it exists in southern New England only in scattered assemblages of northern vegetation. The bark, green with white stripes, is the tree's most distinctive feature and, along with the large, drooping leaves, adds color and pattern to the forest. Striped-maple leaves, twigs, and buds are a favorite food of grouse, deer, and the more northern moose, which accounts for its second common name, moosewood.

Continue along the trail, which curves in and around through this predominantly evergreen forest. Here in the thick conifers several northern bird species may find a winter haven, and others will stay to nest in spring (**C**). According to Connecticut bird authorities, if temperatures in the Far North are extremely cold and food supplies limited, Campbell Falls is a likely spot to find many wintering finches; pine grosbeaks, evening grosbeaks, and pine siskins may come to feed on the many tree fruits and seeds in this southern location. Listen for their loud, distinct whistles and almost constant chattering sounds. In particularly good finch years, red and white-winged crossbills may also congregate here. The crossbills are equipped with slender mandibles crossed much like shears, which allow them adeptly to extract seeds from conifer cones. The bill forces and holds apart the cone scales while the tongue lifts out the seed.

Continue along the trail and across a second YCC bridge. Just a bit farther along, the Connecticut–Massachusetts border is marked by a large concrete post—you are now in Massachusetts. The trail meets the upper parking lot and a second modest picnic area. Go left to a somewhat steep but easily navigable trail that descends to the falls (**D**).

Churning, cascading water greets you as you near the bottom of the narrow 50-foot Campbell Falls. The deep greens of thick hemlock and white pine blend into the lighter shades of green and gray of the white ash and red maple a bit farther downstream. The falls cut through a two-tiered series of rock outcroppings, exposing some of the more-resistant bedrock that was uplifted to create these Berkshire highlands. The rocks here are primarily metamorphic gneiss and schist dating back at least 500 million years to the Precambrian and Paleozoic periods.

Although you will eventually have to retrace your steps along the yellow-blazed trail, it is worthwhile to explore the edge of Ginger Creek as it winds through this steep ravine to join forces with the rushing water of the falls. A kingfisher may surprise you as it bolts down center stream, drawing attention with its sharp, rattlelike call. With patience and careful observation during late spring, you may also be able to catch a glimpse of two warblers that make their home along the stream, the Louisiana and northern waterthrush.

The Louisiana waterthrush is the larger of the two and is distinguished by a broad white stripe over the eye and an unstreaked chin and throat. The northern waterthrush has a strong buff eyestripe and a uniformly brown-streaked throat. Both can be identified by their presence near water and their habit of constantly "teetering" through an upward and downward motion of the tail as they walk—hence the nickname "wagtail warbler." Listen for a loud, musical warble, yet another clue to their presence. The Louisiana's song may be distinguished by its wilder nature, ending in a confused mixture of chippering notes. Both call with a distinctive, loud metallic *pink*.

The northern waterthrush reaches some of its southernmost breeding range in this area. Although it is an abundant migrant, often seen in gardens and shrubbery, it breeds only locally, and rarely in southern New England. On northern nesting grounds it shows a preference for bogs, swamp pools, or lake edges, and nests less often near the rushing streams favored by the more southern Louisiana. At Campbell Falls both species nest close to the water in the streambank, under roots or in a cavity created by the upturned roots of a fallen tree. Nests are constructed of dead leaves, mosses, or rootlets and are lined with finer grasses and soft moss. A streamside nesting location allows the birds close and easy access to their food source: aquatic insects, tiny mollusks, crustacea, worms, and occasionally fish. Look for the warblers among the rocks and aquatic vegetation as they search for food, hunting thoroughly along the stream and picking up soggy leaves to uncover hidden delicacies.

As you head back along the stream to retrace your steps on the incoming trail, note the array of vegetation close to the ground. The world within a steep ravine is quite different from more exposed places nearby. High walls trap the cool, moist air and allow for an abundance of ferns, mosses, and liverworts. It is an enchanting microhabitat amidst the towering hemlock.

Remarks: *The entire walk takes about 1½ hours, but you can get to the falls in 10 minutes from the upper parking lot. Although this site is considered the ''icebox'' of Connecticut, it offers excellent winter birding. Camping is available about 20 miles northeast at Granville State Forest, Granville, Mass. 01034; (413) 357-6611.*

14.

Northeast
Audubon Center

Directions: Sharon, Conn. From Hartford, take U.S. 202 west about 30 miles to Torrington; continue west on Route 4 about 15 miles to Cornwall Bridge. Continue on Route 4 another 7 miles past the intersection with U.S. 7; look for signs to the center (on the right) and the parking lot.

Ownership: National Audubon Society.

Since 1961 this 684-acre property has been owned and operated by the National Audubon Society as one of their five national nature centers. Eleven miles of trails lead you to two large ponds inhabited by beavers, to a hemlock gorge, through open fields, and through a mixed-hardwood forest where bobcats, foxes, and coyotes are known to occur.

Begin walking on the Fern Trail to the edge of Ford Pond (**A**). This 30-acre body of water was created in the mid-nineteenth century as a source of power for a cider and sorghum mill and a sawmill. It was also used for ice harvesting; the old icehouse is directly to the right of the spillway.

Ford Pond is very rich in nutrients, which wash down from local hillsides and through a small stream from Bog Meadow Pond, a few hundred yards to the south. This factor, combined with the pond's shallow depth, silty bottom, and exposure to sunlight, enables it to support an abundance of aquatic vegetation. Cattails, water lilies, pondweeds, and numerous other plants provide the basis for a healthy food web, which accounts for the wide animal community found in and around the water. Brown bullheads, largemouth bass, muskrats, beavers, geese, and ducks are among those that enjoy Ford Pond.

A large wooden nesting box, designed to attract the wary and colorful wood duck (see **#102**), has been placed up in an oak tree beside the pond (**B**). A number of such boxes on the perimeter of this and Bog Meadow Pond have successfully housed clutches of eggs not only of the wood duck but also of the hooded merganser. Although most local ducks nest on the ground, these two species are cavity nesters, usually finding a suitable hole in a large old tree.

Artificial nesting boxes have been erected throughout the country in response to the unfortunate loss of habitat due to the drainage of wetlands and the subsequent cutting of timber. This national effort has resulted in a significant increase in the wood-duck population since the early part of this century.

Proceed quietly along the boardwalk. River otters have been seen frequently at Bog Meadow Pond (**C**), and loud noises may scare them away. Sightings of beavers are also not unusual. Smaller creatures that you are more likely to see or hear include bullfrogs and green frogs, American toads, northern water snakes, and eastern newts. In early spring the frogs, toads, and newts lay their jelly-coated eggs in the still and shallow waters here. Frog eggs usually occur in a large globular mass, while toad eggs are laid in ribbons or strings. Newts, on the other hand, lay single eggs about the size of a sweetpea seed, which is attached to the leaf or stem of a waterplant. If you lie down on the boardwalk and watch the water, you may see some of these amphibians or signs of their activities.

Bog Meadow Pond was also a millpond in the middle to late 1800s, but was drained every summer to allow for the growth and harvesting of a crop of hay. In the fall the outlets were closed, water

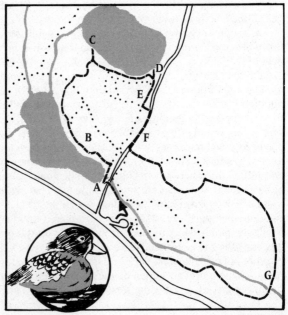

Inset: Wood duck

built up from nearby swamp seepage and rain, and a cider and sorghum mill operated its hydropowered wheel. Eventually this practice was stopped, and the pond filled to its present size.

A huge beaver lodge (**D**) has been abandoned by its owners within the past two years, probably because of human disturbance. If you look down the shoreline to the right, about 150 yards away, you will see the familiar domed shape of an active and recently built lodge. Beavers on this particular pond generally stay in a lodge for about 2 years; when they have depleted the immediate food supply, they move to a new site and fresh source of food. It is possible, however, that the beavers may someday return to this abandoned lodge.

In 1979 and 1980 Audubon staff began clearing brush and cutting trees in this 5-acre area, within the perimeter of several old stone walls (**E**). The carefully conceived plan behind the facelift was to open a space in the woods which would be suitable for the re-creation of a lost New England prairie. Although the Midwest might seem to us a more appropriate region for prairies, botanists have discovered that before the arrival of the Pilgrims New England had fields of grasses and flowers exactly like those found in the Great Plains. The local prairie vegetation died out as the region was farmed and settled and alien plants introduced from Europe began to flourish. Seeds from a number of prairie plants such as little bluestem grass, big bluestem grass, and wild rye have been collected by scientist Bob Moeller and will be sown in this location. Only time will tell if this exciting ecological experiment will succeed and prairie plants once again populate their former environments.

Bog Meadow Road (**F**) is a very old thoroughfare used by farmers, traders, and travelers since 1750. Over the years traffic and natural weathering processes wore down the roadbed, and in places the bedrock is exposed. The schists and gneisses seen here are ancient metamorphic rocks whose origins go back 500 to 600 million years. They are part of the regional metamorphism that engulfed the greater part of New England during the early Paleozoic (see **Taconics, Berkshires, and Green Mountains**). Most of Bog Meadow Road is still a public way, surprisingly enough, but the town stopped maintaining it years ago. No one drives on it except the preserve staff, who occasionally haul firewood in a Jeep.

The Hazelnut Trail slowly winds through a dry mid-slope forest of red and chestnut oaks and down a steep grade toward Herrick Brook, where a grove of white birches gives way to thick hemlocks (**G**). The presence of white birch, a tree usually found farther north, indicates that some kind of disturbance occurred here. All of the accessible portions of land at the Audubon center, including this mid-slope and near-ravine area, were timbered for the charcoal industry during the late nineteenth century. The birches proliferated, most likely because there was a nearby seed source and conditions were right for germination and growth. At the time, open space allowed plentiful sunlight to reach the birch seedlings.

It is no surprise to find hemlocks growing here along the stream ravine all the way back to the main buildings. The cool and shady conditions provide a microclimate similar to their normal range in northern New England. Be on the lookout for ruffed grouse, which eat hemlock needles and buds.

The path (now the Ford Trail) returns to the Audubon center through hemlocks and an old pasture now reverting to forest.

Remarks: *This walk takes about 2 hours. Three detailed trail guides, available near the parking lot, describe an energy walk, a historical walk, and a general nature walk. Trails are open from dawn to dusk; the main building is open Monday through Saturday from 9:00 a.m. to 5:00 p.m. and Sunday 1:00 p.m. to 5:00 p.m. Admission to the property is $1. The annual ecology festival, held in late July, is well known throughout the region for its diverse and entertaining program. The center maintains a small museum with live reptiles and amphibians, an indoor honey-bee hive, and other related displays. An excellent natural history bookstore and library add to the many attractions here. Camping is available at Housatonic Meadows State Park, Cornwall Bridge, Conn. 06754; (203) 672-6139.*

15.

Brace Mountain

Directions: **Millerton, N.Y. From New York City, take the Taconic State Parkway north about 80 miles. Take Route 199 east about 16 miles, then take U.S. 44 and Route 22 north about 1 mile into Millerton. Continue north on Route 22 for 5.4 miles; turn right onto Whitehouse Crossing Rd. Go 0.7 mile to Undermountain Rd.; turn left and go 0.2 mile. Turn right onto Rudd Pond Farms Rd.; drive 1 mile to the very small trailhead parking area on the left, just past a log house.**

Ownership: **Taconic State Park and Recreation Commission.**

The unusually grassy and windswept summit of 2,311-foot-high Brace Mountain is noted for its interesting botany and birdlife and for its outstanding views into three states. Part of the Taconic Range, Brace Mountain is accessible by a steep climb up its wooded sides along a narrow stream valley. Because of the mountain's remote setting within a much larger wild area, it harbors such shy and uncommon mammals as bobcat and snowshoe hare.

From the three-car parking area follow the white blazes of the South Taconic Trail between a posted, private field and privately owned woods. Red and white oaks, red maples, bigtooth aspens, and mountain laurel grow at the base of these mountains, an area most likely cut over in years past for firewood, charcoaling, or pasturing.

Soon the trail parallels a steep creek that cascades down the hillside in musical tones (**A**). The other side of the creek faces slightly northwest and is dotted with shade-tolerant hemlocks (see **#65** and **#73**), while this side slants a bit to the west-southwest and is practically devoid of this flat-needled conifer, though hardwoods are doing fine. This may have occurred because of different sunlight factors that affected competition, or it may be the result of an earlier

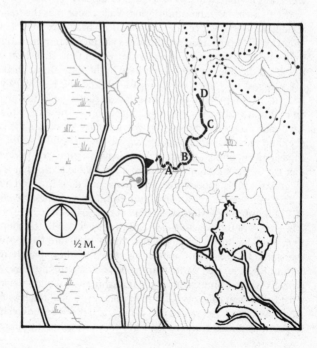

logging. Phoebes and brown creepers sing here in spring and probably nest nearby.

Notice the unusual greenish-blue, wavy rocks and boulders exposed along the slope. Brace Mountain is composed of this foliated
or layered metamorphic rock, which can be characterized as something between a phyllite and a chlorite-muscovite-quartz schist. Like
many other aspects of nature, rocks are often variable and difficult
to classify absolutely. In this case, when the Taconic Range was
formed (see **Taconics, Berkshires, and Green Mountains**), the
distribution of heat and pressure over the mass of sediments in the
region was also variable. Thus the mineralogy and grades of metamorphism differ from place to place.

Brace Mountain is part of the main Taconic system, a series of
high peaks that stretch from Dorset, Vt., south to nearby Sharon,
Conn. Created during the Ordovician period, approximately 450
million years ago, the Taconics are believed to have slid down a low
slope of the Green Mountains when the entire area was uplifted and
folded. The crustal stresses were apparently so great at the time that
huge plates, some many miles wide, were moved in the process.

Watch your step in this extremely steep area as the trail can be
wet and the underlying rocks loose and slippery.

The first views of the rural Harlem Valley appear as the trail skirts
a ridgeside (**B**). Notice the low scrub or bear oak trees (*Quercus
ilicifolia*) rising only a few feet from the ground. Rarely growing taller
than 20 feet high, and frequently much less than that, bear oak is
found on the poorest of dry soils here in the East. Dense thickets of
it are found on Cape Cod, Long Island, and the New Jersey Pine
Barrens. It is reputedly called bear oak because the bear is the only
animal that will eat its intensely bitter acorns. These trees may not
have much success in producing acorns, however, because the windy,
dry, and exposed environment may be too stressful and the trees'
capacities too limited. White oaks growing in protected pockets farther up the mountain produce a more palatable acorn that is eaten
by gray squirrels, rabbits, deer, raccoons, ruffed grouse, and others.

The trail continues to climb and eventually reaches the summit
(**C**) of South Brace Mountain (elevation 2,304 feet), where one has
a fine view of three picturesque bodies of water off to the southeast:
Riga Lake, South Pond, and Grass Pond. These are located within
the state of Connecticut and are protected by the privately owned
Mount Riga Preserve. More than 10,000 acres in this area are owned
by New York, Connecticut, and Massachusetts, creating what ecologist Erik Kiviat calls a wildlife reservoir. For such animals as bobcat
(see **#4**), coyote (see **#110** and **#111**), and black bear, which need
large, undisturbed tracts of land in order to maintain populations,

the natural areas of the tristate region meet some of those requirements.

Dip down into a sheltered hollow where vegetation grows larger
than on the adjacent ridgetops, before climbing again to reach the
grassy bald summit of Brace Mountain (**D**). The views are spectacular! In the distance to the northeast stand the towers of Massachu-
sett's Mount Everett. Alander Mountain is directly to the north, and
the Catskill Mountains rise in the far west. Just to the east, perhaps
a mile or so away, is Connecticut's Gridley Mountain.

Explanations for the unusual pattern of vegetation here at the top
include both natural and man-influenced events. It is known that
the summit was pastured, probably in the late 1700s and early 1800s,
as evidenced by stone walls at the north end. This likely disturbed
and destroyed part of the already thin soil cover. Local investigators
have also found signs of fire in the area. These fires, in combination
with harsh winds, the hot summer sun, and the apparent lack of
soil-catching basins, have produced the present scrubby, heathlike
topography.

Grasses, sedges, and lowbush blueberry are dominant plants, while
crustose and fruticose lichens (see **#7**) can be found on bare rocks
and thin soil respectively. Three-toothed cinquefoil (*Potentilla triden-
tata*), a small member of the rose family that favors mountaintop
habitats in the northern United States, can be found at the edges of
the summit near rocks. Bearberry (see **#46**), unusual for Dutchess
County, is also found here. The few dwarfed trees off to the sides are
red oak, bear oak, gray and paper birch, and an occasional pin
cherry.

Audubon warden Art Gingert of Sharon, Conn., has observed the
birdlife of Brace Mountain and mentions hermit thrushes and Canada warblers as likely breeders in the woodlands below the summit.
The ethereal, flutelike song of the hermit thrush can often be heard
here during late afternoons in warmer months. Rufous-sided towhees are found here too, and barred owls in the thicker woods east
of here. In the fall, different species of hawks fly by during migration
(see **#2** and **#66**), and during the rest of the year one can usually
observe turkey vultures (see **#10**) and red-tailed hawks soaring on
the mountain updrafts.

Follow the same route back to the trailhead, taking care along the
steeper portions.

Remarks: *Round-trip walking time is approximately 4 hours, but plan to
spend more time because of the strenuousness of the walk and the superb
scenery from the top. Bring water and food, and dress for cooler weather.
Do not attempt the hike in winter because of the ice buildup. Be extremely*

alert to property boundaries, especially at the foot of the trail, and do not wander off the route there. Be sure to remove any cans, bottles, or paper you bring along. Absolutely no camping is allowed, but a fine campground can be found just a few miles to the south, on Undermountain Rd., at Rudd Pond. This is part of New York State's Taconic Park. The renowned Bash Bish Falls (see #20) is a few miles to the north, just east of the village of Copake Falls. Detailed hiking maps of the area may be purchased in Millerton at the Oblong Book Shop.

16.

Thompson Pond
Preserve

Directions: **Pine Plains, N.Y. From New York City, take the Taconic State Parkway north about 80 miles to the exit at Lafayetteville. Take Route 199 east about 6 miles to Pine Plains; go south on Route 82 about 0.5 mile. At the corner by the firehouse, turn west (right) onto Lake Rd. Go 1.6 miles to the entrance of the preserve on the left.**

Ownership: **The Nature Conservancy.**

At the foot of Stissing Mountain in rural upstate New York lies Thompson Pond, a picturesque 44-acre jewel created thousands of years ago by the action of glacial ice. An extensive cattail marsh and a notable array of wildflowers, mammals, and birdlife are among the many reasons this preserve has been designated a National Natural Landmark. Golden eagles have wintered here several times during the past decade.

The trail begins near a tiny parking lot at the northwestern corner of the property. At the registration box turn left onto the blue-blazed trail and walk toward the pond through a forest of young gray birch and occasional redcedar trees (**A**). These two pioneer species cover much of the western shore, and they tell us the area was once pasture land. (See **#7** for more on redcedars.) Judging from the age of these trees, the pasture was probably abandoned in the 1940s or 50s. Gray birch is thus appropriately known to some as old-field birch. It is distinguished from its more majestic cousin, the white birch, by its smaller size, its triangular leaf, and its dark branch scars,

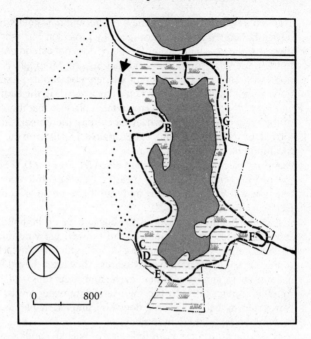

which look like dusky black triangles along the trunk. The gray birches are thriving here and apparently have shaded out and killed most of the redcedars, which are less in evidence than one would expect in an old pasture.

An ancient sunken rowboat lies at the shoreline, where cattails grow in thick profusion (**B**). Thompson Pond is a glacial kettle, formed when a block of ice slowly melted about 15,000 years ago. Its sides were steep then, as sand and gravel from other meltwater streams were deposited around the remnant ice. The kettle thus became a hole in the landscape; the weight of the ice caused it to sink farther into the ground, and its bottom intersected the nearby water table (see **#76**). The kettle originally reached northeast about a mile to the present sites of Stissing and Twin Island lakes but over the years separated into the three present ponds as the buildup of sediments and marshland cut it into pieces. The other two bodies of water drain into this one, and at the southeast end of Thompson Pond, Wappinger Creek begins its 30-mile flow to the Hudson River.

At the edge of this farm field (**C**), just before the yellow-blazed trail heads down along the marshy southern border of the pond, look back to the right for a fine view of 1,403-foot Stissing Mountain.

The geological origin of this mass of Precambrian gneiss is still in question. Scott Warthin, a local geology professor, has written that there is some possibility the gneiss block does not extend downward to the underlying formations and that Stissing Mountain is really a huge fault block, moved from somewhere else into its present position. A fault block is formed when a crack occurs in the earth's crust and upward or sideward movement takes place so that the two sides of the crack no longer match. A block may then break off and be moved by crustal dynamics. The original location of the Stissing Mountain block, however, is unknown.

A huge black-oak tree has fallen here (**D**). Forester Dan Smiley of the nearby Mohonk Preserve measured the circumference of this tree when it was still standing and found it to be an astounding 19 feet!

A shaky boardwalk traverses the boggy edge of the pond, where sphagnum moss and hummocks can be seen growing out of the shallow depths (**E**). The hummocks are formed by tussock sedge (*Carex stricta*) and certain woody plants. They are believed to be an adaptation to changing water levels, and their tops and bottoms roughly correspond with the high- and low-water levels. Woody plants such as alder, blueberry, dogwood, and red maple can be seen growing on top of these hummocks.

The sphagnum moss is an indicator of boglike conditions in this cool, shaded portion of the pond. Thompson Pond has certain bog qualities, but differs in significant ways from the more typical bog communities (see **#11, #74,** and **#76**). It is considered a circumneutral bog: its waters have a neutral rather than acidic pH, clear rather than stained coloration, and vegetation dominated by cattails. The cattail is not adapted to bogs—it is generally found in marshes (see **#33**). Like traditional bogs, this pond has an extensive peat deposit that is the result of incomplete sphagnum-moss decay. In addition, the sphagnum has created floating mats of vegetation as it grows out over the water. Thus Thompson Pond is a complex of many environmental factors coming together to form a unique wetland ecosystem.

As the trail bends to the right near the southeastern edge of the property, an impenetrable alder–purple-loosestrife marsh conceals the beginnings of Wappinger Creek (**F**). Runoff and sediment from dead vegetation have slowly built up this area so that it is no longer open water but a wet thicket. The elevation here, logically enough, is the lowest on the preserve. Thus the marsh serves as a trap for much organic debris.

The loosestrife, seen here and along portions of the shore, is a native of Europe that has spread wildly throughout the region. It fulfills a function similar to that of cattails, slowly filling in sections of marshes, but it provides almost no food for wildlife except for honeybees. For this reason, and because it has taken over areas where more useful plants could have grown, purple loosestrife is known as a pest. It is, however, quite pretty. Look for the four- to six-petaled magenta flowers on a long spike during the summer months.

Continue along the eastern shore past cherry, red maple, ash, and other hardwoods (**G**). The forest here is older and different in composition than on most of the western shore. Hemlock is notably absent in this sunnier location, possibly because other species flourish here and the hemlocks cannot compete. The absence of gray birch and redcedar leads one to conclude that perhaps this side of the pond was used as a woodlot or for other purposes than pasturing.

The trail ends on Lake Rd. Go left, across the causeway that separates Thompson Pond from Stissing Lake, back to the parking lot.

Remarks: *This is a 2-hour walk. Wear rubber-bottomed footwear. The trail to the top of Stissing Mountain is located ½ mile past the parking lot on Lake Rd. Among the many wildflowers one can expect to find here, varying with the seasons, are dutchman's breeches, wild geranium, fringed polygala, lady's slipper, trillium, and white and yellow pond lilies. A collection of essays,* The Ecology of Thompson Pond, *edited by Phyllis Busch, describes the area in detail and may be obtained through the Nature Conservancy office in Mount Kisco, N.Y. The nearby setting of Mud Pond (Twin Island Lake) is featured in an exhibit at the American Museum of Natural History in New York City. Camping is available at Lake Taghkanic State Park, north of Elizaville, N.Y., on the Taconic State Parkway.*

17.
Hudson River
Estuarine Sanctuary
at Tivoli Bays

Directions: **Annandale-on-Hudson, N.Y. From New York City, take the Taconic State Parkway north about 80 miles to the exit at Lafayetteville. Take Route 199 west about 9 miles through Red Hook to Route 9G. Go north on Route 9G about 2 miles; turn left onto Annandale Rd., just north**

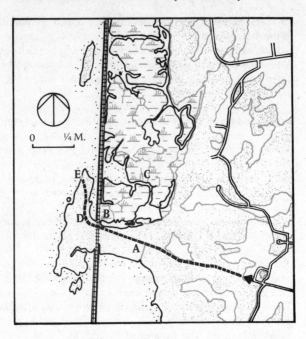

of the entrance to Bard College. Go west about 0.3 mile, where the paved road swings south; continue west on un-paved Cruger Island Rd. (unmarked) about 100 feet to a parking lot, part of the Bard campus.

Ownership: **New York Department of Environmental Con-servation.**

Known as one of the best birding spots in Dutchess County, Tivoli Bays is a 1,400-acre freshwater tidal marsh that recently became part of the National Estuarine Sanctuary system. Dense cattails pro-vide cover for least bitterns, long-billed marsh wrens, common gal-linules, sora and Virginia rails, and other marsh-loving varieties. Numerous kinds of fish and wildlife are also found here amidst the classic beauty of the Mid-Hudson valley.

The road to the marsh is about a mile long and passes through a pine-hardwood forest before reaching the first wetland feature, a red-maple, red-ash, and black-ash swamp. Look carefully in the waters here for schools of banded killifish and mummichogs (**A**). These small (2½- to 3-inch) olive and silvery fish are a vital link in the estuarine food web, eating detritus and small invertebrates such as bloodworm larvae and dragonfly nymphs, and in turn being eaten by larger fish, turtles, kingfishers, and wading birds such as least bitterns. Killifish are widespread in freshwater (and also saltwater) habitats ranging from South Carolina to the Canadian Maritime Provinces and across the upper Midwest to Montana. They spawn in quiet, weedy pools from late spring into late summer, the female extruding a cluster of several hundred eggs, which remain attached to her genital papilla by a fine, transparent thread. An attendant male immediately fertilizes the eggs, which then drop and become entangled in the vegetation. Look for small schools of killifish in this swampy area and in the marsh.

The water at Tivoli Bays is fresh, as the so-called salt front (from the Atlantic Ocean) does not usually move farther upriver than the Poughkeepsie area. This is because of the great volume of freshwater runoff pouring into the Hudson from its source in the Adirondacks, from its many tributaries, and from rainfall. The tides, however, range from 3 to 4 feet and extend all the way north to Troy, where the first dam is encountered. Tidal influence can penetrate as far as the channel bottom is below sea level. This is because an estuary, like the Hudson, is continuous with the ocean.

As one approaches the railroad tracks, the water deepens and the wooded swamp opens up to a large, 350-acre cattail marsh (**B**). Scientists studying Tivoli Bays estimate that perhaps 55 percent of North Bay is covered by narrow-leaved cattail (see **#33**), 15 percent by purple loosestrife (see **#16**), and the rest by a mixture of arrowhead, pickerelweed, spatterdock, arrow arum, and other species. The adaptations of aquatic plants to cope with changing water and oxygen levels, as well as their methods of reproduction, are fascinating in their variety. Large air spaces, for example, in the tissues of most species help keep the plant afloat; otherwise the weight of the stems and flowers would cause it to sink. Arrowhead, named for the shape of its large bright-green leaves, can reproduce not only from seeds but also from bulblike tubers on underground stems. During the winter the main part of the plant dies, but in the following spring, new plants grow from the tubers. Spatterdock, an emergent plant (see **#18**) with floating leaves, has stomata, or gas-exchange pores, on the upper surface of the leaf rather than on the underside, as most plants do. This allows it to secure oxygen and carbon dioxide directly from the air rather than through the water.

The least bittern, a small thin member of the heron family, nests here in the cattail marsh (**C**). You can consider yourself lucky, however, to obtain a good look at this timid and retiring bird, because it prefers to hide in the thickest areas of vegetation. The bittern has a well-known habit of "freezing" when it is approached, pointing its long bill up toward the sky, compressing its feathers, and generally

pretending it isn't there. Its brown coloration provides good camouflage. One may very well hear its song, however, which Roger
Tory Peterson describes as "a low, muted coo-coo-coo." Listen for
bitterns in late May and early June, especially at twilight.

Least bitterns are found throughout the eastern United States, but
are usually limited to areas where aquatic vegetation, cattails in
particular, is densest. Ornithologists believe that marsh drainage,
pollution, and spraying of insecticides have adversely affected the
range of this bird.

The marsh is also a good place to listen for rails, especially in
spring during the early morning hours and around dusk. These elusive birds (mainly sora and Virginia, but occasionally king) are irregular breeders at Tivoli Bays. Consult your field guides for voice descriptions.

A path on the western side of the railroad tracks leads onto Cruger
Island, the site of a former estate (**D**). Cerulean warblers, birds that
occur in small, widely scattered colonies, have nested here among
the larger deciduous trees. Ludlow Griscom, one of the ornithologi-
cal giants of this century, wrote that ceruleans are quite sensitive to
human disturbance, noting that the bird disappeared from various
wooded swamps in the Midwest when they were logged a hundred
years ago. It is good news, then, that the bird seems to be slowly
moving up into southern New England along the river valleys, especially the Hudson and Housatonic. Why this is so is not known
for sure, but it may be because the region is now more heavily
wooded than it was in the past, and taller trees along river valleys
are more numerous.

The cerulean spends much of its time high up in the trees searching for insects and thus may be difficult to see. It has a loud and
persistent song, however, that has been described by Richard Pough
as "a husky, rolling series of 4 or 5 short notes on the same pitch
followed by a higher-pitched shrill." Griscom characterizes the song
as "just a little sneeze."

Warblers of many kinds use Cruger Island as a resting area during
migration in May and September. Several other members of this
insect-eating family nest on the preserve, including the common
yellowthroat and the little yellow warbler.

A spectacular view of the Hudson River and Catskill Mountains
awaits you at the edge of Cruger Island (**E**). The small village of
Glasco is directly across the river, with Overlook and Plattekill
mountains behind.

Remarks: *Walking time is about 2 hours. (During high tide it may be
difficult to get onto Cruger Island.) South Bay, just below North Bay, is*

another part of the sanctuary worth exploring. Migratory waterfowl frequently use both areas and the river itself as stopping-off points. A scope is helpful. Camping is available at Lake Taghkanic State Park north of Elizaville on the Taconic State Parkway, and at Norrie State Park in Staatsburg.

18.
Hudson River
Estuarine Sanctuary
at Stockport Flats

Directions: **Stockport, N.Y. From New York City, take the Taconic State Parkway north about 90 miles. Go northwest about 5 miles on Route 82, then continue northwest on U.S. 9 another 6 miles into Hudson. From the intersection with Route 9G, continue north on U.S. 9 for about another 5.5 miles. Immediately after crossing the bridge over Stockport Creek, turn left onto County Route 22. Go about 1 mile to the dead end; park along the gravel road by the railroad tracks. Canoes can be put in along Stockport Creek on this, the northeastern, side of the tracks.**

Ownership: **New York Department of Environmental Conservation.**

The largest of the four federally and state designated estuarine sanctuary sites along the Hudson River, Stockport Flats covers about 4 miles of islands, peninsulas, marshes, swamps, and shoreline. This lovely configuration provides excellent canoeing and allows access to many places not reachable by foot. An abundance of wild rice and well-developed tidal swamps of cottonwood, silver maple, and ash distinguish Stockport Flats from the other sanctuary properties. Many birds, including marsh wrens, kingfishers, and bank swallows, nest here, while others such as black ducks and mallards use the main marsh for feeding and resting.

Begin paddling down the mouth of Stockport Creek and along the peninsula on your left. The tidal range is about 4 feet, and if you are here during low tide, mudflat areas will be exposed; be careful not to get grounded.

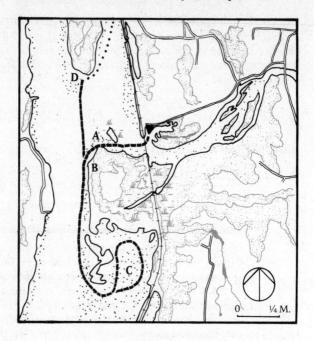

You will find a variety of emergent plantlife, that is, plants that extend significantly above water. Upon closer study, a somewhat predictable pattern of their growth in relation to tidal influence becomes apparent (**A**). Cattails line the upper edges of the marshy areas (see **#33**), and sweetflag grows a little farther out, usually followed by wild rice, pickerelweed, and spatterdock in the lower intertidal zone. This general arrangement has evolved over eons, as plants with different needs and different adaptations competed more successfully in some locations than others. Behind the emergent plants the trees of the floodplain or tidal swamp appear massive and shady. These species, like the aquatic ones, have adapted to a certain ecological niche; here, for example, they are able to tolerate frequent bathing of their roots. The tall cottonwoods, sycamores, silver maples, red ash, and various willows provide dense cover for the small deer population here, as well as for numbers of ruffed grouse and woodland birds such as the pewee and eastern kingbird.

Although the unnamed peninsula you are canoeing around looks quite natural and well established, it is partly man-made (**B**). It began as a naturally occurring gravel bar, but was then added to as the Army Corps of Engineers dredged the river's ship channel earlier in the century and dumped the so-called dredge spoils onto it. The channel now averages 36 feet in depth.

The main marsh is one of the top attractions here, especially for wildlife lovers (**C**). Red-winged blackbirds hang onto the sturdy stems of cattails, singing their familiar *konk-a-ree*. Marsh wrens gurgle their own distinctive songs, while least bitterns (see **#17**) and sora and Virginia rails hide among the dense greenery. A muskrat might be munching on the remains of a root or stalk. Perhaps a great blue heron (see **#40** and **#64**) or green heron will be patiently wading in the shallows, searching for a killifish.

Your canoe can take you up into the small, narrow channels that penetrate the thick cattails and sweetflag, or along the edges of the frequently lush wild rice stands (**C**), where ducks gather in autumn to eat the fallen seeds. Stockport Flats has the most extensive stand of wild rice on the Hudson, and wildlife experts consider it one of the very best foods not only for ducks but for bobolinks, blackbirds, and rails. Fortunately for wildlife, the local citizens do not harvest the tasty kernels.

Wild rice *(Zizania aquatica)* is an annual grass that prefers broad, gently sloping mudflats and slowly circulating waters. It grows throughout a large portion of the eastern United States, west to the Dakotas, and also in parts of the eastern Gulf Coast states. It is intolerant of salinity and therefore does not grow well in the Hudson south of the Poughkeepsie area. It needs full sun and shelter from wind and waves, and seems to do best in quiet marshes such as this one. Look for a tall, graceful grass 5 to 10 feet high, supported by a thick stem. Its seeds start to ripen around the end of August and continue to do so until late September.

As you canoe through the marsh and back out again to the river, you may wonder why the water is so murky. The answer is that an amalgam of everyday occurrences causes a tremendous amount of both organic and inorganic particles to be carried in suspension by the river. The Hudson receives sediment, nutrients, and organisms from the sea as well as from twenty-five major tributaries. The actions of fish, turtles, birds, and muskrats roil the water. Furthermore, sewage and erosion from logging and construction have added to the river's natural turbidity. The deep mud you see in the marshy areas and coves has accumulated over the centuries as these particles settled out in sheltered waters. Plant roots have also played a part in this deposition as they trap more particles and slow down currents.

Paddle north to the southwest end of Stockport Middle Ground Island, where bank swallows have excavated over three hundred nest tunnels in the sandy bluffs or scarp (**D**). This colony is quite large by usual standards and must not be disturbed, either by getting out to land or by dallying too long at the water's edge. A kingfisher's nest is also located here, and the sharply larger diameter of its tunnel entrance stands out against the others. Listen for the rattlelike call of this large and exciting bird.

One can continue around this island and up to Gay's Point for birding, fishing, or simply more paddling. Watch out for sandbars and mudflats that may ground the canoe.

Remarks: *Paddling time is approximately 2½ to 4 hours, depending on weather conditions, wind, and how much time you spend exploring. You can also paddle up Stockport Creek for about a mile to the bottom of a riffle just below Route 9, or through a narrow distributary off to the southwest (during high tide only). Bring warm clothes, lunch, insect repellent, water, and life preservers. Hikers can visit the main marsh by carefully crossing the railroad bridge and walking south. The trains here run at high speeds and are relatively quiet, so exercise caution. Camping is available for boaters on Stockport Middle Ground and Gay's Point courtesy of Hudson River Islands State Park.*

19.

Wilson M. Powell Wildlife Sanctuary

Directions: **Chatham, N.Y. From New York City, take the Taconic State Parkway north about 110 miles. Go west (left) on 203 about 1 mile; turn right at Chatham, and follow Route 66 north about 4 miles to Chatham Center. Just before a bridge over the Kinderhook, turn right onto County Route 13. Follow signs toward Old Chatham; turn right onto Pitt Hall Rd., marked by a sign for the Powell Sanctuary. Turn left onto Hunt Club Rd. and follow it to the parking lot.**

Ownership: **Alan Devoe Bird Club, Inc.**

The Wilson M. Powell Wildlife Sanctuary, established as a refuge in 1959, comprises 143 acres of mixed woodlands, fields, streams, marshes, and a pond. The variety of terrain allows for very diverse bird, animal, and plant populations. The Alan Devoe Bird Club,

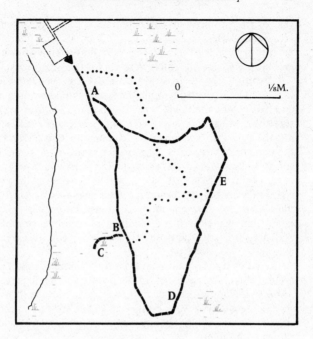

which owns and maintains the sanctuary, has recorded sightings of over 250 different species of birds here.

In parking lot 1, the bird club has set up feeders, which attract red- and white-breasted nuthatches, chickadees, tufted titmice, and various other species. To the right is a small clearing where sparrows and pheasants feed, as well as a shed with maps of the sanctuary, posters to aid bird identification, and a guest register.

Approximately 3 miles of trails wind through the sanctuary. All are clearly marked by red, orange, white, or green blazes. This guide will follow the white-blazed trail, which passes through a variety of habitats but fewer wet areas than the others, and return to the parking lot via the orange-blazed trail.

At **A** the white-blazed trail divides; to the left, down a short hill, is the Eleanor Turner Glade, an open area where towhees, deer, and raccoons might be seen, especially in the early morning. Continuing straight at **A**, the white trail leads through mixed woodlands in an early stage of succession. Watch for dark-eyed juncos and pileated woodpeckers all along the trail. At **B**, marked by a large pile of stones to the right, a short trail leads to Dorson's Rocks. Before reaching the rocks, however, the trail crosses over a seasonal stream

(**C**), which runs between two paternoster ponds. These ponds were created as glaciers scraped the basins along its path and are called paternoster ponds because, when viewed from above or on a topographical map, they resemble a string of paternoster beads.

Dorson's Rocks rise over 900 feet above sea level. From here, the Catskills are visible to the south, the Shawangunks to the southwest, and Albany and the Helderberg Plateau to the northwest. The Hudson River, which cannot be seen from here, lies between these rocks and the Catskills. Even when mist obscures the Catskills and Albany, the panoramic view of the surrounding farmlands is beautiful. Dorson's Rocks is also a spectacular place from which to watch for turkey vultures (see **#10**) and hawks (see **#66**), and for warblers when they are moving through on their migratory travels. The rocks themselves are metamorphic: a combination of shales, slates, and quartz that were twisted and contorted into swirling patterns by heat and pressure (see **Taconics, Berkshires, and Green Mountains**).

The white trail continues on from **B** to a spruce wood **D**. Ruffed grouse, also known as partridge, are common in among these 30- to 35-foot Norway spruce, where they feed on cones and twigs. This species is a ground-dwelling, chickenlike bird with a large body and short but strong wings that allow only brief flights. During its courtship ritual in the spring, and also when defending its territory, the male makes a loud thumping noise that sounds very much like a motor slowly starting up in the distance. He makes this drumming sound by puffing himself up and beating his wings rapidly until the "motor" ends in a sputtering whir. This grove also harbors pine grosbeaks, pine siskins, crossbills, and occasionally pine warblers, which are drawn to the coniferous trees for food and shelter. Year-round it is the coolest and darkest part of the sanctuary, because the spruce block out virtually all of the sunlight. However, because spruce, like hemlock, prefer rockier, wetter soil, the cones of the trees here do not bear ideal seeds, and there are few young trees. Eventually, shade-tolerant hardwoods such as maple and beech will take root and become the dominant species as the evergreens die off.

After the spruce wood, the white trail edges along the top of a ravine. Several of the easily recognized striped, or goosefoot, maples can be seen here (see **#13**). When these trees are young, their green bark is distinctly marked with white horizontal stripes. The leaves, shaped like goose footprints, also make these trees easily identifiable. At **E** is a marshy area, one source of water for the intermittent stream in the ravine below, which is also fed by other springs on the preserve.

The orange-blazed trail, which branches off to the right, follows along a ridge. Here much of the bedrock is exposed, because glaciers scraped away the debris that once covered the rock. Dorson's Rocks, too, were left exposed as glaciers carried away soil and other debris. The bedrock is approximately 450 million years old.

The marshy area to the right along the orange trail is the back part of the pond. The birds on this pond are more easily viewed, however, from a blind near parking lot 2. Take the dirt road to the right of parking lot 1, then a very short and obvious trail to the blind. From this vantage point, looking out on marshy Reilly Pond, herons, kingfishers, and phoebes can be seen, as well as various "puddle ducks"(or dabbling ducks)—including mallards, blacks, and gadwalls—so called because they land in field puddles and feed on the grain (see **#33** and **#79** for more on dabbling ducks). The pond is completely surrounded by woods, and this affects the birdlife. For example, though geese are occasionally seen here, they prefer ponds surrounded by grasses, such as nearby Oom's Pond, which draws snow geese, blue geese, Canada geese, and coots. Hawks, on the other hand—goshawk (see **#48** and **#96**), Cooper's hawk, and sharp-shinned hawk (see **#66**)—are frequently seen on Reilly Pond as they prey on the smaller birds that prefer a pond and woodland habitat. Herds of twenty-five or more deer sometimes gather near this pond, where the second-growth woodlot provides them with food and shelter in bad weather. Look for snapping turtles and painted turtles sunning themselves on rocks and logs in the center of the pond.

Remarks: *Wear sturdy walking shoes, for while the trails are fairly easy walking, there are many wet areas and much poison ivy. Further information about the sanctuary can be obtained from members of the Alan Devoe Bird Club, including Dr. Ed Reilly, Old Chatham, N.Y. 12136; (518) 794-7434. Near the Powell Sanctuary are the Freund Wildlife Sanctuary and Oom's Pond, where more birds can be seen. Also nearby, in Old Chatham, is the Shaker Museum.*

20.

Bash Bish Falls

Directions: **Mount Washington, Mass. From Springfield, take I-90 west 35 miles to Exit 2. Take Route 102 southwest 5 miles to Stockbridge, then go south on U.S. 7 for 7 miles to Great Barrington. Beyond the town center, turn right and take Route 23 southwest to South Egremont. Turn south (left) onto Route 41, and then immediately turn right onto Mount Washington Rd. Follow this up the mountain about 6 miles and turn right onto Bash Bish Falls Rd., which is marked by a sign. There are two parking areas on the left, one at the top of the falls and one at the bottom.**

Ownership: **Bash Bish Falls State Forest, Massachusetts Division of Forests and Parks.**

Hidden high in the rolling Berkshire Hills in the southwestern corner of Massachusetts is an unusually spectacular waterfall that contrasts sharply with its more gentle surroundings. Bash Bish Falls drops 200 feet in a series of cascades that cut through the granite and schist outcrops forming the steep walls of the gorge. While most waterfalls and cascades in New England are found deep in forests, Bash Bish's location on the western slope of Mount Washington affords a panoramic view westward over the Hudson River valley and the distant Catskill Mountains.

The rocky land formation here had its origin in the ancient periods of mountain building, the last occurring about 225 million years ago when the Appalachian Mountain revolution climaxed. About 150 million years prior to that time of upheaval, molten minerals bubbled up to the earth's surface and created deposits in the harder bedrock. An example of this is the white quartz dike that can be seen about halfway up the gorge. Here the hot, silica-rich molten liquid gushed up and filled a crack in the gorge, eventually cooling and solidifying. (See **Connecticut River Valley** and **#82** for more on dikes.)

In much more recent geologic times, the glacial period of 12,000 to 60,000 years ago did much to shape the gorge and falls as they appear today. When the Wisconsin glacier melted, huge mounds of glacial debris that had been picked up and carried by the ice sheet were deposited in the glacier's meltwater streams. As the water pressure built up, these dams broke through, releasing great amounts of water that ran wildly down the hillside. The flow usually followed joints and cracks in the rock structure and created waterfalls. Over the years, the sediments carried by the water have eroded the rock surface of the streambed, smoothing it out and wearing down the rock. Eventually, over several thousand years, the steep drop of the falls will be destroyed by this erosion and Bash Bish Falls will become a small, quiet, meandering stream. For all their force and beauty, all waterfalls are relatively short-lived and share this self-destructive fate.

The waters of Bash Bish Falls begin as a small spring atop Mount Washington. This broad mountaintop, in one of the most remote areas of Massachusetts, provides a large watershed area. Many brooks and streams feed into Bash Bish Brook, adding to the steady flow that eventually winds its way westward to the Hudson River. On the surrounding mountain slopes are a common mix of northern hardwood forest species—maple, oak, and beech (see **Taconics, Berkshires, and Green Mountains** and **#67**)—as well as hemlock. In the spring, many wildflowers can be seen in the understory, including pink lady's slipper, false yellow foxglove, and purple virgin's bower.

Among the open rocky ledges of the hillside are the dens of timber rattlesnakes, a reptile often found in remote, forested hill regions of southern New England. They can sometimes be seen sunning themselves in the gorge, especially in the spring and fall when the air is colder. If you see one, be sure to keep a safe distance, and avoid sticking hands and feet under rocks and logs where they may be settled (see also **#49**).

The most unusual bird seen nesting in the falls area is the worm-eating warbler. It is usually found farther south, but has discovered a suitable habitat here on the wooded slope and in the shady ravine. It is dull olive in color with black stripes on its buff-colored head. Its song is a thin, rapid buzz. In the past, duck hawks, or peregrine falcons, were seen here in large numbers, nesting on the ledges above the brook and soaring high over the gorge. Both birds disappeared in the 1950s due to the effects of the pesticide DDT (see **#44**). Now that DDT has been banned, it is hoped that these species will return. Black bear, bobcat (see **#4**), and fisher (see **#51**) are among the other wildlife that roam the forests surrounding Mount Washington, and Mount Everett to the north. However, it is rare to catch a glimpse of any of these elusive animals.

Remarks: *The gorge is steep and dangerous, so stay on the paths and remain behind the guardrails. Bash Bish Falls is located in the 4,500-acre*

Mount Washington State Forest. There are about 30 miles of marked trails here, and information on hiking routes is available at the park headquarters on East St. above the falls. Backpack camping is permitted on the trails at ten locations. The Appalachian Trail is also nearby. Hunting and fishing, with valid licenses, are permitted, and the streams and ponds are stocked with trout annually. Fishing is not allowed in the falls area. Because of danger from the rocks, swimming is also prohibited there. In the winter, 21 miles of trails are open to cross-country skiing. For more information about park facilities contact Mount Washington State Forest, RFD 3, Mount Washington, Mass. 01258; (413) 528-0330.

21.
Bartholomew's
Cobble

Directions: **Ashley Falls, Mass. Follow directions in #20 to Great Barrington. Continue south on U.S. 7 for 7 miles through Sheffield. Turn right on Rannapo Rd.; go 1.9 miles to Weatogue Rd. and the Cobble entrance on the left.**

Ownership: **Trustees of Reservations.**

Bartholomew's Cobble is an area of incredible biological diversity, which the avid bird-watcher or plant fancier will find endlessly fascinating. There are over 6 miles of well-marked trails throughout its 200 acres that pass through several different habitats, including open grassland, swamp, and old-growth hemlock and hardwood forest.

The dominant features are the cobbles themselves, two limestone knolls of marble (see **#5**) and quartzite that rise about 75 and 100 feet out of the alluvial bottomland along the Housatonic River. They are the product of geological upheaval some 400 million years ago and of subsequent erosion by the elements and glacial activity. The knolls are composed primarily of limestone and magnesium, which were bonded together by heat and pressure deep within the earth. At the time they were thrust upward, the cobbles were much larger than they are today. The Wisconsin glacier removed the top layer of schist, exposing the limestone, which has leached into the soil, leading to the wide diversity of the plant community (see **#34**). The hard quartz that forms the backbone of the cobbles prevents them from eroding away completely.

The outcroppings have created a wide range of soil conditions, which in turn have allowed an unusually large number of plants to prosper. Over seven hundred species of plants have been identified thus far, including almost five hundred wildflowers and one hundred shrubs, vines, and trees. The Cobble boasts forty-nine species of fern, several of which are rare, alkaline-loving types. It is one of the greatest natural concentrations of ferns in the country. The plantlife draws a diversity in the bird population: 236 species have been sighted here during the last 35 years.

A trail guide covering all of the trails at the Cobble is available at the parking area. The most interesting trails for a first visit are Bailey Trail, Craggy Knoll Trail, and Ledges Trail, the first two of which are outlined here.

The Bailey Trail connects with the Ledges Trail from the south end of the parking area. It wanders along the banks of the Housatonic River, over fertile soil that is 80 to 150 feet deep. This area was once covered by a lake, formed as the last glacier melted approximately 10,000–15,000 years ago; the soil is composed of the rich sediments from the lakebottom. After walking through a grove of silver maples, you reach an area (**A**) with especially colorful displays of wildflowers

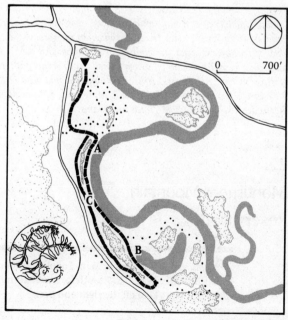

Inset: Silvery spleenwort

in the spring and early summer, including Indian ginger, spicebush, spring beauty, Dutchman's breeches, and cottonwood.

About halfway along the east side of the Bailey Trail Loop are good places for bird-watching, especially during spring migrations. High in the trees near the junction of the Spero Trail are the nests of a red-tailed hawk and a broad-winged hawk. The open fields of the Cobble offer them good hunting of the many small animals found here, such as rabbits and mice.

At **B** is a body of water known as Half River, surrounded by a second-growth forest of maple, poplar, and cottonwood. It was once a part of the Housatonic, but became landlocked when the river shifted hundreds of years ago. Eventually, it will rejoin the river as the shore is slowly eroded by the current.

As you continue along the west side of the loop, at **C** is a fern glen that contains several varieties, including the delicate maidenhair fern and the silver spleenwort (see **#100** for more on ferns). Dogwood, which blooms in the late spring, lines the path returning to the parking area.

The Craggy Knoll Trail crosses the knoll through stands of rare chinkapin oaks, which thrive in the alkaline soil. There are also clumps of redcedar, which are upward of 200 years old.

Remarks: *Bailey Trail requires 1 to 1½ hours; the terrain is gentle. Craggy Knoll Trail is a half-hour walk over generally easy terrain, with some difficult places. Ledges Trail, for which an interpretive guide is available, is recommended for in-depth plant and geological study. There is a good view from the lookout off Craggy Knoll Trail. A cart path leads to the pasture on top of Hubbart's Hill, which offers a fine view of the rolling Berkshire Hills. A visit to the Trailside Museum is recommended, as are the guidebooks to the Cobble's birds and plants.*

22.

Monument Mountain
Reservation

Directions: **Great Barrington, Mass. Follow directions in #20 to Stockbridge. Take U.S. 7 south for about 2.5 miles to the roadside picnic area on the right and park.**

Ownership: **Trustees of Reservations.**

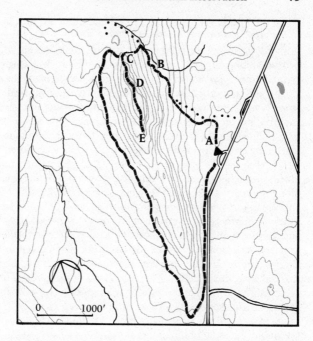

Monument Mountain is a steep, isolated ridge rising 1,642 feet above sea level in the Housatonic River valley at Great Barrington. Flanked by the Berkshire Hills in the east and the Taconic Range in the west (see **Taconics, Berkshires, and Green Mountains**), Monument Mountain's sheer, fractured cliffs soar to a narrow summit of windswept rock crags at Squaw Peak, which offers magnificent views of the lowlands and outlying peaks.

Old legends infuse Monument Mountain with an aura of historical romance. Squaw Peak was named for an Indian maiden who, according to the legend immortalized in a poem by William Cullen Bryant, was flung from the summit as punishment for her love for an enemy brave. The "monument" is an ancient stone cairn at the base of the south slope, said to be built of rocks left by passing Indians as tribute to the maiden. Literary lore also claims the mountain as the scene of the first meeting between Nathaniel Hawthorne and Herman Melville, who, with Oliver Wendell Holmes, later picnicked at the summit on a clear August day in 1850.

The 256-acre Monument Mountain Reservation features two interconnected hiking trails that form a circuit leading to Squaw Peak. The Hickey Trail originates to the right of the roadside picnic area near the display map and trail sign. The most striking feature as you begin the hike is the steep eastern cliff and immense rock fall at its base to the left of the trailhead (**A**). These jagged cliffs are composed primarily of the white marble and pinkish quartzite that form the bedrock foundation of the mountain. This bedrock was originally created some 500 million years ago from sedimentary limestone. During the course of three successive geological upheavals the limestone was transformed by intense heat and pressure into the metamorphic marble and quartzite you see today. The mountain itself was uplifted by these upheavals, while the valley around it was leveled by erosion over the course of the following centuries.

The rock fall, or talus slope, at the cliff's base is the product of erosion, weathering, and the power of glacial ice. As the trail winds along the base of the rock fall, you can see the evidence of the last Ice Age in the fallen boulders around you. The ice sheet descending from the north across New England some 30,000 years ago measured more than a mile in thickness. Flowing through valleys and over mountaintops, it scoured the landscape like a great bulldozer. Cliffs like those above you were scarred and fractured, and boulders toppled from their heights. After the retreat of the glaciers, the cliffs were subject to the natural erosional forces of water and frost (see **#80**), which also loosened rocks from the steep walls. A short distance beyond where the trail divides and rapidly reunites, you can see that the erosion of the mountain continues today. At **B** a ravine cut by a running mountain stream on the right shows how natural erosion can wear away the land's surface.

The trail, which has been gradually ascending the eastern slope of the mountain, now climbs more steeply through the forest of oak, maple, and hemlock. It follows the shady ravine to a fork, where a left turn leads up an even steeper, bouldered slope to a trail junction at the top of the mountain's ridgeline at **C**. The Hickey Trail veers to the left, following the ridgeline to the south. Ahead of you a cragged outcropping of rock offers ledge footholds for the rugged but brief ascent to the summit.

At the summit (**D**), dizzying views appear on all sides of the narrow ridge. Pitch pine, white pine, and mountain laurel grow sparsely among huge white boulders that dominate the trail. Pick your way carefully over the boulders littering the thin ridgeline that in some places is less than 20 feet wide. The high cliffs descend steeply to each side of you as the trail drops down a slope before climbing again to Squaw Peak at **E**. This southern rock knob at the summit ridgeline offers spectacular views of the cliffs and pinnacles of sheared rock. You can also see Mount Everett to the southwest, Mount Wilcox to the east, and other prominent peaks in the Berkshires and Taconics. As you retrace your steps back along the ridge you can catch a glimpse of Mount Greylock (see **#25**), the tallest peak in Massachusetts, to the north. Below you the Housatonic, Green, and Williams rivers are visible, twisting their way through green bottomlands. Overhead, you might sight a raven, which has only recently been recorded in this region as an occasional visitor. The raven is a crowlike bird—though bulkier and longer than a crow—that inhabits the Far North (see **Interior Maine**) and is rarely seen south of the northern mountains in New England. Its method of flight is similar to that of a hawk, alternately flapping and sailing as it flies.

Return down the ridgeline to the trail junction at **C**. A left turn will take you down the gradual western slope along the Indian Monument Trail. As you descend, the white bedrock of the western cliffs will appear on your left through mixed stands of oak, paper birch, red maple, and hemlock. Follow this trail as it takes you along the base of the cliffs, always veering left as unmarked trails radiate off to the right. The trail finally turns northward and runs along an old stone wall where a stand of red pine grows on your right. Soon it emerges on a woods road that quickly leaves the forest and joins Route 7. Walk north on the highway for a short distance to the picnic area to complete the circuit.

Remarks: *The Hickey Trail (¾ mile) and the Indian Monument Trail (1¼ miles) make a 2-mile hike over difficult terrain. Exercise caution while walking the summit ridgeline, where the cliffs drop precipitously on either side. Allow 2 hours for a casual hike. Camping is available at Beartown State Forest in the town of Monterey, about 8 miles away.*

23.
Ice Glen

Directions: **Stockbridge, Mass. Follow directions in #20 to Stockbridge. Go south on U.S. 7 for 0.4 mile. Turn left onto Ice Glen Rd. Go 0.5 mile to the driveway on the left where a sign marks the entrance to Ice Glen. Park on the main road. Alternatively, walk through the glen from the other direction by taking the Laurel Hill Trail from behind the library in the center of town.**

Ownership: **Laurel Hill Association.**

Ice Glen is a deep, dark, and somewhat eerie ravine cut into the southwestern slope of Laurel Hill in the southern Berkshires. It is a jumble of huge rocks and boulders that were carried here by the last glacier and deposited when the glacial ice receded. But although it was created by ice, Ice Glen gets its name from the cold, icy conditions that linger on well into spring due to the ravine's shape and location. It is most spectacular, but also most dangerous, in April and May when the spring meltwaters freeze overnight and create bizarre, free-form ice sculptures on the rock formations.

No matter what time of year you visit the glen, you will immediately notice the change in temperature as you enter the rocky section of the ravine. The unusually cold microclimate of Ice Glen is due to its narrowness, its depth, and its orientation to the sun and prevailing winds. In the last Ice Age, the Wisconsin glacier advanced from the northwest, so that most of its effects are seen on a northwest–southeast axis. However, the hard, granite-based slopes on either side of the present gorge diverted and intensified the force of the glacier in a northeast–southwest direction, where it easily cut through softer shale deposits. As a result of this somewhat unusual orientation, Ice Glen does not receive much direct sunlight, resulting in much colder ground and air temperatures than are found outside the ravine.

This cool climate and the thin, glaciated soil on the steep slopes have led to the growth of a predominantly hemlock forest surrounding the ravine. Hemlocks are common in such areas, where their roots can spread out over a wide area rather than going deep into the soil. They also like the moist air and soil that result from the lack of direct sunlight. These hemlocks are quite old, some of the larger ones dating back about 250 years. They have remained untouched because of the difficulty of logging them over the steep, rocky terrain. The height and density of the trees also block sunlight from the ravine and hold in the colder air, thus contributing to the distinctive climate.

Remarks: *The trail through Ice Glen requires a lot of scrambling over rocks, and the going can be dangerous due to slippery patches of moss. Wear appropriate shoes. Do not attempt to go far into the ravine if there is still ice present. It can be appreciated from either end of the gorge. Remember that Ice Glen is ''air-conditioned'' year-round, and it is a comfortable place to relax on a hot summer day. Total walking time from either direction is between 1 and 2 hours.*

24.

Chesterfield

Gorge

Directions: **West Chesterfield, Mass. From Springfield, take I-91 about 15 miles north to Exit 18; follow U.S. 5 north about 1 mile into Northampton. Take Route 9 northwest about 9 miles to Williamsburg; turn west (left) onto Route 143. Go about 10 miles; after crossing the West Chesterfield bridge, take the first left onto River Rd. Go 0.8 mile to the entrance sign on the left. The short dirt road leads to a parking area.**

Ownership: **Trustees of Reservations.**

The approach to Chesterfield Gorge through the eastern foothills of the Berkshires in western Massachusetts reveals a terrain of steep hills and valleys. From the scenic hilltop village of Chesterfield, Route 143 runs west as the land elevation suddenly drops more than 600 feet in a distance of merely 2 miles. The highway descends into a narrow valley through which the East Branch of the Westfield River flows southward past the low-lying hamlet of West Chesterfield. A typical product of erosion, this valley is but one of countless others that have been carved into the Berkshire Upland over many centuries.

The Berkshires are a southern extension of Vermont's Green Mountains, whose ancient ancestors arose about 500 million years ago as a group of islands in an inland sea. Many millions of years of erosion reduced this uplifted region of western New England to a flat plain—called a *peneplain* by geologists (see also **#65**). Beginning about 12 million years ago, it was further eroded when renewed swellings of the earth's crust animated the region's rivers. Gradually these rivers dissected the Berkshire plateau into a landscape of hills and river valleys closely resembling those of the present day. The later glaciers of the Ice Age wrought comparatively superficial changes in the land surface as it scoured the terrain and its meltwaters formed glacial lakes and streams. Today, the remnant peneplain forms an even horizon of numerous hilltops, such as those visible to the south of Chesterfield.

A superb illustration of river erosion of a more recent age and on a smaller scale lies only a mile south of the state highway in West

Chesterfield, where the Westfield River has sculpted an impressive tribute to its own relentless energy at Chesterfield Gorge. This gorge dominates the 161-acre reservation along the western bank of the Westfield River. A trail from the parking lot begins to the left of a red reservation building and leads down a slope to the river's edge at the northern end of the gorge. From this vantage point at an elevation not much higher than the surface of the water, the river swings into view from around a bend and surges into the gorge to the right. The bedrock wall of the gorge opposite this point on the trail is an impressive work of erosion, for the smooth granite has been scalloped into a wavy surface of rounded lobes and shallow depressions. Jutting out from this naturally eroded granite wall is a man-made stone abutment composed of cut granite blocks, a relic of the High Bridge built in 1739 as part of the Boston-to-Albany Post Road. As you retrace your steps up the slope, notice the abandoned roadway cut into the slope at a point opposite the abutment. Granite stone walls still visible served as road boundaries on each side. A stagecoach route engineered in colonial times, the Post Road was one of the first roads to cross the Berkshire Barrier, so called because the plateau's difficult upland terrain had hindered the settlement of New England's western frontier.

Take the trail, left, behind the red reservation building and follow the fence along the top of the 1,000-foot-long chasm. Eastern hemlocks grow thickly in the thin, acidic soil on top of the bedrock gorge and cling precariously to narrow ledges in the otherwise sheer cliffs of the chasm wall. Glacial boulders of varying sizes line the trail's edge away from the gorge, deposited there by the receding ice sheet. Their irregular shapes stand in contrast to the slablike granite stones (see **#93**) littering the chasm floor. These granite slabs were probably sheared from the chasm's walls by the glacier. The glaciers often made their paths through lower valleys, abrading slopes and cliffs as they advanced. Grooved marks visible in the gorge's cliffs are scars inflicted by glacial boulders carried along by the ice as it passed through the chasm. The granite slabs that were plucked from the side of the chasm are evidence of geological layering in granite bedrock. Sheet joints separating layers of granite run parallel to the rock's surface, producing slablike stones when quarried.

Continue along the fence ringing the top of the cliff and enjoy the impressive sight of the river as it surges over and around the boulders in the 30-foot-deep gorge. Walk the trail to where it meets the reservation road and turn right (north) back to the parking lot.

Remarks: *The trail is an easy 30-minute walk, with time to linger and enjoy the views of the gorge.*

25.

Mount Greylock

Directions: Adams, Mass. From Springfield, take I-90 west 35 miles to Exit 2. Take U.S. 20 northwest about 11 miles to Pittsfield; it is joined by U.S. 7 along the way. Continue north on U.S. 7 about 6 miles to Lanesboro; about 2 miles farther, turn right at a sign for the Mount Greylock State Reservation. Follow the road 6 miles to the summit. Alternatively, the mountain can be approached from North Adams on Route 2.

Ownership: Massachusetts Department of Forests, Parks, and Recreation.

Mount Greylock, the highest peak in Massachusetts, rises abruptly above the Hoosic River valley town of Adams in the northwest corner of the state. The views from the 3,491-foot summit provide a picture of the geological history of the entire Berkshire, Taconic, and southern Vermont regions. On a a clear day, points as far away as Mount Monadnock (see **#72**) (65 miles) and the distant peaks of the Adirondacks (115 miles) can be seen. Mount Greylock presents an enlightening view of the Connecticut River valley and the Holyoke Range (see **#50**), about 35 miles to the southeast. The observation tower provides points of reference for identifying landmarks.

Although the peaks of the Green Mountains in southern Vermont are very close to Mount Greylock, they belong to similar but distinctly different mountain regions. Mount Greylock is part of the narrow Taconic Range, which roughly follows the New York–New England border from northern Connecticut to central Vermont. With the exception of Mount Greylock and Vermont's Mount Equinox, which are the tallest peaks, the range is generally low, rounded, and mature. For many years, the origins of these mountains were open to speculation among geologists. What puzzled them for so long was that the composition of the mountains makes them appear to be upside down. That is, in an unusual sequence of rock deposition, the older layers lie on top of the younger ones, the reverse of the normal sequence.

The Taconic Mountains are about the same age as the Green Mountains, having been formed about 440 to 570 million years ago during the Paleozoic era. However, the bedrock foundation of the

Taconics is different from that of the Green Mountains or of any other area in the Northeast. Shale and slate (see **#29**) are the predominant materials near the surface, which is geologically similar to the region southeast of the Green Mountains. This likeness has led geologists to speculate that the mountains which today make up the Taconic Range originated to the east of what are today the Green Mountains. These shales and slates are composed of clay-based sediments whose origins were in deep ocean waters that once covered the region to the east of the present Green Mountains. The upward thrusting of the earth's crust that created the Green Mountains also lifted huge chunks of shale up and over those mountains; this material flipped over so that the upper, more recently formed shales became buried beneath the older, lower ones. Over the approximately 150 million years since then, erosion has worn away the top layer of shale, revealing a layer of limestone and the younger shales below that. This peculiar arrangement of layers, with the oldest on top and the youngest on the bottom, gives the Taconic Mountains the illusion of being geologically upside down.

During the time that the Taconics were being thrust up and over from the east, the Green Mountains were also being built up. Both processes were the result of plate collisions (see **Taconics, Berkshires, and Green Mountains** and **#30**). As the Green Mountains were thrust higher, the Taconics were pushed farther westward until they slipped down the western side of the Green Mountains and settled approximately where they are today. Water running off the slopes formed rivers and streams that eroded the area between the two mountain ranges and created the valley of Vermont, which runs between them. This entire process can be envisioned and the results clearly seen when you look north to the horizon from the top of Mount Greylock. The mountain itself stands alone in Massachusetts as the biggest reminder of the powerful forces of the ancient mountain-building process.

Remarks: *In addition to the roads to the summit, there are almost a dozen trails, including the Appalachian Trail, that lead to the top. These are fully described in the Appalachian Mountain Club's* Massachusetts and Rhode Island Trail Guide. *Trail maps are also available at the visitor's center at the summit. Bascom Lodge, on the summit, offers food and lodging from May to October. There is camping nearby at Sperry Campground. A naturalist is available for short nature walks around the summit during the summer.*

26.
Atherton Meadow
Wildlife Area

Directions: **Whitington, Vt. From Brattleboro, take Route 9 west 17 miles. Go south (left) on Route 100 about 6 miles to the intersection with Route 122 in Jacksonville. From that point, continue on Route 100 for 6.3 miles to the sign for Atherton Meadow on the right; the parking area is hidden behind the sign.**

Ownership: **Vermont Fish and Game Department.**

Atherton Meadow is a wildlife management area of 1,042 acres with elevations from 1,500 to 2,078 feet. Most of the area is covered with a typical hemlock–northern hardwood forest, but there are also fields, thickets, spruce and fir at higher elevations, and a large beaver meadow for which the area is named. There are several paths here, used by hikers and hunters, but no marked trails.

To reach the meadow, take the right branch at the fork in the path just beyond the parking lot. This path becomes overgrown in places, but there it runs parallel to the stream, so you should not have too much trouble.

The woods at the base of the trail consist of hemlock, beech, and white and yellow birch. There is oil of wintergreen in the sap of yellow birch, which you can smell if you break a twig. Farther up the trail are stands of sugar maple, the tree from whose sap maple syrup is made.

While going through the woods, stop to look under rotting logs, being careful to put them back exactly as you find them. You might see a red-backed salamander, a small, slender amphibian that in one color phase has a yellow, orange, or red stripe down its back. This color phase is apparently most common at higher elevations; at lower elevations an all-gray color phase is more prevalent. In some locations this salamander may be bright orange-red with a black-tipped tail. The red-backed and other members of the woodland salamander group lay eggs in moist woods instead of in shallow bodies of water, as is typical of most other salamanders. Thus they skip the aquatic stage entirely. In some parts of New England the red-backed is said to have the largest biomass of any animal in the area.

Another salamander you might see on the forest floor is the red-eft phase of the eastern spotted newt. The newt spends its first summer as a larva in a shallow pool. After a few months it develops lungs and crawls onto land as the bright orange-red eft. The red eft is poisonous if consumed, and the bright color is believed to serve as a warning to any predator that might have survived a past attempt to eat one. After 1 to 3 years on land the efts turn olive green and return to water, where they will breed. It is best not to handle these or other salamanders as their skin is very thin and easily damaged.

About halfway up, the trail enters a thicket. Alongside the trail, this area is almost impenetrable, thick with blackberries, bindweeds, ferns, and other plants. If you look closely at the standing dead trees you will notice that they have been girdled—that is, the bark has been cut through all around the tree at the base. Girdling severs the nutrient-and-water-carrying tissue of a tree and thereby kills it. This work is part of the Wildlife Habitat Program, which is managing areas for habitat improvement. Deer and other wildlife thrive in a variety of habitats such as young and old forests interspersed with fields, which provide food, and evergreen groves, which offer food and winter shelter. This clearing was created to provide more browse for deer than would a continuous mature forest.

In this thicket you can see one tree, an apple, that has been left ungirdled, since many different animals enjoy wild apples. The growth of this shade-intolerant tree is encouraged by the selective clearing of other trees.

After passing through another wooded area and another thicket, you will see a small marsh off to the right. When the water is low, tracks of animals such as deer or raccoon can be seen in the mud. This marsh was created by a beaver dam, many years ago judging by the fairly large size of the trees that sprang up from the abandoned dam.

As the path continues up, balsam fir starts to appear. Fir and spruce replace the deciduous forest at higher elevations, and the appearance of fir is the first indication of this change (see **#83**). The path rather suddenly opens upon a large, attractive marsh and meadow. Rushes and grasses (see **#101**) and annual plants predominate, with islands of trees on bedrock outcroppings. Seasonally scattered throughout the marsh are pools of water of varying size. This open area was created by beavers, which next to man cause the most change in landscape. In fact, ancient man probably relied on old beaver meadows as ideal home sites.

Beavers are vulnerable on land, where their main source of food, tree bark, exists. Therefore they build a dam to create a pond, which provides a safe place for a home and allows them to reach nearby food without straying too far from safety. When the food around the edge of the pond is eaten, the dam is built higher and the pond rises, giving access to new food.

The standing dead trees are the remains of the forest that was here before the beavers flooded the area. After they left, the pond turned into a marsh. Eventually, if there is no intervention by man or beaver, this area will be forested again.

Around the edge of the marsh are stands of quaking aspen, a common tree of neglected fields and cleared areas in forests. The bark is a favorite food of beavers, and the saplings are used in the construction of their lodges and dams. Aspen buds are a winter staple in the diet of the ruffed grouse, a chickenlike gamebird. Because of this preference, wildlife managers clear some sections of forests to encourage aspens.

A ubiquitous plant in the marsh is the beggar-tick. In the summer these plants are covered with large bright-yellow flowers. By fall they develop the seeds for which they are named. Each seed has a hard coat with two or more barbs that have backward-pointing hairs. The seeds are loosely attached to the plant with the barbs pointing outward so that the slightest contact with fur or clothing assures their transportation to a new area. There are a number of species of beggar-ticks in North America, all having slightly different seed shapes or numbers of barbs.

Follow the same path down to return to the parking lot.

Remarks: *This round-trip hike is about 2 miles and takes about an hour. Avoid hiking at Atherton Meadow during deer-hunting season, which is usually around the end of November.*

Nearby Places of Interest

Molly Stark State Park on Route 9 east of Wilmington has a campground and nature trails as well as longer trails up Mount Olga to a fire tower offering good views. Woodford State Park on Route 9 west of Wilmington has a campground, a nature trail, and swimming and boating facilities on a 20-acre lake.

27.

Stewart Preserve

Directions: **Sand Lake, N.Y. From Albany, take Route 43 east about 10 miles to where it joins Route 66 at Averill Park. Follow the combined highways for 3.5 miles. Turn left onto Methodist Farm Rd.; go 0.8 mile. Turn right onto Stewart Lane and go to the end, where the trail starts.**

Ownership: **The Nature Conservancy.**

The Stewart Preserve is a 123-acre woodland through which winds a lovely mile-long trail, clearly marked by orange discs. Deeds and aerial photos show that much of the preserve was once farmed and logged. Now forest succession (see **#67**) is rather well progressed, and beech and maple seedlings are beginning to supersede the brambles and shrubs in most parts of the preserve.

Along the short access trail at the end of Stewart Lane and just outside the preserve boundaries are the foundations of a barn and a house. The barn foundation is just to the left of the trail; the house foundation is to the right, kitty-corner to the barn. Around this cellar hole are other traces of civilization, such as day lilies and broken bits of crockery.

Throughout the preserve the trail passes over and along old stone walls. These walls served a dual purpose for the farmers: they marked the boundaries of the fields, and they were a convenient place for the stones cleared from the fields. The trail first leads into the east portion of the preserve, which has not been cultivated since 1923. Here small oak, beech, and scattered birch can be seen. To the right at **A** is a stand of mature white pines. A pioneer species in the reforestation process, these fast-growing, sun-loving trees are dying out now as their stage in the forest succession cycle is passing. In time the slow-growing beech and maple, which are tolerant of shade, will replace the white pines (see also **#28**).

Close to and within the old stone walls are some of the largest trees on the preserve. Farmers let these "line trees" stand to provide shade or to help mark field boundaries. Near the white pines, on the left of the trail, are four huge maples. At **B** there stands the largest and oldest tree on the preserve: a white oak whose circumference measures 13 feet just above the crotch. Alongside the oak stands the largest beech on the preserve. The beech is smaller than the oak because it is a slow-growing tree, but both trees probably predate white settlers. A white oak of comparable size, which was downed in the Catskills, was dated back to the 1600s, and these three trees are most likely all of the same generation.

Beyond these two huge trees the forest is less dense. Old aerial photographs show that this area was once very open, and now, as the forest reclaims the farmers' fields, young birch and beech dominate. Partridges and evidence of deer have been seen in this area. Other birds to watch for on the preserve include the goshawk (see **#48** and **#96**) and pileated woodpecker. In the open area near the end of Stewart Lane, one might see scarlet tanagers, cardinals, and titmice. Wild turkeys have been seen crossing the lane itself, but have only been heard, not seen, on the preserve.

Quite near **C**, where the trail turns, two stone walls cross, forming a corner. Within the wall perpendicular to the trail on the left is a large tree stump. While the stump itself is not terribly spectacular, it has been identified as a chestnut, which is interesting. When settlers described this area in the 1870s, they noted the chestnut as one of the dominant trees. By 1920, however, a fungus blight known as the chestnut-bark disease had destroyed every chestnut in large areas

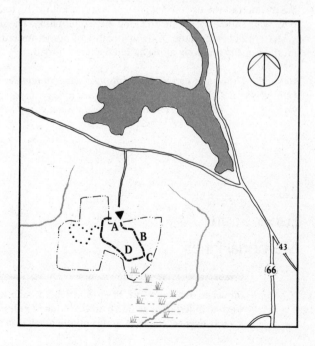

of the eastern United States (see **#67**). Small chestnuts have been found growing around the preserve, but these trees die young, still falling prey to the blight. Chestnut, whether alive or dead, is unusually resistant to decay, as evidenced by this relatively solid stump of a tree that has been dead for about 60 years.

After the trail crosses over the stone wall, it goes down a short hill. Here the land was too moist and steep to be cultivated, and hemlock spruce grew, probably as part of the farmer's woodlot. It is noticeably cooler along this part of the trail as the moisture in this lower area keeps the temperature down. Just beyond the preserve boundary here is a small brook, which runs year-round, fed by runoff from the preserve.

At the next noticeable bend in the trail (**D**) the composition of the woods again changes. Parts of the western portion of the preserve were logged and grazed up until 1950. As the trail leaves the hemlocks behind, smaller growth becomes noticeable. This area has not yet caught up to the stage of succession evident at the beginning of the trail, and there are still grasses, shrubs, and brambles growing here. These shrubs provide shade and prepare the soil for the growth of the maple and beech seedlings that are beginning to appear. The trail that loops through the western portion of the preserve is much like this part of the eastern loop. Here you can follow the trail back to Stewart Lane or continue on along the western loop. The second, western, trail begins rather roughly because of numerous brambles, but then opens up nicely along an old overgrown road.

Remarks: *The eastern and western trails take about 40 minutes each to walk; neither is difficult. Visits in the spring are discouraged because parts of the trail are quite wet. Poison ivy grows abundantly in parts of the preserve.*

28.
Fisher-Scott
Memorial Pines

Directions: **Arlington, Vt. From Brattleboro, take Route 9 west 40 miles, then go north on U.S. 7 for 14 miles to Exit 3; cross over to Route 7A and continue north into the vil-**

lage of Arlington. From there, continue north on Route 7A for 2.1 miles. Turn left onto the dirt road just past the bridge. After 0.2 mile look for the entrance, on the left.

Ownership: **Vermont Department of Forests and Parks.**

This small, 13-acre tract contains the largest white pines in Vermont. While the trees are not quite as large as the Cathedral Pines in Connecticut (see **#12**), they reach lofty heights of about 120 feet, with impressive diameters of 30 to 40 inches. This qualifies them as one of the finest examples of an old-age successional forest. Fisher-Scott is also an illustration of the type of old-age subclimax forest that was once more common in central New England.

Although these trees are very old, they cannot be called a virgin forest. Much of central and southern New England was covered with trees such as these several hundred years ago, but they fell quickly as the region was settled by colonists. Native Americans also burned large tracts of forest to clear areas for agriculture. As a valuable building material, the large white pines were an important part of colonial New England's economy. The king of England ordered the largest of the trees, over 24 inches in diameter, to be used exclusively for masts for the Royal Navy.

The white pine is a "pioneer species," one of the first plants to claim abandoned fields, and it begins the successional process to a hardwood climax forest. These trees are about 175 years old, and thus were established in the early 1800s as agriculture in New England began to decline. Because they have been undisturbed for so many years, white pines dominate this tract. However, they are considered a subclimax tree, meaning they are only one stage in the forest's eventual development into hardwoods. Notice that growing among the pines are many beech, sugar maple, hemlock, and ash trees, some as large as 12 inches in diameter. They are tolerant of the shade cast by the old pines, the same shade that prevents young pines from growing. Eventually, age, disease, or natural disasters such as hurricanes will bring the old trees down, allowing sunlight to reach the hardwoods and causing them to grow more rapidly as they become the dominant species.

Of course, it is impossible to predict how much longer these magnificent trees will remain. But elsewhere there are younger stands that, if left undisturbed, will reach this stage so that future generations can marvel at such giants.

Remarks: The trees are only a few hundred feet from the road. A short, easy trail wanders among them.

29.
Lake Bomoseen
State Park Nature Trail

Directions: **West Castleton, Vt. From Rutland, take U.S. 4 west about 18 miles to Exit 3. Go north on Scotch Hill Rd. 4.2 miles to the park.**

Ownership: **Vermont Department of Forests and Parks.**

Illustrating much of the natural and human history of the area, this trail includes panoramic views of Lake Bomoseen and nearby Glen Lake, and passes through areas that were once pastures, orchards, or fields. One can see how human beings have played a large part in shaping the natural growth of this area. (A guide to the nature trail is available at the park entrance, and several of the areas pointed out here correspond to points on that map.)

At the start, the trail crosses a wooden footbridge over a small marsh. A larger marsh can be seen across from the lakeshore, directly opposite the beginning of the trail. Here kingfishers, ducks, and other waterbirds reside, feeding on grasses, insects, and aquatic life. At the start of the trail, be sure to go to the left. From here the trail is marked with blue blazes.

One of the first areas on the trail is a small open field, grown over with goldenrod and asters. This land was once cleared for farming; today these plants are helping prepare the soil for the rebirth of a forest. A short distance farther is a stand of white pines. Although these trees were planted here, they, like the goldenrod and asters, are part of the process of succession. In natural succession, the stage between the growth of goldenrod and the growth of pines is the appearance of shrubs, which shelter the pines as they get established. In the white-pine thicket the trees have shaded out the shrubs, and they have died. The pine needles also make the soil too acidic for many other plants to grow here. Since the white pine is a fast-growing, sun-loving plant, its seedlings too will die in the shade of the more mature trees. Thus, this stand will eventually give way to such hardwood species as beech and maple, which grow slowly, are tolerant of shade, and like the cool, moist soil conditions under the pines.

Within the white-pine thicket on a short trail to the right is a deer exclosure. Deer were excluded from this area by the Vermont Department of Fish and Game in a study begun in 1969 to determine the effects of overbrowsing by deer. Note that within the exclosure there are many more low branches, shrubs, and saplings than outside it. This experiment has not been very revealing, however, since there is not a heavy population of deer here in winter. (See **#49** for more on white-tailed deer.)

The "gnarled apple tree," Bomoseen's area 6, was probably once a part of an orchard. The farming in this area was done largely by, and for, the people who worked in the slate quarries and mills nearby. Fair Haven is considered a part of the slate belt, and the next open area shows just how accessible the slate here is. *Slate* is a metamorphic rock, formed as the sedimentary rock *shale*, which is layered rock made of materials transported by the glacier, is recrystallized by heat and pressure. Millions of years ago this area was covered by ocean (see **#34**). As the muddy deposits here were compressed, they became shale. Further pressure metamorphosed the shale into slate. The area that was farther out to sea, where crustaceans dwelt, is now the Rutland area. The shells from the crustaceans became limestone, which, under pressure, was metamorphosed into marble. Slate quarries are common near Fair Haven, and marble quarries near Rutland. Both give evidence of the ancient history of the region. As you leave the park, you might note the lovely old houses to the right. The slate in these houses was dug from an abandoned quarry near the park.

At **D** much slate and schist is visible. *Schist* is a silvery rock with tiny flecks of mica in it. It is slate further metamorphosed by heat and pressure. Slate and schist still bear traces of their origins as shale, which was formed from many layers of mud. Slate is harder and stronger than shale, but it also breaks into sheets. Schist, the furthest removed from its layered-mud origins, also retains the mark of its source in the wavy patterns of dark gray that run through the rock. Larger outcrops, areas where the bedrock is exposed, can be seen on the hiking trail that continues on at the end of the nature trail outlined in the state park guide. Just before the end of the nature trail, is a climax forest. In this final stage of forest succession (see **#67**), the dominant trees are beech, sugar maple, hemlock, and birch. If left alone, the basic composition of this or any climax forest will remain virtually unchanged. It is interesting to look at this as the conclusion of the natural succession that began with the goldenrods at the start of the trail.

Remarks: *It takes about 1½ hours to walk the nature and hiking trails. You may wish to walk the trail with the resident naturalist to learn more about the kinds of trees and vegetation growing there; call (802) 265-4242 for information. There are camping and swimming at Lake Bomoseen State Park and at nearby Half Moon State Park, which also offers fishing and another nature trail.*

30.

Mount Horrid
Great Cliff

Directions: **Brandon Gap, Vt. From Rutland, take U.S. 7 north 16 miles to Brandon. Go east (right) on Route 73 for 7 miles to Brandon Gap and a small pulloff on the left, up a small hill. The trail to the Great Cliff overlook begins here; the overlook is 0.2 mile east, marked by a sign on the right.**

Ownership: **Green Mountain National Forest, National Forest Service.**

Rising vertically 700 feet above the road and towering over the small beaver pond at its base, the Mount Horrid Great Cliff is a dramatic sight from the pulloff on Route 73. However, a short hike leads to an overlook on the cliff from which the sights are even more spectacular. Even on a somewhat hazy day, the Champlain Valley and the Adirondacks in New York are clearly visible to the west. Either on a clear day or in the early morning, Lake Champlain may be seen as the sun gleams on the water or the morning mist rises off the lake. To the south are several Green Mountain peaks, and to the west is Braintree Ridge. While the trail to the overlook is mostly steep, it is well maintained, and there are a couple of points at which the trail does level off.

The Green Mountain National Forest, in which Mount Horrid is located, was established as a national forest in 1932 and covers approximately 291,985 acres. This mountain range is one of the oldest in New England, and it is believed to have been formed by a process of folding and faulting of the earth's crust, as explained by a theory known as *plate tectonics.* This theory holds that the continents and ocean beds lie on great plates of either granite or basalt, which are constantly moving and drifting. When plates collide along fault lines, great pressures are created, which result in either deep trenches or mountains as one plate moves over the other. The upward-thrusting pressure is most likely how the Green Mountains were formed some 440 million years ago. Erosion has played a large part in changing the appearance of these mountains, and Mount Horrid Great Cliff clearly shows the effects that the glaciers have had on the mountains.

Mount Horrid is an unusually good example of a glacial process known as *quarrying*, or *ice plucking*. Plucking occurs on the lee side of a mountain, the side facing away from the direction from which the glacier came. When the glacier passed over Mount Horrid, it came up the stoss side, leaving a less steep, scoured slope. It then moved down what is now the cliff. Ice plucking occurs when the ice freezes to rocks and then "plucks" them out as it moves on. These blocks of rock may have been defined by some lines of weakness, such as joints, or water may have seeped in around the blocks, frozen, and then expanded—a process known as *ice wedging*—thereby loosening the rocks and making them susceptible to plucking. These high cliffs are the result of several thousand years of this glacial breaking and plucking process.

At the base of the Great Cliff is a small basin dug by the glacier that now holds a beaver pond. The beaver's lodge can be seen on the far left side of the pond. Look for peregrine falcons in this area. In an attempt to reestablish these birds in the Green Mountain region, the Forest Service recently released many of them at Mount Horrid. The peregrine falcon is an imperiled species because of DDT, which caused the falcon's eggshells to become so thin and fragile that they broke when the birds sat on them. Since the ban on DDT in 1969 the falcons, with human help, are making a comeback. These cliffs provide the rocky, isolated nesting sites the peregrines require, and they can often be seen soaring on the air currents, high above.

Remarks: *The trail leading to the overlook on Mount Horrid is 0.6 mile long and is a part of the Long Trail, which crosses Vermont. One can hike any distance on the Long Trail. Hiking time for the trail described here is about 45 minutes. Allow extra time for breaks, since the trail is rather steep. The view from the overlook is splendid in the fall. Be very careful in the early spring, when thawing occurs: there are some loose rocks on the trail, and it might be dangerous. The Green Mountain National Forest Service has set up a picnic site just past Mount Horrid on Route 73. Chittendon Brook, a small campground that offers fishing, is 2.7 miles east on Route 173 on the right, then 2.5 miles up the dirt road.*

31.

Gifford Woods
State Park

Directions: **Sherburne, Vt. From Rutland, take U.S. 4 east for 11 miles. The park is at the junction with Route 100.**

Ownership: **Vermont Department of Forests and Parks.**

Gifford Woods is a small pocket of deciduous northern hardwoods lying in the heart of the coniferous Green Mountains National Forest. It is a remnant of undisturbed virgin forest that has somehow survived in the midst of Killington Basin's rampant ski-industry development. Vistors are urged to respect its vulnerable situation.

Gifford Woods is the most accessible of the few remaining virgin sugar-maple–beech climax forests in the northeastern United States. You can park your car under towering 300-year-old maples and picnic at a table beside a magnificent eastern hemlock over 3 feet in diameter. Part of the forest's 16 acres has been developed for the state park. The other half lies directly across Route 100 on the shore of Kent Pond, in an almost virgin state. Here stand some of the same trees that were growing here when white settlers encountered the region for the first time. In 1763, Rev. Samuel Peters of Connecticut stood on the summit of Killington Peak less than 2 miles away and proclaimed that the mountains and hills of "Verd-mont" "shall be ever green and shall never die." Gifford Woods seems to stand in support of that proclamation, defiantly resisting human encroachment and natural disaster.

The woods have never suffered a fire, although the Native American people often burned forests to enrich the soil, encourage game, or clear for crops. The woods also survived the clear-cutting that stripped 75 percent of Vermont by 1850. Today the trees make a bridge to a human past. You can gaze up over 100 feet to a leafy canopy that, when the settlers arrived, stretched to the Mississippi River. A Vermont squirrel, it is said, could have reached the river without ever touching the ground. Except for limited tapping for maple sugar, the virgin tract in Gifford Woods has never been disturbed.

Gifford Woods is as small as it can be and still retain its entity as a climax forest. "Climax" means, in part, that it is made up of species that will reproduce themselves because the seedlings can tolerate shade, and that it occurs at the end of a succession of forest types. Gifford woods grows in the highest altitudinal limit of northern hardwood–hemlock forest.

In the spring the sunny floor of the woods contains over eighty-three species of herbaceous flora. Nineteen different kinds of ferns, including maidenhair, New York, rattlesnake, Christmas, and New York, as well as fern allies—club mosses and horsetail—make up over two-thirds of the carpet (see **#100** for more on ferns). The rest is covered by sixty-four species of flowering plants, including round-leaved, downy yellow, and Canada violets, wild ginger, wild lily of the valley, blue cohosh, and Indian cucumber root. The trees that predominate are sugar maple, white beech, yellow birch, and white ash; basswood, elm, and hemlock are also found. Black cherry, hophornbeam (see **#1**), balsam fir, and red spruce appear in scatterings in the shrub layer.

In Gifford Woods the accumulation of decaying leaves and wood on the forest floor has gone on uninterrupted by soil erosion. Typically the soil of a deciduous hardwood forest teems with biological activity, unlike the soil of a spruce-fir forest, which is sandy and acidic. Maple leaves decay quickly. Gifford Woods may contain over a million earthworms per acre. (See **#97** for more on life found in the earth.) The deep tangle of the maple root systems holds the earth in place. As you walk through the woods on the southern end of the forest you will see a massive example of this root system up-ended and exposed at the foot of a toppled tree. This gigantic maple seems to have withered in old age and slid off the granite ledge where it had grown. Thousands of tendrils below the mass of thicker taproots make a root ball 6 feet thick and 10 feet wide.

The soil feels spongy underfoot. It is moist and black. Footsteps release the dank, earthy smells. One imagines that the primeval forest felt like this. Back then it contained caribou, elk, wolverine, and timber wolf. Today you might find a trail of wild-apple cores and droppings marking the path of a black bear during berry season. Beavers are plentiful in the swamps nearby and white-tailed deer are abundant. Gifford Woods is situated near the well-known birding areas around Kent Pond, and although it is squeezed by road and fence, it hosts a variety of bird species. The northern parula, a small wood warbler, rare in Vermont, has been spotted in Gifford Woods. It feeds in the tree crowns and finds the lichen, old-man's-beard, it likes so much for its nests. Its other habitat is cypress swamps, where it finds spanish moss for the same purpose.

Small remnants of original wilderness such as Gifford Woods are becoming extinct. Its size and location make this tract especially precarious and vulnerable. No trails exist on the east side of Route 100, and visitors should avoid making paths in order to minimize soil compaction. Although this forest has taken centuries to develop, any change now in its vegetation would destroy its ecological balance, and its scientific and historical value as well.

Remarks: *Gifford Woods lends itself to detailed study and slow exploration. East of Route 100 one quickly runs into the fence the Vermont Fish and Game Department has put up 50 feet from the pond shoreline. It is best to travel north–south. But if you desire more extensive hiking, you can pick up the Appalachian Trail, which runs right through the park's campground and skirts the southern edge of the woods. Only a mile and a half out of the park, up a steep ascent, is the Maine Junction where the Appalachian meets Vermont's Long Trail, which will take you all the way to Massachusetts. From there it is another half-mile to Sherburne Pass (elevation 2,150 feet) and the Long Trail Lodge. If you take the steep Deer Leap Mountain trail, you will have a demanding 6-mile circle hike back to Gifford Woods. The Appalachian Trail can also be followed around the southern edge of Kent Pond, over trout streams and marshes abounding in birds. A larger, and more remote virgin hardwood stand, possibly older and more impressive, is the Lord's Hill Tract in Marshfield, Vt. Another is Battell Stand in Middlebury, Vt.*

32.

Tinker Brook
Natural Area

Directions: **Plymouth, Vt. From Rutland, take U.S. 4 east and south 17 miles to West Bridgewater. When U.S. 4 heads east again, continue south on Route 100 for 3.2 miles. Turn right onto Northam Rd., which is very steep and rough. After 0.9 mile, there is a rough, rutted dirt road on the left. (You might want to park here, or at the bottom of Northam Rd., and walk in to Tinker Brook.) Follow the dirt road a short distance to the shelter and the natural area.**

Ownership: **Vermont Department of Forests, Parks, and Recreation.**

Tinker Brook Natural Area is a quiet, peaceful wooded site of approximately 45 acres. Located within the 17,949 acres of the Calvin

Coolidge State Forest, this small preserve is home to a virgin stand of large, old-age red spruce and hemlock. The trees are "virgin" in the sense that they have remained undisturbed by humans. Acquired by the Department of Forests, Parks, and Recreation in the early 1900s as part of the "Ingalls Block" (each section of the state forest is named after the donor or previous owner), the Tinker Brook area was declared a preserve because of its natural beauty and relatively undisturbed condition.

The preserve consists of a section of Tinker Brook and the steep ravine banks on either side. In terms of geological history, Tinker Brook is a young and immature stream, roughly 10,000 years old. While more mature streams have wide, possibly terraced beds and meanders, or winding turns, Tinker Brook is quite straight, running from the southeastern slopes of Shrewsbury Mountain (also in the Calvin Coolidge State Forest) to the Black River, which runs along Route 100. Over time, the brook carved this deep ravine through the igneous mica, schist, and granite that are characteristic of the area and can be seen in the many rock outcrops. Here the gradient of the brook's course is steeper than in other spots above and below it. Because of this the brook valley is narrow and the brook's eroding force is more concentrated and sustained.

To the right at the end of the dirt road is a short, steep path leading to the brook. The forest here, not far from the edge of the ravine, is not part of the preserve (the boundaries of which are marked with blue blazes). Approximately 75 years old, the forest is made up of white and yellow birch, beech, white ash, and sugar maple, with some red spruce and hemlock. Before this land was acquired by the Department of Forests, Parks, and Recreation, it was used as sheep pastures and potato fields, and much of it was lumbered. The banks of the ravine, however, were too steep to be used for any of these purposes, so the trees grew without interruption. It is there one finds the virgin stand of red spruce and hemlock, some of the trees with trunks 18 to 20 inches in diameter (see also **#75**).

The conifers become more dominant as the slopes get steeper and wetter. Some of the larger trees here are between 80 and 100 feet tall, and are estimated to be about 150 years old. While they like optimum soil conditions as well as hardwoods do, they do not compete well with hardwoods. Red spruce and hemlock grow more slowly than hardwoods and are therefore eventually "overtopped," or shaded from the vital sun. They dominate near the brook, where it is often quite wet and the bedrock is close to the surface, and where the hardwoods do not do well. On the other hand, on drier, richer soils hardwoods flourish and shade out the conifers.

Along the banks of the brook, mosses (see **#107**) and ferns (see

#100), both of which prefer wet conditions, are abundant. Wild lily of the valley, painted trillium, starflower, dogberry, and various kinds of violets (see #90) can also be found here. The clear, rapid, well-aerated brook contains trout, which need the shallow running water for spawning. The female deposits her eggs under stones or in gravel, and the male later fertilizes them. The forests in the area are home to black bears, foxes, raccoons, coyotes, deer, rabbits, and an occasional wild turkey.

Remarks: *The shelter at the top of the Tinker Brook ravine is open for public use, though stays of longer than 2 days are discouraged. Also open to the public are the stone house and log pavilion farther along on Northam Rd. (both off to the right); the first is 2.8 miles from Route 100 and the second 3.2 miles. There are several hiking trails nearby. The trail to Shrewsbury Peak is at the end of the dirt road 1.9 miles from Route 100, also on Northam Rd. Bring bug repellent if you visit Tinker Brook Natural Area in spring or summer. For further information, contact the Agency of Environmental Conservation, Department of Forests, Parks, and Recreation, Montpelier, Vt. 05602; (802) 828-3375. They can provide information on primitive camping in other areas of the Calvin Coolidge State Forest.*

33.

Dead Creek
Wildlife Management Area

Directions: **Addison, Vt. From Burlington, take U.S. 7 south about 20 miles to Vergennes, then continue south on Route 22A for 6 miles to Addison. Directions to the several access points to the marsh are described below.**

Ownership: **Vermont Department of Fish and Game.**

The Champlain Valley is unique in Vermont, with its flat land and deep soils making it a prime farming area. It has a mild climate due to the moderating influence of the lake and the protection of mountains on three sides. As moisture-laden air traveling from west to east crosses the Adirondacks, it rises and cools. Since cool air is less able than warm to hold water, moisture condenses out, forming banks of clouds and possibly falling as rain. As the air mass drops

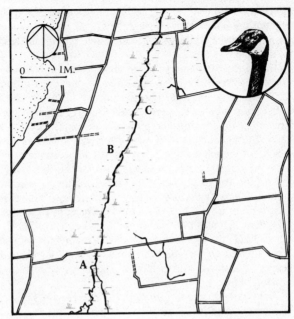

Inset: Canada goose

down the east side of the mountains into the Champlain Valley, it is considerably drier. Thus, the Adirondacks create a "rain shadow," resulting in low rainfall in the valley. However, there is plenty of water available from the numerous streams. Dead Creek is a tributary of Otter Creek, the longest stream in the state. Slow-moving and meandering, it has silt deposits that create an excellent environment for aquatic vegetation. Dead Creek's waterfowl management area is the largest in Vermont. Dikes were created to control water levels and maintain conditions attractive to waterfowl, making this one of Vermont's prime bird-watching areas.

A successful goose management program was begun here in the late 1950s. Before then, little or no nesting occurred here and very few migrants used the area. Canada geese mate for life and are firmly attached to the breeding grounds in which they were raised. In order to establish a local breeding population, wild geese were trapped, their flight feathers were clipped, and the birds were released into a fenced enclosure. Now an estimated 100 to 200 geese are raised each year, and a peak fall concentration of up to 6,000 migrants stops here.

There are several access points to the creek. Starting in Addison go west on Route 17 for 2.2 miles (the headquarters will be on the right at 0.9 mile). After crossing the bridge, take an immediate left into the Brilyea access (**A**). There are two parking areas at the end of the road.

Here a vast cattail marsh covers about 100 acres. Various management practices have been employed to discourage the spread of cattails because they are not as attractive for nesting areas as are other marsh plants. These practices include changing water levels to encourage other plants and protecting muskrats, which eat the cattails. The aquatic muskrat (see **#70**) is a smaller relative of the beaver. Although it eats various plants and occasionally insects and fish, the cattail is its main source of food. The shoots are eaten in spring, the leaves and stems in summer, and the roots in the fall and winter. Muskrats also use the leaves and stems to build their lodges, which range from just over a foot in diameter to 10 feet wide and 4 feet high. People, too, have used cattails in a number of ways throughout history. They have stuffed mattresses with the down from the old flower spikes, and made seating for chairs from the leaves. The flower spikes, pollen, shoots, and roots are all good sources of food.

Around the marsh is a small area of oak-hickory forest. This type of forest is rare in Vermont and resembles smaller woods in the southern Midwest of the United States and New York State. Its presence here is probably due to the rain-shadow effect of the Adirondacks creating dry soils. This type of forest was probably far more extensive in the Champlain Valley before much of the area was cleared for farming.

After returning to Route 17, turn left and proceed 1.3 miles to an intersection. Turn right onto Jersey St. From here there is a good view of the Adirondacks to the west and the Green Mountains to the east. After 1 mile, turn right at the T intersection. Turn left onto Jersey St. again after another mile. The road to the Farrell access (**B**) will be on the left after another mile. This access does not have an extensive view of the creek like the other access points, but like them it is a good place to launch a canoe. Many birds can be seen more easily from a canoe, being less skittish when approached from water.

After leaving the Farrell access turn right and proceed for 2.5 miles to Panton. Turn right again and follow this road for 1.4 miles (a bridge will cross Dead Creek after 1 mile). Turn right onto a dirt road. After 1.3 miles turn right again at a T intersection. This will bring you to the Stone Bridge access (**C**). The parking area overlooks a wide, open marsh with numerous rushes. A path beside the marsh offers good views of the water.

Many birds live in and around the marsh, and many more stop

here during migrations. One that can't be missed in spring and summer is the male red-winged blackbird, flashing his red epaulets as he noisily defends his territory. The brownish female builds her nest in a thick stand of cattails or shrubs near open water. Another bird that is usually easy to see is the magnificent great blue heron (see **#40** and **#64**). It may be spotted either standing motionless in shallow water waiting for small fish and frogs to come near or flying slowly over the marsh. With luck, you might spot the smaller green heron, or perhaps the nocturnal black-crowned night heron flying to its feeding grounds at dusk or on dark days. The American bittern, another heron (see **#64**), also lives here but spends almost all its time in dense growths of cattails. When approached it will "freeze," its bill straight up and its streaked body blending into the background vegetation, making it practically invisible.

One of the more spectacular hunters of the marsh is the belted kingfisher. A small blue-and-white bird with a large head and beak, it will perch on a branch overlooking water or hover in midair until it suddenly plunges headfirst into the water to spear a fish. After catching its victim it flies back to its perch to enjoy its meal.

Ducks can often be seen in the open waters of the marsh, especially during migration. The most common here are mallards and black ducks (see **#41**); blue-winged or green-winged teal and wood ducks are also present.

One of the more common hawks soaring over the marsh and surrounding farmlands is the marsh hawk, or northern harrier. It glides low over the ground with its wings held in a V looking for small mammals. Its most distinctive feature is its white rump. Red-tailed hawks and American kestrels also inhabit the marsh. In warm months turkey vultures soar high over the area. Ospreys and bald eagles (see **#51**) are rare but have been seen here in the fall or spring.

Other birds that may be seen include the ring-billed gull, aptly named for the black band circling its bill, and six species of swallows, which feed on the numerous insects of the marsh. The marsh wren (see **#6**), swamp sparrow, and common yellowthroat are some of the common smaller birds nesting on the edge of the marsh.

Remarks: *The drive, which circles Dead Creek Wildlife Management Area and crosses one portion of it, is about 28 miles. Plan to spend a full day here, in order to view the marsh and its birdlife from the various access points. Dead Creek is open to duck hunters in October; avoid visiting at this time. Nearby Button Bay State Park (see #34) has a camping area. The DAR State Park on the south end of Lake Champlain also has a public campground.*

34.

Button Bay
State Park

Directions: Vergennes, Vt. From Burlington, take U.S. 7 south about 20 miles to Vergennes, then continue south on Route 22A about 0.5 mile. Turn right at the sign for the park onto Panton Rd. Go 1 mile and turn right at another park sign. Follow Basin Harbor Rd. (Lower Otter Creek will be to your right) about 3.5 miles. Turn left, again at a sign; the park is 0.7 mile farther.

Ownership: Vermont Department of Forests, Parks, and Recreation.

Button Bay State Park is surrounded by lowlands and farms of the Champlain Valley on three sides and Lake Champlain on the other. Directly across the lake, the ancient Adirondack Mountains in New York rise in sharp contrast to the lowlands. Within the park are the remains of very diverse and distant times, including a fossilized coral reef (see also **#39**), evidence of an ancient tropical sea and climate, and glacial striations, evidence of much more recent arctic conditions.

The 500-million-year-old coral reef in the Champlain Valley indicates that Vermont was once covered by a warm, shallow ocean. About 345 million years ago, at the time of Pangaea, or the "supercontinent," all of New England was much closer to the equator than it is now, and hence its climate was much different. According to the theory of continental drift or plate tectonics, the earth's surface is composed of several solid plates that float in a semisolid zone beneath the surface (see also **#30**). Pangaea is the name given to the huge landmass that was formed when all of the continental plates were joined together. After 150 million years, the continents once again split up, and North America began to drift northwest, carrying Vermont farther from the equatorial climate.

The next major stage in the formation of the Champlain Valley was the glacial era. While the coral, gastropods, and trilobites found in Button Bay date from a hot era, fossils of clams and shellfish similar to those found in Arctic climates date from this glacial era. The Champlain Valley itself is believed to have been formed by *isostatic disequilibrium,* a condition related to plate movement which caused a great portion of bedrock between the Adirondacks and the Green Mountains to drop to a lower level than the surrounding land. This valley was then modified as glaciers passed through. With the retreat of the last glaciers, about 12,000 years ago, the Champlain Valley was submerged under a postglacial lake called Lake Vermont. Much larger and deeper than Lake Champlain, Lake Vermont was fed by melting glaciers, its northern point blocked by ice and therefore unable to drain. Under the weight of the glacier the land was actually depressed several hundred feet, and as the oceans rose because of glaciers melting, ocean water found its way into Lake Vermont. Referred to as the Champlain Sea, this body of water had about half the salinity of the ocean. As the glacier made its final retreat, the land sprang back, rising high enough to block the ocean. The fossilized clamshells that have been found in the clay-covered areas at Button Bay date back to the time of the Champlain Sea.

Button Bay's Champlain Trail, which is about ¼ mile long, leads from the nature center and follows close to the shore of the lake. At the iron railing, about ⅛ mile from the start, gastropod fossils are easily seen in the exposed limestone. Here, too, as at other points along the trail where limestone is exposed, there are cavities and cracks in the rock. Limestone is a sedimentary rock formed when shells, marine clays, and the remains of marine organisms are cemented together. The main ingredient of limestone is calcium, and these cracks and crevices, known as *solution cavities,* are caused when the calcium is dissolved in a liquid such as rain. Because limestone contains little acid, it helps create a favorable environment for vegetation, and this in part accounts for the great diversity of wildflowers at Button Bay. The more overgrown areas alongside the trail and farther inland are where the clams would be found, preseved in the clay of 10,000 years ago rather than in the older limestone that was formed thousands of years before the Champlain Sea covered the area.

The gastropod and trilobite fossils at the iron railing are the geological highlight of the Champlain Trail. Beyond this spot and for the next ⅛ mile, there is a nature trail. (A guide may be obtained at the nature center.) The same trail leads back to the nature center, with the Cavity Trail veering off to the left. Along this trail are more large solution cavities. The Cavity Trail rejoins the Champlain Trail, which leads back to the nature center.

A short walk from the nature center along the South Trail leads to a limestone point, very close to Button Island. Along this point are many glacial striations—marks left as glaciers dragged their silt and debris across the limestone. Button Island, where the coral reef is located, is small and not very accessible. It is a man-made island, privately created in the early 1900s from sediment from the now eroding Shin Island. Pictures and samples of the coral can be seen inside the nature museum, which also houses many of the "buttons" after which the bay was named. These buttons are clay concretions, formed when clay settled around the stem of an aquatic plant. After the plant died, the hole remained, to be filled in by layers of clay which were then compressed by the weight of the sediment, forming the small buttonlike pieces.

Remarks: *Nearby are the Dead Creek Wildlife Management Area and DAR State Park, which also has fossils. To get to DAR, turn right on leaving Button Bay State Park. Keeping the lake on your right, travel about 11 miles. DAR will be on the right. For further information, write to Button Bay State Park, RD 3, Vergennes, Vt. 05491.*

35.
Camel's Hump

Directions: **Huntington and Duxbury, Vt. From Burlington, take I-89 southeast about 25 miles to Exit 10. Turn south, then east onto Route 100 going through Waterbury. Stay on Route 100 as it turns southwest (right), branching from U.S. 2; go slightly more than 0.1 mile. Turn right again; go 0.2 mile on this road. Where the main road turns sharply left (next to a red schoolhouse), continue straight ahead on the dirt road for another 4.8 miles. Just past a large barn complex, turn left again on another dirt road. Go 3.4 miles to the parking lot at Couching Lion Farm Site.**

Ownership: **Vermont Department of Forests, Parks, and Recreation.**

Camel's Hump is perhaps the most beautiful of the high peaks in the Green Mountains. At 4,083 feet it is the fourth highest mountain in Vermont, and the only one of these major peaks not scarred by a network of ski trails or auto roads. The summit supports a rare and extremely fragile community of alpine tundra vegetation normally found many hundreds of miles to the north (see **#36** and **White Mountains, Monadnocks, and Eastern Connecticut Highlands**).

The various names that Camel's Hump has held over the centuries are a reflection of its unique profile when viewed from a distance. The name "Camel's Hump" was derived from the less-refined "Camel's Rump." French explorers called it "the Couching Lion" while the Waubanaukee Indians named it "the Saddle Mountain."

The state of Vermont started acquiring the land surrounding Camel's Hump in 1911 and now owns almost 18,000 acres. The summit was designated a natural area in 1965, and the protected area was expanded in 1969 in the hope of preserving one of the Green Mountains in its natural state. Consequently, no camping or fires are permitted along the trails on the mountain.

There are a variety of habitats on Camel's Hump, from a northern hardwoods forest at the base, to a coniferous forest, to the rare and endangered alpine community at the peak.

The trails described here are those that start at the west end of the Couching Lion Farm Site parking lot (**A**). Follow the Forestry Trail

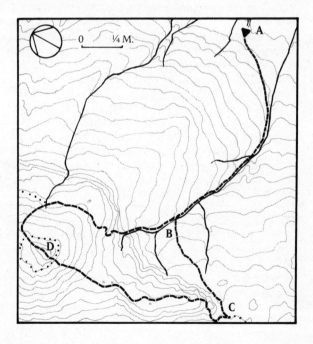

up a moderately steep grade for 1⅓ miles to the Dean intersection. Go west on the Dean Trail, crossing a brook and going through an area of extensive beaver activity (**B**). After 1 mile the trail intersects the Long Trail at Wind Gap (**C**). Turn right on the Long Trail for 1¾ miles to reach the summit of Camel's Hump (**D**). To return, continue on the Long Trail north ⅓ mile to the Camel's Hump Hut Clearing. This clearing was formerly the site of a hotel that burned down. Follow the Forestry Trail from here down to the parking lot.

Hiking on the mountain offers an excellent opportunity to observe changes in vegetation according to the increasing altitude (see also **#83**). Up to 2,600 feet the mountain is covered with a northern hardwood forest in a near-virgin condition. Sugar maple is widespread along with beech and yellow birch. Hobblebush, mountain maple, and striped maple are common shrubs of the understory. A wide variety of herbaceous plants such as red trillium and foamflower cover the forest floor; many of them bloom in the spring before the tree leaves have fully opened.

As the trail goes through the upper zones of the hardwood forest, various changes occur. Yellow and white birch are more common. Scattered conifers, red spruce or balsam fir, appear. At approximately 2,800 feet the woodland grades into a coniferous forest. The distribution of this forest type is controlled by latitude and elevation. At lower elevations it occurs in the northeast area of Vermont and continues north into Canada. At higher elevations it reaches south through the Appalachian Mountains, though beginning at progressively higher elevations. In North Carolina, for example, coniferous forests occur at 5,500 feet.

The coniferous forest on Camel's Hump consists mainly of balsam fir with some red spruce (see **#75**) and heartleaf white birch. There are extensive stands of the white birch, which is often indicative of fires: it is a major pioneer plant, quick to invade open areas. These trees might have become established after the fire that struck the area in 1903. The quantity of red spruce has declined significantly during the last few decades, and the suspected reason is acid rain. The ground cover includes abundant wood sorrel, bunchberry, wild lily of the valley and goldthread. Hikers often enjoy the thirst-quenching sour flavor of the wood sorrel's heart-shaped leaves.

At higher elevations the trees appear dwarfed, with a gnarled and twisted appearance at their crowns. The German word *Krummholz*, or "crooked wood," is used to describe this stage in which the branches are pruned by wind and ice. The trees become progressively more stunted until, at tree line, they are just 1 to 2 feet high and look like shrubs.

The small area of alpine tundra vegetation on the summit, restricted to about 10 acres, is only one of two alpine tundra communities in Vermont. The other exists on the much more heavily traveled summit of Mount Mansfield (see **#36**), 15 miles to the north. These areas are relics of the Ice Age when arctic vegetation was widespread in this region. With the retreat of the glaciers this type of vegetation followed the glacier, leaving behind isolated pockets on the tops of some mountains and a few cliff ledges.

The arctic plants are well adapted to the harsh climate on the summits, which is similar to the climate of the true Arctic. They are low and creeping, taking advantage of protected recesses between rocks where the winds cannot reach them. Most are evergreen and perennial adaptations; as such they do not waste energy growing lots of new tissue in the short growing season here. Water is often scarce in this environment, and the plants have ways of restricting its loss. For example, alpine bilberry has tough, leathery leaves, mountain cranberry leaves are coated with wax, and labrador tea has a woolly covering on the undersides of its leaves. Other plants, such as Bigelow's sedge and mountain sandwort, have tiny narrow leaves that offer little surface area to wind and sun. These plants also grow in dense mats that soak up water when it is available. (See **#107** for more on plant survival at high altitudes.)

Although these plants are quite tough biologically, they are very sensitive to physical disturbances. The soils on Camel's Hump are very thin and easily compacted by footsteps, which kills the plants growing on them. The arctic communities are very slow growers, and bare spots that appear are usually washed clean by rains long before any vegetation can be reestablished on them. To compound the problem, many of these plants look more like grasses and insignificant shrubs than like rare species. Hikers should therefore stay on the trails or the rocks and not walk or sit in any area with vegetation, no matter how commonplace it may look. Special ranger-naturalists patrol the summit from mid-May to mid-October, helping to protect the fragile alpine community by educating the public.

The Green Mountains, including of course Camel's Hump, are a part of a much larger mountain system, the Appalachians. When standing on top of Camel's Hump it is hard to imagine that approximately 500 million years earlier the rock underfoot was a silty ooze on the continental shelf in an earlier "Atlantic Ocean." The materials that make up the present Green Mountains were originally eroded fragments of more ancient mountains that were carried away by streams and rivers. When the sediments reached the quieter waters of the sea, they settled to the bottom. This early ocean began to shrink as the continents on either side drifted together again. The sediments became deeply buried and were then subjected to huge pressures and high temperatures. Under these conditions the sediments and sedimentary rocks were changed to schists and other metamorphics. The enormous forces pushed and folded this newly formed rock to great heights, creating a mountain range far greater than what we see today. Forces of erosion have obliterated this huge range, leaving behind the present relatively humble Appalachians. Given more time, even these may be eroded to a flat plain if uplifting of the land does not intervene.

On a clear day the view from the summit is spectacular. The Green Mountains stretch to the north and south. To the west the much older (over 3 billion years) Adirondacks are visible, with the Champlain lowlands and Lake Champlain in the foreground. To the east are the White Mountains, believed to be considerably younger than the Green.

Remarks: *This is a 5-to-6-hour hike on steep terrain; it is fairly strenuous, requiring some scrambling in spots. There are several other trails on the mountain, including two on the west side that start on a road east of Huntington Center. Check the latest edition of* Guide Book of the Long Trail *for more information and updates on trails. It may be obtained from the Green Mountain Club, P.O. Box 889, Montpelier, Vt. 05602. Hiking is best in late summer or early fall as the trails are then normally drier and less subject to erosion. Lugged soles on hiking boots should be avoided if possible, as they greatly accelerate erosion of mountain trails. Camping is available at Little River State Park, located about 12 miles north in Waterbury.*

36.

Mount Mansfield
Alpine Tundra

Directions: **Underhill and Stowe, Vt. From Burlington, take I-89 southeast about 25 miles to Exit 10. Take Route 100 north about 10 miles to Stowe. Turn northwest (left) onto**

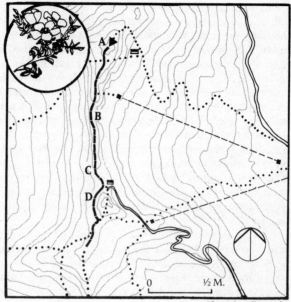

Inset: Flowering diapensia

Route 108; go 9 miles to the entrance of Mount Mansfield State Park and the toll road and gondola to the summit.

Ownership: **University of Vermont.**

The beautiful summit ridge of Mount Mansfield, rising over 4,000 feet high, supports one of the few true alpine plant communities in New England (see **#35**), and is home to several rare plants that are usually found only hundreds of miles to the north on the Arctic tundra. The summit also affords spectacular views in all directions, with Lake Champlain, New York, Canada, New Hampshire, and Maine all visible on a clear day.

Viewed from the northern Champlain Valley, the summit ridge resembles the profile of a human face. The southernmost part is known as the "forehead," while the northernmost and highest point is called the "chin." Between these features, a rocky prominence juts skyward—the "nose." A nearly treeless ridge extends from the forehead to the chin. Stunted fir and spruce trees occasionally occur on the mountaintop where they are sheltered from the strong westerly winds.

Although there are several approaches to the ridge that all lead to different places along the summit trail, this description will begin at the chin. The chin (**A**) contains the largest single expanse of sedge tundra in Vermont. This grasslike vegetation is composed mostly of Bigelow's sedge, few-flowered sedge, and highland rush. The thin, acidic soil found here is almost identical to that of the Arctic tundra.

In the wet depressions on the long, flat ridge between the nose and the chin (**B**) are several small peat bogs (see **#76** and **#103**) harboring unusual boreal vegetation. Mats of sphagnum moss are covered with black crowberry, leatherleaf, bog laurel, and hare's tail cotton grass. The western side of the ridge, where the strong winds prevent trees from developing, sports a heath-type vegetation (see **#74**), dominated by alpine bilberry, mountain cranberry, and low sweet blueberry (**C**). Growing among the wet gravels and rocky soils are clumps of mountain sandwort and scattered three-toothed cinquefoil.

Walking along the ridge toward the forehead, you will see some of the rarest plant species on the mountain. Lapland diapensia, bear-berry-willow, New England tea-leaved willow, and alpine knotweed are all found here. Relatively few birds inhabit the mountaintop because of the scarcity of food and nesting places. However, the dark-eyed junco, white-throated sparrow, and raven are often seen in the summer. The ridge is a good place to look for migrating hawks between late August and early November (see **#66**).

From the nose, the spruce- and fir-forested slopes below are visible, where one can see the trees thinning out and getting smaller as they approach the tree line. The outcroppings of granite here (**D**) show some signs of the glacier that once covered this mountain. Grooves and shattermarks can be found where boulders were bounced and dragged across the top of the mountain. The jutting features along the ridge were created when the glacier pulled the top of this once sharply peaked mountain to the south.

Remarks: *Stay on the trail and do not disturb the vegetation on the ridge. Alpine plants are very fragile, and one misplaced footstep can destroy a plant colony that has taken years to become established. During the summer, warden-naturalists are stationed on the summit to guide visitors and answer questions. On the ridge, the terrain is moderate; getting there on foot, rather than by road or gondola, can take 2 to 3 hours of fairly strenuous hiking. One can easily spend a full day here, but allow a minimum of 2 hours on the ridge to fully enjoy the scenery and the alpine habitat. The weather is usually windy and cool, even in the summer. For other hiking in the Mount Mansfield region,* Guide Book of the Long Trail, *published by the Green Mountain Club, is highly recommended. It contains maps and trail descriptions, and can be purchased in most Vermont bookstores or from the Green Mountain Club, P.O. Box 889, Montpelier, Vt. 05602.*

37.
Smuggler's Notch

Directions: **Cambridge, Vt. Follow directions in #36. Route 108 goes through the notch about 9 miles from Stowe; 0.9 mile beyond the Smuggler's Notch State Park Campground, just beyond a pulloff for the Long Trail, is a picnic area on the right, where the hike starts.**

Ownership: **Vermont Department of Forests, Parks, and Recreation.**

Smuggler's Notch is a spectacular gap with tall cliffs, huge boulders, and caves between Mount Mansfield (see **#36**) to the west and Sterling Peak to the east. The Green Mountains were once an imposing obstacle to east-west travel in the state, and Smuggler's Notch became an important pass through the mountains. As its name implies, the notch was a well-used route for people smuggling goods in and out of Canada before and during the War of 1812. It was also a route to freedom for escaped slaves. During Prohibition, the notch provided a vital passage for contraband.

The magnificent cliffs of Smuggler's Notch reflect a complicated geological history. The bedrock itself is hundreds of millions of years old (see **#35**). The actual carving of the notch represents a much more recent geological event. About 18,000 years ago, during the peak of the last glacial period, Vermont was covered with thousands of feet of ice. Although glacial erosion played an important role in modifying mountaintops and valleys, Smuggler's Notch seems to have been carved by running water rather than by moving ice. When seen from above, the notch has a sinuous shape, which is more typical of water erosion. Viewed horizontally it has a V-shaped cross-section, whereas glaciers typically create a U-shaped valley. Current theory holds that the notch was carved by the large quantities of meltwater from the glacier as global temperatures increased.

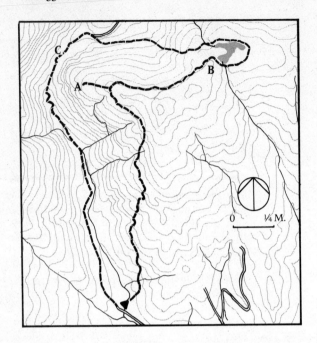

There is strong evidence that the saddle between Mount Mansfield and Spruce Peak had impounded glacial meltwater to its north. Since the glacier blocked the northward flow of these waters, they were forced to flow over the saddle, scouring deeply into the bedrock.

Some of the trails are quite steep and susceptible to serious erosion. For this reason visitors should stay off the trails during the spring when mud makes them extremely vulnerable to damage. Avoid wearing lug soles, common on most hiking boots, which cause much more damage to trails than do flat rubber soles.

The trail described here starts at the south end of the parking lot. Follow the blue-blazed trail as it crosses the brook and climbs steeply up the mountain. As you climb, the vegetation goes through several changes (see also **#35** and **#83**). The yellow birches by the river give way to sugar maple and beech. Higher up the paper birches appear and soon become widespread. Spruce and fir are scattered in the understory. Finally the transition to a coniferous forest is complete; spruce and fir dominate with scattered paper birch and mountain-ash.

While climbing, stop now and then to look at the colonies of plants growing on the lower sides of rocks in wet areas. A variety of ancient plants, mosses and liverworts, grow here. Liverworts, which are inconspicuous flat, fleshy green growths or are mosslike with tiny, thin leaves, are among the most primitive of land plants (see **#101**). They, as well as the mosses (see **#107**) growing here, need to be constantly moist to survive and rely on water for reproduction. These inconspicuous colonies probably resemble the first land plants to emerge from water.

Views of Mount Mansfield soon appear behind you through the trees. This mountain, the highest in Vermont, has extensive areas of rare alpine vegetation on its summit. Just before the spur path to the lookout, views of the notch begin to appear ahead of you through the trees (**A**).

The lookout is above Elephant's Head, a large cliff on the eastern side of the notch. Across the notch are impressive views of the western cliffs with Mount Mansfield to the left. You can see the road, straight below, 1,000 feet down.

In the nooks and crannies of these cliffs are rare arctic plants. The best examples are in the western cliffs across the notch. Although both the cliff flora and the alpine tundra on Mount Mansfield are relics of the Ice Age (see **#35** and **#36**), they are quite different owing to the different climates of the two areas. In summer the ledges are usually moist and shady while the mountaintops are more sunny and dry. In winter the mountaintops are protected by a blanket of snow, the ledges exposed to extremely cold temperatures and ice. Plants growing on the cliffs include the insectivorous butterwort and a variety of rare arctic saxifrages.

Nesting in the cliffs are small flocks of ravens, which live here year-round. This lookout is a good place to view the single birds or family groups as they soar in and out of the notch. A large bird and a native of the Arctic, the raven lives in heavily wooded mountainous regions in this state.

From this point continue on to Sterling Pond (**B**), then take the Long Trail down to the road and follow the road back to the parking area. Sterling Pond, gouged out by the continental glacier, is the largest of several high-altitude ponds in the Mount Mansfield area. On the way down, the Long Trail offers additional views of the cliffs across the notch.

Geological processes in the notch continue right up to the present, as evidenced by recent rockslides (**C**). Water again is the principal agent; in this case, it enters cracks in the rock. Here it freezes and expands, wedging huge boulders away from the bedrock cliffs which eventually break loose (see **#80**). The resulting rockslide is subject to further weathering, both physical and chemical, until the rocky material is reduced to sand, silt, and clay-sized matter that can be transported by streams and rivers. The freshness of some of the rock, indicated by its lighter color, shows how recent these slides were.

The hike back to the picnic area along Route 108 passes beside and through the rubble of these multiple rockslides. A slide that occurred in 1983 actually came across the road, just barely missing a lone jogger.

Remarks: *This is a steep, but not dangerous hike, requiring about 3 hours. If you wish to do any exploring, particularly around Sterling Pond, allow at least half a day. The Mount Mansfield and Smuggler's Notch area has numerous other hiking trails, some of which are* extremely *steep. For details check* Guide Book of the Long Trail, *published by the Green Mountain Club, P.O. Box 889, Montpelier, Vt. 05602. Camping is available at the Smuggler's Notch State Park. Route 108 becomes very narrow, winding, and steep as it passes through the notch. Cars with trailers and oversized vehicles are not allowed on this section. Also, Route 108 in the notch is not plowed in the winter.*

38.
Lone Rock
Point

Directions: **Burlington, Vt. Contact Episcopal Diocesan Center, Rock Point, Burlington, Vt. 05401, for specific directions and permission to visit the grounds.**

Ownership: **Episcopal Diocese of Vermont.**

Evidence of the geological upheavals that shaped our land area some 425 million years ago are seen almost anywhere in New England where there are mountains and hilly terrain. These are usually covered with soil and vegetation, however, so that the composition of this foundation of our land is hidden. Lone Rock Point is an exception. It lies along the Champlain thrust fault, one of the major fault lines in New England, and is one of the best examples of a thrust-fault formation in the eastern United States.

The best view of the outcrop is from the lake, although it can also be seen from the point itself. From both vantage points, the older white dolostone is clearly visible lying on top of the younger black shale (see **#29**). The formation originated approximately 200 million years ago when a crack occurred between two plates of land lying next to each other. This was the fault line. As upward pressure increased, one section of land slid up the slope of the fracture and moved on top of the adjacent land. Eventually, the entire plate of land from one side lay directly on top of the other. Each piece of land was composed of the younger shale on top of the older dolostone (which consists primarily of limestone). Thus the two together created the appearance of white–black–white–black rock. However, erosion and glaciation over hundreds of millions of years have removed the top level of shale and revealed the dolostone. The remaining sequence of dolostone on top of shale on top of dolostone is clearly visible. Some sections of the dolostone are composed of red Cambrian dolostone, which is among the oldest rock known to exist in New England.

Remarks: *The best way to see the point is by boat. Rentals are available at the ferry docks in Burlington. If visiting on foot, allow about 1 hour.*

39.
Chazyan
Coral Reef

Directions: **Isle La Motte, Vt. From Burlington, take I-89 north about 35 miles to Exit 21. Take Route 78 and U.S. 2 west about 12 miles to Alburg; turn south (left) on Route 129. Go south about 5 miles to the bridge; cross over to Isle La Motte.**

Ownership: **Private, but visits can be arranged through the Town Clerk's Office, Isle La Motte, Vt. 05463.**

When one thinks of coral reefs, it is usually in association with warm tropical oceans, not a cold northern New England lake. However, on the small island of Isle La Motte in northern Lake Champlain are outcroppings of the oldest coral reef in the world. It is at least 500 million years old, and serves as evidence to support the growing theory of continental drift. It also provides clues about the nature of our world in the Ordovician period, half a billion years ago. The coral can be seen cropping up all across the island (points **A** through **D**), especially in open fields and old quarries. Many outcroppings are visible from the roads, but arrangements should be made to look at them closely.

Since corals are living organisms that thrive in temperate salt water, it is presumed that this area was once under a vast warm ocean. The theories of plate tectonics (see **#34**), the repositioning of continents over a vast period of time, offer the explanation that at the time these corals were living, the entire region was situated near the equator. The plates of landmass—actually the continents—were divided by fault lines and were separated by the thrusting and drifting movements within the earth.

The continental shelf on which the corals grew, now the substratum of the island, became limestone in the metamorphic process that was occurring at the same time. The limestone today holds fossilized evidence of many crustaceans and other invertebrates found in ocean waters of ancient times. These can sometimes be seen in the areas immediately surrounding the coral outcrops.

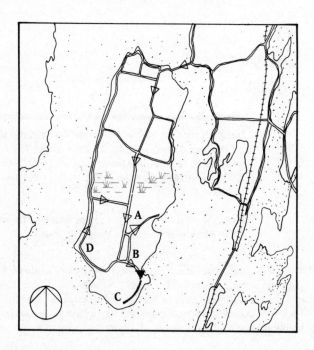

Remarks: *The best areas are only a short walk from the road. Do not remove any coral or fossils from the area, as this speeds erosion and may lead to the destruction of these significant and unusual features.*

40.

Missisquoi
National Wildlife Refuge

Directions: **Swanton, Vt. From Burlington, take I-89 north about 35 miles to Exit 21. Take Route 78 west 3.3 miles to the refuge headquarters, on the left.**

Ownership: **U.S. Fish and Wildlife Service.**

Where the Missisquoi River enters Lake Champlain is an extensive delta formed of silty, sandy deposits (see also **#110**). This kind of environment often leads to the development of marshes and swamps, and that is precisely what has occurred here. The Native American word Missisquoi, meaning a place of "much waterfowl and much grass," describes the area well, as two-thirds of the delta is covered with grassy marsh, providing an ideal environment for waterfowl and many shorebirds. The other third of the delta is a swamp dominated by silver maple. Over 90 percent of the delta falls within the 5,651-acre national wildlife refuge.

Before the establishment of the refuge, the natural process of filling, by both silt and decomposed vegetation, slowly raised the level of the soil. This allowed the growth of brush and trees, which were less attractive to waterfowl than is marsh vegetation. When the refuge was established in 1942, the management instituted a plan to re-create the wet marsh conditions, so important as breeding grounds for waterfowl, as food sources and rest areas for migrating birds.

Before visiting the refuge, call or stop at the headquarters (**A**) to find out which areas are open. After the snow melts, the greater part of the area may be under water. Various sections harboring breeding pools are closed all year to protect the wildlife. There is hunting in some parts of the refuge in the fall.

At any time of year the best way to visit is by canoe, which enables you to explore almost the entire refuge—very little of the marsh itself can be seen from the trails. Also, animals are less likely to startle

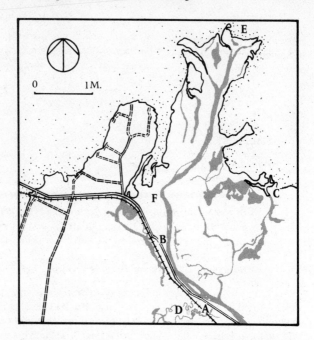

and hide when approached by canoe. There are no canoe rentals close by, so you must bring your own. Among the most interesting routes is a loop that starts on the Missisquoi River, goes to Lake Champlain, then returns to the Missisquoi via Dead Creek (**C**). Allow a full day for the trip, as you will want to explore the numerous inlets and pools in the marsh. The best place to put in is at a parking area (**B**) 1.2 miles west of the headquarters on the north (right) side of Route 78.

The marsh has a wide variety of plants. Water lilies are abundant in the open spaces. Rushes and sedges (see **#101**) form dense stands covering large areas, and cattail colonies (see **#33**) are common as well. Wild rice (which many people regard as a delicacy) grows near Lake Champlain, providing seeds for thousands of waterfowl (see **#18**).

The waters and marshlands of the Lake Champlain area are a main branch of the Atlantic flyway, the route of migrating birds between their breeding grounds in the Canadian prairies and tundra and their southern wintering grounds. This refuge is one of a chain of refuges along the flyway (see **#41** and **#70**).

Impressive numbers of waterfowl can be seen from the canoe

during migration. An estimated 22,000 ducks may be here at one time during peak season. The fall, from about mid-August to the end of September, is the best time. The ducks that migrate through this area come primarily from the lakes and marshes of Quebec and Ontario, especially the Hudson Bay area and the Saint Lawrence River valley. Mallards, black ducks, wood ducks, and common goldeneyes are the most abundant nesting and migrating waterfowl. There are also blue-winged teal and hooded mergansers. Other nesting birds include the American bittern (see **#64**), the common gallinule, and numerous species of songbirds. Various hawks and an occasional bald eagle (see **#51**) may also be seen.

The largest great blue heron colony in the state is in the refuge. An impressive blue-gray bird, this 4-foot-tall heron is often seen standing motionless in a shallow body of water, waiting for its meal to swim by. The large nesting colonies or rookeries, with hundreds of great blues, are found near the outlets of the Missisquoi River. The nests, looking more like piles of twigs, are built high in the trees of the swamps and woodlands. Shad Island (**E**) harbors a particularly rich population.

Behind the headquarters is a 1½-mile nature trail (**D**). Following the Black and Maquam creeks, it meanders through a white-oak and silver-maple swamp with a dense growth of ferns in the understory. Along the river are numerous signs of beaver and muskrat (see **#70**), and you may catch a glimpse of the animals themselves.

The swamps are especially well suited for amphibians. The presence of frogs is particularly noticeable in spring when the males fill the air with their mating songs. The earliest frog to emerge from hibernation is the wood frog, whose hoarse quack sounds more like a duck. The chorus of the peeper treefrog, or spring peeper, is usually next. Its shrill peep can be heard for quite a distance, although this frog is seldom more than an inch long. Other frogs add their voices to the teeming swamp as the season progresses.

Remarks: *A pamphlet describing the nature trail is available at the headquarters building. You may also walk along the Missisquoi River, starting from the canoe-launch point mentioned above. Do not walk here during hunting season. There are camping facilities at Lake Carmi State Park, about 20 miles east in Enosburg Falls.*

41.
Mud Creek
Wildlife Management Area

Directions: East Alburg, Vt. From Burlington, take I-89 north about 35 miles to Exit 21, then Route 78 west about 6 miles to the bridge. After crossing the bridge, continue for slightly over 2 miles to the first parking area, on the right; another is 0.1 mile farther.

Ownership: Vermont Department of Fish and Game.

Unlike nearby Missisquoi National Wildlife Refuge (see **#40**), Mud Creek's marshes are easily accessible by foot. An old railroad bed through a section of the marsh enables excellent close-up views of wildlife while still keeping one's feet dry. A wide variety of waterfowl, both breeding and migratory, can be seen in the open pools. If possible, bring binoculars or a spotting scope for viewing the birds.

The railroad bed is on the left as you enter the first parking area. At the second parking area, cross the bridge, then follow the trail for slightly over 1,000 feet until it crosses the old railroad grade. Along the railroad bed are typical wetland trees such as silver and red maple, swamp white oak, and red elm. Horsetails, with ridged, segmented stems, also grow on the banks of the railroad bed (see **#5**). These ancient plants are smaller versions of their treelike ancestors that were widespread 300 million years ago.

Buttonbush grows in a small marsh area to the left of the railroad bed. This aquatic shrub, with flowers in dense ball-like heads, forms thick stands. In and alongside these thickets are willows and red-osier dogwood, a shrub with bright red twigs and white berries.

To the right of the railroad bed, in the marsh itself, cattails fill large areas, and water lilies cover much of the surface of pools in between. The smallest flowering plant, duckweed, often colors water surfaces a bright green. Looking closely at these tiny floating herbs, you can see that they have a leaflike body, often with tiny rootlets growing beneath them. As their name implies, large quantities are eaten by ducks and other waterfowl.

The most common ducks nesting in the shallow marsh are dabbling ducks such as the mallard, black duck, and blue-winged teal. Because they tip into the water for food rather than dive, they prefer to feed in water depths of no more than 16 inches. This group can also leap into flight directly from a standing or floating position, an advantage in the small marsh pools.

These ducks breed early in the spring, nesting in dense reeds or grasses. Soon after breeding they molt their flight feathers, which renders them unable to fly. For the summer the male changes into a drab plumage similar to the female's. Before the fall migration they molt back into breeding feathers. This enables them to complete their courtship and pair bonding in the winter so they can start nesting early the next spring.

The most common dabbling duck is the mallard. A native of the prairie states, it has moved east, often helped by people who domesticated and then released the birds. Mallards eat primarily the seeds of sedges, grasses, and smartweeds, but also consume leaves, insects, and fish eggs.

A number of other marshbirds are found here. The Virginia rail, hard to see because it spends most of its time in dense vegetation, breeds in the cattails. Its close relative, the common gallinule, is easier to spot as it swims and prowls in the open looking for food, often making chickenlike noises. Swamp sparrows and marsh wrens (see **#6**) are frequently heard in the marsh. Other species breeding here include the American bittern (see **#64**), which is well camouflaged by the vegetation, the green heron, and the black tern. Great blue herons (see **#64**) are common visitors, and you may sight them standing motionless in the water waiting for fish. Marsh hawks, or northern harriers, often soar overhead, easily recognized by the distinctive white patch on the rump.

While walking along the railroad bed, you may see holes dug into the bank surrounded by pieces of leathery eggshells. These are most likely snapping turtle eggs dug up by skunks or other mammals. Of the freshwater turtles, the snapping turtle is the largest. It is mostly aquatic, but does come on land to lay its eggs or migrate to another body of water if there is a drought. Although frequently maligned as a vicious predator, the snapping turtle is actually retiring, feeding on fish, aquatic invertebrates, and, surprisingly, large quantities of vegetation.

The lovely dragonfly also inhabits the marsh. Like the damselfly, its close relative, it is a member of an ancient family with fossil records dating back over 300 million years. Much of its 2-year life is spent as a larva or nymph in the water, where it feeds voraciously on numerous water insects. After molting into a large iridescent adult, it continues its predacious life catching insects on the wing. Dragonfly eyes, the largest in the insect world, can see as far away as 40 yards. Their large diaphanous wings can carry the dragonflies as fast as 30 miles an hour, helping to make them very successful hunters. (See **#104** for more on dragonflies and damselflies.)

Remarks: *The walk along the railroad bed takes only about 30 minutes, but you can easily spend half a day here watching the birds in the marsh. North Hero State Park, located approximately 12 miles south of Mud Creek in North Hero, has camping facilities. Call (802) 372-8727 or (802) 372-5060 to find out when their season ends—it may be earlier than at other state parks.*

42.

Troy Colony
of Great Laurels

Directions: **Troy, Vt. From Burlington, take Route 89 southeast about 25 miles to Exit 10. Go north on Route 100 about 42 miles to Troy. Go past the village 0.6 mile and turn right on the dirt road. Go 0.5 mile and turn left over a bridge crossing a small stream. Go 0.3 mile, park on the side of the road, and follow the path on the right through the woods to the laurel stand.**

Ownership: **Private.**

The great laurel is a large and spectacular rhododendron usually found only in warmer climates than that of northern Vermont near the Canadian border. It is believed that this species was more common in northern Vermont about 6,000 years ago, when the region possessed a somewhat warmer climate. This period of time is known as the *climatic optimum*. As the Temperate Zone moved farther south, the vast majority of laurel stands died off. However, the soil and topographic conditions in Troy combined to allow this colony to slowly adapt to the changing habitat. The soil here is moist, and the colony stands on a small plateau that is warmed by air rising from the surrounding lowlands, creating slightly higher temperatures in which the laurels can grow. They are true relics of ancient times, and they allow the visitor's imagination to wander back to the distant past of ancient New England.

The colony covers only about half an acre in the middle of a relatively young forest of primarily red maple, yellow birch, and balsam fir. What is immediately striking about the area is that this surrounding forest is boreal, or northern, in nature. The laurels have adapted to such an extent that they share the habitat with a drastically different type of vegetation. There is an extensive ground cover of Canada yew, which is also typical of a cold climate.

Like all vegetation, the great laurels are subject to damage and interrupted growth cycles by varying weather conditions in different seasons. In past years, the laurels have grown in dense clusters and reached heights of up to 6 feet. However, several severe winters in the early 1980s have damaged many of the bushes, and they are now struggling to reestablish themselves as a strong, though disjunct, plant community. The bushes are lower to the ground and more scattered than they once were, but as such they are better protected from winter damage and have more space to spread out and grow in the spring and summer months.

The diminished size of the laurels does not detract from either their uniqueness or the beauty of their blossoms in early to mid-June, when they are at their peak. At that time they are surrounded by many other flowering shrubs that cover the moist, mossy ground; these include mountain holly, witherod, dogberry, and goldthread. There are also increasing numbers of mountain ash and velvetleaf blueberry. In the middle and latter part of May, several species of wildflowers bloom, including pink lady's slipper, creeping snowberry, wild lily of the valley, false violet, and the distinctive three-pointed trillium. Clumps of grasslike bladder sedge are scattered in particularly damp spots, along with cinnamon fern and royal fern, which has reached the impressive height of 5 feet here.

This relic colony of great laurels is one of only two that are found in northern New England; the other is in Lexington, Maine. Visitors to this stand are reminded that great laurels are protected from human disturbance by state law, and that the colony needs careful protection in order to regain its former size.

Remarks: *Allow about 1 hour for a visit. Waterproof hiking shoes are recommended during the spring months.*

43.

Moose Bog

Directions: **East Brighton, Vt. From St. Johnsbury, take I-91 north about 10 miles to Exit 23; continue north about 3 miles on U.S. 5 through Lyndonville. Go northeast (right)**

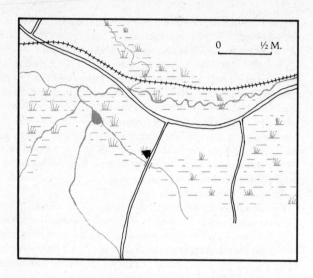

on Route 114 for about 23 miles to Island Pond. Turn east (right) on Route 105; go 7.9 miles (you'll cross railroad tracks at 7.5 miles). Turn right onto a dirt logging road, the South America Pond Rd. After 0.2 mile there will be a dirt track on the the right (if you cross a flooded cedar swamp you've gone too far). Park anywhere you can pull off along the road and proceed on foot.

Ownership: **Vermont Department of Fish and Game.**

Moose Bog is located in the heart of the Northeast Kingdom of Vermont, an area of both high latitude and elevation. With the help of the Nature Conservancy, the Vermont Department of Fish and Game acquired the tract to protect it from possible development.

Underlying the Northeast Kingdom is an extension of the granitic and metamorphic rock that forms the White Mountains of New Hampshire (see **White Mountains, Monadnocks, and Eastern Connecticut Highlands**). The granite causes the soil to be acidic and this, in turn, determines the type of vegetation able to grow here: coniferous forests, which are tolerant of acid, predominate. Repeated advances and retreats of glaciers over the area left thick layers of glacial material and created numerous kettle holes (see **#76**), as indicated by the many ponds, bogs, and swamps in the region.

The coniferous forest in the Northeast Kingdom is part of a similar worldwide forest located between the Arctic tundra and prairies or deciduous forests to the south. This area of Vermont has more in common with northern Maine and southern Canada than with the remainder of Vermont. (see **Interior Maine**). Since the late nineteenth century it has been the center of a vital pulp and paper industry, which relies on the conifers.

Many interesting species of birds can be found in this region of Vermont. The Vermont Institute of Natural Science in Woodstock lists as nesting birds in the Moose Bog area the black-backed three-toed woodpecker, olive-sided flycatcher, gray jay, boreal chickadee, and a variety of wood warblers. Broods of spruce grouse may be seen from June to August. During migration there may be interesting waterbirds at the bog.

To reach Moose Bog itself, follow the dirt path off the logging road. After about half a mile you will see a pond through the trees on the left. Watch carefully for a narrow trail leading down to the edge of the sphagnum-moss mat. This trail on the left of a widening in the road is sometimes hard to spot. The walk down the path from South America Pond Rd. is an excursion into a wonderland of green and gray mosses and lichens growing on either side.

The thin, acidic soils in this subarctic-like forest make this a difficult place for most plants to grow; consequently the tougher lichens that don't do well in competition with other species can become established here. The lichen is actually two plants, a fungus and an alga, which work together, enabling the lichen to survive on such forbidding environments as bare rocks. Lichens grow as spreading stains on rocks, as leafy or ruffled horizontal patches, and as upright, branching filaments. This last type, the fruticose lichens, are represented here especially by the reindeer lichen, a low, shrubby gray-white plant. As its name implies, this lichen is eaten by reindeer. Years ago people in Sweden made flour from it for bread.

As you approach the bog, watch carefully for animal tracks, particularly those resembling a deer's but considerably larger. They belong to moose, which are among the rarest animals that live in the area. Moose get much of their food in and around ponds and, strangely enough, are powerful swimmers (see **#106**). Land clearing in the 1800s pushed the moose out of Vermont, but there are now roughly twenty-five to fifty, mostly in the Northeast Kingdom. Bears and deer have also been seen near the bog.

Several key environmental factors are necessary for the occurrence of bogs. There must be an abundance of water in an area with little or no drainage. Organisms in the stagnant water soon use up any available oxygen. Decomposers such as bacteria and fungi cannot survive without oxygen, so dead plants and animals become pickled in the acidic water. Studies of ancient pollen, preserved at the bottom of bogs, give clues to what trees grew in this region in the distant past. In bogs in northern Europe a number of "bog-men" have been found that are 3,000 years old yet remarkably well preserved.

The most obvious plant in bogs is sphagnum moss. Starting on land, it spreads out as a floating mat over the water (see **#76** and **#103**). It grows from the tips, while the bottom portions die back. Decomposing very slowly, the dead layers accumulate until they reach the bottom. After many years, layers of sphagnum turn into a solid black, compact substance. This is peat, which is sometimes used as fuel in areas of northern Europe. Growing throughout the sphagnum are numerous shrubs whose roots and stems, dead or alive, hold the mat together, often forming a "quaking" bog. These floating mats are frequently strong enough to support a person although they sway and bob with every step. Such is the case with portions of Moose Bog.

Most bog shrubs are members of the heath family, a group that can survive in acid areas (see **#74**). Common heaths seen here include bog laurel, bog rosemary, leatherleaf, labrador tea, and cranberries. These plants and others in the bog are northern in origin. In fact, many of the same plants, such as labrador tea, grow on Arctic tundras. They are Ice Age relics that have survived here in part because of the cool year-round environment of the bog. They cope with the adversities of the bog in a variety of ways. Ironically, the bog water is largely unavailable to the plants because of its acidity. To compensate, sphagnum moss has large dead cells that can store many times their weight in water. The shrubs have tough stems and leathery leaves to prevent excess water loss into the environment. Cotton grass, a common sedge here, has thick stems and narrow leaves, reducing evaporation surfaces.

Several plants of southern origin have a unique solution to the problem of obtaining nutrients in the sterile environment. These are carnivorous plants, which extract nitrogen from their prey instead of the soil. The most conspicuous one here is the pitcher plant. Its large, vase-shaped leaves contain pools of water with digestive enzymes in the bottom. Insects attracted by the leaf odor are trapped in these pools by the smooth leaf surfaces and downward-pointing spines; they are dissolved by the enzymes and absorbed. If you look into a pitcher plant you can often see the indigestible chitinous leftovers (see **#104** for more on pitcher plants). Sundews, also seen here, have small leaves with sticky spines. Insects that land on the leaves become glued as if on flypaper. The leaf curls around the insect until it is digested, then opens for the next meal.

Remarks: *Although it is a short walk in to the bog, plan on spending a few hours exploring. From about late March to early May the dirt road may be closed due to the "mud season." Brighton State Park in Island Pond, about 7 miles west of Moose Bog, has campsites, a swimming beach, and a small natural history museum.*

44.
Lake Willoughby Cliffs

Directions: **Westmore, Vt. From St. Johnsbury, take I-91 north about 10 miles to Exit 23; continue north on U.S. 5 about 11 miles to West Burke. Continue north, after a right turn onto Route 5A; go about 6 miles to a parking area on the left, before coming to the lake.**

Ownership: **Willoughby State Forest, Vermont Department of Forests, Parks , and Recreation.**

One of the deepest lakes in New England, Lake Willoughby is 308 feet deep, long and narrow with towering cliffs on both sides. The area is famous for its rich variety of ferns and flowering plants. Rare arctic plants, relics of the Ice Age, grow on the rocky cliffs (see also **#35** and **#36**).

The geology of Lake Willoughby illustrates two major ways in which glaciers modify the landscape: eroding away material and then redepositing it. Apparently a small valley previously existed between Mount Hor and Mount Pisgah, possibly a result of river erosion. With the advance of the last continental glacier, ice was channeled through the valley, scouring much more deeply than it did as it traveled across flatter land and mountaintops. This kind of glacial carving eroded a U-shaped valley, such as can be seen here today.

The glacier carried within it broken rock fragments of all sizes, which it had eroded from the local bedrock. As the climate warmed, the leading edge of the glacier melted, depositing this rocky material. Here it accumulated to form earthen dams; both the northern and southern ends of the lake's deep basin are blocked by glacial deposits, allowing the clear waters to accumulate. (See **#105** and **#107** for more on glaciation.)

The trail described below climbs Mount Pisgah on the east side of the lake. Much of it parallels the cliff edge with numerous lookouts to the lake and opposite cliffs. The north end of the trail is at Route 5A, 2.7 miles north of the parking area. From here, it is a pleasant walk back on the road beside the lake.

The yellow-blazed trail starts across the road from the parking area (**A**). The forest is a typical example of northern hardwoods with sugar maple, beech, and yellow and white birch. After crossing an area of northern white-cedar swamps, the trail starts climbing steeply through sugar maples. The forest floor is covered with a variety of wildflowers such as blue cohosh, with its deep blue berries, and baneberry, with its unique white berries on red stems. Huge boulders are scattered throughout as the trail goes up over and through the talus slope. Weathering and gravity have combined to create this litter of broken rock material at the foot of the cliffs.

Near the top, a spur path leads to the first of several lookouts. From here you can see the south end of Lake Willoughby with the cliffs rising from the tree-covered talus slopes (**B**). Mount Hor is visible to the left. Concentrated along the cliff face are northern white-cedar, or arborvitae. The cliffs below **C** harbor some of the rarest plants in Vermont. When the climate warmed after the Ice Age, these arctic plants survived in the nooks and crannies of a few

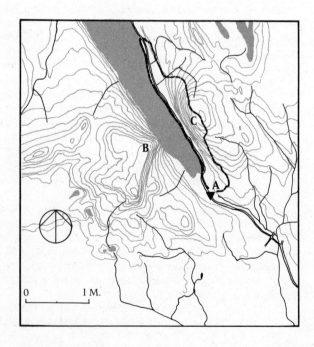

cliffs. Many are calciphiles, receiving their calcium from the mica-schist rocks of the cliffs. Growing on the ledges are purple and yellow mountain saxifrage, sweet broom, and birds-eye primrose. These cliff dwellers are relatively safe from human damage, as only skilled rock climbers can reach them.

Another cliff dweller, the peregrine falcon, has not been as fortunate, having become almost extinct due to human influences. The last known nesting site in Vermont was located in these cliffs in the early 1950s. The reason for the decline appears to have been DDT, which was widely used to exterminate a variety of pests. Because it does not break down in the environment, it started to accumulate in animals of the food chain. Although the quantity of DDT in prey animals was relatively small, the hawks that fed on them soon accumulated extremely high concentrations. If DDT did not kill them outright, it deformed developing embryos or caused weakened eggshells. Thus whole generations as well as individuals were wiped out. The ban on DDT in 1969 helped reverse the decline of many of the hawks. A program to rehabilitate the peregrine in the Northeast was soon started. In 1977 three young peregrines were released at chosen nest sites in the Green Mountains in the hope that they will return when they are old enough to breed.

For spectacular face-to-face looks at many hawks, the best time to come is during their migration. In the fall flocks of hawks, or "kettles," use rising air currents to lift them over the mountains (see **#66**). The north lookout, on a spur trail a quarter of a mile beyond the summit, is the best site for hawk-watching. The area is particularly good for accipiters and falcons, whose migration peaks from late September through mid-October, and large buteos, which pass through from late October to early November. On a good day with westerly winds an observer may easily see one hundred hawks.

Remarks: *The walk is a 7-mile loop, requiring about 4½ hours. It is generally steep and may be slippery in the spring; late summer and early fall are the best times to hike. For more hikes in the Lake Willoughby area, see* Day Hikers' Guide to Vermont, *published by the Green Mountain Club, P.O. Box 889, Montpelier, Vt. 05602. Brighton State Park, located approximately 28 miles to the north and east in Island Pond, offers camping facilities. Call (802) 723-4360 or (802) 584-3826 to find out when their season ends—it may be earlier than in other state parks.*

For more information on hawk-watching contact the Vermont Institute of Natural Science, Church Hill, Woodstock, Vt. 05091; (802) 457-2779. VINS, in conjunction with the Hawk Migration Association of North America, has collected and published data from hawk-watchers around Vermont. VINS also sponsors hawk-watching trips throughout Vermont.

The Connecticut River Valley: Land of Dinosaurs

Born in a handful of springs issuing from the shadowed floor of a conifer forest near Pittsburg, N.H., close to the borders of Quebec and Maine, the Connecticut River flows 407 miles to its mouth between the towns of Old Lyme and Old Saybrook, Conn., on Long Island Sound. The river begins in mountains, some 3,000 feet high, descending through a series of four lakes so precipitously that it drops 1,600 feet in its first 30 miles. From there it angles to the southwest, then flows south, forming the border of New Hampshire and Vermont.

Until it reaches the Massachusetts border, the Connecticut is a stream of modest size, cutting a narrow swath through the crystalline bedrock of the New England Upland. Not terribly deep except where hydroelectric dams, built over the last century or so, have backed it up, it is the home of smallmouth bass and walleye.

Below the Massachusetts border it begins to broaden, becoming a stream of major proportions, more languid than its rushing upper reaches—but still not tame. Its valley widens into an immense trough 25 miles wide, floored by a red earth that contrasts vividly with the comparatively drab soils on either flank. This trough, stretching 100 miles to Long Island Sound, is known as the Connecticut Valley Lowland, one of New England's most fascinating geological areas.

Parts of the valley, some of which lies almost at sea level, are more than 700 feet below the granitic highlands that wall it. The depth of the trough in relation to the land on either side is due partly to the ease with which

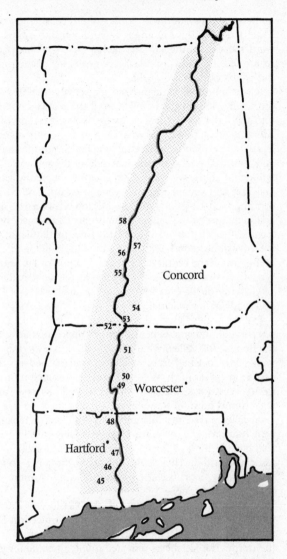

its soft shale and sandstone—which lend the red color to the soil—are eroded. The valley originated, however, from much more violent processes: vulcanism and underground convulsions that wrenched the crust of the earth.

The story of the Connecticut Valley Lowland begins about 200 million years ago, at the beginning of the Triassic period. The landscape was hilly but eventually wore down into a broad plain. Toward the end of the Triassic, perhaps 170 million years ago, the region felt the effects of a series of geological disturbances that left their mark around the world.

It was a time of rampant volcanic activity, as well as faulting of the earth. Fiery magma welled from the planet's interior, seeping into the older rock. Great fields of lava swelled out of volcanoes. Along the eastern edge of what became the Connecticut valley, the earth's crust split into a series of long faults, running between north and south. The land on the east side of these colossal cracks rose while that on the west side sank, creating a towering escarpment.

Rivers and streams surged over the escarpment as time passed, carrying sand, clays, and mud to the land below. There the sediment gradually turned to shale and sandstone. One variety of sandstone, technically called *arkose* and notably from the Portland, Conn. area, is brownstone, a dark red rock favored for building in eastern cities at the turn of the century. Brownstone from Portland quarries—still very much in evidence—was shipped by the bargeload to New York City. Many of the buildings along the main street of Portland are also made of this material.

Even after the valley's shale and sandstone formed, the earth was not through moving. Other upheavals ripped myriad small faults in the floor of the valley, while tilting it 15 degrees to the east. Meanwhile, lava belched from volcanoes and pushed up through the arkose at places such as New Haven, Southington, and Meriden, Conn. West Rock, through which the Wilbur Cross Parkway runs via a tunnel north of New Haven, is one of these intrusions of basalt lava, called a *dike*. Another great ridge of basalt is Talcott Mountain near Hartford. The towering, craggy Hanging Hills of Meriden were also created by lava flows, as were Mount Holyoke and the hills associated with it. They stand high above the softer stone of the rest of the valley floor, because basalt erodes much more slowly than shale and sandstone.

As elsewhere in New England, the Pleistocene glaciers put the finishing touches on the landscape of the Connecticut River valley, not only in the lowland but also in the river's narrower corridor to the north. The ice sheets retreated fitfully, melting for a time, then momentarily readvancing. When this happened, small moraines, deposits of glacial sand and gravel, formed at various spots along the valley. Meltwater pooled into the depressions behind them and backed up into long, narrow freshwater lakes, as if heralding the lakes that in modern times have been created by dams along the river.

One of these glacial lakes stretched from central Vermont and New Hampshire to about where the Moore Reservoir stands on the river today, between Littleton, N.H., and Saint Johnsbury, Vt. The other filled the valley below that, all the way down to Middletown, Conn. Sediment from these lakes remains today in belts that mark the remains of ancient beaches that once lay on their shores. Some of these deposits have proved to be excellent sources of gravel.

As far as the Connecticut valley is concerned, however, it is not the events of the ice ages but those long before, when the region was first forming, that make it especially interesting to science. The first evidence that dinosaurs walked this land was found near South Hadley, Mass., when a Williams College student plowing his father's field discovered a hunk of rock bearing strange footprints similar to those of a giant bird. Since the find occurred in 1800 but the existence of dinosaurs was not suspected for another quarter century, the footprints were indeed believed to be those of a bird—Noah's Raven, it was said.

As the years passed, more footprints of strange beasts were found at sites scattered throughout the valley, tracks that by the middle of the century were attributed to dinosaurs and other prehistoric creatures from the Triassic period. All told, the footprints number in the thousands, this abundance stemming from the fact that during the Triassic period the soft muds and other soils of the valley were conducive to preserving them. Fossil bones, however, are scarce, because the same environment that promoted preservation of tracks—as well as prints of vegetation—worked against fossilization of bones.

From the tracks and a handful of fossils, however, scientists have put together a detailed picture of how the valley looked in Triassic times. Great reptiles, many of them ancestors of the immense dinosaurs of later eras, wandered through a tropical lowland lush with giant ferns, cycads, and immense conifers similar to Norfolk pines. Sluggish streams meandered everywhere among broad mudflats. Ripples from stream water are preserved in the same rock as many of the footprints—at Dinosaur State Park in Rocky Hill, Conn., for instance.

Fish similar to the coelacanth swam in the muddy waters, where they were preyed upon by phytosaurs, large crocodilian look-alikes but not really related to modern crocodiles and their kin. Among the dinosaurs were *Coelophysis*, a swift, aggressive meat-eater about 10 feet long, and *Anchisaurus*, a lightly built omnivorous creature that ran on two legs and, despite its appearance, probably was ancestral to the massive plant-eating dinosaurs of the *Brontosaurus* type, which appeared later.

Nowadays, from the forests of conifers, birches, and maples of its upper reaches through the oak-dominated woodlands of the south, the Connecticut valley still offers habitat for a remarkable array of wildlife. The valley serves as a corridor through which creatures from the more remote northern wilds can wander south to more settled regions. Even moose occasionally thread their way through the mostly rural borders of the river, even showing up periodically in Hartford, Conn., and other urban areas. So, at times, do black bears, which may even at rare intervals penetrate below Middletown—a possibility biologists do not confirm but do not deny, either. Increasingly, too, bald eagles, recovering partially from the pesticides that played havoc with their reproduction, filter down the river and find a haven along its lower banks.

The waters of the river itself provide a thoroughfare for fish, particularly anadromous species such as sturgeon, Atlantic salmon, and shad. Shad and salmon runs, particularly in colonial times, clogged the water with the sleek, silvery forms of fish fighting upstream to spawn and reproduce their kind. Salmon were so numerous that the fish was not a delicacy as it is today, but a staple for the working man. Connecticut River shad, salted and in barrels, were carted to Valley Forge during the Revolution to feed Washington's hungry troops.

Pollution and the construction of dams blocking the river brought an end first to the abundance, and then to the very existence, of the salmon in the river and its tributaries. Shad persisted, but only south of the Connecticut-Massachusetts line. Gradually, however, pollution has been curbed, even if not eliminated. State and federal fisheries agencies have reintroduced salmon into the river. Fishways have been built to bring the salmon and shad over the dams. Ever so slowly, the shad and salmon are returning to their ancestral spawning grounds, living reminders of the river's immense capacity to support life in variety and profusion.

—Edward Ricciuti

45.

Wharton Brook
State Park

Directions: **Wallingford, Conn. From Hartford, take I-91
about 30 miles south to Exit 13, which leads to a connector
highway. After about a mile, turn south (left) onto U.S. 5;
the park entrance is a short distance on the left. Once in
the park, go north (left) to the parking area near the bath-
house.**

Ownership: **Parks and Recreation Unit, Connecticut Department of Environmental Protection.**

As the last glaciers were receding from the region about 12,000 years
ago, their meltwater streams and temporary lakes carried loads of
sand and gravel that eventually settled out to form flat, thick, and
excessively drained outwash plains. Wharton Brook State Park is a
remnant of these disappearing sand-plain communities (see also **#48**),
areas now generally characterized by limited but hardy vegetation
such as pitch pine, little bluestem grass, and scrub oak. One unusual
beachlike area within the park consists of a small stretch of wind-
blown sand set amidst the surrounding forest.

Walk along the dammed end of a trout-stocked pond and bear
left across a mowed meadow and down into the woods. Mature
pitch pines are being crowded out by black and white oak, beech,
and black cherry. Without the intervention of fire here, the pitch
pines will eventually be lost and an oak forest will predominate.
Fires act as trigger mechanisms for the release of the seeds of the
pitch pine, which are stored in tightly closed cones. Layers of pine
needles are burned off from the forest floor, allowing the seeds to
germinate on the bare mineral soil. Oaks are not dependent on fires
for their germination, however, and are not nearly as tolerant of
heat as are pitch pines. Therefore, a fire would assure continuation
of the naturally occurring pine while killing off the invading oak
(and other) species.

This forest represents only one of the variety of botanical communities that are found on Connecticut's sand plains. At Bradley
International Airport, for instance, there is an almost pure stand of
pitch pines. In other parts of the state one may find open, prairielike

grasslands; low, scrubby woodlands of dwarf chestnut oak, scrub oak, and blueberry; and sandy, windblown barrens. Moreover, says ecologist Ann Pesiri, "where past land use or physical factors such as fire history, drainage, or exposure vary across a single site, all or a combination of these cover types may be found."

Common to sand plains throughout the state are their geological origins during the last ice age. As the retreating glaciers melted, material that was previously frozen in the ice was released and carried by the meltwaters, eventually falling out of suspension to form broad sandy and gravelly plains. The rock debris was sorted by the moving water, with the heaviest particles usually settling first and the lightest ones last. In some instances, the sand plains are the beds of former glacial lakes rather than river or stream deposits (see **Connecticut River Valley**).

Each year these unique areas are diminished in size as housing developments, cemeteries, industrial parks, gravel pits, and other businesses are built on their level terrains. In a report for the Connecticut Department of Environmental Protection, Pesiri states that there are fewer than a dozen high-quality examples of sand plains left in the state.

In the northeast corner of the park is a small stretch of sand, perhaps 100 feet wide by 200 feet long, which appears quite suddenly and is rather sparsely vegetated. Little bluestem grass (*Andropogon scoparius*) grows in patches alongside scattered pitch pines. Blueberry, sweet fern, black cherry, and black oak grow around the edges. Researchers believe this surprising landscape to be the result of long-term wind action. Sand particles have been picked up from the surrounding area and deposited here, while the continuing dry and open, breezy location perpetuates the beachlike topography.

A number of moths and butterflies, some of them rare, are found particularly in sand-plain habitats; these include the sleepy dusky wing, the frosted elfin, the hoary elfin, and the Delaware skipper. The relationship between these delicate creatures and the sand plains is related to food supply. The frosted elfin, for example, feeds on wild lupine and wild indigo, two wildflowers that favor dry soils. The larval stage of the Delaware skipper is frequently found on little bluestem grass. Lepidopterist William Howe states that "through much of its range this species is evidently a transient because its apparent food plant is a grass (little bluestem) that is a pioneer on recently burned areas. The grass occupies the area disturbed by fire for only a few years until, through succession, it is replaced by other plants. This demands effective dispersal flight of the skippers, for newly burned areas must be quickly located and colonized during the few years that the site is habitable." Thus we see another fire-related ecological phenomenon, which is more proof that life on earth is connected within a sometimes very subtle web.

Remarks: *Walking time is about 45 minutes. The park, located on the edge of a suburban-industrial area, is popular with swimmers. Sleeping Giant State Park, in nearby Hamden, has miles of hiking trails and camping sites; for information contact park headquarters, 200 Mount Carmel Ave., Hamden, Conn. 06514.*

46.
Higby Mountain

Directions: **Meriden, Conn. From Hartford, take I-91 south about 20 miles to Exit 18; turn east onto Route 66. Take this divided highway east about 2 miles to the intersection with Route 147, then reverse direction and head west on Route 66 for 0.4 mile to the trailhead on the right. Park beside the road just before it becomes divided by a guardrail.**

Ownership: **The Nature Conservancy.**

Higby Mountain is a sheer 892-foot-high basalt ridge that rises sharply above the surrounding valley and provides excellent views in three directions. Chestnut oaks and redcedars, stunted by the wind and harsh climatic conditions, share the rocky summit with isolated patches of bearberry and other hardy plants.

To reach the blue-blazed trail, walk straight up the hillside along an unmarked path that begins at the edge of Route 66. Meet the blue trail in about 60 yards and turn left through a mixed-oak forest.

On the way to the top, be on the lookout for snakes among the blocky cobbles and weathered stones that line a good part of the path. Snakes are cold-blooded animals whose internal temperature fluctuates according to the temperature of their environment. Here, they favor the southern and western exposures on Higby Mountain, which allow for a maximum of sunlight, especially in the cool spring and autumn. Also, the piles of rock in the area create suitable habitat for dens and burrows. Although copperheads are sometimes found

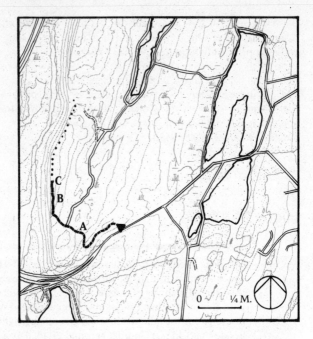

along the traprock (basalt) ridges of the Connecticut River valley, the snake most likely to be seen here is the common garter snake. These snakes are prolific, giving birth in July and August to anywhere from one dozen to six dozen live young. They are one of the commonest snakes in the eastern United States and seem to be one of the few reptiles capable of adjusting to suburbanization and development. This is probably due to their ability to subsist entirely on a diet of earthworms, although they also eat frogs, toads, and salamanders when available.

Walk carefully once you reach the top (**A**)—this is not a place for acrophobics. I-91 is below you and the city of Meriden just beyond. Long Island Sound glimmers to the south, 20 miles away. Notice that the ridge immediately to the south and the one off to the northwest are both sloped gently to the east but have precipitous cliffs facing in a westward direction. Each ridge seems like a duplicate of the other. These ridges are the remains of an ancient series of lava flows that intruded into surrounding sandstone and shale and were tipped or slanted by faultings of the earth's crust (see **Connecticut River Valley**). This occurred during the Triassic period, about 180 to 200 million years ago. Since then, the softer rock has been eroded away, but much of the basalt remained (see **#50**). An examination of the valley floor would reveal the less resistant sedimentary material that persists there.

Notice the roughly hexagonal to polygonal ridges etched on the faces of the exposed rock here at the summit. These are contraction joints, which formed as the basalt cooled from its original molten state. Such shrinking sets up tension in a rock, and a system of short, fairly straight cracks forms, separating each center of contraction from every other. Sometimes this causes the basalt to break into columns and blocks. Examples of this can be seen at the bottom of the cliff and along the south side of nearby Route 66 by the trailhead.

Here and there among the rocks is the low, trailing evergreen shrub bearberry (*Arctostaphylos uva-ursi*) (**B**). A northern plant of circumpolar distribution, bearberry grows in New England and the Mid-Atlantic states in rocky or sandy places. It can be found in thick mats in parts of Cape Cod, Long Island, and the Pine Barrens of New Jersey. The Indians dried the small oval leaves and smoked them with tobacco, calling the mixture kinnikinnick. Look for the small white or pink flowers from May to July.

You might want to explore the ridgetop by continuing northward on the Mattabesset Trail (**C**), but you'll have to follow the route you came in on to get back to your car.

Remarks: *The round-trip walk takes about an hour. Since the mountaintop is fairly close to the road, it may be crowded on weekends or warm, sunny days. Camping is available at Sleeping Giant State Park in Hamden. For information, contact Parks and Recreation Unit, Department of Environmental Protection, Hartford, Conn. 06115; (203) 566–2304.*

47.

Dinosaur
State Park

Directions: **Rocky Hill, Conn. From Hartford, take I-91 south about 10 miles to Exit 23. Go east 0.8 mile; the park, on West St., is highly visible.**

Ownership: **Parks and Recreation Unit, Connecticut Department of Environmental Protection.**

Undoubtedly the best place in Connecticut, and possibly in the Northeast, to see dinosaur footprints is in this unusual state park. Here are five hundred fossilized footprints of carnivorous dinosaurs, some up to 16 inches in length. They are exhibited *in situ* beneath a huge geodesic dome. Interpretive displays and a life-size model of the type of dinosaur believed to have made these tracks help explain the distant past at this unique National Natural Landmark.

The tracks at Dinosaur State Park are approximately 185 million years old, made during the Triassic period of the Mesozoic era. During that time the climate of Connecticut was subtropical, and much of the state was a broad plain, laced with ponds and streams. The footprints made by these 20-foot-long reptiles called *Eubrontes* were preserved in what was then soft, sandy mud of a perfect consistency to retain a clear impression. Other sediments were then washed in over the tracks to "freeze" the imprints. Lastly, the entire area was slowly compressed by additional sediments and turned into sandstone, a solid rock.

No bones have ever been found in this region of *Eubrontes* or of most of the other dinosaurs that lived in the Connecticut valley. Paleontologist Edwin Colbert believes this is because the "conditions conducive to the preservation of footprints were not generally those that would result in the preservation of fossil bones and leaves and tree trunks." These natural relics likely disappeared as a result of oxidation and decay processes within the many layers of sediment that covered them. (For more on dinosaurs, see **Connecticut River Valley**.)

Remarks: *Fifteen hundred other tracks on the grounds have been reburied by scientists until such time that money can be found for their proper display and care. Plans for additional facilities include an auditorium, diorama, greenhouse, formal exhibit hall, and a boardwalk directly alongside the tracks. Background literature and informative exhibits are currently offered at the park. Also on the 45-acre site is a loop trail through a red-maple swamp. Another public location in which to see dinosaur tracks is in a preserve owned by the Trustees of Reservations in Smith's Ferry, Mass., off Route 5.*

48.

McLean
Game Refuge

Directions: Granby, Conn. From Hartford, take I-91 north about 10 miles to Exit 40. Take Route 20 west about 8 miles to Granby, and turn left onto Route 10 going south. Go 1 mile to the park entrance, on the right.

Ownership: Parks and Recreational Unit, Connecticut Department of Environmental Protection.

Geologists maintain that the 3,400-acre McLean Game Refuge is the only wildland tract in southern New England where three major geological terrains—sand plains, traprock ridges, and metamorphic highlands—occur. Twenty miles of trails lead through these formations and through diverse vegetational habitats. Thick conifer woodlands provide nesting grounds for goshawks, white-throated sparrows, pine warblers, and a variety of other birdlife. Dry oak-hickory woods, red-maple wetlands, scenic overlooks, and several ponds add to the unusual diversity here only 16 miles from Hartford.

Begin walking on the blue-blazed trail, which parallels the West Branch of Salmon Brook. Pitch pines (see **#45**) are able to grow well here in the dry, sandy soil, along with scattered white pines, white oaks, and hemlocks. The poor soil owes its origins to sand deposited during the filling and drainage of glacial lakes more than 10,000 years ago (see **#45**). Look in this general area (**A**) for the uncommon pine warbler, a bird breeding only locally in New England but found year-round in the southern states. This little yellow-breasted warbler with white wing bars is nearly always associated with pine trees and has been known to nest in fifteen different varieties within the pine family. It feeds primarily on insects throughout the tree canopy. Listen for its trill song, similar to that of the chipping sparrow but quieter, lower-pitched, and less rapid.

The trail leaves the pitch pines, begins a gradual slope through red and chestnut oaks, continues to a low ridge, cuts down through a hemlock–white-pine forest, and then rises up to a summit of 550 feet on the Barndoor Hills (**B**). From the crest of this erosion-resistant basalt dike, there are good views to the west of rolling slopes and farmland. Formed millions of years ago when a thick wedge of lava was squeezed up into surrounding sandstone, the Barndoor

Hills are one of a series of ridges found in the Connecticut River valley (see **#46**). Their tough composition has withstood eons of weathering, so that now they rise above the eroded lowlands.

As you descend from the summit, look in the high crotches of hemlocks and other trees for nests of the gray squirrel (**C**). Notice that the nests are made primarily of leaves, rather than of sticks and twigs, like the nests of hawks, crows, and owls. Squirrels also like to nest in tree cavities. The nest provides a refuge from bad weather, a place to sleep and to rear young. The nuts from oaks, beeches, and pignut hickories in the refuge make up a considerable portion of the squirrels' diet. When food becomes scarce, squirrels have been known to migrate in large numbers in search of better habitat. This may have been the reason for the startling migration that occurred in September 1933, when over a thousand squirrels were seen swimming the Connecticut River between Hartford and Essex.

A loop in the trail passes along the top of a heavily wooded *esker* (**D**). From the top of this narrow, glacially deposited ridge one can see down about 50 feet. Eskers were formed by the deposits of streams running through tunnels beneath the stagnant ice. When

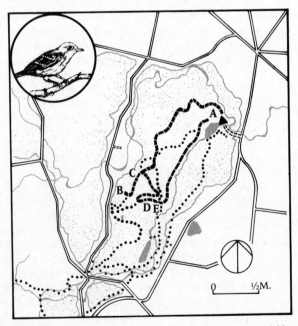

Inset: Pine warbler

the glacier finally disappeared, the old stream deposits were left standing as a ridge. Some eskers are over 100 miles in length, but most are smaller, and almost all are only a few yards wide (see also **#77** and **#108**).

The cool and shady evergreen forest growing on and around the esker is the type of habitat preferred by such northern species of birds as the red-breasted nuthatch, white-throated sparrow, and goshawk (**E**). The goshawk is a fiery and spectacular woodland raptor, not at all averse to diving and screaming at humans who come near its nest. It is also a fearless predator of squirrels, chipmunks, and many birds, including crows. One recent observer watched a goshawk attack a full-grown black duck.

The goshawk is a member of a group of hawks known as *accipiters*: birds with short, rounded wings, long tails, and a remarkable ability to fly at high speeds through dense forests. The sharp-skinned hawk and the Cooper's hawk, two other accipiters also found in the East, are smaller in size. Goshawks breed from northwestern Alaska all the way east to Nova Scotia and from central and northern New England south to Pennsylvania and Maryland.

The trail soon joins Swamp Lane Rd., a pleasant path that leads along the western edge of Bissel Brook. Follow this route to man-made Trout Pond and the entrance gate.

Remarks: *Walking time is about 3 to 3½ hours. The refuge is quite large, and this walk visits only a small part of the holdings. Consult the map available at the refuge entrance for more routes.*

49.
Mount Tom
Reservation

Directions: **Holyoke and Easthampton, Mass. From Springfield, take I-91 north about 20 miles to Exit 18 in Northampton. Go south on U.S. 5 for 3 miles to Smith Ferry (or Bray) Rd. on the right. Follow the road west to the picnic grounds on the right, opposite the Robert Cole Museum of Natural History near the junction with Christopher Clark Rd.**

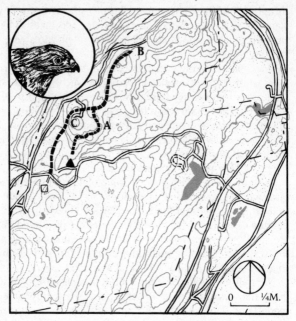

Inset: Broad-winged hawk

Ownership: **Hampden and Hampshire County Commissions.**

Rising 1,210 feet, Mount Tom dominates the skyline of the Connecticut River valley in western Massachusetts. This prominent natural landmark is the highest peak in the Mount Tom Range, a narrow but unbroken chain of small mountains and hills running north to south along the western edge of the Connecticut River.

Mount Tom Reservation, encompassing 1,800 acres, offers spectacular views across the Connecticut valley's flat central lowland to the outlying highlands of the Berkshire Hills in the west and the uplands of Worcester County in the east. Some 20 miles of hiking trails, including a portion of the north–south interstate Metacomet-Monadnock Trail, cover the reservation's diverse terrain of rolling hills, rugged traprock ridges (see **#48**), and steep cliffs. Mountain streams, several ponds, and a forest of mixed hardwoods, hemlock, and white pine provide habitat for many species of wildlife, ranging from the familiar white-tailed deer to uncommon poisonous snakes. Two observation towers serve as hawk-watching stations during spring and fall migrations along the major northeastern flight path of the Connecticut valley.

Several interconnecting trails covering the northern portion of the Mount Tom Range will be described here. Beau Bridge Trail originates from the picnic grounds opposite the nature museum on the north side of Smith Ferry Rd. Look for a trail sign posted at the edge of a coniferous hemlock grove on the east side of a meadow and follow blue blazes along the winding path. As the trail descends the northeastern slope of the range, it weaves through a luxuriant stand of shady eastern hemlock growing along Cascade Creek. A succession of log footbridges crisscrosses Cascade Creek's eroded streambed as it curls down into a cool and quiet hollow. Here the trail crosses the creek for the final time and climbs a slope where hemlock is joined by oak and other mixed hardwoods. Thickets of mountain laurel grow profusely in the understory on the right (**A**), serving as habitat for white-tailed deer. Although you may be lucky enough to see one of these graceful animals, sightings are unusual, since the deers' exceptionally keen senses of hearing and smell quickly alert them to the slightest sign of danger. Their eyesight is believed to be better equipped for perceiving moving rather than still objects. White-tailed deer favor areas of mixed cover rather than dense, extensive forests. They inhabit a home range of as little as 2 or 3 square miles, in forest edges, thicket borders, airy woodland glens, and abandoned orchards and farmlands. Deer usually follow the same routes, or "runways," through their home ranges, which allow them to browse a variety of plants in different cover. Winter snows restrict deer to "yards"—a series of trampled pathways in the snow leading to a central resting place—which are concentrated in good feeding grounds. Winter yards are often located in stands of white pine or hemlock near ponds, streams, or other bodies of water.

Continue up the slope to the junction of Beau Bridge Trail and the Metacomet-Monadnock Trail (white blazes) at the top of the grade. The latter route stretches both north (right) and south (left). Turn right to go to Mount Nonotuck, the northernmost mountain in the range, and bear left at a fork a few yards past the junction with Beau Bridge Trail. A short walk (0.7 mile) brings you to a scenic overlook at Mount Nonotuck's parking lot (**B**). The Berkshire Hills are visible to the west beyond the town of Easthampton. At the base of Mount Nonotuck in the north is the famous crescent-shaped Oxbow Lake in Northampton. This lake represents the former path of the Connecticut River. Once a meander loop in the river channel, the Oxbow became a separate body of water in 1840, when an ice jam forced the river to change course.

Retrace your steps back to the junction of Beau Bridge Trail and bear right along the Metacomet-Monadnock Trail as it now heads southward to Goat's Peak. It winds uphill through laurel thickets and stands of oak and then crosses a road before climbing a short, steep hillside to the top of Goat's Peak (**C**). A short branch trail on the left (east) leads up to the unenclosed observation tower, which affords a fine view of the valley. The Holyoke Range, a continuation of the Mount Tom Range, is visible across the Connecticut River to the east. Mount Holyoke (930 feet) is the westernmost peak in this east–west chain of mountains and hills that bisect the lowland. Both mountain ranges are remnants of extinct volcanoes that arose some 200 million years ago. They share the same distinctive cliffs and ridges composed of basalt rock—commonly called traprock—which was formed from flowing volcanic lava. The lava released by the volcanoes and vents in the valley floor flowed in a north–south direction, but through a complex series of geological events, the Holyoke Range was twisted around into an east–west configuration. (For more on the geological history of the area, see **#50** and **Connecticut River Valley**.)

Goat's Peak Tower is a major hawk-watching station during the fall migratory period. The Connecticut River valley is one of four major northeastern migratory routes for hawks and other migrants. Valleys and mountains attract hawks because the topography interacts with wind and weather conditions to generate thermal currents—rising columns of hot air—which allow hawks to glide rather than constantly flap their wings (see **#66**). During peak migratory periods hawks may appear in groups, or "kettles," as they soar together in the sky.

The largest concentration of migratory hawks in the Connecticut valley during autumn usually occurs from September 10 to September 25. The spring hawk migration (best viewed at Mount Tom from Bray Tower) runs from mid-March to early May. Weather and wind direction can determine the migratory schedule and numbers of individuals on a flight path. In spring, the winds from the south carry hawks north to their breeding grounds in New England and Canada. In autumn, winds blowing from the north transport large numbers of migrants south. The most abundant species seen from Mount Tom is the broad-winged hawk, which may total from 5,000 to 10,000 in the September migration. The sharp-shinned hawk, which may be counted in the hundreds, is the other most frequently sighted species. The osprey migration normally ranges between 50 and 150 birds in autumn.

From Goat's Peak the trail continues southward down a rugged hillside of traprock ledges. On the right, views of the Berkshires in the west appear through gaps in the trees that overhang a steep cliff (see **Taconics, Berkshires, and Green Mountains**). This cliff, which spans the western side of the range, was grooved and broken by the Ice Age glaciers.

The rocky ledges and sunny bluffs of the Mount Tom Range are typical habitat for New England's only two poisonous snakes. The American copperhead and timber rattlesnake are now rare in New England—it is highly unlikely that you will see either species—yet the Connecticut valley's basalt hills are one of the few scattered, isolated localities where they still occur. The copperhead and rattlesnake favor rocky terrain like this traprock ledge, though copperheads often live nearer to wetlands. The copperhead has a triangular yellow head and, like the rattlesnake, elliptical pupils and facial cavities beneath the eyes. It is usually buff or orange-brown with dark crossbands. Averaging 2 to 3 feet long, it tends to remain coiled and sedate unless disturbed. The slightly larger timber rattlesnake is a yellow, gray, or pale-brown color, with black crossbands highlighted in yellow or white; a reddish stripe often runs down the back. Fatalities from copperhead snakebite are extremely rare, since its venom is rather weak. Furthermore, the venom of both species is slow to take effect.

Follow the trail downhill through airy stands of birch, hemlock, maple, and other hardwoods as it shortly returns to the picnic grounds.

Remarks: *Beau Ridge and Metacomet-Monadnock Trail (northern portion) is a 60- to 90-minute hike of approximately 3 miles over difficult terrain. Exercise caution crossing the log footbridges at Cascade Creek, some of which are in poor condition. Goat Peak's traprock ledges may have loose rocks. The Metacomet-Monadnock Trail (southern portion) leads approximately 2 miles (one-way) along the top of the western cliffs to the summit of Mount Tom. Whiting Peak (1,015 feet) and Dead Top (1,100 feet) are included on the route. The reservation's numerous other trails cover the eastern side of the range to the south of Smith Ferry Rd. Several originate from the nature museum, and many are interconnecting. Crosscountry skiing is permitted on trails in winter. Robert Cole Museum of Natural History, Smith Ferry Rd., has geology and geography exhibits, as well as collections of rocks and wildlife specimens. It is open only in summer. Trail maps and other information may be obtained from the museum or from the reservation's headquarters, a stone building at the junction of Smith Ferry Rd. and Christopher Clark Rd. Picnic grounds are located on reservation roads. Fishing and ice-skating are permitted on Lake Bray. A Massachusetts fishing license is required.*

*Nearby Places
of Interest*

Mount Tom Ski Area (access from Route 5) is located on the southern slope of the range. The Arcadia Nature Center and Wildlife Sanctuary in Easthampton includes about 500 acres of woodlands, meadows, and marshland bordering the Oxbow Lake.

50.

Mount Holyoke

Reservation

Directions: Hadley, Mass. From Springfield, take I-91 north about 22 miles to Exit 22 in Northampton. Take Route 9 east about 3 miles to Hadley, then go south on Route 47 for 4.2 miles to the entrance of the state park's summit road, on the left.

Ownership: Joseph A. Skinner State Park, Massachusetts Division of Forests and Parks.

Mount Holyoke's scenic vistas are among the most breathtaking in all New England. Rising steeply above the flat, alluvial reaches of the Connecticut River valley's central lowland, Mount Holyoke is the most famous peak in the Holyoke Range, a chain of mountains ranging east to west across the picturesque interior lowland of Massachusetts.

The contrast between Mount Holyoke's high profile and the comparatively level contours of the surrounding landscape make the mountain appear much higher than its 878 feet. From the summit, one can see almost the entire valley between the state's north and south borders on clear days, as well as such distant, taller peaks as the Berkshires' Mount Greylock (see **#25**) and New Hampshire's Mount Monadnock (see **#72**). The valley itself, flanked on east and west by rolling highlands, is marked by the checkerboard fields of farming villages, the steepled towers of college towns, and the sprawling cityscapes of several manufacturing centers. But it is the

broad, winding channel of the Connecticut River itself that dominates the lowland panorama, curving into sight through agricultural
land from the north, ringing the base of Mount Holyoke's western
slope, and then gradually diminishing from view beyond the southerly cities of Holyoke and Springfield as it drifts southward into
Connecticut (see **Connecticut River Valley**).

Skinner State Park at the summit may be reached by car via the
summit road, or by foot up one of several trails. Hiking, picnicking,
and bird-watching are favorite recreational pastimes on the mountain. On balmy days hawks (see **#49**) and their human counterparts, the hang gliders, can be seen sharing the thermal air currents
as they soar high above the rocky summit or cast drifting shadows
across the river and meadows beneath the slopes. And history enthusiasts familiar with Mount Holyoke's heyday as a nineteenth-
century mountain resort enjoy walking through the old Prospect
House on the summit, one of New England's last survivors from a
bygone age when the region's favorite peaks were dotted with leisure hotels, and rocking chairs lined their verandas. A mountain
railway, built in 1854 but destroyed in the hurricane of 1938, trans-

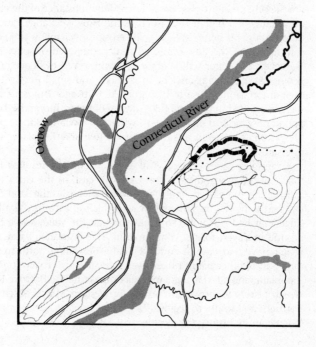

ported visitors 600 feet up Mount Holyoke's western slope to the old hotel, whose more notable guests included Nathaniel Hawthorne, Charles Dickens, and Abraham Lincoln.

The natural history of the Connecticut valley is beautifully illustrated from Mount Holyoke's summit. The origin of the lowland dates from about 200 million years ago, when a fault developed along what is now the valley's eastern edge. Land lying to the east of this 100-mile fissure, which ran southward from the present-day northern border of Massachusetts through central Connecticut to Long Island Sound, gradually rose into a mountain range, whose subsequent erosion deposited sediments across the valley. Lava sheets later spread across the lowland during three periods of volcanic activity, while sediments from the mountains continued to accumulate in the intervals between lava flows. Although the volcanic activity was relatively gentle throughout most of the valley, the lava welling up through vents in the earth's crust at several areas, including the Holyoke Range, caused violent volcanic eruptions to occur.

The rocks found today in the valley were formed in these periods of volcanic activity and sedimentary layering. The reddish sandstone (from sand) and dark gray basalt (from lava) compose many of the cliffs seen in the region. Conglomerate (from gravel) and shale (clay) are the other major types. Basalt formed the substance of the valley's mountains and higher hills, such as the Holyoke Range, since the hard basalt was better able to resist erosion over many subsequent centuries than the now vanished peaks composed of softer rocks. However, the softer sedimentary rocks preserved evidence of such geological features as ancient streambeds and small ponds, before their impressionable surfaces hardened with age. Dinosaur tracks were imprinted in these muddy, silted sediments during the Triassic period of some 190 million years, when the lowland climate probably resembled a tropical savanna. (See Remarks for places to see dinosaur tracks.)

A complex series of geological events eventually resulted in the tilting of the lowland basin from west to east, as the earth's crust sank along the eastern fault line. Simultaneously, the land to the east of the fissure moved southward, which in turn forced a basalt ridge that had run north to south through the valley to be pulled around in a west-to-east configuration. This dislocated basalt ridge, ranging west to east in contrast to the prevailing north-to-south direction of other basalt ridges, was subsequently eroded to form a mountain range. Today these mountains make up the Holyoke Range, which bisects the lowland corridor in western Massachusetts into northern and southern regions.

Later in its history the Connecticut lowland was scoured by Ice

Age glaciers, and several regions were submerged beneath the glacial lakes that formed when the ice sheet melted. Lake Springfield was formed in the area of Middletown, Conn., and eventually spread northward; Lake Hadley occupied an area just north of the Holyoke Range. Visible today are the relics of this period of glacial withdrawal and aftermath. As the ice sheet melted, the earth's crust was released upward from beneath the weight of the glacier, and as the floor of the lowland basin swelled upward, it dispersed the lake waters. The former shorelines of these ancient lakes are today called *kame terraces* and appear as terracelike steps on the valley's hillsides. They mark the level of the sedimentary deposits that had accumulated along an ancient shoreline at succeeding periods, as the shoreline of the lake fell to progressively lower levels with the dissipation of the glacial waters (see also **#77**).

A feature of the valley's more recent history is illustrated from Mount Holyoke's summit in the winding course of the Connecticut River. Across the Connecticut River to the west, notice the highly distinctive Oxbow Lake below Mount Tom outside Northampton Center. The Oxbow Lake was once a meander loop of the Connecticut River until an ice jam forced the river to change course and cut through the base or tongue of the loop. Other *meander loops,* which are curves in the shape of a half oval, can today be seen just to the north of Hadley Center and, more distantly, to the east of Sunderland in the north. The Northampton Oxbow was created as recently as about 1830.

The Summit Trail at Mount Holyoke begins off the summit road just below the Halfway House, identified by a sign for the Halfway Trail. Follow this trail until it connects with the Metacomet-Monadnock Trail, which ascends to the summit. Descend via the Metacomet-Monadnock Trail or take the alternate South Side Trail, both of which emerge at the entrance to the summit road at the base of the western slope.

The Metacomet-Monadnock Trail continues eastward from Mount Holyoke along the crest of the Holyoke Range. After descending Mount Holyoke, the trail crosses a series of hills known as the Sisters (averaging about 700 feet in elevation), which are separated by steep valleys. It then continues east to Mount Hitchcock (1,002 feet) and Bare Mountain (1,014 feet), and after crossing Route 116 at the Notch near the Amherst-Granby town line, it ascends the highest peak in the Holyoke Range, Mount Norwottuck (1,106 feet), noted for its scenic vistas and an impressive cliff on its eastern slope. At the time of this writing, the trail route across the Holyoke Range was undergoing renovation in conjunction with the development of Holyoke Range State Park.

Remarks: *The visitors' center for Holyoke Range State Park, located on Route 116 near the Amherst-Granby town line, has updated trail information and provides general assistance to visitors. Natural history exhibits are on display. The 1,758-acre Holyoke Range State Park in South Hadley borders Skinner State Park (Mount Holyoke) on the south. Dinosaur tracks can been seen at Dinosaur Footprints Reservation, located off Route 5 in Holyoke, Mass., and Dinosaur State Park (see #47) off I-91 in Rocky Hill, Conn. Another rich area for searching both for dinosaur footprints and plant fossils is along the banks of the Connecticut River where it curves westward from the French King Bridge on Route 2 in Gill, Mass.*

Nearby Place of Interest

Mount Sugarloaf State Reservation: From Joseph A. Skinner State Park, take Route 47 north through Hadley to Sunderland Center. Go west on Route 116 across the bridge spanning the Connecticut River, and turn right after the bridge at the sign for Mount Sugarloaf State Reservation.

Mount Sugarloaf rises steeply above the Connecticut River in the town of South Deerfield, some 10 miles north of Mount Holyoke. Excellent vistas of the more northerly end of the Connecticut Valley Lowland can be enjoyed from the summit observation tower, which can be reached by motor vehicle via the state reservation's summit road. Mount Sugarloaf differs geologically from Mount Holyoke, being composed of red sandstone and conglomerates rather than basalt. The mountain's northwest and southwest cliffs were created when the glacier removed loose blocks from vertical joint planes along each side, leaving Mount Sugarloaf as an isolated hill between the joint surfaces. Visible to the south below Mount Sugarloaf is a region of low hills that extend southward along the river's edge for about a mile. These are remnant sand dunes created by wind and floodwaters during the postglacial period.

51.

Quabbin Reservoir

Directions: **Belchertown, Mass. From Springfield, take 1-90 east about 6 miles to Exit 7; go northeast on Route 21 and east on U.S. 202 to Belchertown, about 14 miles. Take Route 9 east from there about 2 miles to Quabbin's west entrance, the first of three public access roads off Route 9. From the entrance follow Administration Rd. past the Metropolitan District Commission headquarters and across Winsor Dam, then take the first left turn. Proceed to the Enfield lookout, a roadside parking area on the left, just a short distance past the Quabbin rotary.**

Ownership: **Metropolitan District Commission.**

Quabbin Reservoir, serving Metropolitan Boston with a 412-billion-gallon water capacity, is one of the largest man-made reservoirs in the world. Stretching north to south for 18 miles through the rolling highlands of central Massachusetts, the reservoir and its surrounding watershed lands encompass 25,000 water acres and 55,000 land acres, including 3,500 acres on sixty islands. Two massive earthen dams impound watershed runoff from an area of 284 square miles.

Quabbin is currently regarded as the largest true wilderness area in southern New England. Its 126 square miles include hardwood and coniferous forests, bogs and swamps, grassy meadows, and rocky, isolated shores, which attract a variety of wildlife. Strict sanitary regulations for safeguarding the water quality afford wild species protection from hunting and trapping and prohibit most other sporting and recreational activities except fishing. Large areas of both the reservoir and reservation lands are closed to the public.

Most of the hiking trails are in Quabbin Reservoir Park (also called Quabbin Hill), located at the south end of the reservoir. Several scenic overlooks serve as eagle-watching stations where a rare migrant population of bald eagles and occasionally golden eagles can be seen in winter. The forest trails reveal the presence of some unusual species of wildlife and vestiges of Quabbin's four "lost" towns—Dana, Prescott, Enfield, and Greenwich—which were largely submerged beneath Quabbin's waters after the Swift River valley was flooded in the late 1930s to create the reservoir.

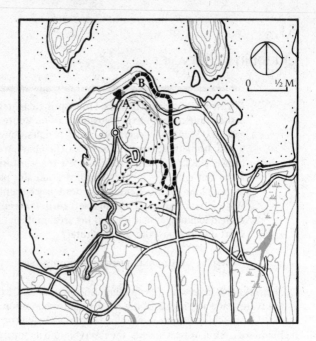

Two interconnecting trails cover both Quabbin's shores and upland forest. The walk begins just northwest of Quabbin Hill, at the
Enfield Lookout, a roadside overlook, which faces west across the
reservoir. This is the best eagle-watching station at the park. In severe winters bald eagles are sometimes seen feeding on deer carrion
on the ice-covered reservoir in the distance; in milder weather they
soar over the open waters in search of fish. With wingspans of up to
7 feet, they are a dramatic sight. Bald eagles also scavenge carrion or
prey upon smaller birds and mammals as large as foxes.

The bald eagle is an imperiled species in North America. Its numbers have been severely reduced by hunting. Destruction of the bird's
breeding habitat and contamination of fish by toxic substances have
further diminished the breeding populations. In New England the
bald eagle once nested extensively along the Atlantic Coast, but land
development has reduced its breeding range to areas in Maine—the
home of Quabbin's migrants. DDT (now banned) produced what
ornithologists called the thin-shelled-egg syndrome: by lowering the
calcium level in the bald eagle's eggshells, DDT contamination resulted in the formation of fragile eggs that broke in the nest.

Bald eagles require abundant food supplies common to large areas of undisturbed wilderness near coastal waters or large inland lakes like Quabbin. In recent years, Quabbin has attracted more bald eagles than any other place in Massachusetts: fifteen were recorded here in 1980, ten in 1981, and twenty in 1982. Wildlife investigators believe that the bald eagle is gradually increasing its numbers in the Northeast, while the nationwide eagle count begun by the National Wildlife Federation in 1979 (which also includes the golden eagle) shows an increase from 9,815 in 1979 to 13,804 in 1982.

Wildlife teams at Quabbin hope to establish a breeding population here. In 1982 a young male and female were introduced to the area and fitted with radio transmitters for flight tracking and behavioral study.

Directly across the road from the Enfield Lookout, a narrow footpath leads a few yards through the trees to a beaver dam (**A**). Beavers here have constructed their own dam of crisscrossed sticks, mud, grass, and other plants, on top of a man-made concrete dam that serves as a spillway for the brook on your left. Beaver dams provide protection from predators and allow the beavers to float sticks and food to their conical lodges. The lodge, which here sits on the edge of this small pond, is composed of sticks and mud. The 1- to 3-foot-thick walls become a hard, impenetrable fortress in freezing winter weather, when predators may gain access to a lodge over the ice.

Walk back across the road and look for the sign posted for Hank's Place Trail, which begins on the edge of the road a few yards to the left (south) of the Enfield Lookout. The trail follows a cart path through stands of white birch and mixed hardwoods, skirting the base of the lookout before descending a gradual grade to the edge of the reservoir. The red-pine grove at **B** is one of many such plantations that were established at Quabbin shortly after it was created. Red pine, which is not native to this area of the oak–white-pine forest of central New England, provides poor cover for wildlife, since few understory plants can grow in such dense shade and in the intensely acid needles that carpet the ground. Quabbin's foresters and wildlife conservationists are gradually clearing the red-pine plantations to make way for new hardwood plantings and open fields. This program will provide more diversified habitat for white-tailed deer, ground birds of open land, and other species.

Just a few yards before the cart path emerges at the water's edge, the trail veers to the right (north) and joins a winding footpath running parallel to the rocky shoreline. Look here for signs of beaver activity: distinctive toothmarks on fallen logs and standing trees whose trunks have been only partly gnawed through. Watch, too, for tracks of semiaquatic mammals, such as muskrat (see **#70**), mink, and otter.

Continue along the path as it crosses a stream and then emerges in an open field that serves as a picnic area. Walk east through the field and cross Administration Rd. to a gate marking the beginning of an abandoned woodlot road. This unpaved road, which skirts the base of Quabbin Hill, is the first portion of Powers Trail. Follow the trail through the woods, where old stone walls and cellar holes now lie overgrown along the route. Old spreading maples and oaks— sometimes called wolf trees—overhang the road, a telltale sign of land that once stood open to the sunlight before the forest grew.

Quabbin's upland forests are home to a wide variety of common mammals. Raccoons, striped skunks, opossums, red and gray foxes, porcupines, the New England cottontail, and the snowshoe hare are among those that may be sighted here, though these species are usually active at night. The sleek, slender bodies of the ermine and long-tailed weasel allow these mammals to slip into crevices in stone walls and cellar holes, such as those (**C**) that appear on the immediate left of the trail. They stalk snakes, chipmunks, and other small rodents, as well as prey larger than themselves, such as rabbits and squirrels.

A small number of fishers, which are uncommon or rarely seen throughout most of southern New England, live at Quabbin, and the population is increasing here as the forests mature. This large weasel eats, not fish as the name would suggest, but small mammals, squirrels, carrion, and especially porcupines. While equally at home in the trees or on the ground, the fisher is considered the most agile and swift arboreal animal in New England. Fishers are solitary, roaming animals, except in the spring mating season. They often take to high ground as they stalk food, sometimes ranging over long distances and making temporary dens in tree hollows or rock crevices, or beneath logs. The fisher was once common in southern New England before logging and agricultural clearing diminished its deep-forest habitat. Today it is commonly found in northern New England and in areas of extensive forest in western Massachusetts.

After roughly a 15-minute hike along the road, a trail sign appears on the right for the second portion of the Powers Trail. A footpath winds steeply up the heavily wooded north slope of Quabbin Hill. This higher, rugged terrain is typical of the habitat favored by the eastern bobcat (see **#4**). The bobcat is the more numerous of the two wildcats present in New England today. (The rare lynx is seldom seen outside the deep forests of the North.) But because of the bobcat's elusiveness and swiftness, it is rarely encountered in the wild.

In the last several decades there have also been a few unconfirmed sightings at Quabbin of the eastern cougar, or eastern mountain lion, the second largest native cat in North America. This cougar, which early New Englanders called catamount, was hunted to extinction in the eastern United States by the turn of the century. The last cougar taken in New England was more than 75 years ago. But sightings of the big cat continue to be reported in the region, mainly in northern New England (see **Interior Maine**) and the Berkshires. The most recent sighting at Quabbin occurred in 1982. Scats were recovered from the scene of the report, but analysis proved inconclusive. If the cougar's presence is finally confirmed, its reappearance may be explained by the rising deer population—the cougar's principal food—resulting from the increase in deer habitat over the last half century. In western Massachusetts a wildlife expert, with the sponsorship of the Worcester Science Center, is currently conducting an investigation of the potentially exciting but still mysterious cougar sightings.

Follow the trail as it completes its ascent up the slope and emerges at the Quabbin Tower parking lot. If you wish, climb to the top of the observation tower for magnificent views of the reservoir and surrounding countryside. The tower is also a fine eagle-watching spot and serves as a hawk-watching station during spring and fall migration periods.

Walk the paved access road down to the Quabbin Hill rotary, and go right on Administration Rd. to return to the Enfield Lookout.

Remarks: *Hank's Place Trail (1¾ miles) and Powers Trail (about 2 miles) together make an approximately 2-hour hike over moderately difficult terrain. There are some potentially wet areas near shoreline and brook, and steep rocky terrain ascending Quabbin Hill. Be especially alert for the posted signs for Powers Trail on the right of the woodland road that directs you up the slope of Quabbin Hill. There are six additional trails, many interconnecting, located in the vicinity of Quabbin Hill. Obtain maps and trail information at Quabbin Metropolitan District Commission headquarters, Administration Rd. Also available is the* Quabbin Area Sportsman's Guide, *an information booklet issued by the MDC and the Massachusetts Division of Fisheries and Wildlife, 100 Cambridge St., Boston, Mass. 02202. Quabbin is one of the finest freshwater fishing spots in southern New England. Coldwater species include lake, rainbow, and brown trout, as well as landlocked salmon and smelt. Warmwater species include bass, pickerel, white and yellow perch, and bullhead. Boat and shore fishing are permitted in designated areas only. Strict regulations govern boat and (mandatory) outboard-motor size. See the* Sportsman's Guide *for boat-*

launching areas and regulations. Pleasure boating and swimming are prohibited. State parks and forests with camping facilities include Erving State Forest, Route 2A, Erving; Lake Dennison State Park, New Winchendon Rd., Baldwinville; Federation State Forest, Route 122, Petersham (four wilderness campsites).

52.

Vernon

Black Gum Swamp

Directions: **Vernon, Vt. From Brattleboro take Route 142 south 6 miles to Vernon. Visitors are asked to check with the town clerk to get directions or to make an appointment for a guided tour. Town Clerk's Office, Vernon, Vt. 05354; (802) 257–0292.**

Ownership: **Town of Vernon.**

Located in the southeast corner of Vermont are at least four swamps that contain aged specimens of blackgum. These contorted and furrowed trees growing in a luxuriant stand of ferns and mosses are an impressive example of a virgin swamp, one that has never been cut over. Although rare in Vermont, blackgum swamps are common at more southern latitudes, indicating that the Vermont stands are relics from a time when the climate was warmer than it is now.

Throughout the last few million years the climate has been swinging between long cold glacial and warm interglacial periods. Although we are now in a warm interglacial (or postglacial) period, from 5,000 to 3,500 years ago the climate was much warmer. During this "climatic optimum" many southern plants extended their range northward into Vermont. When the climate turned colder again, many of these plants died out in the north, shifting the distribution to the south once more. As this happened, pockets of the southern species were left behind in sheltered areas. These isolated stands, or "disjuncts," are often separated by hundreds of miles from other communities of the species, as is the case with the Vernon Black Gum Swamp.

Disjunct communities are not only important as clues to change in climate but also provide information about plants' abilities to adapt and the ways new species develop. Since disjunct communities occur outside the plants' normal range and are therefore subject to different environmental stresses, such a group might acquire a slightly different genetic make-up from the species as a whole. Given time and the right conditions, the few genetic variations between the disjunct and parent population could increase until the disjunct evolves into a separate species.

The blackgum swamps are located in the hills just west of the Connecticut River valley. The climate of the valley is generally milder than that of the rest of the state, and this contributes to the swamps' survival. They are located in old kettle holes, round depressions formed by large chunks of ice that separated from the melting glacier. The ice blocks were buried by glacial sediments and later melted, leaving the depressions.

One of the swamps, about 5 acres in area, is circled by a trail easily accessible from a town road. Walking this trail is like stepping back in history to the time when the magnificent blackgums were widespread throughout the area. The deeply furrowed bark of these trees gives an impressive sense of age. The extensive growth of ferns reflects a far earlier period when they and their allies (such as club mosses) were the dominant plant form on the earth. The typical New England woodland surrounding the swamp consists mostly of hemlock with areas of beech. Hobblebush is the main shrub in the understory, which also contains scattered bushes of mountain laurel, sheep laurel, and witch-hazel.

The blackgums scattered throughout the swamp are as much as 2 feet in diameter. Many of the old trees are hollow, though still growing vigorously. On leaning trees the bark is relatively thin on the upper side but very thick and deeply fissured on the lower side, giving them their ancient appearance. In fact, blackgums are among the oldest trees in New England: trees in a stand in Maine are determined to be more than 400 years old. There are also young blackgums in the swamp, indicating that the stand is still reproducing. (See **#67** for more on blackgums.)

Other trees growing in the swamp include hemlock, yellow birch, and red maple, all typical swamp trees in New England. The shrub layer, which in some areas is quite thick, in others sparse, is dominated by the winterberry holly with its bright red fall berries. Mountain holly, highbush blueberry, and northern wild raisin are also present.

Sphagnum mosses (see **#76** and **#103**) form thick bright green cushions on the floor of the swamp, and tall cinnamon ferns cover the hummocks. Scattered examples of royal fern and Virginia chain fern occur throughout the swamp. Goldthread is abundant on the hummocks, which also contain other wildflowers such as wild sarsaparilla, starflower, and wild lily of the valley.

In order to protect this unique area, the town of Vernon bought a 450-acre piece of land that includes the swamps. The forest is called the J. Maynard Miller Forest after the person most involved in protecting the area. Although the rest of the forest is being developed for logging and recreational uses, a 300-foot buffer zone has been set aside around the swamps. No cutting except for routine trail maintenance is allowed in this zone. Uncontrolled foot traffic and of course logging could cause soil and organic matter to wash into the swamps, suffocating the roots. Even well-meaning visitors can kill the trees and other rare plants simply by trampling on them and compacting the soil. For this reason the town would like visitors to check with the town office so that they can keep track of how often the swamps are visited.

Remarks: *The swamp is magnificent at any time of year; however June offers the widest variety of wildflowers. Fort Drummer State Park, a public campground, is located 1 mile south of Brattleboro.*

53.

Harvard

Forest Blowdown

Directions: **Winchester, N.H. From Brattleboro, Vt., take Route 119 across the river and southeast to the reservoir entrance on the left, east of the town of Winchester.**

Ownership: **New Hampshire Division of Parks and Recreation.**

The process of forest succession is evident throughout New England: old fields are reverting to forest, and woodland habitats are changing as some species reach their climax and others become dominant. It is a fascinating process, but almost everywhere it is one that is heavily influenced by human activity, such as agriculture, logging, and

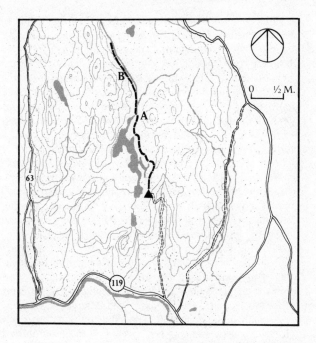

tree planting. However, the Harvard Forest Blowdown is a unique example of a once virgin tract of forest that was destroyed by natural forces—the great New England hurricane of 1938—and is now in the process of recovering without human influence or disturbance. Here we can see how magnificent the primeval forest was, and how nature has recovered from its own destructive forces through the centuries.

The area known as the Harvard Forest Blowdown is a 20-acre tract on the eastern slope of Pisgah Mountain. From the trailhead at the Pisgah Reservoir (**A**), follow Pisgah Brook northward through a hardwood forest for 1 mile. As you approach the blowdown area (**B**), you will have to begin scrambling over some of the giant tree trunks that still lie rotting on the forest floor, several decades after they were felled by the storm.

At the time of their destruction, these trees composed one of the finest stands of old-age woodland in New England. It was a mixed stand, consisting of red maple, beech, and yellow birch, but dominated by white pine (see **#12, #28,** and **#71**) and hemlock (see **#23**), some of which were over 300 years old and reached heights of 150 feet and diameters of up to 4 feet. The forest had been intensively studied by Harvard University for 10 years before the blowdown for clues to the natural successional process and information about the New England forests of centuries past.

On September 21, 1938, the most devastating hurricane of modern New England history moved up the Connecticut River valley, destroying a large percentage of central New England's forests by breaking off and uprooting trees. Because of their great height and width, stands of large, old-age trees were especially vulnerable to the storm's winds. This hurricane struck a blow to the region's timber industry from which it has never recovered. Many landowners were discouraged from raising timber, and forest managers today will not allow trees to reach these huge proportions because of their increased susceptibility to storm damage. Unlike this tract, the Cathedral Pines in Cornwall, Conn. (see **#12**) were spared destruction owing to their protected location on a western slope.

Following the storm, a decision was made not to clear up the fallen timber here but rather to see what nature would do if left alone. Today, among the remains of the fallen giants, we see a young forest mostly of hemlock and beech, although some paper birch, red spruce, and red maple have taken hold. Many of these trees seeded very quickly in the depressions created by uprooted trees, where the soil was exposed and was not covered by the usual thick layer of organic debris on the forest floor. It is somewhat of a mystery that no white pines have become established even though that was a dominant species before the storm. One theory holds that although white pine is a pioneer species, often the first to become established in abandoned fields, the exposure of the subsoil allowed the hardwoods and hemlocks to get a head start in growth. By the time the white pines were seeded, they were shaded from sunlight by the other new growth and therefore lost the battle. However, this is by no means certain, and it remains a puzzling question to forest ecologists, who are looking to the blowdown tract for answers regarding the ancient processes of forest succession that created the original virgin trees.

Remarks: *The trail leading to the blowdown is moderately difficult on a steady though gradual incline. The ground can be muddy in the spring. There is no actual trail through the blowdown area, so it is important to keep your bearings when wandering among the trees. Allow 2 to 2½ hours for the round-trip walk. Fishing is permitted with a state license, in ponds and streams. Camping is prohibited, but there are campsites at nearby Mount Monadnock (see **#72**).*

54.
Rhododendron
State Park

Directions: Fitzwilliam, N. H. From Brattleboro, Vt., take Route 119 across the river and southeast about 27 miles to Fitzwilliam Depot. After 0.5 mile (before reaching the village of Fitzwilliam), turn north (left) onto the access road to the park; look for the sign. Drive 2 miles to the park entrance.

Ownership: New Hampshire Division of Parks and Recreation.

Among the most beautiful of all wildflowers in New England is the mountain rosebay, or catawba rhododendron, a shrub that is very common in the woodlands of the central and southern Appalachians but quite rare in the Northeast. It grows in the wild in New England only in a handful of scattered colonies, and this accessible 16-acre stand is well worth a visit in mid-July, when the large pink blossoms are in full bloom.

Rhododendron is a member of the heath family (see #74) and is closely related to azaleas and mountain laurel (see #69). Most people are familiar with various hybrid members of the rhododendron family, which are common in gardens throughout New England. However, this native stand is a disjunct community, meaning that it is common to another region with different climatic and growing conditions. (See #52 for more on disjunct communities.) It tells us much about the climate of the Northeast in past centuries and about the ability of some plants to adapt to changing conditions.

It is widely believed that after the last glacial period, our climate was somewhat milder than it is today. This warmer period occurred about 4,000 to 6,000 years ago and is known as a *hypsithermal interval,* or *climatic optimum.* During this time, a forest typical of southern regions spread into New England. Some of the trees included pitch pine, chestnut oak, blackgum, and tuliptree. In the shrubby understory, sassafras, redbud, and flowering dogwood were common along with the mountain rosebay. About 1,100 to 1,500 years after the warming trend began, the weather patterns changed, and our climate turned colder. These southern species began to disappear, being pushed back into their native territory. However, isolated colonies remained where factors such as soil, water, and sunlight combined to form a microclimate suitable for continued growth.

That is what happened here, where the acidic, rocky upland soil and the protection of the surrounding oak forest provide an ideal habitat for this remnant colony. The plant is distinguished by its large, oval evergreen leaves, broader and less pointed than those of the mountain laurel. Some of the shrubs look like small trees, having grown to heights of 12 to 15 feet. The light pink flowers often reach 8 inches in diameter, and although they are not always as impressive as the hybrid domestic varieties, the rarity of these wild, native plants heightens one's appreciation of them.

Remarks: *This is a very easy walk on a level path that circles the rhododendrons a short distance from the parking area. The park is a pleasant place to visit at any time of the year, but it is best to come here in middle to late July in order to see the plants in full bloom. Allow about 1 hour.*

55.
Hartness House and Stellafane

Directions: **Springfield, Vt. From Brattleboro, take I-91 north about 30 miles to Exit 7. Take Route 11 northwest about 3 miles into Springfield. Following signs, turn northeast (right) onto Route 143, then shortly turn left onto Summer Hill St. Continue to Orchard St.; turn left to the Hartness House.**

Ownership: **Hartness House: private. Stellafane: Springfield Telescope Makers.**

The Hartness House, a lovely Vermont inn, is listed in the National Register of Historic Places. Located on 32 acres of woodland, it is the site of one of the most remarkable amateur astronomy observatories and museums in the world.

The inn itself was originally the home of James Hartness, an in-

ventor of over 120 different machines including sundials and telescopes. A man of seemingly endless imagination and energy, he also
found time to serve as governor of Vermont. Through the influence
of Hartness, Springfield became the birthplace for amateur astronomy and telescope making in the United States, a field that involves
tens of thousands of people today.

Located a short distance from the inn is the Hartness Turret Equatorial Telescope, designed and built by Hartness in 1910. To avoid
going out in the bone-chilling winter nights so common in northern
New England, Hartness mounted the telescope on the outside of a
large movable turret with the viewing eyepiece inside the insulated
and heated building. (Traditional observatories require that the inside of the building be at the same temperature as the outside air.
Otherwise heat currents passing through the opening in the dome
cause the view through the telescope to deteriorate to a turbulent
jumble. Pointing the telescope at a glass window doesn't work either; the glass would have to be optically perfect, and heat currents
still present a problem.) Hartness's turret had to be aimed precisely
at the north celestial pole, a point in the sky near the north star,
Polaris. This meant tilting the 7,000-pound turret with telescope at
more than a 45-degree angle. When the turret was oriented this
way, its axis of rotation was exactly parallel with the earth's axis. As
the earth rotated, the turret was also turned on its axis at exactly the
same rate but in the opposite direction. Thus it was able to track the
apparent motion of a star field (caused by the earth's rotation) with
the necessary accuracy and with little effort.

To complement his new heated observatory Hartness built a 240-
foot underground tunnel from the observatory to the main house so
that he could go back and forth without suffering the indignities of
winter's chill. Furthermore, he built a five-room underground apartment off the tunnel, next to the observatory, including a library,
workshop, lavatory, study, and lounging room. The apartment, ru-
mor has it, even had a bar.

The present owners of the Hartness House are preserving the Hartness telescope, which is available to all interested individuals and
groups. A view through the telescope of the craters and mountains
of the moon, Saturn's triple ring system, or the Galilean moons of
Jupiter is a memorable sight for child and adult alike. The small
underground apartment is being turned into a museum commemo-
rating Hartness and his colleagues, who helped bring astronomy to
the general public. Foremost among them was Russell Porter, one
of the founders of the Springfield Telescope Makers and a principal architect of the huge, 200-inch Mount Palomar telescope in
California.

Stellafane, "the shrine to the stars," is the site of meetings and observations of the Springfield Telescope Makers. Located about 3½ miles west of the Hartness House, at an elevation of 1,290 feet on Breezy Hill, Stellafane is a perfect meeting of heavens and earth. The 4½-acre cleared hilltop is surrounded by a typical northern hardwood-hemlock forest. The summit itself has many ledges with outcrops of highly folded metamorphic rock, predominately schist with layers of quartz. Small garnets can be found in some of this rock, but do not collect them. To the north, Mount Ascutney dominates the horizon (see **#56**). The Stellafane Clubhouse on Breezy Hill houses the Porter Turret Telescope, built by Russell Porter and other club members in 1931. It is similar to the Hartness telescope, but uses mirrors instead of lenses to gather and focus starlight.

Stellafane is now the site of an annual weekend convention of amateur astronomers and telescope makers held in late July or early August. This event attracts over two thousand people, who range from rank beginners in the world of astronomy to professionals. Daytime activities include the study of telescopes, old and new, many handcrafted by masters.

If skies are clear, participants have the opportunity to view the heavens through telescopes of all kinds and sizes. Huge interstellar clouds of gas and dust, representing the nursery of stars, can be seen to the south in a milky band of light, an arm of our Milky Way Galaxy. Clusters of stars, from a few to many hundreds, are visible through both telescopes and binoculars. The ejected shells of old stars can be seen as faint "smoke rings" or filamentous veils. Stars with companion stars may show unexpected contrasts in color or brightness. In August, Perseid meteors streak across the sky.

The most distant object visible to the human eye appears high in the northeastern sky. This smudge, the Andromeda Galaxy, represents an island of stars, possibly 400 billion in number, larger even than our own Milky Way Galaxy. The light we see is over 2 million years old.

Remarks: *Individuals or groups wishing to visit the Hartness Turret Telescope and Museum should call the Hartness House Inn at (802) 885-2115 beforehand. School and other youth groups are particularly encouraged. Viewing sessions are held almost every clear night. The owners of the Hartness House can provide the name of a representative of the Springfield Telescope Makers if you wish to join them for their meetings, classes on telescope making, or viewing. Details about the annual convention at Stellafane can be obtained from the magazines* Sky and Telescope *and* Astronomy. *Directions to Stellafane and permission to visit their Breezy Hill observatory must also be obtained from the Hartness House Inn.*

56.

Mount Ascutney

Directions: Windsor, Vt. From Brattleboro, take I-91 north about 40 miles to Exit 8. Follow U.S. 5 north 1.2 miles from the intersection; turn left onto Black Mountain Rd. (also called State Park Rd.); go 1.2 miles to the park entrance on the left.

Ownership: Mount Ascutney State Park, Vermont Department of Forests, Parks, and Recreation.

Mount Ascutney is the most conspicuous elevation in the upper Connecticut River valley. For a radius of 20 miles it dominates the landscape, rising 3,144 feet above sea level and 2,500 feet above the valley floor. Ascutney is known as a monadnock (see **White Mountains, Monadnocks, and Eastern Connecticut Highlands,** and **#65** and **#72**). Like Mount Monadnock, its neighbor to the south in New Hampshire, it is not part of a chain, but stands alone because its durable bedrock withstood the tides of erosion that formed southern New England's hilly plain millions of centuries ago.

Owing to Ascutney's commanding isolation, a traveler approaching from any direction is impressed by its beautifully compact and broad conical outline. These softened contours recall the work of erosion and glaciation. However, specific details of the mountain's history can be seen in the various rock formations on any of its three hiking trails.

Ascutney is younger than the nearby Green Mountains (see **Taconics, Berkshires, and Green Mountains**), and, in fact, is more closely related to the craggy White Mountains across the river in New Hampshire. Geologists describe it as a monadnock of igneous rock formed by an involved geological process. What we see today are the basal roots of an old volcano formed over 122 million years ago. Magma, a mass of molten rock, bubbled up from a cavern more than 2 miles below the surface and pushed aside the older sedimentary rock of the crust, filling cracks, pockets, and caverns and, some geologists believe, even erupting on the surface. The magma cooled to form Ascutney's granitic stock, which is primarily biotite granite and a syenite known as nordmarkite and locally as green granite, a granite without crystals.

This granitic core is defined as an *intrusion,* and as such it resem-

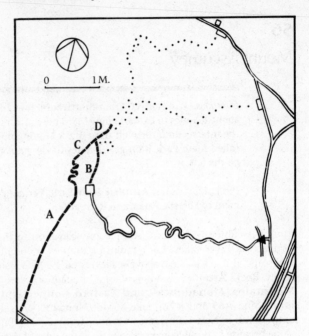

bles the copper veins of Strafford, Vt., 40 miles north, and the granite deposits of East Barre, Vt. However, Ascutney granite and syenite, mined in four different quarries on the mountain, has never been very marketable. Its color is unevenly distributed and is quite unstable, changing from blue-gray to green to brown after prolonged exposure to the air. Nevertheless, enough good stone was found to make the columns of the Columbia University Library and the Bank of Montreal.

The Crystal Cascade (**A**), about three-quarters of a mile up the Weathersfield Trail on the southern side of Ascutney, provides a dramatic illustration of the mountain's ancient life. To get there from Exit 8 on I-91, go west on U.S. 131 for 3.6 miles to the Cascade Falls road on the right. Follow the dirt road, bearing left at the fork where a sign directs you to a good-sized public parking area at the beginning of the trail. White blazes mark the trail as it follows an old woods road along Ascutney Brook. It crosses the brook and picks up another woods road, which you follow up an easy grade. The brook winds down on the right through hemlocks and a birch grove. Several spurs go to the brook's edge, where you can sit for a moment to watch the stream pour over its granite bed.

The trail begins to climb abruptly at the foot of the falls, where you can linger at the bottom of the looming sheer granite face, 84 feet high and over 30 feet across. This abrupt steepening indicates where the magma pushed upward out of the older sedimentary rock. Bands of stone striped in brown, green, and gray from water and exposure indicate lines and layers of a dike, where molten magma oozed out through vertical cracks in the softer crust. The exposed line of contact between schist, the older host rock, and syenite covers a vertical distance of 100 feet.

Where the trail skirts the cascades it is quite steep and can be slippery when the water is running. But for those who do not fear the dizzying height, a scramble out to the rim of the wall provides a lovely view down the valley. Above the big waterfall, in the smaller cascades, you can find evidence of more schists, the thin plates of metamorphic rock pushed aside by the magma.

The trail continues to the summit area through hardwoods and hemlocks, with several fine lookout points on bare rock, notably West Peak (**B**) at 2,940 feet. Here you can hear ravens and look out on the village of Brownsville. West Peak is a favorite launching point for hang gliders, and as you stand at the edge feeling the warm updrafts you can understand why. Hang gliders like the spot for the same reason the broad-winged ravens and migrating turkey vultures do. The thermal uplifts (see **#66**) rising off Brownsville's open farm-lands can carry a flying man or bird far out over the valley. You are likely to find the hang gliders if you hike up to West Peak in the afternoon on a good day. It can be an unexpected thrill to see them jump off.

If you don't have time for a hike, you can drive to within a half mile of the top and leave your car at a summit parking area. Mount Ascutney State Park maintains a 3.8-mile paved toll road with picnic areas along the way. The summit itself (**C**) is spoiled somewhat by the prominent radio, microwave, and television towers and a rotting observation tower. The isolation of the mountain makes it a good receiver and transmitter. However, if you look down at your feet, you will again be reminded of the mountain's ancient history. Among the light granitic stone you will occasionally see brownish-orange deposits. These are xenoliths of trachyte, the volcanic equivalents of syenite that were blown out onto the surface when the inside erupted.

Glacier marks, where the ice mass pulled stones across Ascutney's surface, can also be found on the summit slab. Ascutney has proved to be a significant peak in indicating the movement of the four ice sheets that covered Vermont in the Pleistocene era. As the fingers of the glacier surrounded the base of a mountain, they tended to pick up and distribute rocks and boulders in a fanlike pattern that trailed off to the south or southeast. Mount Ascutney retains an uncommonly wide boulder train (see **#78**) and therefore gives a good idea of how the glacier advanced. Pieces of Ascutney have been found as far away as Sterling, Mass., as part of what is called the Mount Ascutney train.

Ascutney's heights are the delight of bird-watchers. High-altitude birds can be seen easily in the spruce and balsam forest at the summit. Ravens are reputed to nest in the ledges (see **Interior Maine**), and many of the boreal species tend to linger longer in their spring migrations. In the summer you are likely to see Swainson's thrush and the blackpoll warbler. Black-throated blue warblers are abundant and can be seen quite close up. On the lower slopes in the cut-over brambles, there is a colony of mourning warblers.

If you drive to the summit for a view, there is a most spectacular overlook 0.3 mile from the tower: Brownsville Rock (**D**). The trail is clearly marked. Just above the junction of the Brownsville and Windsor trails, take the small side trail to the west where you can climb out to see Killington Peak, Camel's Hump (see **#35**), Pico Peak, and Mount Mansfield (see **#36**). Below the rock there is sometimes a small trickle-fed pool, should you wish to drink before descending on one of the hiking trails or returning to your car at the summit parking lot.

Remarks: *Mount Ascutney State Park, open from mid-May to Mid-October, owns 1,984 acres of the mountain and maintains 36 campsites, 10 lean-tos, a stone shelter, picnic areas, and the paved road to the summit. For further information, telephone Mount Ascutney State Park, (802) 674-2060. At the park you can purchase a guidebook to the three trails maintained by the Ascutney Trails Association, none of which begins in the park. A fourth trail, which begins in the park's upper camping area, is now under construction. The Brownsville Trail on the north side of the mountain is considered the most scenic and diversified; you can pick it up on Route 44, 1.2 miles east of the village of Brownsville, opposite a red brick farmhouse. It is 3 miles to the summit over moderately difficult, rocky terrain, requiring about 2 hours and 40 minutes. The trail begins at the edge of a sheep pasture and then climbs steeply through hardwoods and hemlocks. It joins a wide, easily graded road that leads to the abandoned Norcross quarry. Although grown over with birches, the quarry face is still visible, as is the huge pile of grout, the quarry waste rock, where porcupines make their dens. Farther along the trail is a quiet and stately red-pine wood. The granite stones carpeted with needles make an almost perfect stairway up through the grove. The trail also skirts the top of the Mount Ascutney ski area, where you can follow the upper part of a ski trail. You can come down the Windsor Trail to Back Mountain Rd. and make a circle (roughly 5¾ hours including lunch), ending up about 1.2 miles from your car.*

Wilgus State Park is 3 miles south on Route 5 on the Connecticut River, where there is a boat landing, campsites, and lean-tos.

57.
Islands in
the Connecticut River:
Burnaps and Hart

Directions: **Plainfield and Cornish, N.H. From Brattleboro, take I-91 north about 60 miles to Exit 10. Go east on I-89 across the river to the first exit. Go south on Route 12A for 3.1 miles; look for a sign for Edgewater Farm. Turn west (right) onto River Rd. Go about 100 feet, park at the narrow pulloff on the right (A), and carry the canoe down the dirt road to the river. Burnaps Island is directly opposite the shore. The Cornish landing is 12 miles south of I-89 on Route 12A, then off a dirt road on the right, through a cornfield, in sight of the covered bridge between Windsor, Vt., and Cornish, N.H.**

Ownership: **Private.**

Free-flowing, rapid water and wild-river habitats are becoming increasingly rare in the northeastern United States, but they are still numerous on the Connecticut River, New England's longest and largest river. An easy day's trip from Burnaps Island in Plainfield, N.H., to just above the historic Windsor-Cornish covered bridge, provides a glimpse of river life and its geological history.

From the Plainfield shore opposite Burnaps Island follow a road that leads down a steep bank to the river. A push across the channel will bring you to the island. Looking back at the steep terraced riverbank, you can see a clue to the geological past that the Connecticut River displays so well. The flat banks along which you drove on Route 12A from the interstate down to and beyond the landing at Burnaps is part of a kame terrace (see **#50** and **#77**) left by

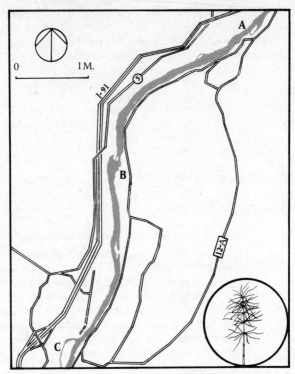

Inset: Marsh Horsetail

melting glaciers during the last ice age of the Pleistocene epoch. As the climate warmed and the great tongues of glacial ice trapped in river valleys began to melt, glacial water and ice washed up great banks of gravel in flat, steplike terraces known as kames.

Melting glacial water flooded the entire Connecticut valley and created a lake stretching from below Middletown, Conn., to Lyme, N.H. It is now known as Lake Hitchcock. When its dam of delta deposits gave way, most of the lake drained, giving birth to the river flowing beneath you. A subsequent, smaller body of water, Lake Upham, arose between Charlestown, N.H. and Lyme. It survived glacial retreat and advance and the gradual springing back of the land from under the weight of the ice sheet. When the glacier finally subsided, Lake Upham shrank to the size of the river channel we see today.

All along the riverbank are exposed layers of gravel, washed up and deposited by the churning waters of the melting glacier. These same cobble-sized stones are found in the gravels on Burnaps Island, suggesting that the island could have been part of the original kame. The upstream end of the island in low water is a long bed of these particular river gravels, covered in part by a variety of unusual plants that have adapted to the uniquely harsh environment on the northern end of an island. Here the ice flows scour the ground each spring, acting like a small glacier. Consequently, hardy, low-growing, prostrate plants like the sand cherry and dogbane are found here. You will also find an abundance of attractive spiky cypress spurge, generally a cultivated plant favored for perennial flowerbeds.

The Connecticut River islands provide a special opportunity to experience the turbulence and dynamism of the river. You can stop in the middle of a channel to witness the rigorous living conditions and particular adaptations required of every organism found in this environment. On Burnaps's upstream end, small stands of grasses are taking hold, trying to become stabilized in the shifting river sands. You can observe silverweed, a cinquefoil growing among the cobbles, whose propagation depends on its low, spreading rhizomes being broken off and reestablished by the spring melt.

The clay along the island's shore makes for excellent tracking. You can follow clearly defined deer, raccoon, and beaver tracks right down to the water's edge. The downstream end of the island has a high steep sandbank that makes a fine picnic site. A note of caution: when you are beaching your canoe, pull it way up on the shore and secure it if possible. Due to the upstream hydroelectric facility at Wilder, the water level can fluctuate as much as 12 feet daily, and you might return after exploring the island to find your canoe floating downstream.

The island's interior contains a good stand of floodplain trees: slippery elm, cottonwood, basswood, silver maple, and some huge red oaks and even a few white pines. Stands of floodplain forest are increasingly hard to find on the Connecticut's banks. Much of the river's fertile floodplain has been cut over many times and cleared for agricultural land. There are no paths into the woods, so pick your way carefully through the undergrowth, avoiding the abundant poison ivy. The forest understory is largely ostrich fern, river grape, raspberry, and horsetail, or scouring rush (see **#5**), an equisetum containing silica that campers can use to clean a burned pot.

From Burnaps, it is a fast and easy flatwater stretch to the difficult and dangerous rapids at Sumner's Falls (**B**). This is a whitewater section of the river favored by experienced kayakers and fishermen. Do not attempt it in a canoe. There is a quarter-mile portage around the falls, which occurs ¾ mile below the three boulder outcroppings called the Rooster, Hen, and Chicken. On the Vermont side there is a public landing off Route 5 for those who want to put in below the falls.

You will find peaceful flatwater paddling from here to Hart Island (**C**) on down to Cornish. The river widens. In the fall migrating hawks pass overhead following the river, a familiar landmark for migrating birds (see **#66**). A lone southbound hawk may be harried for miles overhead by a bunch of orchard crows. An osprey can sometimes be sighted dropping into a treetop carrying a fish in its claws. Hart Island is about a mile below the falls, and in the autumn it is sometimes connected to the Vermont side of the riverbank. It covers 15 acres with an elevation of 320 feet, while Burnaps is one-third that size with the same elevation. Although the forest on Hart Island has been cut recently, the forest floor is still known as a place to see rare or unusual plants and flowers. The rare orchid, autumn coralroot (*Corallorhiza odontorhiza*) has been found here. In summer there are bright red stands of the tall cardinal flower lobelia. The rare Jesup's milk vetch was seen on the island in 1911. In fact, botanists have found 250 species on Hart Island that are not common in Vermont or New Hampshire.

Marsh horsetail and bladdernut are two of these plant types. For all its abundance on Hart Island, bladdernut is considered a typically southern species, like the warty-barked hackberry, also found here. Both plants like soil high in calcium. Their existence on the island may be due to the moderating effect of the river water on the climate of the valley. The elevation is low here. The valley tends in a strong north-south direction; seed dispersion is easier, more direct. For example, somewhere in the Carolinas a migrating duck might pick up a seed in the webbing of his feet and not lose it until Hart Island, N.H. On the river numerous possibilities for plant migration and successions are plausible.

On the Vermont side of Hart Island between island and shore is a protected riffle favored by ducks. The water stays open there through most of the winter, and it is not unusual to startle a large flock of low-flying mergansers, which instantly take off and skim rapidly upstream.

On the downstream end of the island, if you climb up from the river's edge, you will notice a uniform fine-grained clay in the bank, which may be evidence of a glacial lake. It lacks the cobbles and crossbedding characteristic of rapid water movement, found at Burnaps Island. The clay suggests silts from ancient lake deposits (see **Connecticut River Valley**).

Paddling downstream from Hart Island, you will follow a long, wide bar of gravels. This point in the river was the focus of a public outcry that effectively stopped a hydroelectric dam. The gravel beds are considered prime spawning beds for walleye, shad, and possibly Atlantic salmon (see **Connecticut River Valley**). The river here is shallow and fast-moving, making for a highly saturated oxygen content—prime for fish. The Atlantic salmon are eagerly awaited on the upper Connecticut, where they have not been seen for almost 200 years. The slackwater reservoir created by the proposed dam below Hart Island would have flooded a principal salmon spawning habitat, as well as wiped out acres of agricultural land, a rare plant station, the homes of beaver, otter, mink, muskrat, fox, raccoon, squirrel, and mole, and a popular natural recreation site. However, it is becoming a tradition among residents of the Connecticut River valley to try to protect the river's slowly reviving good health.

Federal, state, and local agencies have spent $700 million to restore the river, funding, among other projects, the Atlantic Salmon Restoration Program. The salmon, like the shad, is an *anadromous* fish, which in Greek means "upward-wandering." It spends most of its adult life in the ocean and returns to its river of origin to spawn. A mysterious homing sense, which some think may be a sense of smell, directs the adventurous salmon out of the deeps of the North Atlantic to Long Island Sound and into the rivermouth, and then 400 miles upstream to a mountain stream in inland New England. For the journey to take place in 1983, ladders are being built over hydrodams, and hatcheries are successfully propagating young fish that are imprinted on northern rivers. Water quality is improving. In 1981, 300 salmon made it back to the lower Connecticut River system in New Hampshire. Thousands are expected in the future.

Remarks: *The suggested trip is a leisurely day-long excursion with one portage around Sumner's Falls. Canoes can be rented from the Ledyard Canoe Club at Dartmouth College in Hanover, N.H., (603) 646-2753. The Upper Valley Office of the Connecticut River Watershed Council, Montshire Museum, Hanover, N.H., (603) 643-5672, can suggest numerous other suitable canoe trips in the region. See their publication,* The Connecticut River Guide, *for a complete guide to the river. Safety precautions in the canoe should be observed, with particular attention to securing the boat at the islands against unforeseen changes in the water level. River and weather conditions should be heeded. Both access and landing are just off New Hampshire's 12A. At the head of River Rd. in Plainfield you will see the narrow road down to the river; do not take your car down the road. There is room to pull off and leave it on River Rd. The rocks at the river's edge can be slippery. Although the river is a public resource, much of the bank land is private property and should be approached with permission only.*

The access at Sumner's Falls, 3.2 miles north on Route 5 from the Hartland exit of Route 91, is a public facility with ample parking. At the landing in Cornish, N.H. there is also ample parking. The road down to the river is 0.5 mile from the covered bridge. You can pull your car close to the water here, but watch out for erosion in the sandy bank.

58.

Quechee Gorge

Directions: Hartford, Vt. From Brattleboro, take I-91 north about 60 miles to Exit 10. Go northwest 3 miles on I-89 to Exit 1; take U.S. 4 south and west about 2 miles and through the gorge. There are several places to park: at the gift shop before the bridge; in a pulloff just beyond the bridge; and at a picnic area reached by turning right onto Dewey's Mill Rd. before the gift shop.

Ownership: U.S. Army Corps of Engineers; managed by the Vermont Department of Forests, Parks, and Recreation.

Quechee Gorge is at once spectacular and somewhat frightening. The waters of the Ottaquechee River rush through the steep-walled gorge 160 feet below the highway bridge that spans the ravine and provides the best view. From here you can see the shape of the ravine with its nearly vertical walls of granite (see **#93**), as well as the variety of vegetation clinging to the steep slopes. There is also an easy 1¼-mile trail that follows the length of the gorge along the top and descends to the riverbank at the bottom. This path can be reached by a short access trail in front of the gift shop on Route 4, or from the picnic area and overlook on Dewey's Mill Rd. There is a clear view from there of what was once a millpond, the Dewey Lake Wildlife Sanctuary, the dam and resulting waterfalls, and an earthen dike. To reach these, take a right on the gorge trail and follow it to the end.

The rock formation of the gorge was created 350 to 500 million years ago, during periods of uplifting and thrusting of the earth's crust. It was during this time of the Paleozoic era that molten igneous rock flowed to the surface, cooled, and became the foundation of the mountain systems of New England. About 100 million years later, continued heat and pressure converted these solidified mineral

deposits into metamorphic rock, the basic granite and schist formations commonly found in New England now. These hard rocks remained relatively undisturbed for millions of years until recent geologic time, when the glaciers advanced from the north and covered
the region with a thick sheet of ice. The last glacier, the Wisconsin
glacier of 12,000 to 60,000 years ago, cut through many softer rock
deposits and along natural cracks and fault lines. When the glacier
retreated, the powerful rivers of its meltwaters caused significant
erosion, especially since the rushing waters carried sands and gravels
that had been picked up by the ice. The Quechee Gorge was formed
in this manner when the meltwater cut through the metamorphic
rock, finally settling down to its approximate present level about
6,000 years ago.

Walking along the trail from the lookout area, you can see the
variety of vegetation on the gorge walls and slopes. Hemlock, which
enjoys the cool, wet microclimate of the gorge, is the dominant tree
(see **#23** and **#65**). Some beech, red maple, sugar maple, and white
pine also grow here, but they are not as well suited to the conditions,
especially the thin soil, and do not grow as tall as the hemlocks. In
the understory are hobblebush, mountain maple, and a variety of
wildflowers including purple nightshade, violet (see **#90**), aster, and
little cinquefoil. Some of these plants are commonly found farther
north, but here again the cool microclimate provides a suitable habitat for their growth.

As the trail levels off, there is a dam that was constructed to
control floodwaters downstream and provide power for industries
that operated here from the early 1800s until the 1950s. Behind the
dam is a millpond, and below the dam the erosive powers of the
water can be clearly seen where it has carved small channels in the
schist.

After passing the old milltown site, the trail opens up into a dirt
road that leads out onto the earthen dike separating the millpond
from the lake. There is good trout fishing in both bodies of water.
Warblers, cardinals, flycatchers, and flickers are quite common in
this area. If you are lucky, you might see an osprey, or fish hawk,
hunting over the lake or soaring on the uplifting air currents over
the gorge.

Since access to the trail is near its middle rather than at either end,
it is necessary to double back to see the river below the bridge. The
soil here is quite sandy, a remnant of the glacial deposits of 12,000
years ago and of the sediments carried by the river. Below the bridge,
the trail continues down to the edge of the gorge. About midway
between the bridge and the end of the trail is a small falls and a
series of potholes. These depressions are created when a rock that is

more resistant to erosion than the bedrock becomes caught in a crevice; the rushing water turns the rock around within the crevice, thereby scouring out a basin (see **#81**).

At the end of the trail the Ottaquechee opens up into a wide, meandering river, idyllic when compared with the furious rushing water in the gorge. Here you can walk out to the water's edge on the rock shelves, or fish for rainbow and brown trout.

Remarks: *The rocks along the river can be very dangerous to walk on: stay on the path. Fishing requires a Vermont license. Be sure to bring insect repellent in the summer. There are camping facilities in Quechee State Park, just east of the bridge on the right. For information on accommodations and other features of the park, contact Quechee Gorge State Park, RFD White River Junction, Vt. 05001; (802) 295-2990.*

The White Mountains, Monadnocks, and Eastern Connecticut Highlands:
Above the Timberline

Fog banks roll across the open tundra, wafting between bare, stony crags and obscuring the brinks of cliffs that descend precipitously into deep ravines. It is June, but the weather holds the chance of a storm that will coat the landscape and its low tundra vegetation with ice. Across the fields littered with small boulders and broken stone, across slopes strewn with glacial talus, no sound but the chill rush of the wind breaks the silence. The setting might seem Arctic, but like the sandy beaches of Cape Cod and the red-earthed lowlands of the lower Connecticut River valley, it is really New England.

Trekking the heights of the Presidential Range in New Hampshire's White Mountains is rather like exploring a world that is lost, displaced in terms of geography. By an ascent of some 5,000 feet from the valleys below, a hiker can reach an environment that could otherwise be visited only by a trip of 1,000 miles to the north.

The Presidentials are just far north enough so that timberline occurs at slightly less than 5,000 feet altitude, while the plants above are those of tundra, types found along the northern rim of Canada and on Greenland. The range, moreover, lies in the track of major storms and thus is ravaged by some of the fiercest weather on the continent, indeed, in the world. Again and again these bleak, brooding peaks have claimed the lives of hikers who did not properly respect them.

Roofing New England, the Presidentials and the rest of the White Mountains are the pinnacle of highlands lying east of the Connecticut River. To the north they grade into the mountains of eastern Maine, rugged but not as imposing. In a southerly direction they smooth into rolling hills, ending in the eastern highlands of Connecticut.

The White Mountains can be considered the dominant feature of the New England landscape by virtue of their sheer immensity. Mount

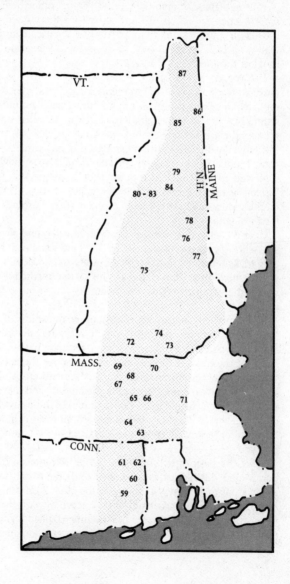

Washington in the Presidentials towers 6,288 feet, exceeded east of South Dakota's Black Hills only by Mount Mitchell in North Carolina, which is just a few hundred feet higher and forested to its peak.

There is an unexpected quality about the White Mountains, which on approach from a distance makes them seem almost an illusion. It is as if such grandly foreboding peaks belong somewhere else, not a scant 2-hour drive from Boston. Ascent via the numerous trails to the heights increases the factor of surprise. They lead up sheer headwalls and edge great ravines where snow can linger to the beginnings of summer.

The rugged aspect of the White Mountains derives from their birth. At first vast layers of sedimentary rock were folded up, cracking, breaking, and disorganizing the earth's crust. Intruding into the sedimentary rocks seeped granite, heated to a molten state by great fires in the earth's bowels but not breaking through the surface. Insulated by the rock around it, the molten granite, or magma, cooled slowly until it had solidified. Some of it was heated again and subjected to pressure, but not sufficiently to revert it to magma. Instead, it metamorphosed into new types of rock, such as gneiss, marble, schist, and slate. Metamorphic rock is extremely typical of the Presidentials.

Over the ages, due to erosion by wind, water, and glacial ice, the soft sedimentary rock disappeared. The hard granite and metamorphic rocks remained as a jumble of peaks and crags, not laid out in well-defined ranges but riotously, due to the discordant manner in which the granitic magma was originally forced out of the earth's interior.

Similar events shaped the landscape to the south of the White Mountains. Granite and metamorphic rocks remain as mountains and hills where older, softer materials over them have eroded away. Some of the isolated mountains that rise above the countryside of southern New Hampshire and central Massachusetts, called *monadnocks*, resisted the erosion that took the altitude and harsh edges off the countryside around them. Most famous of these structures is the one from which they get their name, Mount Monadnock in New Hampshire; Mount Machusett in Massachusetts is another model of the type.

Once the basic structure of the White Mountains, the monadnocks, and the highlands associated with them was formed, the glaciers put their heavy stamp upon the land. Again, in the White Mountains, realm of extremes, the evidence of geological events is most striking. The ice covered the mountains, piled higher than the peaks of the Presidentials. It scattered stones and boulders across the land and scarred the rocks with great scratches and grooves. Glacial ice filled shallow valleys and gouged them deeper into what are called *cirques*, round depressions, steep-sided and filled with talus boulders.

The most celebrated of these glacial valleys in the White Mountains is Tuckerman's Ravine on Mount Washington. Tuckerman's almost retains a glacier today, for snow lingers there until July. Scientists think that if the summer temperature dropped only a handful of degrees, the snow would remain year-round, accumulating increasingly during the winter, until a new glacier was born.

Indeed, the climate atop the Presidentials is so severe that it is not at all difficult to envision the landscape as something from out of the Ice Age. Over the years, the meteorology of the Presidential Range has been carefully documented at the Mount Washington Meteorological Observatory, perched atop its summit. The average annual temperature there is a bit less than 27 degrees Fahrenheit; in the summer months, temperatures average in the middle forties. The mercury has never surpassed 71 degrees on the hottest summer days, and in winter it has dropped as low as minus 47. The coldest month is January, when the average temperature does not rise above 6 degrees.

Temperature readings alone do not indicate how horribly cold it can be on Mount Washington. Wind chill is ever present. Depending on the season, the wind averages between 25 and almost 36 miles an hour, with blasts of hurricane force lashing the mountain every month of the year. In fact, the highest wind recorded on earth, excluding tornadoes, occurred on the summit in 1934—231 miles an hour.

During the summer the mountain is cloaked by ever-present clouds and fog. In winter the snowfall is blinding. The maximum amount of snow to fall in a season topped 28 feet, an extreme perhaps, but on the average it is at least half that.

The heights of the Presidentials are carpeted with true tundra vegetation—scruffy low sedges, grasses, lichens, mosses, and scattered, scraggly shrubs. A short distance below, at timberline, patches of stunted trees called *Krummholz* appear, nestled in cracks and crannies. Many are of the same species as the trees that stand on the lower slopes, such as balsam and black spruce. Growing to 70 feet down below, at the timberline these trees are stunted by exposure into gnarled mats only a few inches high.

Balsam, black spruce, and red spruce growing on the slopes below timberline are characteristic of the conifer forests that are scattered throughout northern New England. Contrary to popular opinion, however, these species do not dominate the landscape except where planted for timber. The main forest type of northern New England is hardwood—with a liberal sprinkling of the conifers—including sugar maple, beech, and birch. This sort of forest rings the base of the mountains and stretches south to Massachusetts.

Near the Massachusetts line the forest undergoes a transition to the oak-dominated woodlands of southern New England. In places such as Harvard Forest, in Petersham, Mass., northern hardwoods with their sprinkling of spruces mix with trees such as chestnut oak, tuliptree, sassafras, and black and red oak. By northern Connecticut, the southern trees almost completely take over. Virtually all of these forests are young, grown in the last century or so after the original virgin forests that stood on the land were cleared for wood or to make room for farmland. The human presence long ago made itself felt in the region, even in its most remote parts. The mountain was first climbed within a decade or two after the Pilgrims landed at Plymouth. By the early 1850s even the summit of Mount Washington had a hotel, built of stone.

Until the cold weather begins, the White Mountains are full of people—hikers, sightseers, birders, and others. With the coming of winter, however, the hordes depart. The peaks are left to themselves for the most part, covered with ice and snow, swept by the rawest of winds. In midwinter, it almost seems as if the great glaciers of the past have returned to the landscape they once covered.

—Edward Ricciuti

59.
Rock Spring
Wildlife Refuge

Directions: Scotland, Conn. From Worcester, Mass., take I-290, then Route 52 south about 50 miles to Exit 89. Take Route 14 west about 11 miles. Turn north onto Route 97 and go 1.4 miles to the refuge sign and entrance on the right.

Ownership: The Nature Conservancy.

Acres to the beautiful Little River is just one of the highlights at this 436-acre preserve in eastern Connecticut's rolling uplands. The cold, clear river is home to trout, smallmouth bass, and other fish, and helps support a small native population of beaver, muskrat, otter, and possibly mink. A sandy glacial esker, several vernal ponds, fields reverting to woodland, a spring, and a fine view of the surrounding valley add to the unspoiled features here.

Follow the white blazes downhill, keeping the map board and sign-in book to your left.

Rattlesnake plantain can be found quite easily, growing on the floor of the hardwood forest adjacent to the trail (**A**). It is a tiny member of the orchid family, a wildflower whose basal evergreen leaves are checkered with white veins that suggest the skin of a snake. In late summer the plant sends up a stalk that averages 6 to 8 inches in length but may reach 16 inches; it is decorated with minute white flowers in a spikelike or spiral arrangement. (An even tinier version, dwarf rattlesnake plantain, is the smallest member of the orchid family in the United States.) A traditional theory called the doctrine of signatures maintains that the shape of a plant may be directly related to its use; in this case, the doctrine erroneously held that rattlesnake plantain might be a cure for snakebite!

The trail leads through old farm fields now grown over with grasses, sedges (see **#101**), redcedars (see **#7**), shrubs, and large patches of tree clubmoss (*Lycopodium obscurum*). Indian Spring, a rivulet of fresh water bubbling from the ground, is just beyond (**B**). The donor of this property to The Nature Conservancy built the small brick and cement cairn around the spring to protect it against contamination. Springs are those places where the water table and the ground sur-

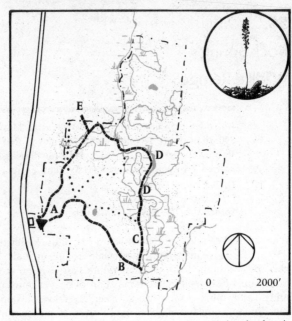

Rattlesnake plantain

face intersect. The underground water that effervesces from beneath your feet is probably flowing over an impermeable rock layer, such as granite, and can only flow laterally. The water is most likely quite pure, but it is generally unadvisable to drink surface water without treating it first.

Retrace your steps a bit and head uphill to the ridgetop of a long sandy esker (**C**). Eskers are common in New England, but many have disappeared due to excavation for sand and gravel. They were formed as deposits of stratified material in river and stream beds that existed under the glacial ice (see **#77** and **#108**). This one is particularly interesting because it affords an opening in the surrounding forest canopy and because it supports a *xeric* (dry) plant community on top of the excessively drained and poor soil. Note several varieties of fruticose (stemlike and branching) lichens here (see **#7**), including British soldier and reindeer lichen (see **#43**). Lichens of this type are frequently found growing directly on the sand in stabilized seashore areas or in inland places where the sand is not blown about by the wind. Notice also the dwarfed condition of the trees, primarily oaks, the presence of a lone pitch pine, and a healthy knot of bayberry. This last shrub is almost always found near the coast but occasionally shows up in other locations with sandy soils. Tree swallows and yellow-rumped warblers are fond of its gray waxy berries. Its thick leaves are an adaptation for holding moisture in windy and dry environments.

The white-blazed trail veers sharply to the right at the edge of the esker and leads through a red- and white-pine plantation where owls are known to roost, and down to the bank of Little River (**D**). One immediately senses the delightfully pastoral nature of this woodland waterway, the lush wildflowers growing nearby, the active birdlife, the undisturbed feeling of the area. If your presence is undetected you might see a muskrat or beaver swimming along the shallow waters, or perhaps a phoebe flying to her nest with food for her young. A brook or rainbow trout may rise to catch an insect.

The source of Little River is 10 miles or so upstream in a series of ponds and springs; about 12 miles downstream from here Little River meets the Shetucket River near Taftville. Beavers have been active in this section for at least 25 consecutive years; there is evidence of their work in the girdled trees and in the remains of a dam they built across the river. Each spring during high water, the dam is partially destroyed and the beavers begin again. They have created a large wet meadow on the other side of the dam. Look for wood ducks (see **#14** and **#102**), which nest in the vicinity.

The trail hugs the river past piles of logs and flood debris, then heads up away from it through white pines and into mixed hardwoods. Meet the white-and-yellow-blazed trail and go right to an overlook of the Little River valley (**E**). A group of obviously dedicated workers have built an amazing stone bench here, complete with cut granite-gneiss blocks. Here you can sit and absorb the beauty of the scene as the Indians (who called the Little River Appaquage) may have done many years ago. It is disturbing, then, to consider that I-84 may be routed through part of the property sometime in the near future. Many citizens in eastern Connecticut have fought its construction, and the outcome is uncertain.

Head back on the white-and-yellow-blazed trail to the point where it meets the white-blazed trail and take this to the right, back to the entrance.

Remarks: *Walking time is about 3 hours. Please sign your name in the guest book so The Nature Conservancy can keep track of how many people are using the refuge. Their office is in Middletown, Conn.; their telephone number is (203) 344-0716. Camping is available at Hopeville Pond State Park in nearby Jewett City.*

60.
James L. Goodwin
State Forest

Directions: **Hampton, Conn. From Worcester, Mass., take I-290, then Route 52 south about 45 miles to Exit 91. Take U.S. 6 west about 11 miles past the intersection with Route 97 to the entrance of the forest on the right.**

Ownership: **Parks and Recreation Unit, Connecticut Department of Environmental Protection.**

Originally farmland and then a scientifically managed tree farm, 1,800-acre Goodwin Forest is an example of a rural area whose recent development has been largely shaped by man. Donated to the state of Connecticut in 1964 by forester and conservationist James L. Goodwin, the property demonstrates how wise environmental planning can serve wildlife and forestry needs at the same time. Three man-made ponds and several hundred acres of pine and spruce plantations blend in with naturally occurring upland hardwoods to provide fine recreational opportunities, including fishing and bird-watching. One pond, Pine Acres, is more than 120 acres in size, and all have a number of nesting wood ducks and other waterfowl.

The yellow-blazed trail immediately enters one of the many groves of red and white pines planted by Goodwin earlier in the century (**A**). Notice the lack of shrubs and understory here in the dense shade of the closely growing conifers. Goodwin's goal of creating a renewable and carefully developed forest was in stark contrast to the pillaging of natural resources that prevailed in America during the previous two-and-a-half centuries. By the late 1800s three-quarters of Connecticut was open land, and vast tracts of woodlands had been clear-cut throughout New England for cordwood, lumber, fuel for industrial purposes, and farmland. The idea of planting trees, the cornerstone of the so-called sustained-yield approach, was a ground-breaking concept at the time Goodwin began his plantations in 1913. In addition to maintaining an orderly planting schedule, the program was designed to allow trees to be cut on a regular basis while others were left to grow. Eventually, Goodwin's views and those of his alma mater, Yale Forestry School, replaced the older rapacious men-

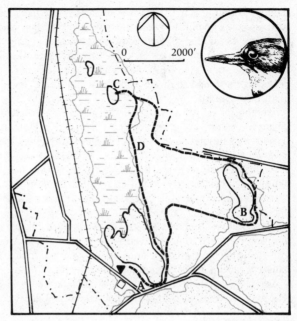

Inset: Belted kingfisher

tality, and forests throughout the state and country are now increasingly managed by professionals.

Continue past an old apple orchard (planted by Goodwin) and a cornfield to Brown Hill Pond (**B**), a pine-bordered body of water frequented by beavers, which was created in 1955 by the damming of a swamp. This pond and the other two on the grounds were created primarily as a water source to combat forest fires and as a refuge for wildlife. At least three characteristic signs of beaver activity—a lodge, downed trees, and teethmarks and gnawings on standing trees—are evident. Beavers do not eat wood, as some people believe, but rather feast on the moist inner bark, especially that of the younger branches. One of the main reasons beavers cut down big old trees is to get at the newer growth on top (see **#14**).

The yellow-blazed trail eventually meets the paved Cedar Swamp Rd. Follow this left until it dead-ends in the woods, then through a green-painted barway and right onto the red-blazed trail. The route leads past moist woods and several small vernal ponds. Be on the lookout for frogs and salamanders.

A narrow dirt causeway crosses over a marshy edge of Pine Acres

Pond and onto lovely Governor's Island (**C**). The marsh is rimmed with sweet pepperbush, white tussock sedge, cattails, yellow birch, and small hemlocks; sphagnum moss and wild calla grow within its confines. A lone tamarack tree, a species usually found farther north, is off to the right (see **#69**). The white pines, red pines, and hemlocks on the island itself are noticeably larger than those in other parts of the forest.

On the far or western side of the island is a wooden viewing platform where you can enjoy an excellent view of Pine Acres Pond. Wood-duck nesting boxes have been placed throughout the wetland (see **#14** and **#102**), and mallards (see **#41**), black ducks, and Canada geese frequent the area. Great blue herons, (see **#40** and **#64**), green herons, and kingfishers are also common. Occasionally, a magnificent osprey will appear and dive into the shallow depths for a fish.

The pond was built in 1935 and originally stocked with trout, but the waters proved to be too warm and the trout died. A number of fish that prefer these temperatures—yellow perch, bluegill, pumpkinseed, catfish, and largemouth bass—now thrive here.

Before the pond was created, it was an Atlantic white-cedar swamp. The cedars were cut during the winter when loggers could gain access on the ice to the mucky wetland.

Note the hundreds of stumps and decaying tree trunks that stick out of the 3-foot-deep waters. These are the remains of trees that died as the pond reached its present size. The brownish color of the water is a result of the large amounts of vegetation that have decomposed here. Look for sundew and cranberries, two acid-tolerant plants, along the edge.

Head back off the island and go right onto the white-blazed trail. After crossing a woods road you will have to pick your way over and through an area littered with hundreds of small granite boulders (**D**). Common to many parts of New England, this local topography is known as a *ground moraine*. A product of glaciation, ground moraines are rocks that have been dumped over the surface of the land as a glacier melts and retreats. Ground moraines usually form gently rolling plains across valley floors and may be deposited as a thin veneer or as a thick mass of rock debris. Here, it appears to be quite thin, but the layers of soil cover may conceal its true dimensions.

Continue along the eastern shore of the pond, through a Norway-spruce plantation, and back to the parking area and trailside visitors' center.

Remarks: *Walking time is about 3 hours. Backpackers using the blue-blazed Natchaug Trail may camp on the grounds at one site, by previous arrangement with the manager. The forest caters to groups and offers planned programs and guided tours. Pond fishing is good; hunting and trapping are not permitted. An interesting living display of woodland shrubs of Connecticut is located just to the north of the visitors' center. In winter, cross-country skiing is encouraged, and trails are marked.*

61.

Boston Hollow

Directions: Westford, Conn. From Worcester, Mass., take I-290, I-90, then I-86 southwest about 30 miles to Exit 104. Go south on Route 89 for 4 miles to Westford. Go northeast on Boston Hollow Rd. about 0.2 mile and park just past the intersection with Chism Rd.

Ownership: Connecticut Highway System, and Yale Forest.

Reminiscent of a northern New England landscape, Boston Hollow is a narrow, heavily wooded ravine known for its excellent birding and picturesque scenery. The hollow lies along an accessible, public dirt road adjacent to privately owned Yale Forest, a 7,000-acre tract of unspoiled woodland. The Nipmuck Trail intersects the Boston Hollow Rd. and winds to the top of 900-foot-high rocky slopes that overlook the ravine and surrounding countryside.

The spring warbler migration is superb here. Local ornithologist Robert J. Craig writes: "Over 30 species occur regularly, and on a good May morning the number of warbler songs issuing from the treetops can be bewildering, with so many species singing at once only an exceptional individual or a wishful thinker could claim to identify them all." In winter you may see pine siskins, crossbills, and grosbeaks in those years when the finches come south from Canada for food.

The walk begins by paralleling a wooded swamp where red maple, spicebush, and thick growths of skunk cabbage and false hellebore create a lush and watery landscape. As one proceeds along the quiet and secluded Boston Hollow Rd. the hillsides get steeper, the swamp thins out to a stream, and shade- and cold-tolerant trees become more prevalent (**A**). Hemlock, yellow and white birch, and beech predominate. The topography of two sharp ridges with a stream-swamp in between leads to the formation of a cold-air sink. Because

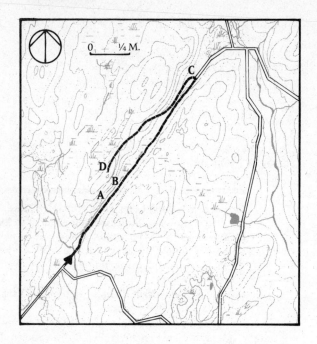

of the narrowness of the hollow, sunlight does not shine directly into it for very long, and consequently the air warms less than it might under different conditions. Cold air from the higher slopes sinks down and creates a microclimate analogous to that found farther north. This environment is conducive to the presence of some northerly species of birds. The birds are not drawn to the climate, however, so much as to the vegetational community that arose with this climate. During the eons of bird evolution, this type of vegetation and location provided the right nesting areas, food sources, climate, and openings in the competitive matrix for a number of species to survive. Winter wrens, and Blackburnian, black-throated blue, black-throated green, and Canada warblers all nest there, along with broad-winged hawks and other species.

As you walk through this shady glen (**B**), listen for the unbelievably long song of the tiny winter wren. Ornithologist Edgar M. Reilly describes this song as a "fifelike, rollicking cadenza of warbles, trills, and rapid and tumbling notes usually ending on a high trill." The outstanding singer is only about 4 inches long and, along with the sedge wren, is the smallest wren found in the East. It most frequently nests in northern New England and Canada but is found breeding south in the Appalachian Mountains to the Carolinas. The winter wren often makes its nest among cavities in the exposed roots of upturned trees, in rock crevices, and in holes in standing trees. The spherically shaped nest of twigs and mosses has a side entrance. Five to six eggs are laid in late spring and are incubated for approximately 2 weeks, the young being able to fly 19 to 20 days later. Winter wrens eat insects, especially beetles, spiders, caterpillars, and ants.

After walking for about 45 minutes, keep a close watch for the blue blazes of the Nipmuck Trail and turn left (**C**). Here is a chance to get up into the woods and see the area from another vantage point. In the spring look for the surprisingly large blossoms of the purple trillium, and the small six-pointed, yellowish-green flowers of blue cohosh.

The trail winds up along the ridgeside and eventually leaves the hemlocks behind, as red and white oak, black cherry, black birch, hickory, and mountain laurel prevail. The worm-eating warbler may be seen in this area. Continue to climb and soon you will reach the summit, a rocky overlook facing east (**D**). For the most part, the view is of expansive woodland with a few farms and houses scattered in the distance.

Part of a 20-mile-long fault that trends or runs, northeast to southwest, Boston Hollow was created when great blocks of the underlying metamorphic rock were cracked and moved during the collision of continental plates. (See **#38** and **#50** for more on faults.) The valley then formed as the tremendous erosive processes of glaciation and running water plucked, washed, and moved away the rock debris.

The Nipmuck Trail continues north and east through Yale Forest and about 2½ miles farther comes out on Kinney Hollow Rd., near Bigelow Brook. To get back to your car, however, go back down the ridge and along Boston Hollow Rd.

Remarks: *Walking time is about 2½ hours but may be much longer, depending on time spent bird-watching. Do not wander off the Nipmuck Trail; Yale Forest is not officially open to the public but does allow a right-of-way for this footpath. Camping is available at Mashamoquet Brook State Park in Pomfret Center. Bigelow Hollow State Park, just north of here in Union, is cited by Dr. Noble Proctor as another good birding area, with species similar to those at Boston Hollow.*

62.

Wolf Den

Directions: **Pomfret, Conn. From Worcester, Mass., take I-290, then Route 52 south about 40 miles to Exit 93. Go west on Route 101 about 5 miles to the junction with U.S. 44. At the junction turn south (left) on Wolf Den Dr.; go 0.7 mile to Wolf Den Camping Area; park in the visitors' lot on the right.**

Ownership: **Mashamoquet Brook State Park, Parks and Recreation Unit, Connecticut Department of Environmental Protection.**

Wolf Den, the legendary cave where Revolutionary War General Israel Putnam slew a great wolf in 1742, is the highlight of this woodland tract in 781-acre Mashamoquet Brook State Park in Pomfret. Wolf Den's rocky, rugged landscape contains interesting boulder formations resulting from glaciation and erosion. Its high ridges and wet ravines also host a variety of native flowering shrubs and wetland plants, including eastern mountain laurel and marsh marigolds.

A major portion of the blue-blazed trail, the longest of the four color-coded routes at Wolf Den, will be reviewed here. Follow the wooden trail posts marked with blue blazes from the east side of the visitors' parking lot at Wolf Den Camping Area. The blazes lead uphill through an open meadow before the trail veers left into the woods. Here it ascends the first in a succession of steep hills and rock outcrops that dominate the hike. On the top of the hill is one of many thickets of eastern mountain laurel that grow throughout the park. This evergreen shrub thrives in the acidic mor humus produced by the decaying leaves of the oak and eastern hemlock trees that largely compose the forest. Laurel is prized for its beautiful displays of white or pinkish flowers in June (see also **#69**). Canada mayflower, another common indicator of acid soil, also grows here. This species of the lily family forms extensive colonies that spread by underground runners. Standing only 3 or 4 inches tall, with two or three light green oval leaves to a stem, this perennial appears in late April and its tiny white flowers blossom from May to July.

The trail crosses several more ridges of bedrock and granite boulders, weaving through a hemlock grove, a laurel thicket, and a declining stand of aging white pine. It climbs steeply uphill to a sign directing you to the Indian Chair. This unusual glacial boulder is perched on a flat ledge topping a 20-foot cliff, which offers a view to the south over the wooded valley. The boulder was naturally cracked into the shape of a chair and deposited here by the Ice Age glacier. The ice sheet that retreated from New England some 12,000 years ago left behind many such glacial boulders, called erratics (see **#78**). Plucked from ledges and strewn across the landscape at varying distances from their source, these loose erratics often came to rest in precarious postures and on bare ledges like the one here.

The trail continues south to a wooden footbridge, where skunk cabbage grows profusely in the saturated soil of a wet ravine. This familiar wetland plant has unmistakable green leaves, which can grow as large as 3 feet long and 1 foot wide and produce a skunklike aroma when crushed. It is one of the first plants to appear in the spring, sometimes blooming when snow is still on the ground. Both the eastern and western varieties of skunk cabbage are believed to have migrated across the land bridge that arose between Siberia and Alaska during the Cenozoic era 2.5 million years ago. The glaciers then pushed it southward from northern North America down the eastern and western seaboards. Most of the nearest related species are found today in Malaya.

Soon the trail runs parallel to a stone wall on the left as it ascends a hill, arriving at the intersection of the blue-blazed and red-blazed trails at the top. For the rest of the hike the two trails follow the same route.

A second footbridge crosses Wolf Den Brook at its outlet from a woodland pond on the right. Marsh marigolds thrive on mossy hummocks in the streambed. This herbaceous plant, also known as cowslip, is arrayed in clusters of small yellow flowers in late April and early May. Its hollow, branching stem grows 1 to 2 feet high, with green, heart-shaped leaves.

The final portion of the hike to Wolf Den Cave runs from the footbridge up a steep, rocky hill, where the cave lies about halfway up the slope. According to legend, it was in this narrow cave that Israel Putnam, a young Pomfret farmer who later became a distinguished Revolutionary War general, slew a great she-wolf in 1742. The wolf had been raiding sheep and evading farmers for many years before Putnam and two fellow hunters tracked it as far west as the Connecticut River, where the wolf then backtracked to its Pomfret lair. Putnam, his ankles fastened with ropes to retrieve him, was then lowered into the cave, where he shot the trapped animal. The story of Putnam's bravery soon entered the annals of Connecticut folklore and is today recorded on a bronze plaque mounted on the granite ledge near the mouth of the cave.

Continue up the slope to the top of the hill. A left turn here leads to a small picnic and parking area. Follow the blue and red blazes along a short access road to its intersection with Wolf Den Dr. (dirt surface). Go right to return to the camping area and visitors' parking lot. You can also continue along the remaining portion of the blue-blazed trail as it resumes on the west side of Wolf Den Dr. opposite the entrance to the picnic area. This last portion of the trail leads through stands of sugar maples and smooth alders before completing the circuit that ends back at the camping area.

Remarks: *The blue-blazed trail is a strenuous 90-minute hike over difficult, rocky terrain. Wolf Den Cave is too narrow for casual or amateur exploration. Experienced cave explorers should contact the park ranger for information and assistance. Visitors who wish to see the cave but omit the hike can park at the picnic area off Wolf Den Dr. Because the upper half of Wolf Den Dr. has a dirt surface with stretches of soft sand, drivers should inquire at the camping area for information on road conditions. The park is open April 15 to September 30. Mashamoquet Brook State Park, Pomfret Center, includes two camping areas: Wolf Den, with 35 open-field campsites; Mashamoquet Brook, with 20 wooded campsites.*

63.

Purgatory Chasm
State Reservation

Directions: **Sutton, Mass. From Worcester, head south on Route 146. From the intersection with U.S. 20, continue south on Route 146 for about 7.5 miles; turn west (right) on Purgatory Rd. and go about 0.5 mile to the second parking area, on the left by a picnic pavilion.**

Ownership: **Massachusetts Division of Forests and Parks.**

Purgatory Chasm is a deep, narrow rock gorge surrounded by low, rolling woodlands in south central Massachusetts. This dramatic geological fault forms an abrupt 60-foot-wide crack in the surface bedrock of a granite hillside, with jagged cliff walls dropping vertically about 70 feet to the base. The dry floor of the fissure is heaped with immense slabs of rock, which in some portions of the gorge are piled more than 20 feet high. The wedged boulders are honey-combed with small caves and crevices, and unusual rock formations occur throughout the chasm and on the heights of the overhanging cliffs. To the minds of eighteenth-century New Englanders, these rock features inspired darkly symbolic names appropriate to their visions of the netherworld: Devil's Pulpit, Devil's Coffin, and the Devil's Corncrib. Today the haunting rock cliffs and the chaos of stone at their base are more likely to arouse awe at the force of the ancient earth upheaval that split the bedrock of this hill. (See **#38, #50,** and **#61** for more on faults.)

The craggy walls of the chasm support very little vegetation beyond scatterd ferns (see **#100**) and lichens (see **#7**). A handful of eastern hemlock trees lean precariously from the uppermost ledges. One old hemlock has wrapped its roots around boulders on the deep floor of the gorge, its ragged crown rearing to the top of the cliff. On the rocky high ground to either side of the gorge grows a mixed forest of oak, hemlock, and white pine.

A trail through the chasm begins at the edge of the parking lot. Follow the blue blazes that lead through the maze of boulders in the gorge, and then go left up a rocky hillside to circle your way back to the parking lot over the high ground and exposed ledges on the eastern heights overlooking the chasm.

Remarks: *The trail is a 30-minute hike. You must pick your way over boulders for virtually the entire length of the chasm; the rocks may be slippery underfoot. The 187-acre Purgatory Chasm State Reservation offers picnic facilities adjoining the parking areas. Rock climbing in the chasm is by permit only; contact the Division of Forests and Parks, Region III Headquarters, Clinton, Mass.; (617) 368-0126. The park is open all year. The 135-acre Sutton State Forest, which adjoins Purgatory Chasm, has facilities for hiking, cross-country skiing, and snowmobiling.*

64.

Quaboag River

Directions: **Brookfield and West Brookfield, Mass. From Worcester, take Route 9 west about 17 miles. Go south (left) on Route 148 for 0.5 mile to a bridge over the Quaboag River and an old white mill building. Before the bridge, park on the left in a dirt turnoff that serves as a**

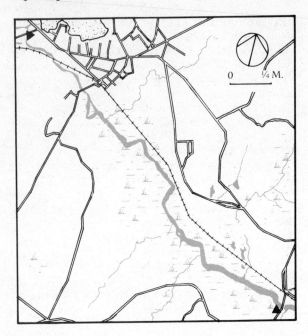

boat landing. To the river access in West Brookfield, continue on Route 9 for 4 miles west of Route 148. Turn south on Route 67, and make an immediate right-hand turn into an unmarked scenic rest stop near the bridge.

Ownership: Towns of Brookfield and West Brookfield; Massachusetts Division of Fisheries and Wildlife.

The birds and aquatic life of the sweeping freshwater marshes along the historic Quaboag River are the highlights of a flatwater canoe journey through a rural valley of inland Massachusetts.

The 24-mile Quaboag River, a tributary of the lower Connecticut River, rises in the town of Brookfield from headwaters in Quaboag Lake and flows westward to the village of Three Rivers. There, the Quaboag merges with the Ware and Swift rivers to form the Chicopee, an industrial waterway that drains into the lower Connecticut.

The upper portion of the Quaboag River, a roughly 9-mile stretch winding through Brookfield and West Brookfield to neighboring Warren, features the most attractive scenery and richest wildlife. It is also a historic part of the waterway. In precolonial times the Quaboag Indians settled on the sandy shores of Quaboag Lake, using the river for a westward passage. In the late seventeenth century the upper Quaboag was the site of the first colonial settlement in the central highlands of the Massachusetts Bay Colony, Quaboag Plantation, which was destroyed by Indians during King Philip's War in 1676. By 1700 the area was resettled as the town of Brookfield, which for more than a century served as a major wayside stop on the legendary Bay Path, an old stagecoach route linking Boston and Springfield. The old Bay Path, which followed the Quaboag valley through the region, forded the river in West Brookfield.

The upper Quaboag is a wide, slow-moving river that meanders through broad, treeless marshes along its first 4½ miles. In areas where the gentle hills that cradle the floodplain descend close to the river, the marshes grade into grassy wet meadows and red-maple swamps. Finally, where the surrounding uplands completely enclose the river channel at the narrows in West Brookfield, its waters flow between higher, wooded banks.

The canoe route described here begins at the narrows in West Brookfield for a roughly 5½-mile upstream journey to Brookfield. The downstream access in West Brookfield is the preferred starting point for a canoe trip when the prevailing winds are from the north or west, since it is more difficult to paddle against a strong northerly headwind through the open marshes than to run against the upper Quaboag's gentle current. In southerly winds canoeists should start upstream at the Brookfield access and paddle with the current and the wind to their backs.

The northern access at the rest stop in West Brookfield lies beside the Route 67 highway bridge. Here the river emerges from beneath the bridge on the left and curves southwest on its way to Warren. A channel entering the bend in the river on the right is the outlet of Wickaboag Pond (seen from the junction of Routes 9 and 67 to the north). Park at the rest stop and slide your canoe down the embankment on the left and paddle southward under the Route 67 bridge. At most times of the year the current flowing against you is very slow; it is faster when spring runoff swells the river.

For the next mile or so the river forms a narrow channel running through woodlands. The water here is shallow, but the bottom is sandy with only a few rocky areas. Turtles may be observed basking on some of the rocks that protrude above the water. The snapping turtle, which inhabits the river, is the largest native turtle in the region. It has a rough 8- to-18-inch upper shell and a long tail. Because its head and limbs are too large to withdraw into its shell for protection, the snapper has evolved strong jaws for defense.

Soon the river passes beneath a second bridge spanning Long Hill

Rd. outside West Brookfield Center, and in the next half-mile fully emerges into the open marshes of the upper Quaboag. During the first mile or so, you have observed a few riverfront houses and other buildings scattered along the shore. But now, as the river twists into the marshes, the scenery becomes surprisingly wild and solitary. The western ridge of hills overlooking the river, known as Long Hill, is heavily forested and fringed in places with swamps. (A large portion is protected as part of the state-owned wildlife management area, which also extends into the marshes.) In the east the hills are swathed in rolling green pastures, hayfields, and woodlands, where you may glimpse only an occasional church steeple or distant rooftop in the surrounding towns.

Slow-moving rivers like the upper Quaboag occur in flat lowlands where the level contours of the land allow the water to spread over a wide area. Its looping meanders are typical of sluggish waterways that in some instances split into several channels or change course within the floodplain. Slow-moving rivers are also rich in nutrients that support abundant aquatic vegetation. The marsh plants further enrich the river by dying back in winter and releasing additional nutrients as they decompose. The upper Quaboag's marshes are good examples of *riverine* marshes, which develop along wide flood-plains. In large watersheds like that occupied by the Quaboag, the yearly spring flooding from melting ice and tributary runoff raises the river above its normal banks, submerging the marshlands for weeks. The flooding prevents the marshlands from becoming invaded by trees while promoting the growth of aquatic plants.

The rich plant growth in marshes is food for a wide variety of fish, amphibians, and birds. Birdlife on the upper Quaboag is at its peak in summer when the wading birds have arrived from their southern wintering grounds. The most numerous species is the great blue heron. At 4 feet tall and with a 6-foot wingspread, the great blue is the largest wading bird in the northern United States. It is long-legged and long-necked, with a sharp bill and bluish-gray plumage. In flight it is easily distinguished from other large birds by its folded neck and trailing legs. On the upper Quaboag these birds often detect your approach before you see them on the shore. Once disturbed, they rise into the air and glide away down the river. Sometimes you can rouse the same bird again and again as you take successive bends in the river, and each time the bird will fly down the channel and drop out of sight beyond the next curve. When standing, the great blue poises motionlessly upon the riverbank waiting for its prey of fish and small amphibians to swim by.

The American bittern is a less conspicuous but frequently sighted summer wading bird here. It is a large heron, 25 to 30 inches long, with a short neck and a brownish color that provides camouflage in the marsh grass. It may be seen standing in its peculiar but characteristic "freeze": completely motionless, its yellow bill cocked skyward. The American bittern's spring song, which it produces by swelling its throat with air and then expelling it in violent bursts, is often compared to the sound of a stake being pounded into the ground.

As you paddle south toward the Route 148 bridge in Brookfield, which marks the end of the trip, you may see muskrats in the water or a lodge along the shore. The muskrat is the most abundant mammal in the marshes, and feeds upon crayfish, mussels, fish, and vegetation. Paddle beneath the Route 148 bridge to the boat landing on the left.

Other recorded marshbirds on the upper Quaboag include the long-billed marsh wren (see **#6**), egret, sandpiper, osprey, and an occasional herring gull. In spring and fall migrations, you can sometimes see Canada geese, common mergansers, and other waterfowl (species vary from year to year). The common loon is a rare migrant on the river.

Remarks: *The upper Quaboag is completely flatwater from the Route 67 to Route 148 bridges. Allow 2 to 2½ hours one-way to cover the roughly 4½ miles of river. The months of May through October are the best time to explore the river by canoe. Spring flooding raises the river far above its banks and submerges the marshes, making it difficult to navigate, but by late May the river is usually restored to its normal water level. There are no canoe rentals nearby—you must bring your own.*

Nearby Places of Interest

The 1,000-acre Quaboag Wildlife Management Area extends into the marshes from the western hills. The forested portion has unmarked woods roads and hiking trails along the east side of Long Hill. The whole area is heavily used by hunters in season. The marsh is also open to hunting, as well as trapping and fishing. There are no visitor facilities. Take Route 148 north from Route 20 in Sturbridge and go 6.7 miles to Long Hill Rd. on the left; or 0.4 mile south from the bridge over the Quaboag on Route 148. Follow Long Hill Rd. 1.5 miles to the sign and parking area (open field) on the right. Nearby Wells State Park, Sturbridge, has 50 campsites, swimming, and a boat ramp

on Walker Pond. It is open May to October and is particularly crowded in July and August. Campsites are available
on a first-come, first-serve basis. The park is located near
the Old Sturbridge Village outdoor museum. From Exit 10
off I-90, take Route 20 east to Route 49 north. Take Route
49 north for a short distance to the state park entrance on
the left.

65.
Wachusett Mountain
State Reservation

Directions: Princeton, Mass. From Worcester, take I-190
north about 10 miles, then go northwest (left) on Route
140 for 2 miles, then go west (left) on Route 62 for 4 miles
to the junction with Route 31 in Princeton Center. Follow
Route 31 north (right) for about 2 miles to the entrance of
the reservation, Summit Rd., and the visitors' center.

Ownership: Massachusetts Division of Forests and Parks.

Mount Wachusett is the highest peak in central and eastern Massachusetts, a monadnock (see below) rising to 2,006 feet above sea
level. Mount Wachusett's natural setting amidst the rolling upland
hills of central New England, combined with its proximity to several
major cities, has made it a popular recreation area. A modern, paved
summit road provides easy access by car to the mountain's spectacular scenic overlooks, where on clear days maximum visibility stretches
to 120 miles in all directions. Crisscrossing the slopes of the reservation's 2,000 acres is an extensive network of trails for hiking, snowshoeing, and cross-country and downhill skiing.

The geological history of the land form we now call Wachusett,
an Algonquin Indian name meaning "by the Great Hill," is part of
the greater chronicle of a particular class of similarly isolated mountains in the upland regions of New England. Geologists have given
the name *monadnocks* to these widely scattered peaks, after the classic
example, Mount Monadnock (see **#72**) in southern New Hampshire. As impressive as Wachusett may appear today in contrast to

the smaller surrounding hills of central Massachusetts, it is actually the vestige of a much larger ancient mountain that arose more than 100 million years ago as the product of a tremendous geological upheaval. This "mountain revolution," as it has been called, created New England's major mountain ranges when the earth's crust folded and cracked from enormous internal forces, heaving upward masses of molten rock that eventually solidified to form mountainous bodies largely composed of granite (see **White Mountains, Monadnocks, and Eastern Connecticut Highlands**). Over the course of millions of years, erosional forces reduced Wachusett and other monadnocks to their present-day size. Other ancient mountains and hills, composed of materials softer than the hard granite of the monadnocks, were completely leveled by erosion, leaving such granite monadnocks as Wachusett to stand alone upon a flat plain.

This erosional plain, known as the *peneplain* (see **#24**), was itself transformed during several subsequent periods of comparatively milder geological upheaval. A gentle uplift of the earth's crust animated the peneplain's once placid rivers, which then carved its flat surface into valleys, ridges, and hilltops, molding the basic terrain of New England as we know it today. The later glaciers of the Ice Age, which covered Mount Wachusett itself with an ice sheet estimated to have been as much as a mile thick, only slightly modified the already deeply eroded peneplain. Today, from Mount Wachusett's summit, the original surface of the central New England peneplain is visible in all directions, surviving as a panorama of countless hilltops, all relatively equal in height, which in the distance appear to merge together as an even horizon.

Wachusett Reservation features 13 miles of interconnecting trails, marked throughout with blue streamers and identified by guideposts, which appear at the trail intersections. A trail map and a viewing guide to the topography as seen from the summit are available at the visitors' center.

Jack Frost Trail begins at the base of the south slope, off a closed administration road. From the visitors' center, drive south before taking a sharp right onto Westminster Rd. Go 0.7 mile to the administration road, located next to a small pond on the right-hand side, and park at the iron gate. Proceed past the gate up the administration road until you reach the guidepost for the Jack Frost Trail.

Many of the plant species seen along the lower half of Jack Frost—especially mountain laurel, American beech, hemlock, and ferns—thrive in the acidic soil found in rocky, granitic terrain, as well as in areas with cool habitats on the higher slopes in this region. After walking a short distance through stands of mixed hardwoods, scattered white pine, and hemlock, the trail twists through a dense thicket of mountain laurel (**A**), whose presence betrays high soil acidity (see **#69**). A few steps away there is an immature grove of American beech trees (**B**), easily recognizable by their exceptionally smooth, light gray bark and straight trunks. The acidic soil increases the beeches' ability to reproduce by seed or by root sprouts, as they have done here in great numbers. Hemlock becomes dominant at **C**, where the trail climbs abruptly up a steep, boulder-strewn slope. The tall hemlocks growing from the slope's side display shallow root systems almost fully exposed aboveground, where the roots have tortuously wrapped themselves around the protruding boulders. Hemlocks are often present on low rocky slopes and especially in ravines where the climate is cool and moisture is plentiful.

Jack Frost continues to climb steeply until it reaches the top of a rocky, wooded hill (**D**). At 690 feet, the effects of an increasingly cooler climate and greater wind exposure are evident in the shorter stature and twisted trunks of the trees, a phenomenon that becomes even more noticeable higher up the mountain. Hemlocks cannot survive in this drier and more exposed habitat. Lack of soil moisture from drying winds, rapid water runoff, and a deep water table almost always exclude hemlocks from the typical hilltop plant community

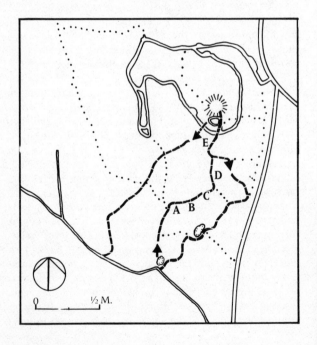

in southern New England. While their shallow root system can absorb moisture in areas of thin soil, such as the slopes below, this feature also makes hemlocks vulnerable to the unobstructed force of the wind on exposed heights. Thus, mixed hardwoods occupy the hilltop, including many chestnut oaks, a common species on dry hilltops where sunlight is plentiful.

After dipping into a protected hollow harboring another, smaller hemlock grove, the trail again ascends through a forest of small mixed hardwoods, and finally intersects with the Mountain House Trail. As the two overlapping trails now approach the summit, a second immature grove of beech trees (**E**) offers a striking contrast to that which appeared earlier at the lower elevation. Again, the effects of wind exposure and drier terrain are dramatically made clear by these beeches' stunted, twisted forms. Continue on the trail for a very short distance until it emerges onto the summit road. Follow the road to the right before making a quick turn to the left, where a short stretch of road leads to the summit. At the summit you will have a virtually unobstructed view of the central New England peneplain, appearing as an even horizon of blending hilltops. But also notice the exposed bedrock surface of the summit itself; the worn granite is evidence of the erosion that for millions of years shaped the New England landscape.

Here you have a choice of several trail routes, each of which leads back to Westminster Rd. and your car. Harrington Trail (1½ miles) descends the south slope through beech forest. Mountain House Trail (1 mile) descends southeasterly through a heavily eroded hardwood forest, with many oaks and an open understory carpeted with ferns. At a point very close to its end, Mountain House connects with a section of the southerly Bicentennial Trail, which winds a short distance through a young hardwood successional forest crisscrossed with stone walls before connecting with the lower half of High Meadow Trail. High Meadow takes a route through a reverting farm pasture, blanketed heavily with common juniper and scattered redcedar. Echo Lake Trail then leads through a red-maple swamp and plantations of white pine and white spruce before emerging onto Westminster Rd. at the gate to the administration road.

Remarks: *Jack Frost Trail (1½ miles) is a 50-minute hike, ascending 600 feet. It is moderately difficult at its steeper intervals. The mountain laurel blooms there in June. North-slope trails include Bolton Pond Trail (½ mile, 30 minutes), featuring a glacial rock formation known as Balance Rock. This connects with Old Indian Trail (2 miles, 90 minutes), which has two overlooks on the way to the summit. The Mid-State Trail crosses Wachusett Reservation. Beyond the reservation it continues northward to Redemption*

Rock, Crow's Hill in Leominster State Forest, before connecting with the Wapack Trail in southern New Hampshire. To the south, the Mid-State Trail continues to Barre Falls. The summit road is open from mid-April to October 31. The reservation is open all year. The visitors' center has a small exhibit area, focusing on native wildlife and vegetation and the history of Mount Wachusett. Mount Wachusett is the foremost hawk-watching point in Massachusetts during peak migratory periods in spring and fall. Nearby Wachusett Meadow Wildlife Sanctuary, Princeton, is also a prime birding area. Its lands adjoin Wachusett Mountain State Reservation on the south.

66.

Wachusett Meadow
Wildlife Sanctuary

Directions: **Princeton, Mass. Follow directions for #65. From Princeton Center, continue west on Route 62 for 0.7 mile. Turn right onto Goodnow Rd.; go 1 mile to the sanctuary parking lot on the left.**

Ownership: **Massachusetts Audubon Society.**

A rolling upland of woodlands and meadows, quiet ponds, and a red maple swamp provides diverse natural habitats for a teeming array of birdlife at Wachusett Meadow in rural north-central Massachusetts. The great blue heron, Canada goose, bobwhite, belted kingfisher, and yellow warbler are among the many birds observed on the 900 acres of reverting farmland here, with its 10½ miles of hiking trails. Spectacular vistas of the surrounding hill country from the top of the sanctuary's Brown Hill include nearby Mount Wachusett (2,006 feet), bordering Wachusett Meadow on the north, the highest peak in southern New England east of the Berkshires. Mount Wachusett's upper slopes are a dramatic backdrop to the flights of migratory hawks in spring and autumn.

Goodnow Rd. bisects Wachusett Meadow and divides the sanctuary's trail system into north and south parcels. The north portion traverses the higher terrain, including Brown Hill; the south portion occupies a mixed terrain of pasture, forest, and a red-maple swamp and brook spanned by a boardwalk. All trails begin at the parking lot, where maps are available at a small visitors' center. Trails are identified by paint blazes and occasional signposts. Blue blazes indicate a trail leading away from the parking area, yellow identifies returning trails, and white designates connecting trails. At some points, the color-marked trails overlap. A self-guiding, descriptive trail brochure for the Maple Swamp Nature Trail (available at the visitors' center) interprets points of interest along a lengthy stretch of the sanctuary's southern portion; several trails in the northern half of the sanctuary will be described here.

Cross the road from the parking lot and enter a meadow where the northerly main trail originates to the right of a colonial homestead. As you follow the trail up the gentle slope of the hayfield (**A**), watch for the bobolinks in the spring or summer grasses. The bobolink builds its ground nest in hayfields. In spring the male is easy to identify: black below and largely white above. This reversal of the normal tone pattern distinguishes the male from any other songbird. In winter both the male and the female closely resemble sparrows, with buff-yellow coloring below and dark stripes on the crown and upper parts. Once more prevalent in New England than at present, the bobolink population has dwindled with the disappearance of meadowland in the wake of the region's agricultural decline.

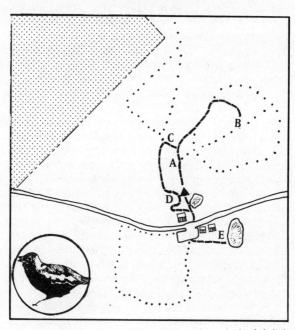

Inset: Spring bobolink

The main trail leaves the hayfield as it crosses a stone wall, blue markers guiding you through a reverting field of sumac and common juniper before entering a pine grove. Weaving among pines and thickets of aspen, white birch, and red maple, the trail ascends more steeply and finally climbs the terraced ledges of bare bedrock leading to the summit of Brown Hill (**B**). As you follow the blue markers over the exposed bedrock, winding your way through carpets of juniper and haircap moss, an uninterrupted view of the landscape below stretches in every direction except to the north, where the slopes of Mount Wachusett rise above Brown Hill. From here bird observation is excellent in the open sky.

In the peak migratory periods of late spring and early autumn, as many as two to three thousand hawks have been sighted in one day over Mount Wachusett. Many species breed in the northern states and Canada during spring and summer; they fly south as far as the tropics for better winter feeding. Flying singly or sometimes in groups, hawks follow migratory routes with geographical features conducive to generating thermal updrafts, such as broad valleys and river plains, or ridges and mountain slopes. Thermals are columns of rising air that are produced when wind is deflected upward by an obstruction, such as a mountain or even a tall building. They can also form when air is heated by the land, which absorbs or reflects radiation depending upon whether its surface is forested (reflecting heat) or bare (absorbing heat). When a hawk soars or circles in the air, it is said to be "riding" a thermal current, which means the heated air is rising as fast as or faster than the bird is dropping. Hawks are attracted to thermals and moving weather fronts that allow the birds to glide easily.

Fifteen species of hawks, falcons, and eagles are commonly seen in southern New England during migration. Among the more common hawks seen at Wachusett is the broad-winged hawk (14 to 18 inches), with the characteristic broad wings and broad-rounded tail of the buteos. Soaring in wide circles high in the sky, the broadwing is the smallest buteo, no larger than a crow, with white-and-black tailbands and light underwings. It breeds from central Texas and the Gulf Coast north to Saskatchewan, Quebec, and New Brunswick, migrating in winter to Florida and the tropics. Another common hawk at Wachusett during migration is the sharp-shinned hawk (10 to 14 inches), with its dark blue-gray back, rusty chest, and distinctive square, notched tail. The sharpshin is also no bigger than a crow and, as an accipiter hawk, has that family's short, wide, rounded wings, long tail, and flap-sail method of flight. It breeds from the Gulf Coast north into Canada and winters in northern states.

The turkey vulture has also been seen at Brown Hill. With a wingspread of 6 feet, this almost eagle-size bird can be differentiated from eagles and hawks by its very small head and slimmer tail. The turkey vulture often soars in high, wide circles, rocking and tilting as it flies (see also **#10**).

Descend Brown Hill and retrace your steps back along the trail until a branch trail appears (white blazes) that leads off to the right into a pine grove. This short woodland trail heads northwesterly to an impressive glacial boulder (**C**) known to geologists as a glacial erratic, a rock carried by the glaciers of the Ice Age and deposited some distance from its original location (see **#78**). This large erratic was perhaps torn away from Mount Wachusett by the ice sheet.

Notice here several dead pine trees with large holes bored in their trunks—a sure sign of the pileated woodpecker (17 to 19½ inches), the largest member of the woodpecker family and the only one with a crest. The red crest, black-and-white coloration, and size of this bird make it highly conspicuous.

Veer left after passing the glacial boulder and follow a stone wall in a southerly direction. Along this stretch of the trail are groves of shagbark hickory trees, easily identified by their scalelike bark. The trail soon returns to the hayfield where you began your walk.

As you descend the hayfield, turn right at a signpost for the Crocker Sugar Maple Tree (**D**) and follow a branch path to the field's western edge. The sugar maple seen here is one of the largest of its kind in the country, standing 70 feet high with a crown spread of 100 feet and a trunk circumference of 15 feet, 15 inches. A relic from the days when Wachusett Meadow was a working farm, the tree was already large enough to preserve when the land was cleared and stone walls established in 1786. Estimated to be at least 300 years old, this sugar maple achieved its magnificent size owing to lack of competition and an abundance of water from a nearby spring.

Ruffed grouse and bobwhite can sometimes be glimpsed in the vicinity of the sugar maple. The ruffed grouse (16 to 19 inches) is the only large, chickenlike bird found in deep woods. Its plumage is a reddish- or grayish-brown, and its fan-shaped tail has a wide black band. The bird is usually invisible in the underbrush, so that the sudden drumming of its wings, which creates a loud, whirring sound, can be startling (see **#19**). The bobwhite, a quail that is also chickenlike but much smaller (8⅓ to 10½ inches) than the ruffed grouse, utters the distinctive whistle for which it is named—*Bob-white!* It is commonly seen in farming regions.

Return to the parking lot and take a path through a meadow to the east beyond the barn to the wildlife pond (**E**). The great blue heron, black-crowned night heron, Canada goose, mallard, and black duck are among the waterfowl sighted at the pond. Also watch for the belted kingfisher, a slightly larger bird than the blue jay, with a bushy crest and large bill. It will hover above the pond's surface before diving into the water, sometimes emerging with a fish in its beak.

The Maple Swamp Nature Trail in the south portion of the sanctuary features a lengthy boardwalk through a red-maple swamp and an observation platform at a brook. Among numerous birds that frequent this area are the red-eyed vireo, yellow and palm warblers, yellow-bellied flycatcher, and least flycatcher.

The Crocker Trail connects with the Maple Swamp Nature Trail. It weaves through pasture, pine woodlands, and the small "Fire Pond." The scarlet tanager, hermit thrush, ring-necked pheasant, and veery are among the species reportedly sighted.

Rock Pasture Trail, a connecting trail leading back to the parking area off the Crocker Trail, winds through hemlock forest, thickets of mountain laurel, and scattered wet swales and red-maple groves before emerging into a meadow. The pileated woodpecker and brown creeper have been sighted along this trail.

Remarks: *The northerly trails (as described) are a 45-minute hike. The terrain is relatively easy, except for Brown Hill (moderately difficult). The southerly trails, forming a loop that includes the Maple Swamp Nature Trail, Crocker Trail, and Rock Pasture Trail, are altogether a 1-hour hike over easy terrain. Use caution walking on the boardwalk; although it is in generally good condition, occasional wooden planks or supports are weak and can bow unexpectedly underfoot. Nearby Wachusett Mountain State Reservation, Princeton (see* **#65**), *is the foremost hawk-watching point in Massachusetts. Bird observations are made from the summit, accessible via motor vehicle.*

67.

Harvard Forest

Directions: Petersham, Mass. From Worcester, take Route 122 northwest about 25 miles to the junction with Route 32 in Petersham. Go north (right) on Route 32 for 3 miles beyond the town common to the Harvard Forest entrance on the right.

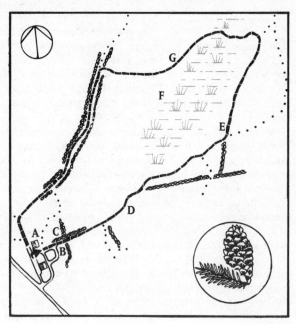

Inset: White spruce

Ownership: **Harvard University.**

Situated in the gently rolling hills of north central Massachusetts, Harvard Forest serves as headquarters for Harvard University's Forestry School. An ideal place for visitors to begin learning about the evolution of central New England's woodlands, Harvard's forestry museum and nature trails trace the history of land use in the rural town of Petersham for a period spanning almost three centuries.

The varied array of exhibits at Harvard's Fisher Museum introduces visitors to both the past and the present character of the landscape, and to the natural and human disturbances that have altered it. These exhibits reveal the effects of forest fires, hurricanes, and such diseases as the chestnut blight and Dutch elm disease, as well as the impact of agricultural development. Especially noteworthy is a series of highly detailed dioramas depicting historical patterns of land use in Petersham, from early European settlement, beginning soon after 1700, through the first half of the twentieth century. Successive stages of agricultural clearing and natural reclamation are depicted in these models, which ultimately represent the history of land use in the central New England region as a whole.

Two nature trails illustrate the relationship of Harvard's forest tracts to prior agricultural uses, compare reforestation areas of naturally seeded hardwoods to conifer plantations, and show varied types of forest succession. Trail maps, available at Fisher Museum, identify former pastures and fields and the composition of forests now growing upon them. Since the Natural History Trail features excellent descriptive trail markers, only the Blackgum Trail will be reviewed here.

Marked with yellow streamers, the Blackgum Trail begins along a gravel farm lane that runs from the parking lot between the Fisher Museum building and the Sanderson Farmhouse (**A**). Built sometime after 1763, the farmhouse was the homestead of the Sanderson family, whose farmlands are now part of Harvard Forest.

As the trail follows the farmlane behind the buildings, it enters a forest stand of naturally seeded mixed hardwoods growing on a field abandoned in 1920, which appears on the immediate right. At **B** compare this natural hardwood stand with a bordering stand of red pine planted in 1926, which is being succeeded by hardwoods in the understory. While hardwoods would have eventually succeeded the red pine over the natural course of time, a root fungus has accelerated the process: it destroyed many of the red pines in 1950 and prematurely thinned the forest canopy, allowing sunlight to penetrate to the hardwoods beneath. The emergence of a new generation of trees in a forest is always triggered by the thinning of the overstory trees. This is true both of a successional forest, where the young trees are of a different species than the overstory trees, and of a climax forest, where both young and old species are the same. As seen here, disease or other external factors, such as insect attack, wind, or lightning, may thin the overstory. Otherwise senescence—the period in plantlife from maturity to death—causes overstory trees to become less efficient in their ability to produce food. Such trees then become less able to tolerate climatic extremes and drought and may become too weak to resist insects or diseases. Competition between overstory trees in stands of mixed species can also open the canopy as one species finally tops and suppresses another. Once an opening appears in the canopy, it is likely to become enlarged over the years by wind and storm damage to the exposed edge trees.

Some of the factors that determine overstory mortality may also influence the growth of a young forest. Directly across the trail a mixed stand of white pine and white spruce (**C**) planted in 1924 reveals how an insect attack has affected competition between these two conifers. The white pine weevil attacked the pines' terminal shoots or leaders when the trees were young, retarding their upward growth. The forked trunk that results from the loss of the terminal shoot is a typical mark of infestation by this beetle. White spruce then gained a competitive advantage and was able to dominate the overstory. As the closed canopy of this stand eventually thins out with age, the white pine may be the first to decline. The crowns of white pine that have been surpassed by the spruce will recede for lack of sunlight, and the upper branches of the least competitive trees will be pruned away through friction as the crowns sway back and forth in the wind.

Like the red pine at **B**, the white pine and white spruce will eventually yield to successional species that are more tolerant of understory shade than the second-generation seedlings of these sun-loving pioneer trees. Somewhat more tolerant of shade than the red or white pine, the white spruce illustrates how understory hardiness of a species can vary according to such factors as locality, soil type, climate, and the surrounding plant community. White spruce can sometimes succeed itself on cool, exposed sites of poor, marginal soils within its natural range in northern New England. But these conditions are absent at Harvard; the white spruce here was introduced as reforestation plantings beyond the southern limits of its range. A warm climate and fertile soils have instead favored the growth of hemlock and hardwoods in the understory, which in the future will compose a mature stand of mixed species.

Although white spruce may never again form a dominant stand here, it has managed to seed itself naturally in limited numbers. Small white spruce seedlings grow on the edge of the trail as it continues ahead, and at **D** a seedling bed of white spruce is seen on the right. Once introduced outside their range, most non-native species find it difficult to seed themselves naturally because of climatic differences and other factors. Here the white spruce grows in moss, which insulates the vulnerable seedlings against temperature extremes and retains moisture in dry periods.

While white spruce is not native to this region of central Massachusetts, a number of other northern species are found at Harvard Forest. The northern portion of central Massachusetts lies in a forest transition zone that contains tree species common in the northern hardwood forest as well as the more southern central oak forest. Northern hardwoods, such as beech, sugar maple, yellow and paper birch, poplar, and basswood, occupy more protected, cooler terrain such as lowlands, ravines, and north- or east-facing slopes. Of the Northern conifers, red pine and hemlock (more plentiful in the north, but also common farther south in the central oak forest) are native to this area; and in some isolated spots, red and black spruce grow in wet bogs. The predominant species of the central oak forest found here include hickory, black birch, and especially black and red oak. The central hardwoods generally grow in the warmer, drier, and more exposed south- and west-facing sites. Also native here are trees common to both the northern and the central forests: red maple, white ash, black cherry, and on dry, sandy soils, white pine. Many of these various transition-zone species appear along the trail (see also **White Mountains, Monadnocks, and Eastern Connecticut Highlands**).

After the trail crosses the stone wall marking the north boundary of the Sanderson farm, it passes a plantation of red pine on the left, with oak, maple, and hemlock growing in the understory. These are the dominant late-successional species on well-drained sites in this area. On the right, naturally seeded white and gray birch have invaded an area that was cut clear in 1951. Both species of birch are pioneer hardwoods on well-drained sites in central New England.

Soon the trail swings left on a woodland path through a former farm woodlot now dominated by hemlock. Up until now the trail has passed through forest tracts that were either pasture, cultivated cropland, or hayfields in the past agricultural period. The woodlot was never cleared for grazing or cultivation, although it may have been logged for timber. Woodlots typically constituted only a small percentage of farm acreage during the height of New England agriculture in the nineteenth century. A study of Harvard Forest lands found that on this particular tract (Prospect Hill) only about 9 percent remained as forest, whereas 91 percent had been cleared for agricultural purposes at one time or another. These figures reflect the intensity of nineteenth-century farming in New England. It is estimated that in the peak farming years only about 25 percent of the overall region was forested, and of this the major portion was being cut continuously for firewood. Today, on the other hand, it is estimated that more than three-fifths of New England is covered with forest.

Visible to the left of the trail in the woodlot are the relics of chestnut trees killed by the devastating fungus blight (**E**). The chestnut blight was introduced from Asia in about 1903, and by 1920 it had eliminated almost every chestnut in New England. Before the blight, the tree was so common it competed with oaks for dominance of the central forest. A fast grower, the tree commonly reached 100 feet and constituted an important New England timber resource. Chestnut was once prized for its majestic size, beauty, and resistance to decay; here the limbless, weathered trunks have survived for as long as 50 years. Today these trees grow from sprouts only to shrub-size, quickly dying from the blight as they begin to approach flowering maturity. Watch for these small, diseased saplings along the path as the trail leaves the woodlot, curving left to join an old farm road.

At **F** blackgum trees quickly become visible in a swamp off to the left. The blackgum, or more properly, black tupelo, is a species of the central oak forest, which usually occupies shallow swamplands in cool upland regions (see **#52**). Its wide range extends from southwestern Maine to New York and southern Ontario to northern Florida and eastern Texas. Its simple, untoothed leaves are glossy green in summer, but flame to a brilliant scarlet in late August and early September. Small green flowers appear in spring as the leaves become full, and are a source of nectar for bees. The tree is dioecious, meaning that a specimen is either male or female. The female trees produce purple, berrylike fruit in the fall, which is the preferred food of certain birds, including flicker, wood duck, cedar waxwing, brown thrasher, starling, wood thrush, eastern kingbird, and red-headed woodpecker. Foxes and black bears also consume the fruit, and beavers browse the foliage and branches.

Down the trail on the right is an area of relatively immature hardwoods (**G**), which sprouted after a fire struck in 1957. The trees growing here—red maple, red oak, and white and gray birch—are among those species that can quickly sprout from stumps on burned lands. Notice that hemlock and white pine are completely absent here because of their inability to sprout, whereas they proliferate on other sites at Harvard. Follow the yellow markers along the lane, turning left onto another gravel road that leads back to the parking lot.

The Natural History Trail (¼ mile) is a short, 20-minute walk over easy terrain. Marked in red, the trail has interpretive descriptions at numbered posts. Winding across former farm lots, it examines the composition of conifer plantations established between 1924 and 1926 and areas naturally seeded to mixed hardwoods and white pine. Also highlighted are farm relics (apple trees, stone walls), trees damaged by ice storms and disease, and the complex root system of a maple grove. Many of the posted trail descriptions are complemented by exhibits at the Fisher Museum. This short trail is especially suitable for a hike with younger children.

Remarks: *Blackgum Trail (1½ miles) is a 1-hour walk over easy, flat terrain. Some low stretches bordering the swamp may become wet underfoot after periods of rain. Harvard Forest is closed on weekends and holidays.*

The Fisher Museum's other exhibits include silvicultural practices and forest-fire control. Maps show paths of New England's three major hurri-

*canes in 1635, 1815, and 1938. (See **#53** for discussion of the 1938 hurricane.) Charts and topographical maps trace the history of Petersham; the evolution of the Sanderson farm through generations of the family. Other varied exhibits are devoted to aspects of forest science. An illustrated booklet of the dioramas at the Fisher Museum, with accompanying text, is available for a small fee.*

68.
James W. Brooks
Woodland Preserve

Directions: **Follow directions in #67. To the Swift River tract, take Route 122 east from the junction with Route 32 for 1.5 miles. Turn north (left) on Quaker Dr.; go 0.2 mile to the first barred gate on the right beyond the bridge. To the Roaring Brook tract, take East St. from the east side of the town common off Route 32; go 1 mile to the barred gate on the left.**

Ownership: **Trustees of Reservations.**

Old-growth forest, secluded ponds, and whitewater cascades are the scenic attractions at James W. Brooks Woodland Preserve in Petersham. This 408-acre preserve in the rural highlands of north central Massachusetts is divided into two parcels that border the East Branch of the Swift River and several tributary streams. Once territory of the Nipmuc Indians and the site of early Yankee farms, the preserve features early-nineteenth-century stone walls and cellar holes on abandoned pastures and fields that have succeeded to a mature forest dominated by oak, white pine, and hemlock. Five miles of hiking trails and forest roads traverse wetlands and dry upland habitats, which support a variety of native woodland plants and many common mammals, including porcupine, beaver, and white-tailed deer.

The Swift River Tract is the larger, southern parcel in the preserve. It includes more than 1 mile of the East Branch of the Swift River and portions of Moccasin and Rutland brooks, as well as ponds and marshes. Connor's Pond Loop covers the southern end of this tract. It begins at the barred gate on the south side of Quaker Dr., where a trail junction is identified with the posted number 65. Go right at this junction and follow the forest road that runs parallel to the Swift River on the right.

Eastern hemlock and scattered stands of white pine dominate this portion of the tract. The old-growth stands of hemlock and pine here are about 80 years old, dating from the end of New England's period of agricultural decline. As New England farmers moved west to more fertile lands throughout the latter half of the nineteenth century, the forest began to reclaim the open land. In Petersham, old-field succession was typical of the region as a whole. By 1870, the majority of Petersham's farmers had left the farmlands that had been settled and cleared more than one century earlier. Consequently, the Petersham forest doubled in size between 1865 and 1885, and then doubled again by 1905, when it encompassed 55 percent of the town's area.

At **A** the road emerges at a shady knoll overlooking the northern end of Connor's Pond. An unmarked footpath on the right descends to the edge of the Swift River at its inlet to the pond. This river, a major watershed for massive Quabbin Reservoir (see **#51**) some 5 miles to the southwest, provides a wetland habitat for many plants

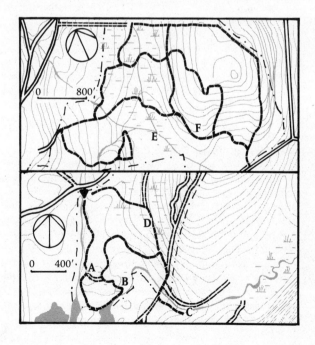

and animals. In spring, jack-in-the-pulpit, trillium, skunk cabbage (see **#62**), and maidenhair fern thrive on moist, shady ground along the pond's and river's edges. These plants serve as a food source for porcupines (see **#73**), which at night follow trails to the water from their dens among boulders in upland areas. Raccoons are also common nocturnal visitors to the pond, where they hunt for crayfish, fish, turtles, and other food. White-tailed deer (see **#49**) browse on a variety of plants along sunny edges near the water. Occasionally otter and mink fish here, especially where the water runs swiftest in the river.

Continue to follow the footpath along the wooded slope as it curves to the northeast, leading away from the Swift River to Rutland Brook. At **B** a small beaver dam has been constructed from sticks, plants, and mud. A portion of this dam has been removed by sanctuary personnel to allow the water to flow without obstruction to Connor's Pond. Beavers build dams to flood low-lying terrain, thereby creating ponds in which to take refuge from predators.

A footpath swings westward and quickly rejoins Connor's Pond Loop. At junction 67 it soon intersects with another trail, Rutland Brook Rd., where a right turn leads across a footbridge into adjacent Rutland Brook Sanctuary. Beyond the bridge, take a footpath on the left into a hemlock grove at **C**. The path here skirts Rutland Brook, where an attractive cascade plunges around boulders in the deeply eroded streambed.

Retrace your steps across the footbridge and go left at junction 68 down Rutland Brook Rd. Though no side trail leads off the road to the Reuben Stone Cellar Hole (**D**) in the woods on your left, a short detour will provide a glimpse of the stone foundation of a vanished farmhouse.

Bear left at junction 64, which rejoins Connor's Pond Loop and returns you to the gate on Quaker Dr.

The Roaring Brook Tract is the northern parcel of Brooks Woodland Preserve. The trail begins at a barred gate on the north side of East St., and then divides into numerous interconnecting routes at a series of numbered trail intersections. Oaks, American beech, and other hardwoods common to the transition forest of this region dominate the tract, which includes species associated with both the Northern Hardwood Forest and Central Oak Forest (see **#67**). Large, rotting oak logs, toppled in a violent storm in the 1950s, are widely strewn across the forest floor. A 10-acre swamp (**E**) that lies in the watershed of Roaring Brook was created as a storage pond in colonial times and now serves as habitat for beavers. Of special horticultural interest are specimens of a variant form of eastern hemlock growing in the understory along a stretch of Fiske Rd. at **F**. These low-growing, horizontal shrubs represent genetic variations that are not uncommon for this species. Over one hundred natural variants of hemlock, with a wide range of shapes, sizes, and colors, have been discovered in the wild.

Remarks: *Connor's Pond Loop, with connecting trails, is a 60-minute hike over moderately easy terrain. Other trails in the Swift River Tract connect with hiking routes in three adjoining reservations. To the south of Quaker Dr. lies Rutland Brook Sanctuary, a Massachusetts Audubon Society property. (Entrance is on Route 122 south of the junction with Route 32, at the southern end of Connor's Pond on the left.) To the north of Quaker Dr. is the J. Fiske, Jr. Wildlife Sanctuary (privately owned), with trails providing access to the northern portion of the Swift River Tract. Adjacent to the tract's northeastern corner is the R. F. Johnson Sanctuary (privately owned). The Roaring Brook Tract adjoins several additional reservations. North Common Meadow lies at its southwest corner. This open meadow, owned by the Trustees of Reservations, has frontage on the east side of Main St. (Route 32) in Petersham Center, and is the site of the historic James W. Brooks Law Office. J. and R. C. Fiske Sanctuary is located on the south side of East St., opposite the entrance to Roaring Brook. This privately owned sanctuary has trails connecting with those in the northern portion of the Swift River Tract. Reservations and sanctuaries listed above are open to the general public. The preserve is open all year.*

69.
Elliott
Laurel Reservation

Directions: **Phillipston, Mass. Follow directions in #67 to Petersham town commons; continue north on Route 32 about 1 mile. Turn east (right) onto Route 101; go about 3.6 miles to the reservation sign on the left. Park off the road beside a stone wall bordering the reservation.**

Ownership: **Trustees of Reservations.**

In late spring, the Elliott Laurel Reservation is radiant with the blossoms of eastern mountain laurel. Quiet and secluded, this 33-acre hillside tract in the rural hills of north central Massachusetts occupies

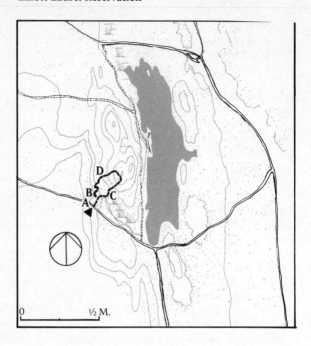

former pasture that has largely reverted to a successional forest of conifers. A short woodland path loops across the western slope of a hill, where old-field white pine, eastern hemlock, and scattered hardwoods shade an understory of luxuriant mountain laurel.

Enter the reservation from the roadside through a gap in the stone wall. A trail sign stands in a small, sunny clearing (**A**) a few steps past the stone wall. Here the bedrock underlying the acidic soil at Elliott Laurel is exposed as flat ledge. Several mature specimens of common juniper grow in the clearing. Familiar relics of former pasture land, the junipers were unpalatable to browsing cattle in the years when the property was used for grazing livestock. These prickly evergreen shrubs have assumed a healthy, spreading form in the sunlight of the clearing. Unlike mountain laurel or eastern hemlock, common juniper is intolerant of shade, which explains its absence in the dark understory on the trail ahead.

Seedlings of tamarack, also called eastern larch, grow in the warm, insulating bed of haircap moss that covers patches of the bedrock ledge. Tamarack is the only native New England conifer to shed its needles in late autumn, their light gray-green color turning vivid yellow before they fall. The delicate conifer is easily identified by its drooping branches, and by the distinctive distribution of its needles in clusters or tufts that radiate in a circular fashion from both spur and leader branches. Once fully mature, these trees can reach heights of 40 to 80 feet.

The presence of tamarack at Elliott Laurel indicates the intermingling of species in this area from two forest regions. Elliott Laurel is situated in a forest transition zone, where plants common to the warmer climate of the more southern Central Oak Forest and the cooler Northern Hardwood Forest overlap (see **#67**). Tamarack, for instance, is abundant in the cool northern forest; here it is close to the southern limit of its range. Typically it prefers dry upland soils, such as those found here; but where tamarack does appear in rare, scattered colonies farther south in the oak forest, it grows in the soggy soils of swamps or bogs in cool inland areas. (Only a few other tree species, such as Atlantic white-cedar, black spruce (see **#11**), and red maple, can tolerate the intensely acidic conditions of a bog.) Two other northern species appear ahead: the striped maple, a very infrequent species in southern New England, and white or paper birch, which is a familiar tree in central New England but far more numerous in the north.

From the clearing the trail leads north, following alongside a stone wall that borders an open field on the right. To the left on this short stretch of the trail (**B**) is Elliott Laurel's most charming natural feature—a dense thicket of mountain laurel. Here the mountain laurel grows along with eastern hemlock (see **#73**), two species that are often found together in central New England. Both are common inhabitants of rocky sites where acidic soil conditions have been created from an underlying bedrock of granite or granite-gneiss.

Mountain laurel is one of New England's most abundant and popular native shrubs. In central Massachusetts it is very common in both southern and northern sections, preferring the region's characteristic upland slopes. It can grow as tall as 13 feet or may compactly hug the ground when young. Sometimes used as ornamental planting, it sprouts vigorously after being cut back to encourage new and fuller growth. A member of the heath family (ericad), this evergreen has glossy, dark-green leaves, which are poisonous to livestock. It often grows in dense thickets such as the one seen here. "Laurel slicks," "heath balds," or "laurel hells" are among the more common terms used to describe these often impenetrable thickets. The mountain laurel's white or pinkish spring blossoms, however, are the feature that have deservedly earned the shrub popular appreciation. At Elliott Laurel the spring bloom peaks about the third week of June, when the forest understory becomes cloaked in a luminous mantle of white-and-pink flowers.

From the thicket the trail emerges into a grove of white pine, where a second trail sign marks a fork in the path. Follow the trail to the right, guided by white blazes painted on tree trunks. The trail at first gradually and then more steeply ascends the boulder-strewn hillside through groves of white pine and hemlock. Finally it reaches a high, flat ledge (**C**), where through a gap in the trees a view to the southeast appears, with purple hills in the distance.

The trail continues along the top of the hill, then quickly descends through the dark understory; mountain laurel and scattered hardwoods, such as red maple, white birch, and oak, grow beneath the high canopy of white pine. About halfway down the slope (**D**), be alert for the distinctive striped maple, easily recognized by its conspicuous bark—very smooth, bright green, and marked by vertical white stripes. A small understory tree or shrub that rarely reaches more than 23 feet in height, the striped maple in southern New England can only be seen where isolated areas of northern vegetation are found (see **#13**). Usually it grows in ravines or other cool sites. The bark is food for deer, beaver, rabbits, and moose. Follow the trail until it rejoins the main trail at the fork and retrace your steps to the road.

Remarks: *The trail is a short, 30-minute walk over moderately easy terrain. Hikers should exercise some caution, however, since the terrain is strewn with numerous small boulders, some of which may be concealed beneath deep mats of conifer needles. White-paint blazes on tree trunks at frequent intervals make the trail easy to follow.*

70.

Great Meadows
National Wildlife Refuge

Directions: **Concord, Mass. From Boston, take I-95 (Route 128) to Exit 46. Go northwest on Route 2 for 5 miles. Turn northeast (right) onto Route 62; go 1.2 miles. Turn left onto Monson Rd. and follow it to the refuge entrance.**

Ownership: **U.S. Fish and Wildlife Service.**

The wetlands and meadows adjoining the historic Concord and Sudbury rivers represent one of the finest bird habitats in inland Massachusetts. Great Meadows National Wildlife Refuge encompasses almost 3,000 acres of this outstanding wildlife area and claims more than two hundred species of migrant and indigenous birds. Upland forest and meadow, river, and freshwater marsh are also habitats for many mammals, including fox, raccoon, squirrel, weasel, cottontail rabbit, white-tailed deer, and an abundant muskrat population. Plant-life at the refuge reflects its primary wetland character, featuring water lilies, duckweed, purple loosestrife, wild iris, American lotus, and cattail, among others.

Great Meadows is located in a historically significant region. Stone Indian artifacts have been recovered in the area, many dating back to 2,000 B.C. A later epoch found early colonial pioneers harvesting hay from the floodplain of the Concord River, before a milldam raised the water level in the early nineteenth century. Subsequently, the submerged floodplain saw increasing numbers of waterfowl inhabiting a major wetland now appreciated by the naturalist and ornithologist. Henry Thoreau, whose famous cabin at Walden Pond stood only a few miles from the present-day refuge, was a frequent explorer of Great Meadows and a student of its animals, birds, and plants.

Great Meadows, which lies just 20 miles from downtown Boston, comprises two separate refuge units that together include 12 miles of frontage on the Concord and Sudbury rivers. The most heavily frequented area within the refuge is a 250-acre tract at the Concord unit, situated about 1 mile from Concord Center. This visitor area encompasses the refuge's original lands, which were acquired in 1944. Extensive trails provide access to a freshwater marsh adjacent to the Concord River, a stretch of the river itself, and abutting wood-lands. Dikes contain the marsh from the river and also serve as trails. A display board at the parking lot features trail routes and topo-graphical maps. Trail leaflets and wildlife checklists are also available at the display board.

The Dike Trail rings the freshwater marsh and affords the best vantage point from which to observe the refuge's many species of waterfowl, as well as the large muskrat population. Follow this trail from the right side of the observation tower that stands on the park-ing lot to the open spaces of the freshwater marsh. The trail runs along the top of a dike that bisects the marsh into two separate pools: the Upper Pool (left) and the Lower Pool (right). During spring and fall migratory periods, these marsh pools provide habitats for large flocks of migrant species. In southern New England, migratory birds tend to follow routes along the Atlantic Coast or the large river valleys. While Great Meadows lies inland, it is close enough to the coastal area to attract birds whose coastal routes find them circling around the urban region of Boston and its suburbs.

Numerous migratory species that breed in New England have been recorded nesting at Great Meadows. The wood duck is a conspicuous nesting species here by virtue of the male's showy, variegated plumage, the most colorful of all ducks in North America. The male in spring and summer has vivid white face markings, a long, square dark tail, a white belly, a chestnut breast, and iridescent wings, with a back of green, purple, blue, and white. In fall and winter it resembles the duller, dark brown female, but retains a distinctive red-and-white bill. These ducks nest in wooden boxes scattered throughout the marsh pools or in hollow stumps or trees, sometimes as high as 60 feet (see **#102** for more on wood ducks). The handsome mallard (see **#41**), recognized by its green head and white neck ring, builds its nest on the ground in reeds or high grasses near the water. The black duck is a familiar, often permanent member of southern New England; both sexes are dark brown, with yellow-brownish heads, violet wing patches, and unmistakable white wing linings visible in flight. Usually nesting away from the water, the black duck hatches its young on the ground in protective grasses or brush. Each of these species is common throughout the marsh at varying times of the year.

The refuge is also popular with long-legged wading birds; great blue herons, green herons, black-crowned night herons, pied-billed grebes, and least and American bitterns have all been observed nesting here. Great blue herons, which may be seen in the summer and fall, are the most abundant. The largest wading bird in the northern states, this elegant heron stands about 4 feet tall, with a wingspread as large as that of an eagle. The long neck, long legs, and sharply pointed bill are typical characteristics of the heron family, but the great blue heron's impressive size and gray-blue coloration are its distinguishing features. While it usually nests in colonies, it will also nest singly.

As you walk along the dike between the marsh pools, look for conical mounds of mud and vegetation protruding above the surface of the water. These are muskrat lodges, ranging in size from 1 to 4 feet high and 5 to 10 feet in diameter. It is unlikely you will see muskrats during daylight hours, for, like beavers, they are nocturnal animals. Dusk is perhaps the best time to observe a muskrat as it ventures outside its lodge to feed in the marsh, or else the early morning hours before it retires for the day. Of all the members of the rodent family, the muskrat is the most aquatic species, seldom leaving the water except to feed occasionally on shore plants. A fascinating creature to watch, the muskrat is best differentiated from the larger beaver by its skinny, vertically flattened tail. Webbed hind feet help it swim with surprising swiftness, and its brown fur prevents water from penetrating to the skin. Muskrats feed on crayfish, snails, fish, and freshwater clams or mussels. The muskrat does not hibernate in winter, but instead enters the water through "plunge holes" in the ice near its lodge. These mammals can stay submerged underwater for up to 12 minutes, foraging for a typical winter diet of nonwoody plants, such as the rootstalks of cattails. Cattails also provide the muskrat with building material for its lodge, which is cemented together with mud. The muskrat digs one or more chambers above the water line in this mound and enters through an underwater hole. Certain waterfowl such as Canada geese, which gather in large numbers at Great Meadows, sometimes build their nests on top of muskrat lodges.

After you have crossed the dike dividing the marsh, a trail sign directs you to the right, where the Dike Trail continues around the edge of the Lower Pool. The trail on the left—marked Concord—follows the Upper Pool. This trail then continues southwest along a portion of the Concord River and leaves the refuge before arriving at Concord's Old North Bridge on Monument St. If you wish, take this trail left as far as the end of the Upper Pool and then retrace your steps back to the Dike Trail as it skirts the edge of the Lower Pool, providing excellent views of waterfowl and muskrat lodges.

Notice the marsh vegetation that grows profusely along this stretch of the trail. American lotus floats on the surface of the marsh, the only place in Massachusetts where its golden blossoms can be seen in such large quantities. The cattails growing in the marsh are a sign of wetland succession to dry ground. As the cattails' rootstalks spread over the water on the edge of a pond or lake, decaying organic material accumulates over the years, trapping silt or other matter. Gradually the shallows of the pond are transformed to an increasingly drier condition, and other forms of vegetation invade the area. The cattails, in turn, are forced to spread farther into the pond or lake.

Two trails branch off from the Dike Trail as it leaves the Lower Pool and the dike behind. The Timber Trail (left) and the Edge Trail (right) both wind through forested areas. The Edge Trail leads back to the parking lot as it wanders through the woodlands bordering the Lower Pool. A photo blind located on the Edge Trail overlooks the marsh. (Hikers can also choose to follow the Dike Trail a short distance beyond its junction with the two branch trails to an access road, where a right-hand turn will take you back to the parking lot.) Once back at the parking lot, the Black Duck Trail may be followed south through a woodland bordering a creek. This is a springtime nesting habitat of the black duck.

Remarks: *The Dike Trail is a 45-minute hike over easy, flat terrain, highly suitable for children. Limited parking at the Concord unit restricts visitor access via motor vehicles on weekends and holidays, especially during peak visitor months. Alternate parking is available off Monument St. in Concord, opposite the Old North Bridge, where a trail leads into the refuge. Great Meadows' Sudbury unit serves as refuge headquarters. A visitors' center features natural history exhibits and wildlife education facilities. A short trail off Weir Hill Rd. in Sudbury traverses an upland forest, with overlooks of the Sudbury River. Directions are available at the Concord unit's visitors' display.*

Nearby Places of Interest

Walden Pond State Reservation, Route 126, south of Concord Center. Here one may hike to the site of Thoreau's cabin.

Minuteman National Historic Park, Concord and Lexington. Visitors' centers are located at the Old North Bridge in Concord (off Monument St.) and off "Battle Rd." (Route 2A East).

71.
Carlisle Pines

Directions: Carlisle, Mass. From Boston, take I-95 (Route 128) to Exit 44. Go northwest on Route 225 for 7 miles to Carlisle Center; continue on Route 225 for 1.5 mile farther. Turn right onto Curve St.; go 0.4 mile. Turn left onto Forest Park Dr., and go to the entrance of Carlisle State Forest at the end of the road. Park off the road on the right.

Ownership: Carlisle State Forest, Massachusetts Division of Forests and Parks.

The Carlisle Pines at Carlisle State Forest in eastern Massachusetts are one of the few ancient stands of enormous white pines that survive in New England today. The twelve white pines that stand in this small, 22-acre preserve are a remnant of a more extensive grove of towering trees that was almost completely destroyed by logging and by the 1938 hurricane (see **#53**). Although few in number, they compare in size with the 150-foot-tall Cathedral Pines in Connecticut (see **#12**) and the 120-foot Fisher-Scott Memorial Pines in Vermont (see **#28**). The Carlisle Pines well exceed 100 feet in height, the tallest measuring 136 feet, with a trunk diameter of 3½ feet.

Like New England's other ancient stands of white pine, the Carlisle Pines are not virgin trees from the precolonial forest. Rather, they represent an unusually early example of old-growth successional forest from the nineteenth century. In a 1980 study, state forest personnel determined the Carlisle Pines to be between 140 and 160 years old. The trees were seeded and became established between 1820 and 1840, a time that witnessed the beginning of agricultural decline in New England and the early succession of abandoned open fields to white-pine forest. The greater part of this old-field white pine was extensively logged for valuable board timber around the turn of the century; much of what remained was toppled in 1938 by the most violent hurricane to strike New England since 1815.

A short, unmarked trail loop begins at the state forest entrance at the end of residential Forest Park Dr. Go left at the fork in the trail a short distance beyond the entrance. The trail dips downhill through a stand of eastern hemlock and white pine. These trees offer a comparison in age and stature with the huge pines that lie ahead. The oldest trees in this stand are generally no more than 50 to 70 years old—a typical age for much of the mature white pine common in the region.

After crossing several stone walls, you will find the first of the Carlisle Pines to the left of the trail. Its straight trunk, which measures about 8 feet in circumference, soars high above the canopy of the forest. Another, even larger pine is visible beyond the first tree, standing farther off the trail on the left. This tree has a trunk circumference of roughly 11 feet.

More of these magnificent trees appear as you walk along the trail. The Carlisle Pines offer a glimpse of how white pine must have looked to seventeenth- and eighteenth-century New England settlers, when precolonial trees commonly stood 150 or more feet high and measured as much as 4 feet in diameter.

Watch for an old eastern hemlock growing on the left side of the trail. It rises 93 feet high and has a trunk diameter of over 3½ feet—the maximum growth range for the species—and it has produced seeds in such great abundance that the forest is now dominated by young hemlocks. This shade-tolerant species will sustain itself here for many generations, long after the sun-loving white pines have vanished.

Soon the trail intersects with a woodland road. Go right and follow the road as it returns to the entrance.

Remarks: *This unmarked but well-defined trail loop is a short, 30-minute hike over easy terrain. A thirteenth Carlisle pine, struck and killed by lightning in 1981, stands still deeper within the state forest. Hiking, horseback riding and cross-country skiing are permitted here throughout the year.*

Nearby Place of Interest

Great Brook Farm State Pond on North St. in Carlisle is a popular, 934-acre state recreation area, with facilities for boating, fishing, hiking, horseback riding, and cross-country skiing. It is open all year.

72.
Mount Monadnock

Directions: **Jaffrey and Dublin, N.H. From Nashua go west on Route 101A, then on Route 101, to Dublin, about 35 miles. Go south (left) on Jaffrey Center Rd., marked by a sign for Mount Monadnock State Park.**

Ownership: **Mount Monadnock State Park, New Hampshire Division of Parks and Recreation; Society for the Protection of New Hampshire Forests; and the town of Jaffrey.**

Grand Monadnock Mountain is the most prominent landmark in central New England, rising 3,165 feet above sea level and 1,500 to 2,000 feet from the surrounding hill country of southwestern New Hampshire. With the exception of Mount Washington, no mountain in New England rivals the fame of Mount Monadnock. For more than a century the mountain has been a popular sightseeing and hiking area, ranking as one of the peaks most frequently climbed in the eastern United States. Historically, it is associated with the names of many nineteenth-century naturalists, artists, and writers, including Henry David Thoreau and Ralph Waldo Emerson. These earlier

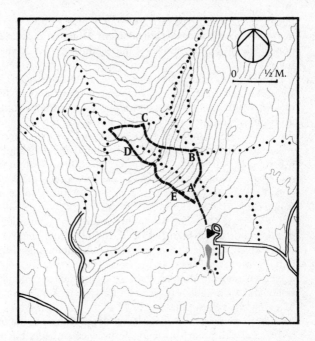

explorers, like the tens of thousands who now visit Mount Monadnock annually, marveled at its splendid vistas, its rich plant and bird life, and most of all, the stark grandeur of its ice-scarred cliffs, boulder-strewn ledges, and gaunt, treeless summit.

Mount Monadnock is visible on clear days from numerous points across Massachusetts, southern Vermont, and New Hampshire. Its prominent silhouette, rising above the horizon of endless hilltops on the eastern upland of central New England, has endured the centuries of erosion that reduced the surrounding landscape to a rolling terrain of small hills and narrow river valleys. Mount Monadnock is a classic example of an isolated mountain of resilient rock that stands above the eroded surface of an upland. Indeed, geologists have borrowed its name to describe other solitary mountains that share a similar geological history. For instance, the central New England upland features a number of scattered "monadnocks" which, like Grand Monadnock, are remnants of much larger ancient mountains created more than 1 million years ago in a period of major earth upheaval. Some of these smaller monadnocks are visible from Mount Monadnock's summit, including its close eastern neighbor, the 2,280-foot Pack Monadnock, and 2,006-foot Wachusett Mountain in northern Massachusetts. (See **#65** and **White Mountains, Monadnocks, and Eastern Connecticut Highlands** for a description of the geological history of the central New England monadnocks.)

Mount Monadnock offers over 20 miles of hiking trails, including summit routes on all sides. (There is no motor road to the top.) The majority of the trails are located on its southern slope, originating from the site of the former halfway house (no longer standing) at the end of the abandoned motor road, and on the eastern slope, where the most popular trails begin at the parking area for Mount Monadnock State Park. The trails described here, beginning at the state park, include an ascent along the first portion of the Cascade Link Trail and the Red Spot Trail, and a descending route over the White Cross Trail and Spruce Link Trail.

The Cascade Link Trail is a gradual ascent along the eastern slope of the mountain. It branches off the White Cross and White Dot trails (which run together at the base of the mountain) at the junction known as the Falcon Spring Trail Center (**A**), located about half a mile beyond the starting point at the Ecocenter building in the state park. Turn right at the sign for Cascade Link at Falcon Spring, following the yellow dots.

The trail climbs gently up the lower slopes of the mountain, which is forested with mixed lowland species such as paper birch, white ash, red oak, sugar maple, and red maple, as well as young red spruce and older yellow birch. This variety reflects the milder climate at the lower altitudes of the mountain. It also represents the New England forest of brilliant autumn color, which, from the summit of Monadnock, forms a breathtaking tapestry of red and gold across the outlying lowland in early October. Some of the trees here also reveal past disturbances to the forest. In the late eighteenth century Monadnock's lower slopes were cleared of timber and turned into sheep pasture. After the pastures were abandoned in the mid-1800s, the lower slopes were reforested, but the second-growth trees below 2,000 feet were logged in the early years of this century. More recently, the 1938 hurricane (see **#53**), the worst storm to strike New England since 1815, devastated the exposed woodlands on the southern and eastern slopes. A fire in the state park in 1953 caused further damage. The attractive grove of paper birch on the first portion of the Cascade Link grew up in the wake of these recent disturbances. This sun-loving tree often invades open spaces after storms or fire, and is a good indicator of forest disturbances in this region.

As you continue up the trail, the composition of the forest undergoes noticeable changes. By the time you reach the 2,000-foot elevation near the point where the Birchtoft Trail appears on the right, the diverse hardwoods of the lower slope have largely been supplanted by abundant red spruce (see **#75** and **#99**) and yellow birch. These northern species are the dominant trees on the middle slopes at elevations between 2,000 and 2,500 feet. They are joined by typical understory vegetation common to northern forests, such as mountain and striped maples (see **#13**). The yellow birch seen here is a major component of the northern forest and one of the largest hardwoods in the North Woods. In colonial times some trees were reported to have stood over 100 feet high. It is the most hardy, shade-tolerant, and long-lived of the birches. The young yellow birches have curly bark that is a lustrous yellowish-gray. The bark of older trees is reddish-brown and furrowed.

Shortly after the Cascade Link encounters the Birchtoft Trail, it meets the Red Spot Trail (a portion of which includes the Old Ski Trail) on the left at **B.** Leave the Cascade Link and follow the Red Spot Trail (marked with white and red spots) as it begins a steeper and more direct ascent to the summit up the eastern slope. It weaves up a succession of rock ledges that serve as fine eastern overlooks at heights between 2,200 and 2,500 feet. A prominent landmark, Thorndike Pond, lies below you at 1,159 feet (about 1 mile northeast of the state park).

Pick your way over the large heaped boulders that dominate the steep terrain on the last portion of the Red Spot Trail. These boulders were wrenched by glacial ice from ledges during the Ice Age 30,000 years ago, or in some instances were loosened by frost action (see **#80**).

As you pass the 2,500-foot elevation, the dense vegetation that cloaks the middle slopes begins to thin out. Soon you enter the scrub zone of the upper slope, where soil and plants become increasingly sparse among the bedrock ledges. Notice how the vegetation becomes shrubby and stunted. The sparse dry soil and the shearing wind limit plantlife in the scrub zone to the hardiest species. Red spruce is by far the dominant plant in the scrub zone, ranging between 50 and 70 years of age across the upper slopes. Yet many of these spruce are no more than shrub-size because of the high wind exposure. As you climb through the scrub zone, watch for shrubs including mountain cranberry, low sweet blueberry, rhodora, withe bush, bush honeysuckle, black chokeberry, and mountain winterberry. Some of these, such as cranberry and rhodora (see **#74**), also manage to live in the wet, boggy areas on the treeless summit cone.

Before you leave the belt of red spruce ringing the upper slopes, the mountain's bare rock summit will appear ahead. Prior to 1800 this gaunt rock peak was completely forested with mature red spruce. But in 1800 a smoldering fire consumed the organic soil across the summit and the spruce were felled. (The great hurricane of 1815, which was comparable in force to that of 1938, may also have flattened some of the spruce.) Then, according to legend, the dense tangle of fallen timber was set on fire in 1820 to drive out timber wolves that had sought haven on the summit while raiding sheep on the lower slopes. This tremendous fire completely engulfed the summit cone, stripping it of timber and its remaining soil. As we have seen, the upper slopes of the mountain have been partially reforested by scrub vegetation, but the summit today remains barren except for mosses, lichens, and small alpine plants. Thousands of years must pass for decaying rock and organic matter from decomposed small plants to produce enough soil for trees to take root. In its history of catastrophic fires, as well as timber cutting and land clearing, Monadnock can truly be said to stand for all New England's mountains, which to varying degrees have suffered disturbances of their forests since European colonization.

Soon the Red Spot Trail joins the Pumpelly Trail at **C,** which leads over the last several hundred feet to the summit. (Paint blazes and rock cairns mark the route.) At the summit you can enjoy a commanding panorama of the surrounding countryside. Vermont's Green Mountains stand on the distant western horizon, while the Massachusetts Berkshires appear in the southwest (see **Taconics, Berkshires, and Green Mountains**). To the north lie New Hampshire's White Mountains, and in the south the merging hilltops of the central New England upland extend into the distance like a flat plain.

From the summit you can also appreciate some of the physical features of the mountain itself. Most noticeable is the large, bowllike depression that dips from the summit and rises again at the northernmost prominence of Pumpelly Ridge. This depressed ridgeline represents what geologists call a "fold," a bend in the rock that occurred after it was formed. Mount Monadnock was originally composed of sedimentary rock that was laid down 400 million years ago when the region lay beneath an ocean. The horizontal layers of mud and sand deposited in the ancient ocean bed eventually became hard rock. Great compressional forces within the earth, caused by the upwelling of molten granite from the earth's center, resulted in the folding of the sedimentary rock layers. The heat and pressure accompanying the compressional forces also transformed the sedimentary rock itself, changing it into metamorphic quartzite and schist.

On the southeast side of the summit are paint markers pointing the way to the state park. Pick up the trail identified by white crosses and white dots as you descend the open ledges. For some distance the White Cross and White Dot trails run together down the eastern slope. Take the White Cross Trail as it branches away to the right at **D,** which along the upper slopes offers fine views to the southeast. This trail also features stands of American mountain-ash. This showy tree bears large clusters of bright red berries in the fall, which give it a rather exotic appearance. On Monadnock's heights the mountain-ash grows only to the size of a large shrub, but in some regions it can reach 30 feet.

The Spruce Link Trail appears on the right at **E** as you near the end of the White Cross Trail. This short connecting route leads through a pure stand of red spruce on the lower slope. Note the many spruce seedlings that are thriving in the deep shade cast by the taller trees. Unlike many conifers such as white pine, the red spruce is very tolerant of shade, and young seedlings can grow to healthy maturity in the dark understory. Spruce forests like this one are far more common in the Far North where the climate is harsh. This tree's ability to withstand a cold climate and poor soils explains its presence on high, exposed mountain slopes.

Follow the Spruce Link as it reconnects with the combined White Cross and White Dot trails, which shortly return you to the parking lot.

Remarks: *The ascent via the Cascade Link and Red Spot trails takes about 2½ hours. The descent via the White Arrow and Spruce Link trails is about 2 hours. Allow 5 hours for the round trip, with a 30-minute pause on the summit. The terrain is steep, rocky, and strenuous, but not extremely difficult for reasonably fit hikers. The rocks are slippery after rain, and hikers are advised to wear sturdy, gripping footwear. During warm-weather months the high winds that frequently arise on the mountain can be cold and raw, and climbers should consider carrying light, windproof clothing. Mount Monadnock is open throughout the year. The Monadnock Ecocenter, located at the start of the trails in the state park, provides information about geology, natural history, and trails. It is open from mid-June to October. Queries can be addressed to Monadnock State Park, Jaffrey Center, N.H. 03453; (603) 532-8035. Monadnock State Park has 21 campsites. Write to the address above or call (603) 532-8862. Greenfield State Park, Greenfield, is located north of Mount Monadnock on Route 136, 1 mile west of Greenfield Center. It has 252 campsites, swimming, pond fishing, and boating, and is open from May to October. For information telephone (603) 547-3497. The Society for the Protection of New Hampshire Forests, which operates the Ecocenter, also publishes the most current, comprehensive guide to the mountain,* Monadnock Guide, *by Henry Baldwin. Write to the society at 5 South State St., Concord, N.H. 03301. Maps showing the main trails are available at the state park. More comprehensive trail maps are included in the* AMC White Mountain Guide.

73.

Beaver Brook
Natural Area

Directions: **Hollis, N.H. From Nashua, take Route 130 west about 7 miles to Hollis. Turn south (left) onto Route 122; go 1 mile. Turn right onto Ridge Rd.; go 0.7 mile. Turn right onto Brown Lane and follow it to the office and barn at the end.**

Ownership: **Beaver Brook Association.**

Beaver Brook lies in the gentle hills, woodlands, and fields of the southern New Hampshire countryside. This roughly 1,800-acre woodland reservation serves as an outdoor laboratory for forestry and wildlife management, and as a "living campus" for environmental education. Although the greater portion of the reservation is used for forestry and wildlife management, a 20-acre tract has been set aside as an undisturbed natural area. It features a self-guiding nature trail that displays the native plants and geological features of a representative central New England woodland.

The nature trail begins behind the farmhouse opposite the barn. The trail is identified by a sign, and throughout its length is posted with a series of numbered markers. It initially runs through a small portion of a wildlife management area, with an apple orchard and small groves of mixed hardwoods, hemlock, and white pine. It arrives in a mature woodland at **A**, where hemlock and white pine are the dominant trees. By now the trail (after passing trail marker 37) has entered the natural area at Beaver Brook and begins a descent across a steep slope and cliff. This high ridge forms the east side of Beaver Brook valley, which lies below you on the right. The bedrock ledges on each side of the trail are composed of an ancient rock called siltstone. Several hundred million years ago this region lay beneath an ancient sea. Over the centuries silt settled at the bottom of the sea and eventually was compressed into solid sedimentary rock. Approximately 100 million years later this rock was altered by heat and pressure in the earth's crust and transformed into metamorphic rock. Over thousands of years the valley you see today was carved by natural erosion as the ancient ancestor of Beaver Brook flowed over the land's surface, wearing away the topsoil and finally the bedrock itself. During the Ice Age the glacial ice that flowed through the valley abraded the cliffs, which were further eroded by torrential postglacial meltwaters that streamed through the valley as the climate warmed some 12,000 to 15,000 years ago. More recently, the action of frost has loosened rocks in the ledges and sent them tumbling to the base of the cliff.

The white pine and hemlock growing on the slope are about 100 years old. They are the most common conifers in the central New England forest, though their ecological roles are quite different. The eastern or Canada hemlock is a species of cool, moist areas, usually found growing on north- or west-facing slopes like this one, where the sunlight is indirect. The white pine is at the center of its natural range in southern New Hampshire; here it grows under a variety of conditions, ranging from shallow, porous soils to deep, moist loams. Unlike hemlock, it can tolerate very dry conditions, but its seedlings cannot mature in the shade like those of hemlock. Hemlock will thus perpetuate itself here indefinitely, while the white pine will largely disappear from the slope as these trees die off. As seedlings they probably benefitted from more abundant sunlight at a time when the land was more open (see **#12, #28,** and **#71**).

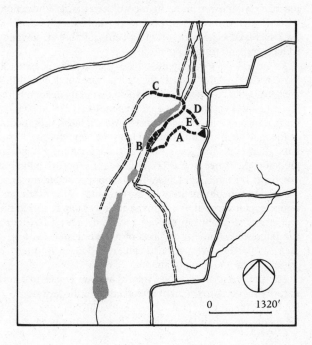

The trail gradually descends about 100 feet below the top of the ridge to the present floodplain of Beaver Brook. Here it briefly leaves the natural area and enters a forest management area (at trail marker 73) where silvicultural practices are in evidence. You soon enter a white-pine grove growing in an area that was a potato field about half a century ago. The pines are numbered for purposes of pruning and thinning to produce a timber stand of commercial value.

Follow the trail as it winds southwestward to the edge of a swampy wetland (**B**) adjoining Beaver Brook. This wetland, known as Beaver Meadow, was flooded by a beaver dam as recently as 1983. However, unauthorized trapping of the beavers reduced their numbers so that they no longer maintained the mud-and-stick dam, and the pond dried up. The beaver is the only mammal that can appreciably manipulate the natural environment to form a suitable habitat for itself. Their dams create ponds that provide them with aquatic food and with protection from predators. Beavers are likely to return to this area soon from other ponds at the reservation. Then the pond at Beaver Meadows will doubtless reappear.

The trail swings northeastward and weaves across low ground between the stream on the left and the bottom of the cliff on the right. On the sides of the path grow bunchberry and clintonia, two northern wildflowers more frequently seen in the White Mountains than in this region. Small evergreen plants also appear along the trail, such as checkerberry (wintergreen), goldthread, dewberry, partridgeberry, and fringed polygala.

As the trail passes along the base of the slope, notice the rubble of loose rocks, or talus, which has fallen from the ledges. This rocky area is a habitat for porcupines, which den in the ledges. Porcupines prefer hemlocks as food, and are sometimes seen aloft in high branches during the daytime. Loggers consider porcupines a nuisance because of the damage they can inflict on trees by eating twigs and stripping bark. However, the resurgence of the porcupine's major natural predator, the fisher (see **#51**), may help to control the population. The fisher is a large, minklike weasel whose population was severely reduced in agricultural times by the clearance of the extensive forests it requires for survival. For many years it was found only in northern wilderness areas, but in the last several decades it has returned to the reforested southern portions of New England. In some timber areas of the Far West it has been reintroduced by foresters as a natural control on the porcupine.

The trail joins a woodland road that soon comes to a fork. The nature trail bears to the right on its return to the farmhouse. On the left a woodland road leads across Beaver Brook into a forest management area where an unusually fine stand of hardwoods grows on a slope at **C**. A short walk along this road is worthwhile, for the wide variety of hardwoods in this stand are between 80 and 160 years old. The species here include red, white, black, and chestnut oak as well as shagbark hickory, pignut hickory, basswood, white ash, and beech. There are also red and sugar maples, as well as black, yellow, and paper birches. Most of these trees were defoliated by the gypsy moth caterpillar in the summer of 1981. That year witnessed the worst infestation of this harmful insect since it was accidentally introduced into New England's forests early in the century. In the larval or caterpillar stage, the gypsy moth favors a diet of oak leaves. But at the peak of the cyclical population explosion in 1981, it consumed the foliage of other species as well. The least hardy of the broad-leaved trees succumbed to the gypsy moth attack, but perhaps the insect's worst damage to healthy individual trees was its defoliation of needle-bearing conifers like hemlock and white pine. Unlike deciduous trees, these evergreens could not produce new foliage in the same year they were defoliated. Lacking the needles required for photosynthesis, the conifers had little chance for survival. A number of old hemlocks killed by the gypsy moth still stand here along the path, though they are gradually being cut and removed.

Follow the trail until a grove of white pine appears, and then retrace your steps back across Beaver Brook and go straight on the nature trail as it heads southeastward on its return to the office. As you ascend the slope of the woodland road, an attractive mixed forest (**D**) has excellent specimens of white oak, pignut hickory, red maple, alternate-leaf dogwood, hophornbeam (see **#1**), and on the right, tall white pines.

The trail shortly skirts a fencerow (**E**) bordering an open field on the right. Here grow many species typical of sunny edges along fields or open farm roads, such as arrowwood, witch-hazel, barberry, black alder, butternut, and flowering dogwood. Follow the road along the fencerow as it returns to the barn and office.

Remarks: *The nature trail is a 1-hour hike over relatively gentle terrain, with only a few steep slopes and high grades. A comprehensive interpretive trail booklet, including map, is keyed to the 127 trail markers along the route. It is available at the office on Brown's Lane for a small fee. A large map of the reservation is posted at the parking area in front of the office. The trail is open all year. Hiking, horseback riding, cross-country skiing, and snowshoeing are permitted. Beaver Brook's facilities at Brown Lane (office and renovated barn) house a natural science library and a collection of mounted birds, small mammals, rocks, insects, and botanical specimens. The office is open Monday through Friday from 9:00 a.m. to 12:00 p.m., throughout the year. Maple Hill Farm is Beaver Brook's horticultural facility. This scenic New England farm, located on Ridge Road a short distance south of Brown Lane, has large gardens and a wildflower trail. An exhibit barn is used for demonstrations, shows, and summer programs in nature studies for elementary school children. A horticultural library is housed in a former cooper's shop on the premises. Beaver Brook is a nonprofit educational corporation supported by private funds. For more information concerning special programs, nature tours, and scheduled events, as well as opportunities for environmental studies, contact Beaver Brook Association, P.O. Box 34, Hollis, N.H. 03049; (603) 465-7787.*

74.
Ponemah Bog
Botanical Preserve

Directions: **Amherst, N.H. From Nashua, take Route 101A west about 7 miles. Turn north onto Route 122; take the first right onto Stearns Rd., and follow it to the refuge sign on the right. Turn right at the sign and park at the gate.**

Ownership: **Audubon Society of New Hampshire.**

Ponemah Bog is an exceptional example of one of nature's most fascinating ecosystems, the sphagnum bog. On this roughly 100-acre preserve in southern New Hampshire, a boardwalk circles an open bog surrounding a small pond. The boardwalk provides an excellent opportunity for observing an unusual array of plants.

Compared with freshwater marshes or other types of wetlands, the sphagnum bog supports a relatively narrow range of plants because of its intense acidity and shortage of vital plant nutrients (see #76). Bog plants are specially adapted to its marginal conditions for growth. They include species that are found in no other natural habitat, such as the insectivorous pitcher plant. Here, too, are coastal pitch pine and various alpine shrubs, whose ecological requirements allow them to succeed in bogs outside their normal geographical ranges and more common habitats.

A short trail leading to the bog originates to the left of a small picnic shelter at the end of the entrance road. It soon drops down an embankment to the boardwalk at the edge of the bog. Along this

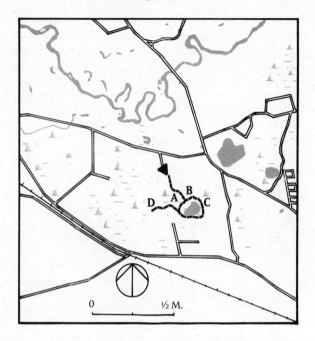

0   ½ M.

stretch of the boardwalk (**A**) grow four members of the American heath family. Heaths prosper in acidic, sterile soils that are unfavorable to most other plants. They are so characteristic of bogs that the term "heath bog" is often used interchangeably with "sphagnum bog" or "peat bog."

One of the most adaptable of the heaths is highbush blueberry, which is also common to moist woodlands, shrub swamps, and lakeshores. Its twisting stems grow 3 to 10 feet high, and its smooth, elliptical green leaves turn brilliant scarlet before dropping in the fall. Its purple berries, which are eaten by many songbirds, appear in late summer.

Also seen here is bog rosemary, a low heath shrub that only reaches a height of 20 inches. Its narrow leaves with rolled edges are blue-green above and whitish underneath. Small, bell-shaped white or pink flowers droop in clusters from the stems.

Two heaths that grow both in bogs and in the alpine zone of northern New England are leatherleaf and rhodora. In their mountain habitat at elevations above the tree line, an almost constant wind produces arid conditions. To conserve moisture the plants have evolved a small leaf to resist dehydration. This adaptation rather surprisingly allows the plants to survive in bogs. Although the bog is saturated with water, its intense acidity makes it difficult for most plants to absorb moisture. However, it allows alpine plants to grow at low elevations by providing them with an insulated microclimate that remains cool throughout the year. The evergreen leatherleaf has elliptical leaves and grows 3 feet high. In early spring it sends out urn-shaped white flowers, which are distributed in rows at the ends of the stems, with each flower opposite a tiny leaf. Rhodora, too, is a low shrub, but its gray-green leaves are deciduous. It has showy, magenta flowers that bloom in late spring.

Look for the pitch pine growing to your left at **B**, where the boardwalk nears the perimeter of the open bog mat. A common conifer across the dry, sandy barrens of Cape Cod and the northeastern Coastal Plain, pitch pine seems an unlikely member of the wet bog community. Yet in the nutrient-poor bog, it finds an environment that is not totally dissimilar to the sterile soils of the coastal sand plain. It occurs regularly in bogs in the southern portions of northern New England where, like the drought-tolerant alpine plants, it tolerates acidic conditions. Also watch for tamarack trees along this stretch of the boardwalk. The tamarack, or eastern larch, easily recognized by its pale lime-green needles, is a common conifer in northern bogs (see **#69**).

At the edge of the open bog mat on the northern side of the pond, go left as the boardwalk branches in two directions. At the eastern edge of the bog, a large colony of pitcher plants appears to the right of the boardwalk (**C**). The insectivorous pitcher plant captures insects to obtain vital nutrients lacking in the bog. Its hollow purple leaves are tubular, or pitcher-shaped, and contain a mixture of water and sticky fluid that attracts insects. The small, down-pointing hairs on the inside of the leaves allow the insects to enter but prevent escape. The insects soon drown in the liquid, and their soft body parts are absorbed by the leaves of the plant.

This area of the bog mat is carpeted with various shrubs and wildflowers, including bog rosemary, swamp loosestrife, and cranberry. The water willow seen here (it is not related to the willow family) is an especially attractive wildflower. Reaching 1 to 2 feet high, with willowlike, upright leaves, it bears small white flowers with purple markings in summer. It is also found in marshes, lakes, and streams.

Black spruce grow all around the perimeter of the bog. This species, also called bog or swamp spruce, is the most common bog tree in northern New England. Anchoring themselves in the bog mat, its roots often never touch the mineral soil underlying the water and peat. It frequently reproduces by "layering": notice how the lower branches of the larger trees have taken root in the bog mat, thus producing one or more smaller seedlings around them. In time a growing colony of black spruce will spread across the bog mat, and later it may occupy the entire wetland. The existing open-water pond may become completely engulfed by the encroaching bog mat as it creeps inward from the shores, providing a platform on which the black spruce can grow. (See #11 for more on black spruce.)

At **D** a short side trail leads through an area where the process of bog succession is more advanced and the open water has become completely overspread by the bog mat. The scattered black spruce trees you see here will someday form a dense stand of bog forest. Ultimately, this forest will thoroughly dry out, which will allow it to support more diversified vegetation, like the red maples and other hardwoods that are common in the surrounding upland and the region as a whole.

Retrace your steps back to the main boardwalk, and follow it around the western edge of the pond to the fork. Go left to join the trail that leads back to the entrance road.

Remarks: *The boardwalk is a 60-minute circuit over flat, sodden terrain. Portions of the boardwalk are spongy and sink slightly under human weight. During rainy periods it may become too wet for comfortable hiking. Hikers are advised to wear waterproof footwear and should refrain from straying off the boardwalk. The preserve is open all year. There is camping nearby at Greenfield State Park on Route 136, 1 mile west of Greenfield Center. From Ponemah take Route 101 south from Amherst and follow it west to Route 31 north in Wilton. Take Route 31 to Greenfield Center.*

75.

Paradise Point
Nature Center and Sanctuary and
Hebron Marsh Wildlife Preserve

Directions: **Hebron, N.H. From Concord, take I-93 north about 30 miles to Exit 23. Follow Route 104 west for 6 miles to Bristol. Turn north (right) onto Route 3A; go about 8 miles to East Hebron, then continue about 1 mile farther.**

Turn left onto the northern shore road for Newfound Lake; go west 1 mile to the Paradise Point Nature Center on the left. For Hebron Marsh, continue west from Paradise Point for 1 mile and turn left onto a dirt road beyond the red cottage. Park on the roadside near the refuge sign.

Ownership: Audubon Society of New Hampshire.

Situated on the north shore of Newfound Lake in northern New Hampshire, the 44-acre Paradise Point Nature Center and Sanctuary embraces 3,000 feet of rocky, unspoiled lakeshore bounded by a mature northern forest of hemlock, red spruce, and white pine. The nearby Hebron Marsh Wildlife Preserve borders a freshwater marsh occupying the lake's northwest corner. These two reservations, with their contrasting wildlife habitats of northern forest and treeless wetland, reflect the diverse ecology of a northern New England lake.

Paradise Point, which serves as a summer nature educational facility, has five self-guiding interpretive trails. The Swamp Trail leads from the nature education building adjacent to the driveway through a forest dominated by eastern hemlock, red spruce, and white pine. Hemlocks are the most abundant species here, and the most mature individuals, averaging 150 years old, may be remnants of a virgin stand. Although there is evidence of timber cutting here in both the distant and the more recent past, probably only selected white pines and red spruces were logged. Take note of the hemlocks' exceptional height and the absence of lower branches due to natural pruning by wind and friction. These characteristics are typical of old forest trees.

The trail soon weaves along the edge of a small lowland swamp where red spruce and red maple are numerous. The red spruce is the most common variety of spruce in the White Mountain region. It is also one of the most adaptable trees in the forest, thriving on rocky soils along lower mountain slopes, where it mingles with hemlock and northern hardwoods like beech, maple, and birch, as well as at high elevations just below mountain timberlines, where it is often joined by balsam fir. The red spruce occurs farther south than any other spruce, growing above 3,500 feet in Virginia and 4,500 feet in the mountains of North Carolina and Tennessee.

As the trail mounts a slight rise, look for two huge white pine trees posted as the "Alcott and Helen Elwell Pines." These beautiful straight-trunked trees, which are the oldest pines in the stand, have been estimated to be about 175 years old. Such ancient specimens are rare in New England, where white pine is a highly valued timber tree. In mountainous northern New England white pines inhabit lowland valleys, where they often grow around lakes. Because of their great height, those trees near water are sometimes struck by lightning. Several white pines thus injured and killed can be seen ahead after the trail swings eastward to follow the lakeshore. (See **#12**, **#28**, and **#71** for more on old-age white pines.)

Go left as the path reaches a high, forested bank overlooking the water and then winds through the trees on a parallel course to the rocky shore. While enjoying the view of the lake to the right, you may also observe the rich birdlife. Families of common merganser may be seen in the water along the shore. This diving duck, which often behaves like a loon, can disappear for minutes at a time underwater. The males may be distinguished by their green heads and orange beaks, the females by their reddish heads and crowns. Watch for northern woodland birds among the trees, including the Blackburnian warbler, northern waterthrush, dark-eyed junco, golden-crowned kinglet, and pileated woodpecker.

Follow the trail as it runs along the shore until it reaches the beach in front of the nature center, and then ascend the gradual slope to the parking area.

Hebron Marsh Wildlife Preserve features an observation tower with views across the open marshlands on the northwest side of Newfound Lake. Walk across the open field from the refuge sign at the roadside to the woodlands that separate the field and marshes. An unmarked but well-defined path leads from the edge of the field through a narrow woodland swamp to the observation tower. Climb the steps to the open platform at the top of the tower.

Lake marshes develop in shallow areas where a slow current allows aquatic vegetation to creep out from the shore into the open water. One of the most common marsh mammals is the muskrat (see **#70**), which has built here its characteristic rounded lodges of cattails and grasses. Muskrats eat rootstalks, seeds, fish, and mussels. They are usually active at night, but in the early morning or twilight hours the wake of a muskrat may signal its presence in calm water.

Marshes are also important feeding grounds for many species of waterfowl. Migratory black ducks, mallards, and other species may be observed in the marsh during their spring and fall migrations.

Pause here and enjoy the view of the marsh, and then retrace your steps to the road.

Remarks: *Paradise Point Nature Center and Sanctuary is open from late June to Labor Day. The Swamp Trail is about a 45-minute hike over easy terrain, with some moderate grades and large rocks. Interpretive pamphlets for the self-guiding trails are available at the nature center, which also houses indoor exhibits. Hebron Marsh Wildlife Preserve is open all year. Binoculars are necessary for satisfying bird and wildlife observation. The marshlands themselves are property of the town of Hebron, which permits duck hunting in season. No hunting is allowed in the preserve.*

76.

Heath Pond Bog

Directions: **Ossipee, N.H. From Concord Take U.S. 4 and 202 east 11 miles. Take Route 28 northeast (left) about 45 miles. Turn north (left) on Route 16 for about 5 miles. Turn northeast (right) onto Route 25 and go 2 miles to a parking area on the right at the edge of the bog. A boulder with a bronze marker indicates the beginning of the short loop trail.**

Ownership: **New Hampshire Division of Parks.**

Northeast of Lake Winnepesaukee, and south of the peaks of the White Mountains, is an outstanding example of one of northern New England's most distinctive ecological communities: the quaking sphagnum bog. Beautiful and unspoiled, Heath Pond Bog has been designated a National Natural Landmark. It is located at the edge of Route 25 and is easily accessible by a short trail.

This Ossipee Lakes and Mountains region of New Hampshire has a rich geological history that was heavily influenced by the most recent glacial age about 12,000 to 60,000 years ago. Like most northern bogs, Heath Pond is located in a kettle hole, a deep, steep-sided depression formed when a large chunk of ice broke off from the retreating glacier and became embedded in the glacial till deposited by the meltwaters. As the once mile-thick sheet of ice melted, other sands and gravels that were embedded in it settled on top of the isolated chunk of ice, covering it and keeping the water frozen for many years after the retreat of the main ice sheet. As the climate warmed and the ice block melted, the soft glacial till, often of granitic origin, surrounding the ice block was formed into the shape of the block, thus accounting for the depth and steepness of the kettle hole. Eventually the ice melted completely and a pond was formed. The surrounding lands once again became vegetated with both southern and northern (or boreal) plants, the latter having been pushed south by the glacier. Many of these plants remain in bog communities such as this today, remnants of a time when the New England climate was significantly cooler.

Primary among this vegetation are the trees surrounding the pond: predominately spruce and tamarack (see **#69**), with a few silver maples scattered throughout. The vegetation on the edge of the kettle-hole pond played a major role in its development into a bog. Like most kettle-hole ponds, Heath Pond Bog does not have an outflow of water from the pond; the water has very little oxygen content and becomes acidic. As a result, decaying vegetation from the nearby trees does not decompose as it would in a wetland environment with more oxygen, such as a stream-fed swamp or pond. This decaying organic matter builds up in the kettle hole and eventually forms a mat of peat that floats on the surface. As the bog mat becomes established, it becomes thick enough to support vegetation, including trees, and grows in both area and thickness as dying plants add to the mat. Sphagnum moss, a soft-looking, spongy material, is often the dominant surface vegetation in bogs, as it is here at Heath Pond (see #103). Growing out of the sphagnum are many plants that are found only in the low-nutrient, acidic waters of the bog: orchids, leatherleaf, bay laurel, rosemary, sedges, insectivorous plants, and many plants of the heath family (see #74). From late spring to midsummer, many of these plants bloom in a diverse array of colors.

As the mat of sphagnum moss grows, it covers the open surface of the water and moves the evolutionary process of bog development toward the point where the water will be completely covered. From the lookout area along the trail, you can see that the open-water area is very small, surrounded by the thick, quaking mat of sphagnum. Eventually, the entire area will form a firm layer of peat, capable of supporting a dense growth of shrubs and trees. Much of Canada, Russia, and Scandinavia is covered with bogs in all stages of succession, and the commercial use of peat for fuel and fertilizer (see #103) is a centuries-old tradition.

Fortunately, Heath Pond Bog is protected from development, so that the slow process of bog development and eventual disappearance can be observed.

Remarks: *A short, looping half-mile trail follows the edge of the bog, leading from the parking area and returning there. All of the trail is on firm ground, although there are some areas of the bog mat that can be explored with waterproof footwear. Allow about 1 hour for a visit. Black flies and mosquitoes are abundant in spring and early summer, so be prepared with repellent.*

77.

Pine River

Esker

Directions: Ossipee, N.H. From Concord take U.S. 4 and 202 east 11 miles. Take Route 28 northeast (left) about 45 miles. Turn south (right) onto Route 16 and go 2.7 miles to the old entrance road to the abandoned Summer Brook Fish Hatchery on the left side of the highway. Park here and walk a short distance on the entrance road to the old fish pools at A.

Ownership: New Hampshire Division of Fish and Wildlife.

Eskers and their related glacial formations—kames, kame terraces, and crevasse deposits—are among the most common surface features in central New England. The Pine River esker is one of the largest esker systems in New Hampshire, and is well known among geologists for its length, 7 miles, and its height of 120 feet. Although a portion of the esker has been destroyed by development, it is still an outstanding example of glacial land formation, with a variety of vegetation on the site including some of the largest red and white pine trees in the state. In fact, the destruction of a middle portion of the esker provides a good "cutaway" view of its shape and allows close examination of the fine sand and gravel that make up the formation.

An esker is a long, winding ridge shaped like an inverted V that was formed when caverns deep in the glacial ice were filled with sediments carried by the glacier's meltwaters. As the mile-thick ice sheet of the Wisconsin glacier began to melt about 20,000 years ago, the waters cut tunnels deep within the ice and large icebound river systems were formed. In the meltwater were the sediments—sand, clay, and gravel—that had been picked up and carried by the glacier over the previous 40,000 years. As the waters rushed through these tunnels with great force, the clay-based materials tended to stay suspended in the water, while the sands and gravels dropped to the bottom, eventually filling up the tunnels.

The pressure of the meltwater's flow and the ice breaking up also caused large cracks, or crevasses, to form. These were usually at right angles to the main flow, and they also filled up with meltwater

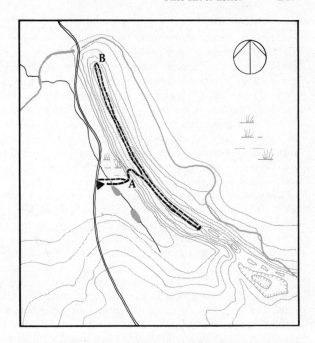

sediments, forming smaller ridges known as crevasse deposits. The nearby kames, scattered among these deposits, are small rounded hills formed by glacial deposits that filled cavities in the ice. They generally contain some clays as well as sand. Kame terraces, also part of the esker system, are broad, elevated plains, usually running parallel to the esker. They were formed by the buildup of deposits in a lake created by the meltwaters at the edge of the melting ice mass. Kame terraces are not as high as the esker, and usually border a river or stream that was formed as a result of glacial action.

All of these glacial features are easily distinguishable at the base of the esker at the end of the entrance road (**A**). Stretching away from the esker itself are the long, low crevasse deposits, the rounded kames, and the plateaulike kame terrace. From this vantage point it is easy to see how these formations are all interconnected, and how they were formed when the ice mass rose a mile high over this spot.

Also at this point are some fine examples of old-age mixed pines, which grow well in the dry, sandy soil of the esker. The towering 125-foot white pine here (**A**) may be the tallest in New Hampshire, although at 250 years old it is probably not the oldest. On the other side of the concrete fish pools and a short way up the path stand some very old red pines, approximately 200 years old and 30 inches in diameter. The third species of large pine here is the pitch pine. These do not grow as large nor live as long as the other two species, usually about 150 years compared with 200 and 300 years respectively for the white and red pines. The easiest way to distinguish these three types of pines from each other is by the number of needles in each cluster: white pines have 5 needles, red pines have 2, and pitch pines have 3. It is unusual to find old-age trees of all three species growing together; here this may be a result of the right soil conditions and the steep slope that has prevented their harvesting. Several naturalists in New Hampshire believe that it is the finest stand of mixed pines in the state.

The path leading up the side of the esker to the road at the top of the ridge is quite steep. Turn left on the road and walk a short way to the point of excavation of the esker (**B**). Here, with a beautiful view of Mount Washington (see **#84**) as a backdrop, one can see that about ¾ mile of the esker has been cut away by a gravel company that owns part of the land. Across the excavated area is the other end of the esker, showing a perfectly formed inverted V shape and stretching several more miles to the north. Notice the fine, clean sand at your feet that covers the entire work area below. Called washed sand and gravel, it was indeed washed by the running glacial meltwaters. Such material is highly valued for use on winter roads and in construction. Although the rest of the esker is currently protected as state property, it could be sold and destroyed as the middle section has been. Several conservation groups in New Hampshire are working to protect the remainder of the esker and its related formations and vegetation for the study and enjoyment of future generations.

Remarks: *Return to the entrance by retracing your steps. The path is marked by blazes on the trees, and is quite steep, so caution is advised. Be very careful around the edge of the excavation on the esker's ridge. Allow about 1½ hours for a visit.*

78.

Madison Boulder

Directions: **Madison, N.H. From Concord go north on I-93 about 30 miles to Exit 23. Go east on Route 104 about 8 miles, then north on U.S. 3 about 2 miles through Meredith.**

Turn right onto Route 25 and go northeast about 21 miles to Whittier. Turn left onto Route 113, go northeast about 10 miles to Madison; bear left and continue on Route 113 for 1.6 miles to the large sign on the left marking the entrance to Madison Boulder. Continue to the parking area at the end of the road, and the short walk to the boulder.

Ownership: New Hampshire Division of Parks.

The Madison Boulder is a dramatic testament to the power of the last massive ice sheet to cover New England. This huge piece of granite, located on a 17-acre tract in east central New Hampshire, is the largest known glacial boulder in North America. As such, it has been recognized by the U.S. Department of the Interior as a National Natural Landmark.

North America has experienced several ice ages over the last 2 million years. The most recent, known as the Wisconsin glacial stage, occurred between 12,000 and 60,000 years ago. Plant and animal species were driven southward as the continental ice mass moved down from Greenland and the Canadian Arctic at the rate of about 6 to 8 inches a day. In valleys where the glacial force was channeled and concentrated, the ice could move up to 12 to 18 inches a day. Eventually the ice built up to about 1 mile in thickness, and markings on the summit of Mount Washington show that the ice covered even that 6,288-foot peak (see **White Mountains, Monadnocks, and Eastern Connecticut Highlands**).

As the ice sheet moved over the landscape it picked up loose rock and soil, grinding and carrying it along on its southerly path. The hard granite of the White Mountain region was often broken from exposed ledges in huge chunks. These breaks were usually along joints and cracks in the rock that were formed when the molten rock cooled some 200 million years ago. The material carried by the glacier was later deposited by the glacier's meltwaters, and the rocks and boulders came to rest where the ice melted—often about 100 miles from their original location. Rocks that traveled this far were usually much smaller than Madison Boulder, and formed what are called *boulder trains,* a trail of rocks indicating their place of origin. Boulder trains have helped scientists map the flow of the glacier through New England, since it often moved in different directions as it advanced over and around hills and mountains.

The largest rocks that were carried by the glacier are known as glacial erratics, and are more common in areas where bedrock ledges stand exposed on the earth's surface. Such is the case with Madison Boulder, which was plucked from a high ridge to the northeast in Albany, N.H., about 2 miles from where it sits today. Geologists have been able to determine exactly where it came from by comparing its composition and shape to that of the ridge, a process somewhat similar to solving a big jigsaw puzzle.

Approaching Madison Boulder is something of a humbling experience, for this monument to glacial history is 83 feet long, 37 feet wide, 23 feet high, and weighs about 7,650 tons—roughly the same as an ocean freighter. It is a dense mix of biolite and quartz feldspar known as Conway granite. That it survived its icebound journey under tremendous stresses and pressures indicates that the boulder contains no fractures. Theoretically, a stone cutter could form an 83-foot-long solid column out of this rock without encountering any cracks. However, the relatively smooth, rectangular shapes of the boulder's surfaces do indicate that it broke from its parent ledge along several different joints. The smoothness of its surface, which is similar to the effects of glacial polishing, is actually from a process known as exfoliation, which began long before the coming of the glacier. Exfoliation is the chemical weathering of the rock's surface over many thousands of years by corrosive elements contained in rain, snow, and atmosphere. The weathering process peels off layers from the rock surface, much like separating the layers of an onion.

Walk around the boulder and notice how it rests on the ground: around its base are smaller rocks, gravel, and coarse soil known as glacial debris. This is material that was picked up, ground by the ice, and deposited here. It probably came from a location many miles farther to the north than the boulder, traveling easily over large distances because it is relatively light. While pondering the power of the glacial ice, it is sobering to stop and realize that the same process may happen again. We are now living in an interglacial period, and in a few hundred thousand years, perhaps another glacier will cover New England and move Madison Boulder once again.

Remarks: *This site is just a few hundred feet from the parking area along a well-worn, level path.*

79.
Pondicherry
Wildlife Refuge

Directions: **Jefferson, N.H. From Concord, take I-93 north about 65 miles to Exit 33; continue north, now on U.S. 3, about 23 miles to the junction with Route 115. Continue**

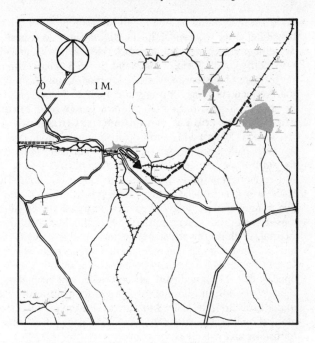

on U.S. 3 about 4.5 miles and turn right at the sign for the
Whitefield Airport. Take the road east for about 1.7 miles
and turn right again at the airport sign. Drive to the airport office and park.

Ownership: **Audubon Society of New Hampshire.**

The 305-acre Pondicherry Wildlife Refuge comprises two separate
parcels of woodland surrounding two natural shallow bodies of water, Cherry and Little Cherry ponds, which are set in a small valley
in the western foothills of the White Mountains. These remote, little-
known ponds lie about half a mile apart within an unspoiled, road-
less tract of northern New England forest at the border of Jefferson
and Whitefield townships. Cherry Pond, the larger and more accessible pond, is a magnificent 100-acre open-heath bog fringed with a
bog forest of tamarack and black spruce trees, as well as patches of
freshwater marsh vegetation. It is a habitat for many of the mammals
found in New England's sparsely populated northern realm, including moose, beaver, otter, mink, muskrat, and coyote. Its birdlife is
unusually rich for the inland mountain region, with over forty-eight
reported species of resident and migratory birds. In addition, Cherry

Pond's scenery ranks among the most beautiful in the entire state, becoming truly spectacular in the autumn foliage season. In late September golden-needled tamaracks cast their brilliant reflections on Cherry Pond's surface and stand in relief against the red and purple hues of the soaring western slopes of Mount Washington and the Presidential Range. Rising some 4,000 to 5,000 feet, these are the highest peaks in New Hampshire (see **White Mountains, Monadnocks, and Eastern Connecticut Highlands**).

To reach Cherry Pond, follow an abandoned railroad right-of-way (a cinder path) from the east side of the Whitefield Airport. Look for the start of the unmarked path in a grove of trees several hundred feet east of the airport's two adjacent hangar buildings. This path leads over flat, wooded terrain to the present tracks of the Boston and Maine Railroad; follow them in a northeasterly direction to the crossing with the present north–south running tracks of the Maine Central. Walk northward along the tracks of the Maine Central and look for the refuge sign on the right of the railbed after the crossing. Cherry Pond, which partially bounds the railbed on the west, will appear several hundred yards ahead on the right beyond the refuge sign. Watch for an informal, overgrown footpath leading through underbrush from the railbed to a small clearing on a wooded bank at the shoreline. This strip of higher terrain at the pond's edge is used for fishing and wildlife observation.

From the shore you can see the roughly 60 acres of open heath mat that occupies the eastern and northern portions of Cherry Pond. Behind the open mat lies a bog forest of tamarack and black spruce. Both these trees are common in bogs in northern New England. Tolerant of the bog's characteristically acidic growing conditions, the trees can take root in the floating heath mat of sphagnum moss without ever becoming anchored in the soil. Black spruce (or bog spruce) and tamarack (or larch) are generally restricted to northern regions of cool climate. In fact, tamarack grows farther north than any tree in North America. It is also the only conifer on the continent that is deciduous (with the exception of baldcypress in the South). In the fall its lime-green needles turn gold and then drop, leaving the branches barren until new foliage emerges in the spring. Fresh-water marsh vegetation is also visible along portions of Cherry Pond's shallow margins. A spike rush (*Eleocharis robbinsii*) and a pondweed (*Potamogeton robbinsii*), as well as other aquatic plants, add to the pond's ecological diversity. Marsh plants provide food for resident muskrats (see **#70**) and cover for summer waterbirds like the great blue heron (see **#64**), American bittern (see **#64**), and Virginia and sora rails.

Aquatic plants are also a source of food for moose at Pondicherry.

The moose browse a large array of plants, but in summer they often wade into shallow ponds and streams to forage for food and escape from biting insects. They are most active during early morning and twilight. Look for their large hoofprints on the railbed leading to the pond. (See **#106** for more on moose.)

Pondicherry is an important breeding ground for two rare summer bird residents in New Hampshire, the green-winged teal and ring-necked duck. The green-winged teal is a dabbling or surface-feeding duck, which consumes aquatic organisms as it dips its bill into the water while swimming. Teal are considerably smaller than most ducks, measuring only 13 to 15 inches long as compared with the average 20-inch wood duck or the 21- to 25-inch black duck, which also nest here. The male is largely gray, with a distinctive white stripe on its wing, and a green patch on the sides of its brown head. The female is a speckled brown. Teal commonly breed from James Bay south to the upper Midwest and winter from the Midwest to the Gulf of Mexico. The ring-necked duck is a diving species, which swims underwater to obtain its food. It is a member of the scaup family, and is 16 to 18 inches long. The male's upper parts and chest are black, and its sides are light gray with a white stripe in front of the wings. The female is brown with a white belly, grayish wing-stripe, and white eye-ring. These birds breed from central Canada south to the Great Plains, and locally across the upper Northeast. They winter as far north as the Great Lakes and southern New England.

Cherry Pond is also a breeding ground for one of the most famous resident waterbirds of the Far North, the common loon. Roughly the size of a goose at 28 to 36 inches long, the loon has a more sharply pointed bill and shorter neck. Its summer breeding plumage consists of a black head, black back spotted with white, and white under-parts, whereas its winter plumage is dark gray with white under-parts. In breeding season the loon's famous call sounds like an eerie imitation of human laughter or a series of yodels. It is a deep under-water diver, feeding mainly on fish, crabs, and algae (see also **#86** and **#108**).

Other summer bird residents recorded at Cherry Pond include the pied-billed grebe, marsh hawk, common snipe, long-billed and short-billed marsh wrens, boreal chickadee, ruby-crowned kinglet, rusty blackbird, Lincoln's sparrow, yellow-bellied flycatcher, and assorted warblers. Many waterbirds are seen at the pond during spring and fall migratory periods. Late afternoon is an excellent time to observe migrants as they land on the pond.

Retrace your steps back along the railbed and old railroad right-of-way to the airport.

Remarks: *The hike from the Whitefield Airport along the abandoned railroad right-of-way and railbed is flat and easy walking. Allow roughly 4 hours for the round-trip hike (approximately 3 miles one-way.) Portions of the abandoned right-of-way may be somewhat overgrown, but the present railbed is entirely open. Hikers should be alert for passing trains, which still occasionally use the tracks. Access to Little Cherry Pond is by a rough path located about 200 yards north of Cherry Pond along the Maine Central tracks. The 30-acre Little Cherry is also an open-heath bog, surrounded by dense stands of tamarack and black spruce. This path crosses through wet lowlands and should only be attempted with a knowledgeable guide. For more details contact the headquarters of the Audubon Society of New Hampshire, 3 Silk Farm Rd., P.O. Box 528-B, Concord, N.H. 03301; (603) 224-9909. Both Cherry and Little Cherry ponds are "Great Ponds," or public bodies of water. Hunting and trapping are prohibited, but fishing (without motorboats) is allowed. The refuge is operated jointly by the Audubon Society and the New Hampshire Fish and Game Department. It is open all year.*

80.

Franconia Notch
State Park

Directions: **Franconia, N.H. From Concord, take I-93 north about 65 miles to Exit 33; continue north, now on U.S. 3, about 3 miles as the highway enters the state park. Continue on U.S. 3 as it goes through the notch until I-93 picks up again at the northern boundary of the park.**

Ownership: **New Hampshire Division of Parks and Recreation.**

Franconia Notch, known for over a century as the "Gateway to the White Mountains," is New Hampshire's most spectacular state park. Since the early nineteenth century when mountainous northern New Hampshire was opened to road travel, Franconia Notch has enchanted millions of visitors who came first by stagecoach and later by railroad and automobile. The notch's fame arises from both its breathtaking mountain scenery and its unusual geological features, including the Old Man of the Mountain, a beautiful rock profile; the

Flume, a deep stream gorge; the Basin, a giant glacial pothole; and many others. These formations are concentrated within a relatively small area, which today is encompassed by the 6,441-acre state park and, at the higher elevations of the notch's surrounding peaks, by the White Mountain National Forest.

The notch itself is a deep, narrow mountain pass running north to south for some 8 miles between the Franconia and Kinsman ranges. Its steep mountain walls rise 2,200 feet from the floor of the valley, where the Daniel Webster State Highway (Route 3) follows the

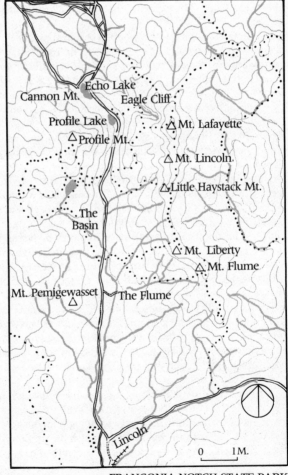

FRANCONIA NOTCH STATE PARK

banks of the Pemigewasset River along its entire length. The western wall of the notch is formed largely by 4,040-foot Cannon Mountain (also called Profile Mountain). Its eastern face is dominated by a huge, vertical cliff, climbing 2,500 to 3,500 feet above the valley, with a massive talus slope, or rockfall, rising up its lower slopes. The notch's eastern wall is composed of the lofty Franconia Range, which forms a scenic ridgeline extending from 4,327-foot Mount Flume in the southeast to the most prominent peak, 5,249-foot Mount Lafayette, in the northeast. The Franconia Range features the second largest arctic alpine area in New Hampshire (after Mount Washington), where rare alpine plants grow under severe, arctic-like conditions above the 4,600-foot tree line on Mount Lafayette and adjoining peaks.

In the notch, State Route 3 (soon to become part of I-93) provides access to many natural areas located along the highway. Driving northward into the notch, Route 3 passes the entrance and parking areas for the Flume (see **#82**) and the Basin (see **#81**), while excellent views of Cannon Mountain's east-facing cliffs rise on the left (see **#83**). Covering roughly a half-mile-square area south of Profile Lake, these cliffs rank as the White Mountains' most magnificent. The 1,500-foot-high talus slope, occupying an area of 320 acres along the lower portion of the cliff, is the most extensive formation of its kind in the state.

The geology of the cliffs and talus slope is interwoven with the larger history of Franconia Notch. The notch is an ancient river valley, which beginning some 60 million years ago was gradually cut into the surface of the land. Prior to the valley's formation, the land had been a flat, rolling plain, broken only by placid, meandering rivers. It was only in the wake of an ancient earth upheaval (see **White Mountains, Monadnocks, and Eastern Connecticut Highlands**) that the notch came into existence, as the ancestor of the Pemigewasset River began to erode the land into a V-shaped valley. The earth upheaval had lifted the land surface some 5,000 feet above sea level, transforming the once gentle rivers on its surface into swift, erosive streams. Throughout the White Mountain region the land was deeply dissected by rivers, leaving only the summits of Mount Washington and the Presidential peaks as isolated remnants of the old land surface.

A more recent natural disturbance produced the cliff of Cannon Mountain. This event was the last ice age, which began some 60,000 years ago. The mile-thick glaciers descending from the north scoured the surface of the entire region. In the notch the ice flowed through the valley and over the mountaintops, widening the canyon's walls and smoothing its surrounding peaks. The ice carved cliffs and steepened slopes, producing a U-shaped valley that became vulnerable to natural weathering (frost, ice, rain, and wind) after the glaciers' retreat some 12,000 years ago. The freeze-thaw frost cycle then loosened rock on Cannon Mountain's cliffs, forming the huge pile of toppled boulders that lie along its lower slopes.

The Old Man of the Mountain is also a product of postglacial weathering from frost. Drive north past Cannon Mountain's cliff and talus slope to Profile Lake on the left side of the road. A short path leads from the parking area to the north shore of the lake, where you can find the best place to view the Old Man. Perched 1,200 feet above Profile Lake at an elevation of 400 feet, the Old Man of the Mountain is a remarkable rock outcropping on the east flank of Cannon Mountain which assumes the form of a human profile when seen from the lakeshore. It was created by the heaving of frost in its ledges, which broke the outcropping. The Old Man, or "Great Stone Face" (as Nathaniel Hawthorne called it in his 1850 story of the same name), is one of the great natural landmarks in New England and is the state symbol of New Hampshire.

Other natural features that appear on Route 3 include landslide scars on the western slopes of Mount Lafayette, which are visible across the highway from Profile Lake. Eagle Cliff, also seen from Profile Lake, is a craggy cliff on the western flank of Mount Lafayette. At the top stands the only virgin forest in Franconia Notch, a small patch of virgin red spruce and fir. (The Greenleaf Trail, which begins on the northeast side of Route 3 across from Profile Lake, leads to the cliff.) Echo Lake, situated just north of the Old Man of the Mountain (near the parking area for the Cannon Mountain Ski Area), and Profile Lake are both glacial basins on the Pemigewasset River that were created during the Ice Age. Migratory waterfowl are frequently seen on the lakes.

Remarks: *There are numerous trails for day hikes, backpacking, cross-country skiing, and snowshoeing throughout the state park. The vast majority have access on Route 3. The Appalachian Mountain Club maintains two huts for hikers on both the western and eastern sides of the notch, with overnight accommodations. Contact the AMC, 5 Joy St., Boston, Mass. 02108, for information and reservations. AMC White Mountain Guide contains trail maps and descriptions of the Franconia region. Lafayette Campground, a public campground situated in the state park, offers 98 campsites for tents and trailers on a first-come, first-served basis. It is open daily from late May to late October. For further information call (603) 823-5563 or (603) 823-7751. The campground is located between the Basin and Profile Lake, 5 miles north of the Flume parking area, on Route 3.*

Franconia Notch State Park is to undergo redevelopment by the state of

*New Hampshire in the next decade. Park renovations, including improved
parking and visitor facilities, will coincide with reconstruction of the present
Route 3 as an extension of I-93. Controversial plans for a four-lane express-
way have been scaled down, and the highway through the notch will
remain a two-lane road. Because of future park renovations and additions
to existing facilities, the descriptions of park areas in this text are subject to
change.*

81.

Franconia Notch State Park:
The Basin

Directions: **Franconia, N.H. From Concord, take I-93 north
about 65 miles to Exit 33; continue north, now on U.S. 3,
about 5 miles to a parking area for the Basin on the left.**

Ownership: **New Hampshire Division of Parks and Recreation.**

The Basin is a giant glacial pothole sculpted in solid granite by ice
and water. One of the most unusual geological formations at Franconia Notch State Park, the Basin is an impressive illustration of the
power of natural erosion through the centuries. The scenic woodland surrounding the basin harbors a cascading brook and a rare
ancient white pine surviving as a centuries-old remnant from the
virgin forest.

The Basin lies on the west side of the parking area off Route 3. A
trail and footbridges lead you along the perimeter of the Basin,
where the torrential waters of the Pemigewasset River spin around
a circular cavity that is sunk in solid granite bedrock. This glacial
pothole is 30 feet in diameter and 15 feet deep at its center. It was
created some 25,000 years through erosion by glacial meltwaters
and then further ground down by spinning water-borne sediments
in the river.

The Basin-Cascade Trail begins after you cross the lower footbridge. Look for a trail sign where a path branches into the forest.
The trail soon leads to Cascade Brook, which spills down a series of
broad granite ledges. As you follow the trail along the right side of

the brook, watch for the bleached and limbless spire of a soaring white pine leaning into the open sky over the brook. The trail leads directly to this tree, which straddles the rocky banks of the stream below an attractive cascade. Another, smaller old pine, which has died, stands a few yards away.

The great white pine is dead from the top of the crown to about halfway down the trunk, though its thick lower branches are still green. Its size is magnificent: over 100 feet high, with a trunk diameter of over 4 feet. But the pine's most striking feature is its exceptionally thick, deeply furrowed bark, which is only characteristic of a truly ancient specimen. The age of the white pine, estimated to be between 300 and 400 years old, dates to the precolonial virgin forest. Its exact age, however, will remain a mystery forever, since rot in the inner trunk makes a scientific ring count impossible. While it still stands, the great pine at Cascade Brook is unrivaled in its combination of age and size.

Retrace your steps along the path as it follows the brook back to the parking area. Or you can extend the hike by taking the trail farther upstream (west) to scenic Kinsman Falls.

Remarks: *The Basin-Cascade Trail is a short, 30-minute hike to the old pine and back. The terrain is moderately difficult, with some large rocks but a fairly level grade.*

82.
Franconia Notch State Park:
The Flume

Directions: **Franconia, N.H. From Concord, take I-93 north about 65 miles to Exit 33; continue north, now on U.S. 3, about 3 miles to the parking area for the Flume on the right.**

Ownership: **New Hampshire Division of Parks and Recreation.**

The Flume is a dramatic natural gorge stretching 800 feet along the lower slopes of Mount Liberty at the south end of Franconia Notch. This narrow fissure ranges in width from 12 to 20 feet, with steep granite walls rising to 90 feet above the foaming waters of Flume Brook. The Flume is the most prominent natural feature in a small but spectacular area within Franconia Notch State Park. A network of hiking trails links a boardwalk in the Flume with two waterfalls and a deep, stream-carved granite basin spanned by a footbridge.

A bus transports you the 1 mile between the parking lot and the major trail at the Flume. (There is a footpath for those who prefer to walk.) The trail begins to the left of the Boulder Store at the bus stop. Follow it to the Flume boardwalk and begin your walk through this impressive fissure.

The Flume is an example of what geologists call a dike, which is formed by an intrusion of one kind of rock into another. Over 200 million years ago the Conway granite that forms the walls of the Flume was buried deep within the earth. Vertical fractures in the granite were invaded by fluid basalt, or magma, which flowed under pressure from deep within the earth. This basalt dike forced the granite apart and then cooled, solidifying into a fine-grained rock. After millions of years the dike became exposed above the surface of the land, which had been eroded into the present mountain land-scape. Once exposed, the soft basalt rock eroded more rapidly than the harder granite surrounding it, a phenomenon geologists call dif-ferential erosion. Eventually an eroded valley appeared where the Flume now lies, and after the Ice Age, Flume Brook began to carve the gorge you see today. As you walk along the boardwalk you can see the vestiges of the basalt dike at the bottom of the Flume and in portions of the walls. The basalt is a distinctive reddish-brown rock, while the granite is dark gray.

After leaving the boardwalk, you can go right (east) for a short distance to Avalanche Falls, where Flume Brook pours down a 45-foot waterfall, spilling into the canyon. On the left, the Rim Path skirts the upper edge of the Flume and then quickly merges with the main trail, which returns you to the bus stop.

The Wildwood Path leads from the parking lot to the Sentinel Pine Bridge and Pool. It starts to the right of the Flume Store, and enters a forest dominated by hemlock, yellow birch, and beech. The trail features many large glacial boulders, or erratics (see **#78**). Many of these are covered by colonies of common polypody, a small fern with leathery evergreen fronds. An opening in the trees on the right appears about three-quarters of the way down the path, offering fine views of 4,460-foot Mount Liberty on the left and 4,327-foot Mount Flume on the right.

The trail weaves down a grade and then branches in opposite directions. Veer right and go down the short slope to the overlook of Sentinel Bridge and the Pool. In front of you the Pemigewasset River cascades over massive granite slabs before tumbling into the pool.

The Pool is a deep rock basin, 40 feet deep and 150 feet in diameter. It was created some 25,000 years ago during the last ice age through erosion by silt-laden glacial streams. The 130-foot cliffs above the pool are spanned by Sentinel Pine Bridge. The covered footbridge is supported by an enormous white pine tree stretching across the Pemigewasset River from cliff to cliff. For centuries the Sentinel Pine had stood upon the high cliff, but it was blown down in the 1938 hurricane. It ranked among the largest white pines in the state, with a huge trunk circumference of 16 feet and a height of nearly 175 feet.

Walk back up the slope and go straight along the branch of the trail you passed earlier. This leads to the covered footbridge, allowing you a closer look at the pine and another perspective of the Pool. At the time of this writing, the Sentinel Pine Bridge was closed to foot traffic for safety reasons. If you look carefully at the pine, you will see it has developed a severe crack from rot. For many, the passing of this great pine will mean the end of an era in the notch.

Retrace your steps to the parking lot. Other attractions at the Flume include Liberty Gorge and Cascades, a scenic waterfall flowing into a narrow gorge, reached by taking the Ridge Trail off the Rim Trail at the Flume.

Remarks: *The Flume trail and boardwalk is a 30-minute hike over easy terrain from the bus stop. The bus ride takes only 5 minutes, with short waits between trips. Visitor information is available at the Flume Store. There is an admission charge for the Flume (bus ride included).*

83.
Franconia Notch State Park:
Cannon Mountain

Directions: **Franconia, N.H. From Concord, take I-93 north about 65 miles to Exit 33; continue north, now on U.S. 3, about 10 miles to the parking area for the Cannon Mountain Aerial Tramway on the left.**

Ownership: **New Hampshire Division of Parks and Recreation.**

High on the blustery peak of Cannon Mountain live the yellow-rumped and blackpoll warblers, gray-cheeked thrush, and other birds of the Canadian north woods. Far south of their natural home, the great coniferous forests of Hudson Bay, these northern birds thrive in the stunted fir and spruce forest growing on the cool, rocky heights above Franconia Notch. For avid bird-watchers and casual nature lovers, the northern birds are to be enjoyed alongside Cannon Mountain's other outstanding attractions: its bird's-eye view of Franconia Notch and dazzling panorama of the northern New England mountains.

Cannon Mountain (or Profile Mountain) climbs to an altitude of 4,040 feet to form the grand western wall of Franconia Notch. The eastern side of the mountain is an immense vertical cliff looming 2,500 to 3,500 feet above the floor of the valley, with a massive talus slope, or rockfall, rising up its lower slopes. The mountain's best-known feature is, however, the "Old Man of the Mountain," or the "Great Stone Face," a beautiful natural rock silhouette on its eastern flank that forms an unusual human profile (see **#80**).

The summit of Cannon Mountain is one of the most accessible peaks in New England. The Cannon Mountain Aerial Tramway whisks you there in a modern, enclosed cable car in 5 to 10 minutes. Although neither the great cliffs nor the Old Man is visible from the tramway, you can see exciting scenery and get an excellent overview of the mountain vegetation.

The vegetation of Cannon Mountain changes markedly in composition as you ascend to higher altitudes. The mountain's plant communities, referred to as vegetation or life zones, reflect the climatic conditions at different elevations. The successive changes in the flora as you climb the mountain are much the same as those that would appear along a journey from northern New England to the far northern reaches of Canada. (In New England, each gain of 400 feet in elevation produces a climate similar to that found 100 miles farther north.)

As you climb up the lower slopes, the forest below you reveals familiar trees of the northern-hardwood zone growing throughout the floor of the valley. The dominant trees—sugar maple, American beech, and yellow birch—are all deciduous species, which in early autumn paint the low slopes in brilliant red, orange, and yellow.

The spruce-fir zone begins at a height of 2,500 feet. This forest, composed of almost pure red spruce and balsam fir, extends to an elevation of about 4,000 feet. When observed from the floor of the notch, it appears as a wide blue-green band ringing the middle slopes of the mountain. These two species are commonly found in the high elevations of the White Mountains where climatic conditions resemble those of the great spruce-fir boreal forest of upper Canada.

As you approach the summit, there is a transition to the scrub-fir zone above 4,000 feet; however, the shift is less distinct than that between the hardwood and fir-spruce zones. The most noticeable difference is the stunted, gnarled appearance of the dominant balsam fir. There is also the addition to the forest of mountain-ash and paper birch. The white bark of the birches, and especially the bright red berry clusters of the mountain-ashes in early fall, are conspicuous even from the windows of the cable car.

Although the scrub zone occupies the summit of Cannon Mountain, the peaks of higher mountains reaching about 4,500 feet above sea level feature the arctic alpine zone (see #107). Here trees are supplanted by small northern wildflowers and shrubs that are commonly found in the Arctic tundra. Mount Lafayette and several other peaks in the Franconia Range across the notch from Cannon Mountain have arctic alpine zones above 4,600 feet.

The Rim Trail, beginning to the rear of the Summit Station for the tramway, offers spellbinding vistas of the notch and surrounding mountains as it circles the summit of Cannon Mountain. Take the path as it branches southward into the trees from the clearing. You will immediately notice the stunted, deformed shapes of the balsam fir, as well as scattered red and black spruces. The small size of the trees results from a lack of soil and, to a lesser degree, the climatic conditions. Though the mountain summit technically is not alpine in character, it does have some species of alpine vegetation along the trail. On the side of the path opposite the first lookout you can see labrador tea, mountain winterberry, sheep laurel, mountain cranberry, bilberry, and other small plants.

Northern bird species in the scrub zone may be observed throughout the trail. Most common are the gray-cheeked thrush and the yellow-rumped and blackpoll warblers. The gray-cheeked thrush, measuring 6 to 8 inches long, has a gray-brown back and spotted white breast. The yellow-rumped warbler is best distinguished from the blackpoll by its yellow rump in both its spring and fall plumage. The spruce grouse (see #97) is occasionally glimpsed in the scrub zone. This large, dusky ground bird is an inhabitant of moist coniferous forests in the far north, but appears locally in the New England mountains. It is a chickenlike bird 15 to 17 inches long that scratches in the ground for food. Other birds in the scrub zone include the ruby-crowned kinglet, junco, and white-throated sparrow.

An observation platform along the trail offers a fine vantage point from which to appreciate the mountains that unfold in all directions. The Green Mountains appear in the West, and in the immediate east is the Franconia Range, running north to south: Mount Lafayette (5,249 feet), Mount Lincoln (5,108 feet), Little Haystack Mountain (3,338 feet), Mount Liberty (4,460 feet), and Mount Flume (4,327 feet).

Enjoy the view, before completing the trail circuit that brings you back to the tramway station and your ride down the mountain.

Remarks: *The Rim Trail is a short, casual 20-minute walk over easy, flat terrain. Cannon Mountain Aerial Tramway leaves from the notch station for round trips at regular intervals. Both the notch and summit stations have snack bars and rest rooms. The tramway is open daily all year. A fee is charged. Cannon Mountain Ski Area has extensive facilities for downhill skiing. The site of the first aerial tramway in the nation, it has long been one of the leading ski centers in New England.*

84.

Mount Washington and
the Presidential Range

Directions: **Mount Washington State Park, N.H. For the Mount Washington Cog Railway, take I-93 north from Concord about 65 miles to Exit 33; continue north on U.S. 3 about 20 miles to Twin Mountain. Take U.S. 302 east for 4 miles to Fabyan; follow the Base Road about 4 miles to the Base Station of the Cog Railway. For the Mount Washington Auto Road and AMC Pinkham Notch Camp, take I-93 north from Concord for 18 miles to Exit 20. Follow U.S. 3 north for 17 miles to Meredith. Take Route 25 northeast 22 miles to West Ossippee. Turn left and follow Route 16 north about 29 miles to Pinkham Notch, or 34 miles to the Auto Road.**

Ownership: **New Hampshire Division of Parks and Recreation; U.S. Forest Service.**

Rising more than a mile from the mountainous heart of northern New Hampshire, Mount Washington is the highest peak in the

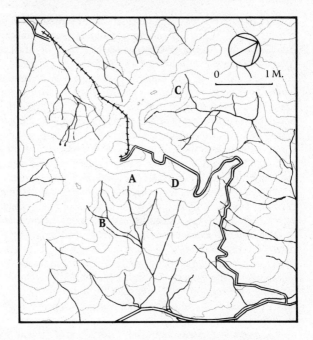

Northeast. This 6,288-foot mountain looms at the center of the Presidential Range—the backbone of the New England landscape—an imposing chain of eleven peaks running north to south for about 15 miles through the northeastern portion of the White Mountain National Forest (see **White Mountains, Monadnocks, and Eastern Connecticut Highlands**). Six of these peaks—Mounts Clay, Madison, Jefferson, Adams, Monroe, and Franklin—climb more than 5,000 feet; four others—Eisenhower, Clinton, Webster, and Jackson—range between 3,900 and 4,700 feet. The tallest of the Presidentials, including Washington, rank as the five highest mountains in New Hampshire.

The Indians called Mt. Washington Agiocochook, or the "Mountain of the Snowy Forehead," for its gaunt crown of white stone and its shining mantle of winter snow. Indeed, for stark, rugged grandeur Mount Washington and its lofty sister peaks are unrivaled by any mountains east of the Rockies. Although the Great Smokies are slightly higher, the Presidentials are more impressive: the gentle slopes of the former are forested to their summits, while the latter have bleak, treeless peaks and steep, jagged contours with extensive exposures of bare bedrock. The Presidentials also project far above the surrounding countryside. Mount Washington towers about 4,500 feet above the land, its rock crest visible on clear days from the Atlantic Ocean some 70 miles to the east.

Visitors to Mount Washington may ascend to the summit via a wide network of hiking trails, Mount Washington's famous Cog Railway, or its historic Auto Road (called the "Carriage Road"). A newly built visitors' center at the summit contains the Mount Washington Museum and other facilities (see Remarks). In addition to commanding views across northern New England, one finds at the summit a fine array of alpine flora. The ridgeline that extends across the highest of the Presidentials breaks timberline at about 4,800 to 5,200 feet. At these elevations frigid winter temperatures, high wind exposures, and abundant precipitation produce arctic conditions in which only alpine species can flourish. Here they grow far south of their natural range in the tundra of Labrador. Although several other high New England peaks in both the White Mountains and elsewhere display similar arctic species, the alpine zone of the Presidential Range is the largest of its kind in the eastern United States, extending for roughly 8 square miles from Mount Madison in the north to Mount Eisenhower in the south. Scientists theorize that alpine vegetation arrived in New England during the late stages of the Ice Age and retreated to the cool elevations of the mountaintops as the climate warmed. The alpine plants are diminutive species, such as sedges, heaths, mosses, grasses, and wildflowers, which, unlike tall trees, can withstand the shearing force of the wind on the summit and lie protected from the extreme cold in winter beneath an insulating blanket of snow. Windshorn black spruce and balsam fir trees—called *Krummholz*—growing at the upper edge of timberline dramatically convey the effects of wind chill and dehydration here. These shrub-sized evergreens form low, dense mats of twisted branches, which despite their miniature size are sometimes quite old. Frigid blasts of air prune away all branches that protrude above the snow layer in winter.

The alpine plants in the Presidential Range number about 75 species, and about 30 subalpine species grow in the most sheltered spots above treeline. Perhaps the best-known of the alpine plants are the attractive wildflowers, which generally bloom in June. Mount Washington's Alpine Garden area (**A**) is the most popular point in the range for seeing wildflowers and other tundra plants because of its relatively close proximity to the Auto Road near the summit. This area is reached by hiking the Alpine Garden Trail, which connects the Auto Road with the Tuckerman Ravine Trail. Situated about 1 mile below the summit on the eastern side of the mountain, the Alpine Garden is composed of grassy "lawns" where you can see some of the showiest of the mountain wildflowers. Among these are the Lapland rosebay, a small rhododendron with pinkish-magenta flowers and leathery, evergreen leaves. The tiny alpine azalea has ¼-inch long bell-shaped flowers, which are pinkish or rosy in color. The white flowers of the diapensia are among the earliest to bloom on the mountain. Other excellent areas to see these species and other alpine vegetation include Mount Washington's Bigelow Lawn, Mount Monroe's Monroe Flats, and Mount Jefferson's Monticello Lawn.

Two of the most spectacular geological features on Mount Washington are the glacial cirques of Tuckerman's Ravine and the Great Gulf. Cirques are bowl-like depressions formed when glacial ice scooped out shallow valleys on the high mountain walls. Similar in shape to an amphitheater, cirques have very steep headwalls and rather gentle valley floors. Tuckerman's Ravine on the east side of Mount Washington (**B**) is the most famous cirque in the Presidentials, though one of the smallest. Its 800-foot headwall is about half the height of the 1,500-foot headwall of the Great Gulf (**C**) on Mount Washington's north slope. Huntington's Ravine (**D**), located on the east side of Mount Washington, is another major cirque.

A great body of scientific and historical writings has been devoted to the White Mountains, and to Mount Washington in particular. The two basic trail guides—the *AMC Guide to Mount Washington and the Presidential Range* and the *AMC White Mountain Guide*—should be obtained before hiking in the region. Each guidebook is periodically revised with updated trail and camping information. Another useful guide, *Mount Washington: A Guide and Short History*, by Peter Randall, contains excellent skyline profiles that allow you to identify the mountains and other geographical features visible from the summit. Also included is a bibliography of valuable out-of-print books on the White Mountain region. The *AMC Field Guide to Mountain Flowers of New England* is an invaluable aid for exploring the alpine zone of the Presidentials.

No guide to Mount Washington and the Presidentials is complete without a warning to hikers and sightseers about the rapid weather changes that commonly occur on the mountains. Wind gusts of over 100 miles an hour have been recorded in every month of the year at the summit of Mount Washington, and even in warm-weather months hikers in the exposed alpine region have literally been knocked off their feet by unexpected wind gusts. In cool months sudden, severe snow and ice storms are common. In all seasons the mountains experience frequent "white-outs" from fog and clouds. Reduced visibility not only hampers views from the summit but can be dangerous to hikers above treeline, who must rely on stone cairns to find the trail.

The Mount Washington State Park occupies the summit area of

Mount Washington. The rest of the mountain and its adjoining peaks are part of the federally owned White Mountain National Forest.

Remarks: *The Mount Washington Railroad has a parking area (fee charged) near the Base Road off Route 302. The railroad operates from May to October. Call (603) 846-5404 for schedules and information. The trip to the summit takes slightly more than 1 hour. The Auto Road begins off Route 16 opposite the Glen House site in Pinkham Notch (toll charged). It is also open from May to October. For information call (603) 466-3988. The visitors' center at the summit is operated by Mount Washington State Park and contains refreshment and restroom facilities. It is open from May to October. Dolly Copp Campground is the only public camping area for motor-vehicle use in the Presidential Range area of the White Mountain National Forest. It provides a base for climbers to Mount Washington and the northern Presidentials, as well as to the Carter-Moriah Range. Located 6 miles south of Gorham off Route 16, it has 194 tent and trailer sites available on a first-come, first-served basis from late May to mid-October. Dry River Campground at Crawford Notch State Park is the nearest state-owned camping area to the Presidentials; it is located 12 miles north from Bartlett off Route 302. It offers 30 tent sites on a first-come, first-served basis from mid-May to October. For further information call (603) 374-2272.*

Wilderness camping is allowed in designated areas of the White Mountain National Forest. The Appalachian Mountain Club maintains a number of trailside shelters, tent sites, and huts for overnight camping. The AMC Pinkham Notch Camp, off Route 16 in Pinkham Notch, serves as a major information center for hikers in the range and accepts advance reservations for all AMC huts. It also provides updated trail information and regulations for the White Mountain National Forest. It is open every day of the year; call (603) 466-2727. For further information on camping and hiking regulations in the national forest, write or call the Forest Supervisor, White Mountain National Forest, P.O. Box 638, Laconia, N.H. 03246. Permits to camp in certain restricted areas of the forest, campfire permits, and brochures are available from this office. Also consult the most recent edition of the AMC Guide to Mount Washington and the Presidential Range. *The regional headquarters of the AMC is at 5 Joy St., Boston, Mass. 02108.*

A complete listing for state, federal, and private campgrounds in New Hampshire can be obtained from the New Hampshire Division of Economic Development, Concord, N.H. 03301. For detailed information about state parks, write to the New Hampshire Division of Parks, Concord, N.H. 03301.

85.

Dixville Notch

Directions: **Dixville, N.H. From Concord, take I-93 north about 65 miles to Exit 33. Continue north, now on U.S. 3, another 75 miles to Colebrook. Take Route 26 east for 12 miles.**

Ownership: **New Hampshire Division of Parks and Recreation; the Balsams Hotel.**

New Hampshire's northernmost notch offers some of the most rugged and splendid scenery in northern New England. Smaller than Pinkham, Crawford, and Franconia notches (see **#80**), Dixville also differs in shape. Its precipitous cliffs form almost vertical walls in a V shape, wide enough only for the highway at the bottom; whereas the other notches are U-shaped, with rounded floors.

All the New Hampshire notches are the result of deep glacial scouring; however, at Dixville the effect is totally different. The rocks have no rounded, water-worn appearance. Rather, they are tall, jagged spurs forming sharply defined pinnacles that look like fallen castle spires. Dixville Notch has been described as the second Petraea, because it so closely resembles the ancient ruins of that Arab city.

The notch is part of a northeast–southwest–trending ridge that follows the valley formed by the Mohawk River, dammed at Lake Gloriette and Clear Stream. This high-grade metamorphosed and sedimentary rock ridge was so resistant to erosion that the various glaciers succeeded primarily in plucking and pulling the rock rather than rounding and smoothing it. Nevertheless, the talus found today at the bottom of the notch walls provides a vivid indication of the continuing process of erosion: boulders break loose in the contraction and expansion of freezing and warming (see **#80**) and sometimes fall into the road itself.

The climate of the notch is particularly rugged, owing to the high winds channeled to even greater velocity by the steep walls of this narrow passage. Consequently the vegetation—red spruce, balsam fir, and white birch—that clings to the poor talus soils has a stunted appearance like that of trees near the timberline, even though the elevation of the notch (1,990 feet) is well below the natural timberline level. This small low-altitude alpine environment attracts the rare and inconspicuous gray-cheeked thrush, a bird usually found only after a hike into much higher and more remote elevations. If you look up to the cliffs either early or late in the day during nesting season, you are very likely to hear its thin, eerie song.

Remarks: *It is easy to see the notch from your car, and you can pull off at two parking areas by the side of the road. There are also several short, steep hikes that offer superb views of the notch and the surrounding landscape. The first trail you encounter as you enter the notch from the west leads to Table Rock. Beginning on the right side of the road, it is ¾ of a mile to the top of the rock which projects up 167 feet. From here you can see parts of Maine, New Hampshire, Vermont, and Quebec. Do not attempt to scale its ledges unless you are an experienced rock-climber. One mile east of this site, off the main road on the left is a short, 200-foot trail through woods to a waterfall called the Flume. Flume Brook drops 250 feet through a granite chasm, then tumbles through several graceful cascades. At one spot you will see a pothole (see **#81**) 7 feet deep and 4 feet across.*

The area on the east side of the notch also offers views of Mount Sanguinari, which sometimes appears blood red at sunset, and Mount Abenaki, which towers above sparkling Lake Gloriette. Information about hiking trails can be obtained from the Balsams Hotel on the west shore of the lake.

86.
Umbagog Lake

Directions: Errol, N.H. From Concord, take I-93 north about 65 miles to Exit 33; continue north, now on U.S. 3, about 23 miles. Go northeast (right) on Route 115 about 11 miles, then east (right) on U.S. 2 about 12 miles. Go north (left) on Route 16 about 35 miles to Errol. To put in a canoe on the Magalloway, go north 5.5 miles farther on Route 16 to where the road first meets the river at a sharp elbow (A). Take out 2.5 miles down the Androscoggin, where that river meets Route 16 (B).

Ownership: Private.

In the marshy northwestern corner of Umbagog Lake, at the confluence of the Magalloway and Androscoggin rivers, is the finest wildlife region in New Hampshire. A short canoe trip covering portions of both rivers and the northern end of the lake will take you through an intricate complex of meandering river oxbows and ponds and a wilderness wetland of northern heath bog called the Floating Islands, which is bordered by a mixed swamp forest.

The backwaters of Umbagog, as this region is known, have evolved from the damming of the Androscoggin at Errol and the subsequent flooding of Lake Umbagog. Umbagog, an Abenaki Indian name meaning "clear lake," is a sparkling, shallow lake. It is the southern-most of the Rangeley chain of lakes that begin in Maine, and it is bisected by the Maine boundary. In this region the Abenaki hunted caribou and gave the Magalloway its name, meaning "dwelling place of the caribou."

Although the caribou are now gone, the wilderness marshlands on the edge of the lake continue to support a vast variety of vegetation and wildlife. In fact, marshes are the most biologically rich of all ecosystems. These wetlands produce more pounds of vegetation per square foot than does either a forest or grassland. They are spawning grounds and nursery for mollusks, crustacea, worms, insects, reptiles, and fish, and are the hunting grounds of mammals. The surprisingly aquatic moose (see **#106**) is often seen on Umbagog. It is not unusual to glide silently in a canoe quite close to one of these

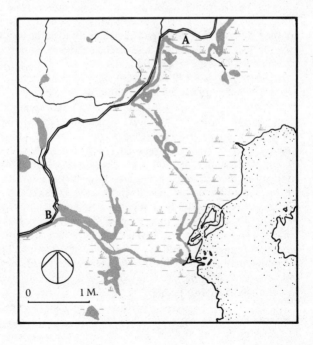

enormous mammals, which will sometimes feed on water plants with head totally submerged. Or you may see a moose swimming from one shore to another. If you startle him, he may bound away, splashing the water dramatically, or he may simply look at you and slowly wander away. The black bear is another mammal that frequents this area. One canoeist was recently surprised to find a bear swimming across the lake a short distance from the canoe.

The trees of Umbagog Lake and its islands range from the southerly red oak to the jack pine, a northern, high-altitude tree occurring nowhere else on New Hampshire's lowlands. This broad range, including northern conifers as well as bog species, is quite unusual and attests to the richness of this region.

Birdlife on the lake and adjacent marshlands is quite extensive as well. Fish-hunting birds favor its shallow waters, and there is a great variety of nesting and migrating waterbirds, including many species of diving and dabbling ducks. Birds not normally found nesting anywhere else in New England can be found on Umbagog. For example, the palm warbler with its rapidly flicking tail nests on the boggy floor of Floating Island. The lake region was the last known nesting place of bald eagles (see **#51**) in New Hampshire, and they can often be sighted here, although nest locations are no longer known. The lake region is also the only known nesting place in New Hampshire for the osprey. The 1983 listing of endangered species counted eighteen nests here. As you paddle through the backwaters, look for their enormous nests high in the tall, pointed forest trees or in dead trees killed by swamp flooding.

The loon (see also **#79** and **#108**) still exists comfortably on this wilderness lake, undisturbed by civilization. In 1983, twelve active nests were counted. You can hear its eerie and lonesome laugh coming across the water, accentuating the wilderness solitude. But the lake was not always so peaceful. In the late nineteenth century, steamers plied its waters and unlimited market hunting was rampant around it. Although the loon is not considered a gamebird, it was nearly exterminated by market hunters who often shot from the lake steamers at anything that moved within their sights. The loon population is, in fact, declining throughout New England. Its precarious existence is due in part to its nesting habits. On Umbagog its persistence depends on a constant water level. The loon produces only one or two eggs a year, and any disturbance of the nest will prevent the young from surviving. Boating, lakeside development, and camp-following raccoons that prey on loon eggs have all but driven this shy bird out of the Northeast.

Remarks: *The canoeing for this trip is all on easy, smooth water. But because of its shallowness, Umbagog can become quite choppy in a wind.*

Head to shore if there is a sudden change in the weather. The numerous bends and islands can also be confusing heading from the Magalloway to the Androscoggin. Pay close attention to the channel and the land forms in order to stay on course. Camping information and canoe rentals are available from the Brown Owl Camps 5.5 miles north of Errol on Route 16; telephone (603) 482-3274.

87.
East Inlet
Natural Area

Directions: **Pittsburg, N.H. Follow directions in #85 to Colebrook. Continue north on U.S. 3 another 43 miles, past the Second Connecticut Lake, until a sign on the right for East Inlet marks a private dirt road, maintained by the St. Regis Paper Co. Follow the dirt road 1.7 miles to the dam at the southwestern end of East Inlet Pond. The virgin stand is reached by a logging road and footpath that leave the dirt road on the left, 3 miles from the dam.**

Ownership: **St. Regis Paper Co.**

East Inlet Natural Area lies deep in the northernmost range of New Hampshire's logging wilderness, 6 miles from the Canadian border. In the 1950s the entire upper Connecticut Lakes region was virgin forest. Now there is only one remaining tract of virgin north woods: 143 acres of red spruce and balsam fir at Norton Pool on East Inlet Stream. This magnificent tract has been reserved from cutting by the St. Regis Paper Co., which also maintains as a buffer zone for the forest the extensive moose pasture bog above East Inlet Pond.

The only man-made alteration in East Inlet, except for the road, is the dam at the southwestern end of the pond (**A**). It was built in order to back up enough water to float log drives, and it is a good place to put in a canoe. You can paddle this natural trout pond (where only fly-fishing is allowed) and look for moose and ducks.

Moose Pasture Bog (**B**), a spruce-tamarack bog, lies on the long northern shore of the pond and can be reached on foot or by canoe. Be prepared to get your feet wet if you venture into this intriguing ecosystem. Bogs are generally saturated with water, and there are no boardwalks here.

The bog began as a pond. Its sodden surface with its beautiful and exotic flora is made up of a floating mat of sphagnum moss, sedge, and other plants that gradually grew outward from the pond edges and covered the water. A bog differs from a marsh or swamp in that its waters are nearly stagnant, and it supports a type of vegetation that survives in strongly acidic environments with few plant nutrients. A bog mat of sphagnum moss (see **#103**) can hold many times its weight in water. However, rainwater is a primary source of moisture, and it is low in nutrients. Furthermore, although there is water everywhere in a bog, the high acidity makes it difficult for plants to absorb it. Consequently, plants of the heath family (see **#74**) with their woolly and leathery leaves that reduce moisture loss are common in bogs, as are sedges with their thick stems and narrow leaves that also retard evaporation. Bog laurel, andromeda, rhodora, labrador tea, and leatherleaf are all found at Moose Pasture, and in the spring the attractive flowers of this heath group bloom in profusion.

You will also find the exotic pitcher plant in Moose Pasture. This plant has adapted to the lack of nitrogen in a bog environment by trapping and digesting insects in water-filled leaves (see **#104**). Insectivorous plants (sundew and butterwort) and the exquisite and

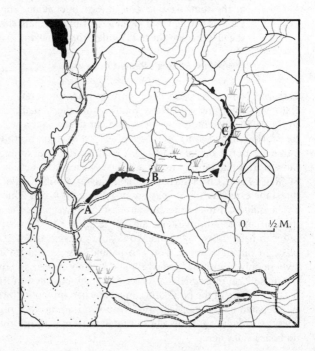

delicate bog orchids (grass pink, rose pogonia, and white-fringed orchis) are of a tropical genera and coexist happily in this wetland with plants of the Arctic tundra, such as leatherleaf, labrador tea, and cotton grass. This is because the bog offers conditions of low nutrients and high acidity that are common to both tropical rain forest and tundra.

East Inlet virgin forest (**C**), which can be visited with permission from the St. Regis Paper Co., is a magnificent stand of red and white spruce, balsam fir, and some yellow and paper birch (see **White Mountains, Monadnocks, and Eastern Connecticut Highlands**). The ground is flat and gently sloping in this climax forest, where some trees reach over 90 feet in height, with a 2-foot diameter at breast height. The forest floor is covered by a thick, spongy blanket of moss. Where the wind has toppled aging trees, the moss carpet has crept over and buried them so that many generations of dead trunks are seen as only ridges serving as seedling nurseries for the new growth. This cold site, with its deep winter snows and short growing season, attracts some unusual boreal bird species such as the black-backed three-toed woodpecker, yellow-bellied flycatcher, gray jay, and red and white-winged crossbills, and in the bogs one can find the Lincoln's sparrow.

Remarks: *For permission to visit the virgin forest, contact Lewis Ruch, District Operations Manager, St. Regis Paper Co., West Stewartstown, N.H. 03597; (603) 246-3331. The rest of East Inlet Natural Area is open to the public. It is best to visit during late summer when the black fly season is well over and the swarms of voracious mosquitoes have somewhat subsided. Camping is available at Moose Falls campground, north on Route 3, 0.5 mile past the East Inlet turnoff; the campground entrance is on the left.*

Interior Maine:
Northern Wilderness

Knife Edge. The Allagash Country. Caribou. Moosehead. These names, evocative of big wilderness, belong to places in the interior of Maine, as rugged an expanse of great north woods as can be found this side of the Canadian border—or, for that matter, above it. About 50 miles inland, the towns and cities that cluster so thickly by the sea thin out amidst forests of spruce and fir, maple, birch, and beech. Lakes and ponds shimmer seemingly everywhere among the trees. Bogs dot a landscape roughened into stony hills and barren mountains.

The mountains of interior Maine geologically resemble the White Mountains of New Hampshire (see **White Mountains, Monadnocks, and Eastern Connecticut Highlands**). They are built upon granite, formed when magma pooled and then slowly cooled without breaking through the crust of the earth.

The highest of Maine's mountains, Mount Katahdin, at 5,273 feet, rises from the vast forests in Baxter State Park in the central part of the state. It is topped by bare rock and alpine tundra, just like the Presidentials in New Hampshire. Its flanks were scarred and gouged by Ice Age glaciers, which probably lasted much longer here than in other parts of New England. South of Katahdin's summit, the ice long ago sliced the rock into a ridge so sharp and narrow it is called Knife Edge.

Southwest of Katahdin lies the most rugged mountain region of Maine. This area, adjacent to the White Mountains across the state border, is known as the Mahoosuc Range. It is traversed by the Appalachian Trail—which

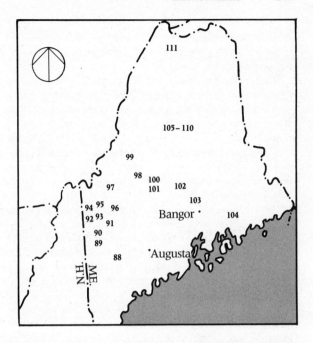

ends on Katahdin—and is probably the most hazardous and demanding portion of that 2,000-mile-long hiker's path. In one part of the Mahoosuc Range, for instance, the trail crosses Old Speck, a mountain of 4,180 feet, and then drops 2,600 feet over the next mile and a half to Grafton Notch, where the rock has been carved by erosion (and possibly, geological faulting) into intricate and spectacular gorges, rare in the northeastern part of the country.

In northern Maine the mountains become scattered, in the form of isolated peaks rather than ranges. Several peaks, notably Mount Kineo and Big Squaw Mountain, rise around the perimeter of 117-square-mile Moosehead Lake, the biggest body of fresh water in Maine.

According to some estimates there are two thousand lakes in the big woods of Maine, many of which feed into the state's major rivers. Moosehead, for instance, supplies water to the Kennebec River, which flows across southern Maine to the sea. The waters of the Kennebec below Moosehead are white and wild as the river flows for 15 miles over rocky cataracts, dropping a total of 450 feet.

The Kennebec is one of three major rivers that drain the interior of Maine. The others are the Penobscot and the St. John. The headwaters of the Penobscot are in the northwestern border country. Streams flowing out of the hills and from several small lakes eventually join to form the main river, which runs south to the sea below Bangor.

North of the Penobscot, the St. John begins its journey to the sea, following a route that is remarkably indirect. It too starts along the state's northwestern border, but instead of flowing south goes north, arching over the northern tier of the state and the defining border with Canada. Along the way it is joined by the Allagash, a name that to many outdoorsmen is synonymous with wilderness because of the primitive country it traverses. From the border, the St. John flows southeast through New Brunswick, where it finally empties into the Bay of Fundy.

The area drained by the St. John is the heart of the Maine woods. To the horizon stretch spruces—black, red, and white—together with balsam fir, scattered hemlocks, and hardwoods. The forests have been logged, often repeatedly, so despite their vastness they are not mature. Because streams, lakes, and ponds fill almost every valley and depression, the forest is moist; because of its northern latitude, it is cool as well.

Throughout the Maine woods, ponds in the process of evolving into forest have created innumerable bogs. Conventionally, the bogs feature a pool of open water in the center ringed by concentric zones of vegetation, starting with floating aquatic plants in the middle and grading through shrubs into spruce and other trees.

The conditions in Maine are ideal for the formation of bogs. The cool, moist climate is an important factor. So is the soil—mainly gravels and sand from granite—that underlies much of the Maine woods and is poor in plant nutrients. Only certain plants can thrive under these severe conditions. Among them is sphagnum moss, which forms mats over the water of the bog, blocking air from the water below and retarding decay of dead plants, which in turn promotes acidity. The acid nature of the bog further restricts the variety of plants that can live there.

Plants that can survive bog conditions, however, grow thickly, until they cover the water with a dense, soggy carpet of vegetation. Underneath, the remains of dead plants, only partly decayed, form deposits of peat. Eventually, if the vegetation accumulates sufficiently, shrubs such as labrador tea and buttonbush take root. If the process continues to completion, the bog fills in entirely and becomes woodland, first a shrubby area that resembles a clearing, then heavier forest.

The animals inhabiting the Maine woods are a mix of creatures from the north and south, but all must be able to withstand an environment that is cool and moist in spring and summer, with heavy snow and bitter cold in winter. Perhaps the animal that most typifies these creatures is the moose, which is adapted to foraging in shallow lakes and streams as well as forest. Moose wade into the water, dip their great heads below the surface, and come up with heaps of dripping aquatic vegetation in their jaws, the males further festooned with vegetation on their broad antlers. Depleted earlier in the century, moose have made such a comeback under careful wildlife management by the state that they are now a common sight in many areas.

White-tailed deer are also abundant in the Maine woods, although this species approaches the northern limits of its vast range there. As the name of the community of Caribou testifies, another member of the deer family is native to the state, but the caribou no longer exists within its borders. It may be possible, however, to reintroduce the creature into parts of the interior.

Like the caribou, the wolf that once preyed upon it has disappeared from Maine. Within the last few decades, however, another large canine predator has taken up residence. It is the eastern coyote, newly recognized as a coyote subspecies. The coyote probably arrived in New England by a long, slow migration across Canada from the west. Along the way, as it journeyed toward a new home and evolution into a new race, it seems to have picked up a healthy supply of wolf genes through interbreeding. Thus, even if the wolf has left the state, a reasonable facsimile now lives in the woods.

It is also probable that yet another big predator prowls the Maine woods. This creature, which travels as silently as the night breeze, is the eastern subspecies of the cougar, once believed extinct but now known to survive in very small numbers. Cougars entering Maine probably come from a tiny population that persisted in nearby Canada after the big cats were eliminated elsewhere. They may be expanding their range as forests have overgrown abandoned farms and areas stripped by logging, and as the white-tailed deer—a chief food source—has rebounded from a period of decline.

Myriad other mammals rove the woods—Canada lynx and bobcats, fishers, martens, and mink, red and grey squirrels, and voles. Porcupines are so numerous they become camp pests. Beavers build their lodges in the waterways.

Birds, too, are abundant and numerous. The branches are filled spring and summer with twittering, jittery wood warblers. Year-round, ruffed grouse and spruce grouse thrive. So do chickadees, various owls, and evening grosbeaks. Warm weather brings loons and grebes to the waterways, lakes, and ponds. Gray jays, true birds of the north, edge below the Canadian border along the Maine frontier. Rufous-sided towhees, which venture only a short way north of the border in summer, skitter about the underbrush.

The vast North Woods that stretch inland beyond the Maine coast also are home to the raven. Unlike its smaller look-alike, the crow, the raven lives only in big timber, or remote places like tundra and northern seacliffs. The presence of ravens, great black birds that croak hoarsely while riding the air currents, means that an area is truly wild, for they fare poorly where people are numerous. Ravens of the Maine woods signify that New England, along with its picture-book farmlands, cozy seaside villages, great universities, and sophisticated cities, still has a face that is primal and wild, gentled, perhaps, but not fully tamed.

—Edward Ricciuti

88.

Douglas Mountain

Directions: **Sebago, Maine. From Portland, take Route 25 west about 20 miles, then take Route 113 northwest about 7 miles to East Baldwin. Turn north (right) on Route 11; after less than 2 miles, Route 107 branches off to the left. Take Route 107 north 3.2 miles, then turn left onto Dyke Mountain–Douglas Hill Rd. Go 0.8 mile, then turn left and go 0.5 mile to a small parking area on the left. Please avoid blocking the road and local driveways.**

Ownership: **The Nature Conservancy.**

Douglas Mountain, rising some 1,200 feet above Sebago Lake, is the northernmost and tallest of the Saddleback Hills. Farmed on its more gentle portions and lumbered and grazed on its steeper slopes, it was devoid of forest cover well into the 1900s. Today, hemlock and hardwood forests have returned, some trees having gotten started over 70 years ago. Here you will see Douglas firs growing among eastern conifers, Sebago Lake spread out upon the Coastal Plain, an old beech harboring a colony of carpenter ants, a grove of goosefoot maple saplings with their exquisitely striped and tinted bark, and much more.

The trail up the mountain, marked by white blazes, starts off through the stone gateway that you can see from the parking area. The conifers in this section include eastern hemlock, red spruce, and white pine, all typical of this area. Among them, though, is a stranger: the Douglas fir, a western species planted here by Dr. Blackman, the former owner of the preserve. Three-inch cones with three-parted bracts protruding from between the scales are a sure identification sign. Indians of the Pacific Northwest Coast tell that when the Great Spirit made the trees, he made only a few Douglas firs and therefore forbade the mice to eat of their seeds. The mice did so anyway. They would sneak beneath the cone scales and munch the seeds, but their tails and hind legs always hung out beyond the protective cover of the scales. One day, the Great Spirit spied them thus. Enraged, he clamped the cones shut, trapping the mice . . . and there you can still see them today, their tails and hind feet hanging out between the cone scales.

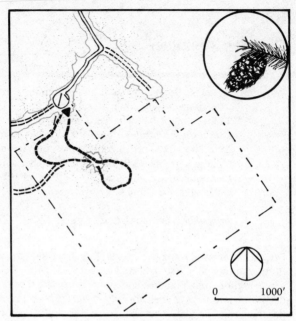

Inset: Douglas fir

As is evidenced by their presence here, Douglas firs *can* grow in the East. Why, then, are they here only where people have planted them? The grand mountain ranges of the West, the Rockies and the Sierra Nevada, and even the extensive flatlands of the Great Plains, are obstacles to the dispersal of many organisms. The fluffy seed of a dandelion may be able to travel up and over quite long distances between places of suitable habitat, but the relatively more cumbersome seed of the Douglas fir is much more limited (see **#96**).

The short walk to the summit passes through mixed coniferous and deciduous woods. Open patches are often crowded with the aromatic fronds of hay-scented fern (see **#100**). Each fall, their foliage dies back, but the rhizomes (underground stems) continue to live, producing new fronds each spring. In this manner, the hay-scented fern can densely colonize wide expanses without having to reproduce. In the open, rocky areas near the summit, juniper is a common ground cover. Its tough coated seeds need to be scratched before they can germinate, and this often occurs in the stomachs of birds that swallow them.

Perched on the summit is a stone tower, built by Dr. Blackman. From the top, you can see for miles: inland (northwest) into an upland area rising gradually to the White Mountains; seaward (southeast) over a coastal plain of low, rocky ridges and broad valleys. Imagine being here some 10,000 to 20,000 years ago: the glaciers were melting and sea level was rising; Douglas Mountain was finally poking above the level of the ice; and the seawater–glacial-ice margin was just a few miles on the other side of where Sebago Lake is today. Outwash streams deposited tons and tons of sediments along that margin, creating the relatively flat plains that underlie the area from Gorham (southeast) to Upper Gloucester (northeast).

At the north end of Sebago Lake, extending a half mile southward from the mouth of the winding Songo River, you may be able to see another delta, this one built much more recently as the river cut (and still cuts) down through a bed of glacial outwash sand. Currents have carried some of this sand to form beaches on the lake's northern shores (see **#109**).

The rocks around the base of the tower tell more of the ancient history of this area. The outcrops with wavy bands are schists (see **#29**): 400 to 600 million years ago, this area was the floor of a shallow sea; layers of mud and silty sands consolidated and were later metamorphosed into the garnet-bearing (the garnets are small) schists exposed today. The other outcrops are granitics. Cooled from magma some 350 million years ago, the exposures here are but a tiny portion of a batholith that underlies the entire Sebago Lake area. In the large-grained pegmatite (see **#1** and **#91**) intrusions, you may find a few dark, rod-shaped crystals of tourmaline.

An orange-blazed nature trail begins on the south side of the tower. (As of this writing, the Nature Conservancy is still working on the brochure.) From the fairly open upper slopes, descend into hemlocks and then deciduous woods. The ruddy furrows in the bark of the older red oaks may have been the impetus for their common name. The forest at the bottom of the mountain is mainly beech and maple, with scattered yellow birch (see **#72**). Look left for a scarred old beech with the original top gone. A couple of lateral branches have turned upward and become thickened like new major trunks. Cambium is slowly curling over the edge of the wound, but fresh "sawdust" indicates that, though the exposed carpenter ant tunnels are rotted, the ants are still active higher inside. The cambium regrowth thus appears to have been futile, since it was not fast enough to protect the interior of the tree from invasion. In many situations, though, cambium regrowth does get completed before organisms that might invade discover the site. Such a growth mechanism is therefore beneficial (see **#89**).

As you proceed, more deciduous and coniferous species join the forest membership. In late fall and early winter, witch-hazel is adorned with straggly yellow blossoms. An extract made from its bark may be on a shelf in your house, for it has long been used for medicinal and tonic purposes. Bellwort, with dangling flowers or triangular pods, lurks among clumps of marginated and intermediate wood ferns. A beech leans over the trail, braced by other trees. It must have been tilted for a while, since the section growing upward is quite long.

Just before you reach the summit again, you pass through largish hemlocks and deciduous trees. The trunk of a maple bulges with a scar shaped like a giant clamshell, where the cambium has closed over a wound.

"Non Sibi Sed Omnibus" ("not for one, but for all"). Since 1921 the glacial erratic (see **#78**) at the summit has borne this proclamation, which coincidentally also reflects the philosophy under which Douglas Mountain was established, in 1971, as a Nature Conservancy preserve.

Remarks: *The walk is 1½ miles over moderate terrain, with fairly smooth footing. Day use only. Please stay on the trails. No fires; no pets. Use the litter bins! This is a fine snowshoe trip in winter. There is camping at Sebago Lake State Park from May 1 to October 15. For information, contact Sebago Lake State Park Headquarters, Harrison Rd., Naples, Maine 04055; (207) 693-6612.*

Nearby Place of Interest

Sebago Lake State Park also exhibits some intriguing geomorphological features, including kame terraces, sandy beaches, and the Songo River valley. *The Geology of Sebago Lake State Park* by Arthur Bloom is a useful guide to this area. It is available from the Maine Geological Survey, Department of Conservation, State House Station 22, Augusta, Maine 04333. Brownfield Bog Wildlife Management Area and the Saco River are nearby.

89.

Sabattus Mountain

Directions: Center Lovell, Maine. From Portland, take U.S. 302 northwest about 38 miles to Bridgton. Continue west on U.S. 302 about 2 miles, then turn northwest (right) onto Route 93. Go to Lovell, about 11 miles, then turn right and go north on Route 5. After about 2 miles, Route 5A joins Route 5 in Center Lovell. Continue north on Route 5 for 0.7 mile. Turn right onto Sabattus Rd.; after 1.5 miles, take the gravel fork right and go 0.3 mile to the parking space on the left.

Ownership: P. H. Chadbourne Co. and Diamond International Paper Co.

They say that some of the nicest things come in small packages, and Sabattus, a little member of the scattered Oxford Hills of southern Maine, seems to fit that statement well. It is the sort of place one might choose for a late Sunday afternoon stroll, through woods sprinkled liberally with wildflowers. Signs of small woodland animals are numerous, and the mountain itself is a classic example of a glacially sculpted *stoss and lee* landform (see text below). It is also a fine place for sunset gazing.

The trail, marked with yellow *S*'s painted on trees, begins across the road from the parking space. Step into the tall pine forest (**A**). Although the eastern white pine is currently Maine's state tree, it is not as prominent today as it once was, and there were times when it was virtually absent. Examination of pollen buried in bogs suggests that as the glacial ice margin retreated, first spruces and then jack pine became dominant. It was not until 4,000 to 7,000 years ago, coinciding with a warming trend, that white pine became a prevailing species. During the cooling trend of the following centuries, its population seems to have declined again. In recent times, the number of grand old individuals has been further diminished by man's appetite for masts and other building materials (see #102).

Although some of the pines on this site are quite large, the old fieldstone wall which you join on the right at **B** is an indication that the virgin forest (uncut, ungrazed by domestic animals, and undisturbed by human-caused fires) has not existed here for many, many years. The present grove of white pine is growing on an old field

287

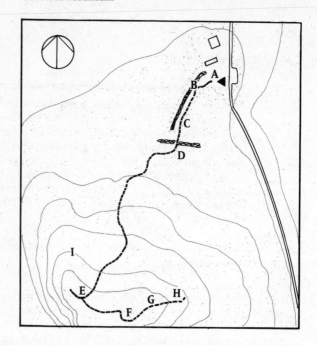

(see #28). Selective browsing of broad-leaved species, good seeding years locally for white pine, a minor warming trend, or a long period between fires may have aided its establishment.

Beyond a little seep, look left for partially healed holes in a pine trunk (**C**). These large, deep, rectangular-shaped holes were made by pileated woodpeckers searching for insects, which have invaded the tree. Generally, the bark and cambium layers of a living tree protect the inner wood from such attacks, but as this pine illustrates, this protection is not totally inviolable. Now the cambium, the thin and only living part of the tree trunk, is slowly growing over the holes. If it can cover them entirely, the dead rings of support wood inside the trunk will again be protected from outside attack, but since insects have already been able to establish themselves inside, the tree's strength may continue to be undermined. This would weaken the pine's ability to withstand high winds, yet it may still stand and grow for years to come.

On the opposite side of the trail, a maple is in the process of falling. As long as some of its roots can maintain connection between soil and leaf, via the food- and water-moving cambium, a section of the tree may survive, even though the disconnected parts die. A red squirrel has been using the root mass as an elevated feeding perch: look for piles of cone scales and "cobs."

Cross a stone wall and walk into a primarily deciduous thicket (**D**) with large, flat-topped stumps half-hidden beneath delicate Lilliputian forests of lichens (see **#7**) and mosses (see **#107**). This short and crowded community is the kind of environment that grouse, many songbirds, and hares frequent: it is full of tasty leaves and seeds and provides many places to hide. As you hike on to the summit, especially in late spring or early summer, note the numerous wildflowers that have joined the larger plants in the chase for space, sunlight, and nutrients. Among them are starflower, Canada mayflower, Indian cucumber root, asters, three-toed cinquefoil, pipsissewa, trailing arbutus, and wintergreen, along with bracken and wood ferns. Starflower blooms quite early. This timing may be related to the fact that it takes a lot of energy to produce flowers and seeds. Blooming when the tree leaves above them are still small and somewhat translucent may allow starflowers to take advantage of more plentiful sunlight than will be available later in the summer.

Walk out onto the ledges (**E**) at the edge of the summit. Compare the steep drop of this southern side with the gentle rise of the slope up which you have just hiked. To the southwest stands another mountain with a profile similar to that of Sabattus: a gentle slope on the northern side and a steep slope on the southern side. Geomorphologists call this shape *stoss and lee*. It is typical of many mountains sculpted by continental glaciers. The northern side, facing into the glacier's flow, was left rather smooth and gentle, partly because ahead on the ridge there was always higher rock, which physically inhibited the glacier from plucking off chunks below. The southern side, facing downstream with the glacier's flow, was left steep and rugged, in part because here blocks could be plucked with less hindrance; the slope downstream was declining rather than ascending, and therefore it provided no obstruction.

Follow the path that heads east (left) along the summit ridge. At **F** is a white patch that at first sight may look like snow. This is an outcrop of quartz, which intruded as a molten blob into the bedrock material, solidified, and has now been exposed at the surface by erosion. Intrusions may vary widely in size and composition. Sometimes they incorporate minerals that form semiprecious crystals, such as garnet and tourmaline. Oxford County is well known for such deposits (see **#91**).

Farther on, a sloped outcrop (**G**) is covered with the delicate, fingered foliage of pale corydalis, a close relative of bleeding heart and dutchman's breeches. In the summer months, look for its yellow-tipped pink flowers, rounded at the base into a bulbous spur. Notice that the leaves are slightly thickened and juicy. This characteristic of holding moisture inside leaves is called *succulence*. It is one of the adaptations that allow plants to live in dry climates or, as here, in places where thin and/or highly porous soil does not retain moisture for long.

The trail ends at a tall glacial erratic (see **#78**) (**H**). Like Sabattus, it is of granitic composition, but you can tell that it comes from elsewhere because its crystals do not match the crystals of the mountain's bedrocks. Under the base of the boulder, you might find some ¾-inch oblong pellets, evidence of a porcupine that has found shelter here.

If you have planned this walk for the purpose of seeing an Oxford Hill sunset, stop at the western ledge edge (**I**) on your way back down the mountain.

Remarks: *The trail is about 1 mile long, round trip; the terrain rises gently most of the time. Sabattus is within easy driving distance of the White Mountain National Forest, where there are campgrounds and numerous hiking trails (see **#90** and **#91**).*

90.

Caribou Mountain

Directions: **Gilead, Maine. From Portland, take Route 26 north and west about 70 miles to Bethel. Follow U.S. 2 west 10 miles to Gilead. Turn south (left) onto Route 113 and go 4.2 miles to the roadside parking space opposite the Caribou Mountain trailhead.**

Ownership: **White Mountain National Forest, U.S. Forest Service.**

Caribou Mountain raises its 2,800-foot summit above the winding valley of Evans Notch. It is an invitation to explore deciduous woods and to enjoy a 360-degree panorama of the White Mountains of New Hampshire (see **White Mountains, Monadnocks, and Eastern Connecticut Highlands**) and the mountains and forests of western Maine. Here, too, you can see some effects various logging practices have on forest growth. This trip can be particularly special in the spring, when the snows are "melting into music" (Muir), swelling the brooks, or in early October, when the woods are bright with autumn colors.

Most of the hike up Caribou Mountain is through deciduous and mixed coniferous-deciduous forests flanking Morrison Brook. In the first section (**A**), rising like pale ghosts among the shaded ground-cover plants are slender Indian pipes, which can be identified in spring, summer, or fall. Although they have no chlorophyll, their leaves reduced to white scales along their stalks, Indian pipes are true flowering plants, closely related to pyrolas (see **#99**). Like many fungi and a few other flowering species, they get their nutrition from decaying organic materials in the soil. When the white flowers bloom, they nod, giving the plant the pipelike shape from which it got its name. As the seeds mature, the capsules turn upward, and eventually the entire plant turns blackish.

In some of the more open woods, spring brings forth an array of violets on the forest floor. These flowers are related to pansies. Look closely at their purple, white, or yellow petals, which are often veined, especially the lower central ones. Botanists believe that these striking

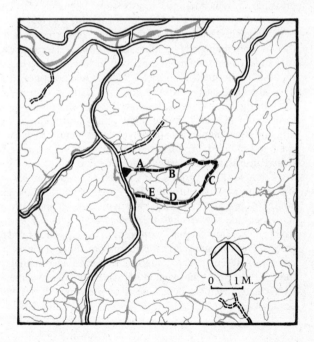

lines help guide insects into the central part of the flower, where the pistil (the female part of a flower) waits to be pollinated. Many species of violet also have beards or hairs in their throats. These brush pollen from the surface of the insect as it probes inside the flower for nectar. There are many species of violet in New England, with habitat needs ranging from marshy to moist and shady to dry and sunny. Violet leaves are high in vitamins A and C and are used by edible-plant enthusiasts as salad greens, cooked greens, and an okralike soup thickener.

If the wind is from the north or east, you may discover that the air has a sulfuric smell. The odor comes from the Bethal pulp mills, into which many of the trees from the White Mountain National Forest are fed. Although the forests here are federally protected, they are managed for multiple use: some trees are cut for timber; others are left as wilderness. It was in the early 1900s that concern over uncontrolled logging on private lands in the White Mountains area began to be expressed on a wide scale. Enough people were vocal about the threats of stream erosion and fire, which were frequently associated with these logging operations, that Congress passed the Weeks Act in 1911, permitting federal acquisition of forest lands in the east. In 1960, the Multiple Use/Sustained Yield Act defined the principles by which national forests would be managed to satisfy the needs of a wide variety of Americans (see also #91).

In the White Mountain National Forest, somewhat more than half the lands are managed for timber harvest. Harvest levels are adjusted periodically, and limitations are set on such practices as clear cutting (cutting all the trees in an area). Soil, slope, and watershed conditions are some of the factors taken into account. Current management in the forest seeks to increase the proportion of species useful to the pulp industry, among them yellow and white birch, white ash, and sugar maple. Two basic types of timber management, even-aged and all-aged, are practiced. In *even-aged management*, forest is cleared from areas of several acres or more, and the new crop of trees that seeds in (from such sources as a seed tree left standing specifically for that purpose) thus covers a considerable extent of land. This practice results in forests with trees all approximately the same age and size. In *all-aged management*, trees are cut on only small patches, and the new crop seeds in closely surrounded by older woods. Forests managed in this manner maintain a mix of tree ages and sizes. Recent research suggests that even-aged management is more effective for reproduction of "desirable" hardwoods, whereas all-aged management better meets the demands of recreation and aesthetics.

In the stretch around **B**, the brook is a series of falls, cascades, slides, and pools flanked by forests. Here you will find yellow birches (see **#72**), some young and golden, others ancient and shaggy. In the fall, they and the other local hardwoods envelop the area in a warm, yellow glow. As you climb higher, in either fall or early spring, you may discover needle ice crunching under your feet in wet sections of the upper parts of the trail. Water freezing near the surface draws more water molecules up between the soil grains. This water also freezes, pulling even more water up from below, until thin needles of ice accumulate in the upper layers of the soil. While this process creates many air spaces in the upper soil when the ice melts, it is very hard on the plant roots. In areas that accumulate needle ice each year, the small plants are often annual species, which die in winter.

In the saddle between the peaks of Gammon and Caribou, turn right onto the Mud Brook Trail. About halfway between this junction and the summit, the Caribou Shelter sits with its back to the trail. As the vegetation becomes shorter, yellow blazes on the rocks lead to the open summit and then west and south among the slabs of the summit ridge (**C**). In June, pocket bogs are sprinkled with white clusters of labrador-tea blossoms. The leathery, evergreen leaves have downward-rolled margins and densely woolly (rust-colored) lower surfaces. These characteristics inhibit moisture loss from the lower side of the leaves, where the stomata (pores) are located. Dried and then steeped for 5 to 10 minutes in boiled water, these leaves make a mild tea, which in large enough quantities is a laxative. Some arctic-alpine species also live in the upper reaches of Caribou Mountain, where the temperatures are quite cold and the growing season is short. Look for mountain sandwort and tundra bilberry among the plants that crowd the cracks in the bedrock (see **#107**).

Following yellow and blue blazes, descend into spruce-fir and then mixed deciduous forests (the blazes end here). There are some very lush miniature "forests" of shining clubmoss in these woods (see **#107** and **#110**). Beyond the Mud Brook crossing, the hardwood forest (**D**) includes white and yellow birch, sugar and red maple, beech, ash, and an occasional red spruce. Note the various bark patterns. The younger trees of any particular species generally have smooth bark, whereas the mature trees of the same species will be cracked or furrowed. This is because trees grow in girth from the cambium layer, which is inside the bark layer. Most bark is not very stretchy, so it cracks as the tree grows. The bark of each kind of tree cracks in a pattern characteristic of its species, so with a little practice, you may find that you can identify most of the trees in a forest like this by their bark alone.

The lower part of the trail (**E**) passes through younger, fairly even-size trees, which suggests that the area may once have been clear-cut. Overgrown sections of an abandoned logging road periodically intersect the woods road, which the Mud Brook Trail follows here. In this area, where most of the twigs and leaves are above the reach of deer, thicket and weedy patches provide enough forage to enable deer to live here. An all-aged forest tends to have a relatively continuous supply of saplings, which may support a deer population for quite a long time. An even-aged stand tends to contain an abundance of saplings in early years and very few later on; thus it may support a deer population only in its youthful years, and those deer will probably disperse into other areas as the forest grows too tall for them.

If you are passing through this area in the late afternoon, you may be lucky enough to see a deer come to drink in the brook. Beyond here, at the foot of the mountain, the last bit of trail passes through dense, young spruce and emerges on Route 113. Go right about 0.4 mile to your car.

Remarks: *This is a 7-mile loop over both gentle and steep terrain. The elevation difference between the trailhead and the summit is about 1,700 feet. For camping and other hiking in the area, see* **#91.**

91.

Bickford Brook

Directions: **Bethel, Maine. Follow directions in #90 to Gilead. Turn south (left) onto Route 113 and go 10 miles to the parking area at the Brickett Place, on the left.**

Ownership: **White Mountain National Forest, U.S. Forest Service.**

One of the delightful qualities of the White Mountains is their large amount of water, dancing in streams and rivers, mirrorlike or wind-ruffled in ponds. Flowing down the wooded slope of Spruce Hill, Bickford Brook is small but exquisite. The trail from the Brickett

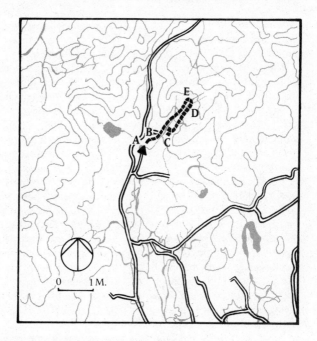

Place passes a swath of blown-down forest and later winds along a section of the brook that includes two sliding falls.

The hike begins on the old woods road behind the 1812 brick house. Just upslope at **A** is a cutover tract. This cutting has been done as part of salvage operations initiated after storm winds in December 1980 blew down extensive numbers of trees. National forests were established as multiple-use lands, to be managed so that as many resources as possible, including scenery, recreation, wood, water, wildlife, and wilderness, would provide long-term benefits to people. When trees on these lands are killed by wind or other environmental phenomena, the timber is sold as salvage. In the 1980 storm, it was estimated that over 60 million board feet were damaged. Of this, about 50 million board feet are scheduled to be salvaged, the remaining trees to be left untouched because of fragile soils, inaccessibility, or too-low volume of timber per acre. The areas from Robbins Ridge (north of South Chatham, Vt.) north and west to Deer Hill, Adams Mountain, and Albany Mountain were hit hardest, with some 5,000 acres of trees reported as completely snapped off or root-sprung (that is, the roots were pulled out of the ground when the tree fell). Many of these areas will be left to reseed from a "seed tree," an older tree left standing for the express purpose that it produce the seeds that will grow into the new forest.

The right-hand road edge in this section is an old stone wall. Although lichen (see **#7**) is abundant on the rock surfaces, close inspection reveals a variety of rock types, including contact zones where two kinds of rock join. A few of the rocks have very large grains. These are the kinds of rocks in which crystals of tourmaline, garnet, amethyst, and smoky quartz are sometimes found. Deer Hill and Lord Hill, just south of here (access road still closed for storm salvage operations in 1982), are among the localities in this area favored by rockhounds who seek the minerals for collections and for use in making jewelry. Mines in this county (Oxford) have produced some excellent specimens. Although these minerals form in both igneous and metamorphic rocks, the largest and most perfect crystals are usually found in extremely coarse-grained igneous rocks, called *pegmatites*, which are composed mainly of feldspar, quartz, and mica. Geologists generally believe that these pegmatites represent one of the last stages in the cooling of granitic magmas, a time when they are enriched in water and rare elements and cool very slowly, thus giving mineral grains time to grow large.

On the left, at **B**, an ancient sugar maple clings tenaciously to life. Most of the trunks and branches are rotting, but one major limb remains alive at the time of this writing. The trunk is like a hotel serving many guests: insect borings honeycomb the interior, woodpeckers have left holes where they fed near the base, a slug hides in a cool cranny. Throughout, the white filaments of dry rot are wedged between the wood cells. It is the work of this fungus that gives the decomposing interior its blocky appearance.

Meet the fire road and go right, then go right again when you reach the Blueberry Ridge Trail junction. Follow pale-yellow blazes down into cool hemlock woods along the bank of Bickford Brook. Just before the brook, take the side trail, right, down to Lower Bickford Slide (**C**). The water courses down a narrow channel that seems to follow the horizontal joint component of the bedrock. Below, the cascades tumble into a pool whose bottom exhibits the contrasting colors of a contact between the whitish bedrock and a blackish dike, which intruded it. The dike (see also **#82**) runs along the base of the cliff on the far bank. More easily erodable than the bedrock, its presence was probably a key factor in the formation of a falls and cliff at this point in the canyon.

Retrace your steps upstream to the main trail and head toward Upper Bickford Slide, crossing the brook shortly after the trail junction. Look for three big red oaks to the right of the path, the nearest one with a 10-foot-long scar rising from the base of its trunk. If the scar extended higher up the tree, one might suspect that lightning had caused the wound. Alternately, if the scar were on the upstream side of the trunk, and other trunks were scarred as well, one might look to the stream for the origin of the wound: rushing water may have battered the tree with rocks. Here, though, it seems more likely that the tree was injured by another tree falling against it.

Continue on the trail, passing some cascades, crossing and recrossing a branch of the stream, and then go directly up the bank (rightish; there is no blaze here) to an old road where you cross a side creek and pick up the yellow blazes again. At **D**, you get a view of the Upper Slide from below. At the junction marked with CTA signs, go right. As you follow the gorge above the slide, the infrequently blazed trail becomes difficult to see. In order to minimize erosion in this delicate area, please try to stick to the blazed route.

Just above another small cascade, the trail crosses the brook for the final time (**E**). Turn over some of the stones that are in the water. You may find ½- to 1-inch-long tubes in the streambed, constructed from sand grains. These are the homes caddis-fly larvae build to protect themselves. The species here use sand for making straight cases. Other species use bits of grass or other plant material, sometimes arranging the pieces lengthwise to form a slender tube, sometimes arranging short pieces crosswise to the circumference making a short, nubbly cylinder. All haul their homes around with them the way a hermit crab carries its snail-shell protection wherever it goes. Most caddis-fly larvae feed on aquatic plants, a few species making silken nets for catching floating materials. After pupating in these cases, the adults emerge as dull-colored insects with rather fluttery and jerky flight, active mainly at night.

From here, the trail heads away from the stream. Go left when you meet the woods road, and return to the Brickett Place.

Remarks: *This is a 2½-mile round trip over bumpy but not steep terrain; the vertical rise is about 400 feet. The trail is difficult to follow through one section because of infrequent blazing. There is fishing in all lakes and streams. Licenses are required. Brook and rainbow trout are the commonly caught species. There are a number of campgrounds in the national forest, four of them accessible from Route 113. They are open year-round, but water is available only from May 15 to October 15. For information, contact the forest's district headquarters at Evans Notch Ranger District, Bridge St., Bethel, Maine 04217; (207) 824-2134. Rockhounding is allowed in the forest with hand tools only, and sites must be restored to near-natural conditions by the end of each day. There is a display of minerals in the forest office in Bethel. Perham's Maine Mineral Store, located at the junction of Route 26 and Route 219, has a wonderful museum display of minerals. They also have a handout with directions to major rockhounding sites in the vicinity.*

92.

Mahoosuc

Notch and Arm

Directions: **Gilead, Maine, and Berlin, N.H. Follow directions in #90 to Gilead. Continue west on U.S. 2 about 14 miles; turn north (right) onto Route 16. Go 6.7 miles to a traffic light in Berlin; cross the Androscoggin on the Twelfth St. Bridge. Immediately, turn right onto Hutchins St. and go 0.4 mile to the stop sign at Morris Lumber Co. Turn left, cross the railroad tracks, then turn right by the Liberty Market. Go 0.4 mile; turn left onto the second and better-traveled dirt road, between large pulp piles—this is Success Pond Rd. (which may be closed at times in winter). Be alert for large, fast-moving trucks. Stay on the main dirt road, passing the Goose Eye and Carlo Col trailhead at 7.8 miles and the Notch trailhead at 10.5 miles. At 11.1 miles, stay on the right-hand fork. The Speck Pond trailhead is at 11.9 miles.**

Ownership: **Brown Paper Co.**

The Mahoosuc Range extends southwest from Old Speck Mountain along Maine's border with New Hampshire. It is striking and rugged country. This hike traverses numerous habitats: second-growth hardwood forests, wind-swept spruce-fir ridges, the edge of Speck Pond, bogs and alpinelike slopes on Mahoosuc Arm, and jumbled boulder mazes in Mahoosuc Notch.

The trail begins as an old dirt road flanked by wet ditches crowded with uniformly tall alder bushes (**A**). Other wetland species include aspen and willow. Shortly, the trail turns from this road, crosses a trickle of water, and enters a mixed deciduous and coniferous forest with abundant clumps of wood ferns. As you proceed, watch for

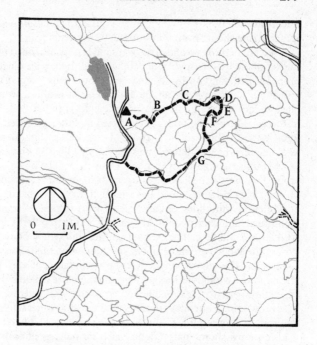

blue blazes and AMC (Appalachian Mountain Club) signs; in the first 2 miles, the route switches frequently from one old road to another.

In some of these lower sections, black cherry is a common member of the slender forests. Notice that many of the cherries are dead. A number of reasons might explain this: (1) black cherry has a fairly short life-span, and these individuals, which probably seeded in with the rest of the forest after logging, may simply be at the end of their span; (2) this cherry is a relatively small and sun-tolerant species and perhaps cannot compete successfully with other species at this time; (3) a cherry disease may be active in the area.

In springtime, look for the white petals of painted trillium to unfold their magenta-blazed centers in the shadows of some of the cooler and more acidic woods. While an aster may make hundreds of flowers in a season, the trillium makes only one—but what a spectacular one!

At **B**, walk through a gravelly patch of pearly everlasting. Just beyond some half-log "boardwalks," a big stump sustains an exceptionally large conk of shelf fungus. Farther on are others, though smaller in size. If you look closely at the underside, you may find numerous tiny insects prowling in and out of the pores or perhaps a spider taking shelter from raindrops, dew, or predators.

A section of more recently cut-over land is now inhabited by a tall thicket of birch and aspen, studded here and there with older trees, probably left standing by logging operations. This is good ruffed-grouse habitat (see **#19**). In fall and winter, it is also a wonderful place to look at tree buds. They are at eye level rather than 50 feet in the air. Most of the buds are protected by little, hardened scales, often very strikingly colored. Those of viberums, though, are naked. The tiny, usually hairy leaves are simply folded close together.

As you rise along the lower ridge, follow the trail along a contour around the northern slope of a ridge nubble, or knob, and continue on the upper ridge (**C**). You pass through a number of coniferous and birch communities, some carpeted with shining Lycopodium, goldthread, and clumps of intermediate wood fern, others crammed with spruce and fir saplings seeded on sites thinned by blowdowns. Where the woods are more open, spreading wood fern crowds the forest floor. Though one might describe a general set of soil, climate, and exposure conditions for the ridge and therefore expect a uniform vegetation pattern, the variability especially of wind (both in degree of severity and frequency) produces different amounts of stress from one spot to another; this results in different groups of inhabitants.

Listen for a short, sharp *kik* or watch for patches of bark scaled from dead conifers. Both may reveal the presence of a black-backed, or arctic, three-toed woodpecker, a boreal species that does have only three toes per foot rather than four. Its preferred habitat is cold spruce and fir forests, but even there it is not common. Maine is the southeastern corner of this bird's range.

At the Cutoff junction, stay left on the Speck Pond Trail. Nestled in a basin in the saddle between Old Speck and Mahoosuc, Speck Pond (**D**) reflects the moods of the sky. As the great continental ice mass was melting, a remnant alpine glacier plucked rock chunks from the headwall of its valley, forming a depression that later filled with water. A pond formed in such a manner is called a *tarn*. Join the Appalachian Trail (white blazes), heading right, down to the pond.

The trail skirts the pond, passing the shelter and tent platforms, and then winds up Mahoosuc Arm (**E**), a truly special place. Amble among dwarfed and tough conifers (including a few larch) and white birches, open ledges, and little pocket bogs (see **Interior Maine**) edged in early spring with the magenta flame of rhodora blooms. Bend down and explore the tangled mat of vegetation that inhabits one of the poorly drained, acidic pockets. If you have explored bogs elsewhere, even in the lowlands, you may find much that is familiar: sphagnum mosses, small cranberry, black crowberry, leatherleaf, labrador tea, pale laurel, rhodora, cotton grass, black spruce. (See **#103, #74,** and **#11** for more on bogs and these species.) Tolerant of cold temperatures and short growing seasons, these species grow from sea level to mountaintops in New England and as far north as the Arctic.

Near the top of the ridge, meet the other end of the Cutoff Trail and go left. Differential erosion, in which certain layers erode more easily than other, more resistant layers, creates a surface of thin ridges and valleys on schist ledge outcrops (**F**). Faint glacial striations diagonally cross the rock bandings.

Descend over rocky, rooty, and steep terrain into forests again. Cloverlike leaves of oxalis, or wood sorrel, can refreshingly pucker your tongue with the bite of oxalic acid (a little like vinegar). Listen for a nasal series of "*ank . . . ank . . .*" If you imitate the notes or go "*psh, psh, psh,*" you may attract a red-breasted nuthatch. With its sharp little beak, it probes bark cracks for insects. Often, you will see it upside down, searching a tree trunk from top to bottom.

From a large, compacted flat area, the trail turns right and enters Mahoosuc Notch (**G**). Great boulders fallen from the cliffs above now lie in a jumble between steep walls, forcing you to scramble over, under, and around. Gardens of polypody fern, labrador tea (see **#90**), and mosses cap the rocks. Underground runoff gurgles below, sometimes near, sometimes far, and then not at all. Some people say they have found ice in some of the deep caves, even in the middle of summer. In the fall, watch ice clatter down the cliffs as they warm in the midafternoon sun.

At the head of the notch, go straight at the trail junction, leaving the AT and following a couple of white and then blue blazes toward Success Pond Rd. Abandoned beaverworks in grassy and shrubby openings are almost hidden now. As the trail crosses back and forth, the trickle of water you follow rather rapidly grows into a babbling brook.

Below the registration box, you meet a logging road. Go right, passing a camp (left), turn left onto the well-used dirt road, and finally go right onto Success Pond Rd. 1½ miles to your car.

Remarks: *This is a 10½-mile loop; much of the terrain is steadily rising, with some very steep sections. Be prepared to scramble over boulders through the notch. The Mahoosuc Range is a popular backpacking area. It is very rugged and full of ups and downs. Mahoosuc Notch has the reputation of being about the slowest mile on the entire Appalachian Trail. There are lean-tos and tent platforms along the route. A small overnight fee is charged. Other AT access trails from Success Pond Rd. also make nice day trips. Success Pond Rd. has many potholes. The trip from the Twelfth St. Bridge to the trailhead may take an hour.*

93.

Old Speck

Directions: **North Newry, Maine. From Portland, take Route 26 north past Newry to Grafton Notch State Park, about 85 miles. Parking for Old Speck and the Appalachian Trail is 3.6 miles inside the park (0.8 mile beyond Moose Cave), on the left.**

Ownership: **Grafton Notch State Park, Maine.**

Old Speck, the northernmost peak of the Mahoosuc Range and the third highest mountain in the state of Maine, rises some 2,700 feet above the floor of Bear Brook valley. Like the rest of the range, it is rugged and steep-sided, a challenging hike, perhaps, for the uninitiated, who will do well to go slowly and enjoy the wildlife and rich vegetation as it changes with increased elevation.

From the edge of the parking lot, follow the white blazes of the Appalachian Trail (AT) for 0.1 mile, then go right, onto the orange-blazed Eyebrow Trail. The surface of a large boulder resting in a slight depression on the left invites close investigation by fingers as well as eyes: finely banded sections of metamorphic rock are sandwiched by large, randomly arranged igneous grains of feldspar, quartz, and mica (granite). Some mountains in Maine, such as Penobscot on Mount Desert Island, are formed of basically just one kind of rock. They exist in places where the bedrock is uniform over large areas. Other mountains, such as Old Speck, are composed of a variety of rock types, reflecting bedrock that is fragmented and that may be composed of rocks that have formed by differing processes and during widely divergent time periods. As you hike Old Speck, you will be able to see some of this variety. Most of the top of the mountain, like the randomly grained parts of this boulder, are granitic rock, but you will readily see from the appearances of the rocks that even the single term *granitic* covers rocks of a variety of structures and compositions. By definition, granitic rocks form underground, from magma, and their major minerals are feldspar, quartz, hornblende, and mica; but the percentages of the various minerals, the grain size, and the grain arrangement may vary quite a bit. Elsewhere on the mountain, you may discover schists and gneiss, banded rocks that often look as though they are flowing, albeit ever so slowly, like cold molasses. They are formed from layered or granular rocks that have been restructured by heat and pressure.

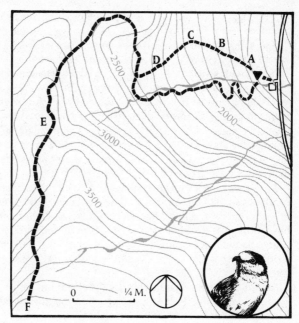

Inset: Gray jay

The forest on this lower slope (**A**) is composed mainly of beech, yellow birch, and maples. There are scattered clumps of Christmas fern and intermediate wood fern (see **#100**). Eastern chipmunks are common and often very active. If you look beneath the edges of rotting logs, old tree stumps, or rocks, you may discover the unobtrusive, 2-inch-diameter opening of one of their burrows. Most active in spring and fall, chipmunks in these northern parts spend the bulk of winter in their dens, torpid for 1 to 8 days at a time and munching on their cache of food (sometimes as large as ½ bushel!) in between. As they prowl the forest floor the rest of the year, they seek a wide variety of foods, including nuts, berries, insects, worms, eggs, mushrooms, and even small birds and snakes. The capacity of their cheek pouches is quite impressive: there have been found, variously, 13 prune pits, 32 beechnuts, 70 sunflower seeds, 145 grains of wheat!

A big yellow birch on the right sports a noselike knob about 8 feet up the trunk. The swelling may be caused by a viral infection.

Shortly beyond, the trail heads essentially straight up the steep flank of the Eyebrow (**B**). Fortunately, the roots of trees here manage to hold at least some soil. Many of the trails in our parks have sort of "happened" as numbers of people used the same route over and over again. Little thought was given to the possible effects on the surroundings. If this trail were to be planned today so that it would create as small an impact as possible on the forest, it might be designed with switchbacks traversing the slope. The less-steep angle of the trail would cause runoff to flow at a lower velocity and with less eroding power. In addition, at the end of each traversing segment, the water would be directed into uncompacted forest floor, where it could be absorbed. Although it is a bit more tiring, this trail is preferable for the ascent route because the numbers of people who hike it these days will do less damage to the trail and slope hauling themselves up it than they would sliding down it.

As the trail swings up and right at **C**, a beaten but unblazed path continues straight on to the base of an overhanging cliff. Weaknesses in rocks, such as cracks or softer minerals, are generally eroded more rapidly than the rest of the rock. The patterns of the weaknesses play a large part in determining the shapes of landforms. Here, frost- and root-wedging along a set of vertical joints (cracks) have formed a cliff.

Return to the main path: you have climbed into spruce, fir, and white birch country. Hobblebush, spreading and intermediate wood ferns, goldthread, wood sorrel (oxalis), shining lycopodium, and mosses are common shrub and forest-floor species.

From the Eyebrow Cliffs (**D**), look back down the broad, glaciated U (see **#85**) of Grafton Notch (see **#94**) and over to the steep, gullied slopes of Old Speck. If you are here in the late fall, a dusting of snow may mantle the top of the mountain, ending in an abrupt edge contouring the slopes at the elevation where the air temperature was warm enough for the snow to turn into rain.

Descend to meet the AT again. Go right at the junction, following white blazes once again. Signs of high winds are abundant: shorter stature of trees, toppled trunks, bleaching snags. The spruce and fir (see **#83**) common here have numerous characteristics that allow them to survive the rigors of this environment. Their roughly conical shape and highly flexible twigs allow them to tolerate or shed snow loads and gusty winds; their waxy and tough-cuticled needles allow them to conserve more of the little unfrozen moisture available; and their shallow root system can anchor them in thin soil. They are not totally immune, though. Each individual has its own tolerance levels, and wind stresses up here often surpass them.

As you ascend the long ridge of Old Speck (**E**), there are numerous places where the overstory is spruce-fir and the understory is dense fir with some spruce. Botanists differ in interpreting the future of such forests. Some suggest that fir is a more prolific seeder than

spruce but that it also has higher "adolescent" mortality from competition. As the canopy trees eventually die and the understory saplings grow up to form the new canopy, more young spruce will
survive than firs. The new forest, then, will be nowhere near as
dominated by firs as this dense, youthful understory population.
Other botanists note that although firs do produce heavy seed crops
more often than spruces, the two species have similar tolerances and
rates of mortality as they grow. Thus, the forest that will occupy this
site in the future may well reflect the relative abundance with which
fir appears in this sapling stage.

In summer and fall, among the mosses and blueberries of the
forest floor, you may spot the bright red tops of *Russula* mushroom
caps. Bend down and look up at their exquisite white gills, which
appear very even and closely spaced. Take a closer look and you will
see that the gills are not arranged with exactly even spacing or with
a repeating pattern of lengths. That, too, is part of their beauty.

Beyond some log steps and stone sections, a curve-banded outcrop presents a mosaic of textures due to differential erosion (see
#92 and **#5**). The hard, crystalline granite is roughly pitted; the
softer, banded inclusions form depressions now with lightly ridged
bottoms where the layers of minerals have eroded at slightly different
rates.

Harsh squawks, a soft *whee-ah,* or a bright and watchfully cocked
eye may announce that a gray jay (or two or three) has discovered
you. "Bold" is an understatement for most of them. Leave no sand-
wich unattended—"camp robber" is another one of their North
Woods names. Like other jay species, this jay of boreal coniferous
forests is an opportunist when it comes to food, eating nuts and
seeds, fruits, insects, carrion, apple pie, and even hot peppers when
available. Gray jays also occasionally raid nests of unwary songbirds.
Most birds, though, are very alert, especially during the nesting season, and you may frequently see small birds dive-bombing a jay that
has approached too closely. On the other hand, you may be surprised to discover that the source of very mellow, whistling bird calls
is none other than one of these bold and often raucous jays.

From the top of the observation tower (**F**), you can look into
Mahoosuc Notch and along the length of the Mahoosuc Range,
some 15 miles as the crow flies and close to 25 by trail. Old Speck
rises by the drainage divide of the valley that Route 26 follows: the
waters north flow into New Hampshire and Canada via the Cambridge River; the waters south flow into Casco Bay via Bear Brook
and the Androscoggin.

For the descent, retrace your way to the AT–Eyebrow Trail junction and stay right on the AT to the parking lot.

Remarks: *The trail is 7½ miles round trip. On the way up, it rises steadily, with some steep sections on the Eyebrow Trail. Many people begin hiking the Mahoosuc Range from this trailhead (see #92). For camping and other hiking in the area, see #95.*

94.
Grafton Notch
Gorges

Directions: **North Newry, Maine. Follow the directions in #93. From the boundary to Grafton Notch State Park, Screw Auger Falls is 1.0 mile, Mother Walker Falls 2.1 miles, and Moose Cave 2.8 miles.**

Ownership: **Grafton Notch State Park, Maine.**

Gorges are not common in Maine, nor in New England in general, and to find three in close proximity in Grafton Notch is a rare treat. Gorges are formed in various ways, and usually by a combination of processes. In some cases, recent uplifting of horizontally bedded sedimentary rocks has led to the erosion of huge gorges, such as the Grand Canyon or Canyonlands. In the east, where the rocks are igneous and metamorphic and there has not been recent uplift, gorges are indeed smaller, but often rich in detail. Screw Auger Falls, Mother Walker Falls, and Moose Cave are dynamic illustrations of the effects of diverse gorge-creating phenomena.

One mile north of the park boundary, stop at the parking lot on the left (**A**). Walk out onto the flat ledges near Bear Brook, above the falls. The bedrock exposed here is fairly fine-grained granite (see #93) with dike intrusions of coarse-grained pegmatite (see #91) in which it is easy to identify the large crystals of its major minerals: white feldspar, translucent gray quartz, and shiny, clear mica. This broad, flat area has been eroded along a horizontal joint in the granite. Look for it as a long crack flush with the base of the bank on the far side of the brook.

A short walkway leads to Screw Auger Falls. What a fantastic sculpture of winding curlicues! The Bear Brook of today, even in its flood stages, could not create such a gorge, although it *is* modifying the topography it has inherited. The major erosive agent here was probably a heavily laden glacial meltwater (see **#58**). Thomas Brewer, who studied gorges in Maine for the Critical Areas Program, suggests that the course of this gorge was inscribed into the bedrock by a stream that originally flowed on or in the dead ice of this valley's receding glacier. Such streams generally had high-volume flows and carried large loads of abrasive rock fragments. This stream eroded its sinuous course through the ice, reached bedrock, and continued, incising the curves into the rock. Smoothed grooves and holes well above the present brook's banks further attest to the large volume of water that must have flowed through this valley as the glacier continued to melt northward. Notice that the stream has undercut some of the side walls and has even left a free-standing wall with a "window" through it!

Drive another 1.1 miles to the Mother Walker Falls pulloff on the right (**B**). The right-hand fork of the trail leads to an overlook of the lower portion of the gorge. This gorge appears to follow a contact zone in the bedrock where granitic and partially pegmatized metamorphic rocks meet. A contact zone is often a region of weakness. In such places, erosive forces may work more rapidly or, as here,

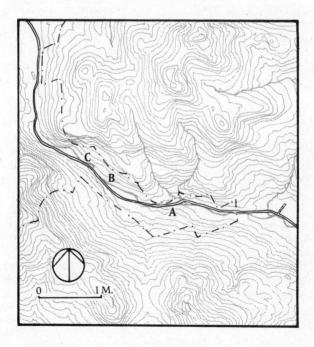

0   1 M.

tensions in the rocks may be released through movement producing a fault, or crack (see **#38** and **#50**). The interpretive sign at the overlook illustrates a model that geologists use to explain their current understanding of the processes that created Mother Walker Falls gorge. Remember that this model may change as our perceptions and understanding of this phenomenon grow. Similarly, an early research team in this area had proposed a different model, in which large volumes of glacial meltwater eroded a small waterfall or gorge along the weak contact zone in the bedrock; in recent times, Bear Brook eroded this into a steep-walled slot. They only *suspected* that faulting might also have occurred in that zone.

Walk up the trail to the top of the gorge. Smooth grooves above the current streambanks mark former water channels. The "natural" bridge here and the one at Screw Auger Falls are the only two known in the state.

Drive another 0.7 mile to the Moose Cave pullout, also on the right (**C**). Walk left around the short loop trail as it winds down to the gorge and returns via the "Moss Garden." On the first big bend, a yellow birch (see **#72**) illustrates its tenacity and flexibility: it has fallen over, and two of its major branches have been cut off, but a third major branch is growing upward as a new trunk. The plant hormone auxin, which in low concentrations promotes cell elongation (growth) of shoots, also indirectly helps stems to grow upward toward sunlight. Auxin is destroyed by sunlight; more auxin was destroyed on the sunnier side of the birch branch than on the shadier side, so the branch cells elongated more on the shadier side, and the new growth turned upward toward the sunlight.

Fork left twice to reach Moose Cave, a narrow section of gorge with a great slab of rock hanging over it. As with Mother Walker gorge, geologists think that this gorge has formed in a fault zone. Listen to the water gurgling below. It sounds as though it may be falling somewhere in its subterranean crack. Below the big downstream boulder is a pool, visible from a point farther along the main trail. The water is so still in this pool that it is difficult to believe that the brook running through Moose Cave connects with it, yet it may somewhere down near the bottom of the pool.

Continue left on the main trail. The "Moss Garden," sadly, is a good example of what happens to delicate vegetation when too many people pass through, however good their intentions. Most of the moss and lichen that once covered these rocks has disappeared. In this particular case, destruction of the plant community may be temporary, and the same type of community *may* reappear if we simply leave the area alone. This is not the case for all communities in all environments, though. Destruction of a tropical rain forest for even a few years changes the environment so much that, even if we tried to, we could not establish another forest there or even a domesticated crop. Temperate lands are much more tolerant of human uses than are tropical ones, but *all* environments are sensitive to overuse.

Remarks: *There are picnicking but no camping facilities in Grafton Notch State Park. The season is from May 15 to October 15. The Old Speck hike begins 0.7 mile beyond the Moose Cave pulloff. The Step Falls Nature Conservancy Preserve (#95) is 2 miles outside the state park.*

95.
Step Falls

Directions: **North Newry, Maine. From Portland, take Route 26 north to Newry, about 75 miles. Continue north on Route 26 for 7.6 miles to the dirt-and-grass parking field on the right just before the road crosses Wight Brook; there is no sign.**

Ownership: **The Nature Conservancy.**

In Step Falls Preserve, the waters of Wight Brook tumble in a series of cataracts and small pools before they join Bear Brook, and then the Androscoggin River and Merrymeeting Bay, on their way from the flanks of Baldpate Mountain to the Gulf of Maine. The desire of the former owners to see this scenic and geologically instructive area protected, combined with a fund-raising drive, led to the establishment of Step Falls as the first preserve of the Maine Chapter of The Nature Conservancy in 1964. A wonderful place for a family picnic, the falls are visible after a short walk; the top of the falls is accessible with only a little more exertion.

The trailhead is at the back end of the grassy area, where an apple tree bears a nearly hidden white arrow. The Nature Conservancy welcome sign is a few yards farther in. From there, the trail is marked with white blazes and arrows. Begin walking through a cool coniferous forest (**A**). The trees, in the main, are fairly young. Here, as in so much of the state, the forests have been cut over probably more than once. Red spruce, and to a minor extent balsam fir, feed the ever-increasing demand for paper products, while white pines are turned into boat masts and boards.

Farther in, lustrous golden-yellow birches occupy a flatland near the river (**B**). The forest is now a mixture of conifers and deciduous trees. In summer and fall, look on the ground for white-to-lavender branched clumps of coral fungus. The upper part of each "antler" is the spore-bearing surface, akin to the gills of the mushroom. Spore production is an asexual (one parent) form of reproduction. It does not have as much built-in flexibility as the genetic combining of sexual reproduction, but on the other hand, asexual individuals do not need to spend energy on finding a mate. Both strategies have been found successful: some organisms use one, some the other, and a few organisms, such as ferns (see **#100**) and aphids, use both in alternation.

Snags (standing dead trunks and limbs) in the cool conifers beyond show signs of recent woodpecker activity (**C**). The woodpecker tongue, which is stretchy, narrow, pointed, and barbed, is a marvelous tool for extracting insects from their woody hiding places. It is

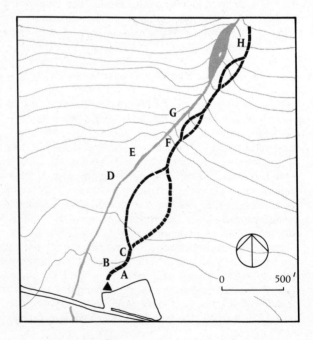

very long, is attached near the bird's forehead, and curves around the back and bottom of the skull! The tongue is also part of the shock-absorbing system that prevents woodpecker concussions.

Stay left at the fork (and also the ones farther up) and join Wight Brook where it bounces among numerous boulders (**D**). This process mixes a good deal of oxygen into the water, helping to make good habitat for brook trout.

The vegetation on the far bank (**E**) contrasts markedly with that through which you now walk. Hardwoods occupy the highly sunny (south-facing) and well-drained slope opposite, whereas hemlocks and other conifers dominate the cooler, less porous soils of this riverside land (see **#32**).

A bit farther on, the trail follows a riverine terrace (**F**) left as the brook cut down through glacial till deposited some 10,000 years ago. In these shadowy woods, trillium, goldthread, and partridge-berry share the forest floor with abundant mosses (see **#107**). As you enter more open areas upstream, blueberries, mountain cran-berry, and trailing arbutus are more common.

Nearly the whole of the falls is visible from its base (**G**). The bedrock over which the water cascades is granite (see **#93**) intruded by mineralized veins consisting of thin white lines of quartz and by pegmatite dikes (see **#91**), which compose the extremely coarse-grained bands. These dikes contain crystals of pink feldspar, gray quartz, and almost transparent mica. All these features are of igneous origin. As the magma cooled, it shrank in volume, and cracks, or joints, developed. Others formed later as earth tensions heaved crustal rocks into mountains. Granite often fractures into perpendicular sets of parallel joints. Here one set of cracks is nearly horizontal, the other almost vertical. As joint blocks of bedrock were excavated by the stream, the series of falls formed with the height of the drop of each corresponding to the spacing between the vertical joints.

From a large boulder (**H**) a few yards below the red boundary markings, you can look down into a classical pothole scoured by waterborne rocks and sand (see also **#81** and **#110**). Most of these potholes and grooves were formed initially by eddies, which eroded the weak joints or pockets of softer rock (as in an inclusion or a dike).

Remember before you leave to look outward, over the falls, to the view of mountains to the south.

Remarks: *The trail is 1 mile round trip over smooth, sometimes rocky, terrain. It rises gently to the falls area. This is a wonderful place for a sunny-day picnic. Day use only; no fires permitted.* Caution: *the rocks*

*around the falls may be slick even when they are dry. Camping is available
year-round at White Mountain National Forest, 20 miles southwest, although water is available only from May 15 to October 15; also at Mount
Blue State Park, 65 miles north, May to October 15.*

96.
Tumbledown Mountain

Directions: **Weld, Maine. From Bangor, take I-95 then U.S.
2 west about 85 miles. Turn right onto Route 156; go 14
miles northwest to Weld. Continue northwest, now on
Route 142; after 2.2 miles, turn left in Weld Corner onto
Byron Rd. After 0.5 mile, continue straight ahead onto a
dirt road (the tar road swings left, toward Mount Blue
State Park). From this point, follow the major dirt road;
at 2.2 miles you will pass two dirt roads on the left; at 3.7,
two on the right; at 4.6, two old woods roads. Parking for
Tumbledown Mountain is on the left, opposite the trailhead, at 5 miles.**

Ownership: **Diamond International Paper Co.**

Tumbledown Mountain pokes its 3,000-foot peaks up from the logging country of west central Maine. It offers a rugged and engaging
climb through a variety of habitats. Downy woodpeckers and goshawks are among the year-round residents of the area. Fascinating,
convoluted bedrock patterns are exposed on the open eastern peak,
which also offers comfortable picnic spots overlooking Tumbledown
Pond and the lower regions to the south.

The trailhead is on the north side of the road. The sign is frequently stolen, but red-and-orange blazes mark the route and are
usually visible at the road edge. The first part of the trail passes
through mixed deciduous and coniferous forests and thickets, crosses
a creek once occupied by beaver, and leads through a section of very
densely packed young conifers, which reduce the trail to just barely
body-width.

Many factors influence what species of plants grow where. Plants
generally spread to a new location via their seeds. Especially in late
summer and fall, look for seeds in this area. Some of them, like those

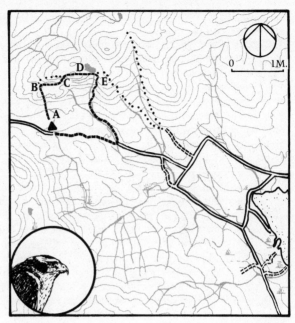

Inset: Goshawk

of asters, are very light and have feathery structures that allow them to be blown over great distances. Other seeds, like those of beeches and oaks, are heavy and disperse over only very small distances unless they are carried away and *not* eaten by animals. Seeds, like those of maple, spruce, and fir, are intermediate in weight and have a winglike appendage that allows them to be airborne over short distances. Still other seeds, like those of burdock and mistletoe, have barbs or sticky coatings by which the seeds can adhere to animals until brushed off later in their travels. Whatever way they travel, they are fairly randomly scattered and do not necessarily land in a spot that is suitable for their growth. A seed that landed on the duff below the thick conifer growths at **A** would have little chance of survival, no matter how "healthy" its genetic makeup.

While dispersal may not be highly selective, germination is. Each kind of seed needs to absorb a certain amount of water in order to germinate. If it gets some but not enough, it may just rot in the soil. If it gets too much, it may rot also or drown from lack of oxygen. The seeds of aspens germinate within 2 or 3 weeks from the time they fall from the trees in June. They are very small and tend to establish themselves successfully only where their tiny roots begin to grow in direct contact with bare soil. Beechnuts, on the other hand, spend the winter in a dormant state on the ground. Photoperiod (length of daylight versus darkness) and temperature are key factors in stimulating the spring resumption of growth in these seeds. The combination is important as a safety factor. If temperature alone were involved, a seed might germinate during a January thaw, only to be frozen to death by the chills of February. Many kinds of seeds can lie for a year—or for many years—on a field or forest floor, waiting for proper conditions to occur. Once germinated, a seedling must survive the rigors of its first summer or, if a perennial, its first few years, in order to become firmly established. High ground-surface temperatures, surface drought, and frost heaving are among the common causes of seedling mortality. Some plants must make incredible numbers of seeds in order that at least a few survive the rigors of infancy. The presence of plants in the woods and fields here is thus not only a matter of proper soil and climatic conditions, but also a result of the vagaries of dissemination, the particular sequence of microclimatic events, and the particular adaptations of each species.

In the more open woods of the area, you may spy downy woodpeckers industriously searching for insects and other small creatures hidden inside wood or within cracks of bark. This type of food is readily available throughout winter as well as summer, so downy woodpeckers do not need to migrate, and you may see them in Maine year-round. For birds, food-supply availability is a major factor influencing whether or not a species will migrate. Cold is not particularly a problem for them, since they sport the original down parka. However, birds that winter here must be able to find protection from the elements. With their chisellike beaks, downy woodpeckers excavate a small roosting cavity in the trunk or a branch of a tree. Around this spot, each bird defends a winter territory large enough to supply it with food until the spring breeding season. The young are usually reared in a different cavity, excavated by both parents. In early summer, you may hear an incessant, plaintive chippering issuing from a tree. Look for a nest hole anywhere from 15 to 50 feet above the ground. If you conceal yourself and wait patiently, you may have the good fortune to see parent downy woodpeckers as they arrive to feed their calling young.

About a mile from the road, the trail begins to climb steeply up the first ridge of the mountain. In order to minimize erosion here, please walk on rocky surfaces as much as possible. From the top of this ridge (**B**), you will be able to see the western summit of Tumbledown. The rusty, but not yet lichen- and algae-covered section of the peak's face is the scar that remains from a large rockfall not too many years past. Imagine the roar that must have arisen when all the lighter-colored rocks on the talus slope below came tumbling and crashing down from their former positions on the cliff!

From the large pile of stones, known as a cairn, follow the right-hand fork of the trail, marked by red, yellow, and white blazes and arrows. As you ascend the gully between Tumbledown's east and west peaks, the bright, sunny green of hay-scented fern fronds (see **#100**) spills down a side gully (**C**). This fern commonly clogs openings in Maine's moist woods. At the top of the gully, climb up and through a short boulder tunnel. Two rusted iron rungs inside provide added foot and hand holds. From the notch, follow the right-hand fork of the trail up the east peak of the mountain (**D**). If you have climbed peaks in other glaciated areas, you will probably recognize signs of the Ice Age: glacial striations, especially on the north-facing surfaces, and the steep southern face of the mountain mass itself (see **#89**). The rock surfaces exposed along the ridge have wonderful patterns and textures. Differential erosion (or erosion at different rates due to differences in the resistance of given materials) of various contorted layers of minerals has left the surface wrinkled in parallel sets of tiny ridges and valleys.

From the summit, a pleasant alternate descent route is via Tumbledown Pond and the Brook Trail (**E**). Follow the summit ridge down toward the pond, picking up any of a number of trails that join along the shore and lead to the outlet on the south side. The Brook Trail begins just on the far side of the outlet stream. There are red, yellow, and white blazes, but they are not easy to follow. The red blazes go all the way to the end. Cross the brook near the bottom, and shortly thereafter meet a very rocky woods road. Go left.

While walking this road, I saw a goshawk, which had caught and was feeding on a snowshoe hare. Its prey was so heavy that the hawk could fly with it for only very short distances, and even then, the long legs of the hare dragged along the ground. The goshawk is a member of the broad-winged and long-tailed group of hawks known as *accipiters*. These hawks generally hunt in wooded country, their long tails providing the ruddering capability needed for quick and agile flight between trees. Goshawks are rather secretive hawks of northern forests, where they subsist mainly on birds and, to a lesser extent, on small mammals (see also **#48**). Stay left at the next junction. When you meet Byron Rd., go right 1⅓ miles to your car.

Remarks: *This is a 5½-mile loop that includes a good deal of steep and rocky terrain. The Chimney Trail, which takes off left from the cairn at* **B,** *is very steep and rugged. If you are a skilled hiker and scrambler and decide* *to follow this route, it is advised only as an* ascent *passage, returning via the trail described here. Camping is available at Mount Blue State Park, May 30 to October 15.*

97.

Bigelow Mountain:
The Horns

Directions: **Stratton, Maine. From Bangor, take I-95 then U.S. 2 west about 80 miles to Farmington. Take Route 4 north about 2 miles, then turn north (right) onto Route 27; follow it about 25 miles through Kingfield and Carrabassett Valley to the road to Sugarloaf Mountain on the left. From this point, continue 3.1 miles on Route 27, then turn right onto the dirt road to Stratton Brook Pond. With care, you can drive the 1 mile to the trailhead, where the new Appalachian Trail heads up to Horns Pond and the Horns. There is a little space just west of the trailhead where a few cars can fit just off the road, and there is space right at the trailhead for another car or two.**

Ownership: **Maine Bureau of Parks and Recreation.**

The Bigelow Range stretches some 17 miles across the logging and ski country of west central Maine. The long ridge-crest of Bigelow Mountain, with its two pairs of conical peaks, affords superb travel through boreal habitats where you may discover such creatures as spruce grouse and springtails.

Follow the white blazes of the Appalachian Trail (AT) north from the Stratton Brook Pond Rd. toward Horns Pond. The first part of the trail passes through the forested lowlands that surround the base of Bigelow Mountain (**A**). Numerous tree species that live here, for instance almost all of the conifers, have ranges restricted to northern latitudes. Others, like red maple and American beech, grow southward all the way to Georgia and Florida. No matter what their range, all the individuals that survive up here, where winter temperatures drop well below freezing, have special adaptations that help prevent winter injury. These injuries may be from such external forces as loads of ice, which make branches and trunks more susceptible to breakage by wind or simply from the sheer weight added to the structure. Damage may also result from internal forces such as freezing: ice crystals may mechanically disrupt cells, or a plant's metabolism may be disturbed by loss of water or by too rapid release of water in thawing. Both lengthening of nights and repeated exposure to near-freezing temperatures seem to be involved in stimulating the changes (collectively called the hardening process) that protect the plant tissues from these potential injuries.

Ice forms inside both frost-hardy and non-frost-hardy plants, but while in non-hardy plants it forms inside and outside the cells and destroys them (as in frostbite), in hardy individuals it forms only between the cells (as in frost nip). Some of the changes that allow this are (1) the permeability of the cell membranes to water increases so that as ice crystals begin to grow outside the cells, water is drawn from the inside of the cells into the intercellular spaces, leaving the antifreeze factors (such as sugars) within the cell more and more concentrated as ice continues to build up in the less sensitive areas outside the cell walls; (2) the structure of the protoplasm and the cell membranes becomes less viscous and thus less susceptible to mechanical injury by ice crystals. Although botanists have

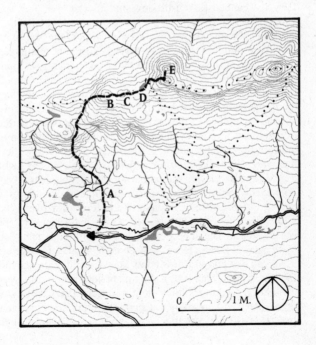

been able to identify a number of the mechanisms involved in the hardening process, many of the details remain mysteries. Whatever the whole picture may turn out to be, we know that if we tried to transplant Florida's vegetation into Maine, most of the plants would be unable to survive the winter here.

When you meet the Bigelow Range Trail, go right, still toward Horns Pond, and ascend into dense, dark spruce and fir woods (**B**). This is the home of spruce grouse. Like other grouse, these birds have heavy, chickenlike bodies, strong legs well adapted for walking, and short, broad wings that make a loud, flapping sound when the grouse fly. Spruce grouse seem relatively unafraid of humans, and with a little caution and patience you may be able to watch some fascinating behavior. Male spruce grouse display for their ladies in spring, summer, and fall. Watch how the size of the male's bare red "eyebrow" increases as he puffs out his body feathers and spreads his gorgeous tail erect. If you listen carefully, you may be able to hear a soft rustle, as of silk, as he broadens the fan of his tail and then reduces it again. Females sometimes make this sound, too, while they walk with tail less widely spread and in its regular low position. Spruce grouse spend a good deal of their time in coniferous trees where they prowl the branches and feed on needles and buds. They also eat berries, mushrooms, and insects.

Take a side trip, right, to the marked outlook (**C**). To the north, Flagstaff Lake spreads in a huge crescent around the base of Bigelow. This huge puddle in the Dead River is currently maintained by a control dam at the northeast end of the lake. That is Flagstaff today. In the days of the Revolutionary War, when Benedict Arnold led his campaign against Quebec, he poled, paddled, carried, and hauled up the rough Kennebec River and then spent days and days among the tortuous windings of the Dead River; no lake was reported then. Geologists believe that when the glaciers were retreating, thousands of years ago, a barrier of till in the area of the current outlet locked meltwaters into a lake, whose surface was some 30 feet higher than the current lake level. The till barrier presumably was breached by an ancient outflow stream, which subsequently eroded its channel deep enough to drain the lake to the level of a river—that with which Benedict Arnold contended. Visible in the southern and western ends of the lake are extensive deltas built from sediments brought by the glacial meltwaters as they entered the ancient Lake Flagstaff.

As you descend to Horns Pond, keep straight at the junction with the Horns Pond Trail (this is the trail of your return trip). Numerous compacted sections of forest floor in this area (**D**) are now marked off and labeled Forest Floor at Rest. The trampling of too many feet has taken its toll on the life-supporting capabilities of the soil, both for the large organisms such as trees, which we readily see above the surface, and for the smaller organisms such as fungi, bacteria, and insects, which inhabit the underground environments. The "dirt" you might pick up in your hand is really a complex event. It is composed of interacting bits of minerals weathered from the bedrock below or brought into the area by erosive agents, organic material in various stages of decay, water in the pores between the grains or coating the grain surfaces, pockets of air, roots, insects, earthworms and their tunnels, fungi, and billions of microorganisms. This underground world is a very restless place. Most of the mobile organisms move upward and downward in response to fluctuations in such factors as water, heat, food, and oxygen. For instance, if oxygen is cut off by extended flooding, nonmobile organisms and small organisms not strong enough to overcome the surface tension of a film of water may suffocate and die. Anaerobes (organisms that do not need oxygen) will probably do just fine. Animals like moles may burrow deeper, while others, like earthworms, may crawl up to the surface. Some, like the adult forms of many insects and millipedes, have a waterproof cuticle that enables them to wait out temporary flooding. Numerous species, especially insects, that do not inhabit the soil during the warmer months spend the winter in the insulated protection of the soil.

If you are here in the early spring when the snow is melting and saturating the soil with water, you may discover that the snow and ground surfaces are alive with masses of tiny crawling and jumping dark spots. On close inspection, these elongated "spots" can be seen to have six legs and a springlike appendage. These are springtails, the most generally distributed of all insects, coming to the surface to escape the flood below. They reportedly feed on decomposing organic matter that is in the soil or has accumulated on the snow surfaces.

From the lean-tos, it is about a half-mile climb up to the open peak of the South Horn (**E**). Across the valley to the south is Sugarloaf Mountain, its north face ribboned with ski runs. At one time, a similar fate was planned for Bigelow and gave rise to a ten-year battle between developers and conservation groups. A petition drive resulted in a referendum vote that established the Bigelow Preserve, some 35,000 acres including the entire Bigelow Range and a buffer zone around its base.

From the peak, head back down to Horns Pond, taking a side trip up the North Horn if you are ready to tackle another summit. Beyond the lean-tos, go left down Horns Pond Trail. You descend from terrace to terrace, pass the marsh visible from the peaks, and travel through mixed deciduous and coniferous woods where pileated woodpeckers may holler loudly to one another. Go right at the junction with the Firewarden's Trail, left at the junction with the woods road, and right when you reach Stratton Brook Pond Rd. As you walk the 1¼ miles back to your car, you are on or flanking an esker segment (see **#77** and **#108**).

Remarks: *This is a 10-mile hike over both gentle and steep terrain. There is camping at Rangeley Lake State Park about 30 miles southwest of Stratton; the season begins when the late ice breaks up and continues to October 15. In Eustis, 10 miles farther up Route 27, there is a unique stand of old-growth red pines. For other hikes nearby, see listings in* 50 Hikes in Maine, 50 More Hikes in Maine, *and the* AMC Maine Mountain Guide.

98.
Big Squaw
Mountain

Directions: **Greenville, Maine. From Bangor, take Route 15 northwest to Dover-Foxcroft and west (joined by Routes 6 and 16) to Abbot Village, about 50 miles. Turn north (right) with Routes 6 and 15 and go another 22 miles to Greenville. Turn west (left), still with Routes 6 and 15. After 5.3 miles, you pass the Squaw Brook Forest Service Campsite on the right, then cross the brook; 0.1 mile farther, turn left onto a Scott Paper Co. dirt road. Go 1 mile to a small turnaround; there is parking space on the left.**

Ownership: **Scott Paper Co.**

According to an old Indian tale, Maquaso, wife of a legendary chief, Kineo, left her wicked husband and eventually died on the top of a mountain. The Indians named the mountain for her, and today we call it Big Squaw. The tower on the summit offers a panoramic view dominated by Moosehead, the largest lake in Maine, which the Indians called Mspame, or "large water." The hike up Big Squaw, rising some 2,000 feet from the lake's southwest shore, takes you through some lovely hardwood forests and up into wind-pelted co-

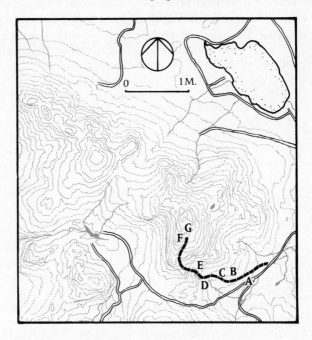

nifers. Wildflowers abound in the wetland thicket near the beginning of the trail. Red foxes are among the numerous animals that roam the wooded slopes.

The trailhead, marked by a rough sign and some plastic flagging, is across the road from the parking space. There are no blazes, but the old woods road and trails are well worn and easy to follow. The wet area at **A** is colonized by numerous species of wildflowers and ferns. In August, shady places may be brightened by the orange, spurred flowers of jewelweed. Small green pods will replace the blossoms in the fall. Touch one. If it is ripe, you may jump as the pod snaps and shoots its seeds into the surrounding brush. This dispersal mechanism has given rise to the plant's other common name, touch-me-not. Nettle, whose stinging hairs even more vividly suggest "touch me not," also lives in moist places, sometimes intermixed with jewelweed. Coincidentally, the juice from crushed jewelweed stems and leaves is an old remedy used to alleviate the sting of nettles.

Forests of northern hardwoods with scattered conifers cover the lower slopes of Big Squaw (**B**). Beneath them in some sections grow thousands of beech and sugar-maple saplings. This profusion of tiny trees could originate from a variety of conditions, which botanists are just beginning to glimpse and to comprehend. It seems that stress on the canopy trees, from disease, drought, fire, cutting, and/or overall climatic changes, may commonly trigger increased reproduction. Flurries of root shoots appear under some infected trees, such as beech. Excellent seed-production years of other species seem often to correlate with changes in climate. During a dry period in the eastern states around the 1950s, for example, there was a significant dieback of birch and, to a lesser extent, of sugar maple trees. Abundant seed production here might be linked to the stress of that drought or another similar occurrence, after which the seeds lay on the forest floor for years perhaps, until proper germinating conditions arose.

Scat (animal droppings) 2 inches long, slightly twisted, usually pointed at both ends, and often deposited on flattish rocks along the trail indicates the presence of foxes. The materials in the scat offer clues as to what the foxes have been eating; you may find fur, pieces of bone, teeth, claws, seeds, fruit skins, grass fibers, and insect exoskeletons. The red fox is an opportunist when it comes to food. Although mice make up a great portion of its diet, in summer and fall, a quarter of its intake may be plant materials. Purple scat from July and August blueberry feasts is a common sight in many upland and barrens areas. Mainly nocturnal, red foxes hunt a wooded or brushy territory about 5 miles in diameter, caching under leaves, grasses, or snow any food they do not consume immediately. Great horned owls have been known to take pups, but humans and dogs remain the major fox predators in New England. Despite this, people have reported watching red foxes that seemed to be intent on befriending dogs. Red foxes have also been seen leaping around caribou and bighorn sheep, bumping and nipping them and bouncing away, as if asking to play, then resting among the flocks when they lay down. As far as biologists know, this playful-seeming interaction is unusual between animals of two different species. More commonly observed are predatory, territorial, and mutually tolerant interactions.

Beyond a fairly level area of sugar maple seedlings growing beneath a canopy of mixed deciduous trees, the trail climbs a bit. As it flattens again, look right for a 6-inch-diameter sugar maple whose bark is growing around a piece of wire to which an insulator is attached (**C**). In 1982, the insulator was about 3 feet above the ground. How much higher up will it be in another 20 years? Why, no higher at all. A tree trunk thickens as the cambium grows new rings of wood cells, but it increases in height only at the tips of the branches, where cell elongation takes place (see **#94**). The insulator will remain at its current distance from the ground no matter how tall the tree grows.

Find some mountain-ash trees as you cross the creek on a bridge (**D**). In the fall, you may meet a flock of migrating robins stopping to feed on the bright red-orange berries, which not only supply juicy nutrients to birds but also helped botanists to classify mountain-ash as a close relative of roses rather than of true ash trees. Take a few minutes to watch the robins (see **#100**), for although they are common, they, too, are among the marvels of life. Notice subtle details of their coloring, such as the white ring around each eye, the patterning of grays on the back, the white tips on the outer tail feathers. Watch the birds as they interact with other members of the flock with which they spend their winter months. Ornithologists believe one advantage of flocking to be that, although a group is more conspicuous than a single bird, each individual has a higher chance of survival from a predator if it is in a flock rather than alone; not only is it possible to receive an earlier warning due to the watchfulness of many eyes, but there is also the "safety in numbers" factor. A goshawk would have trouble zeroing in on one robin among the many in a flock taking flight from one of these mountain-ashes, but if one bird were to stray in a different direction, it would provide an easy target. The precision with which flocks move and turn together has probably grown from this selective pressure.

In a glade at **E**, an old warden's cabin lies abandoned amidst a profusion of hay-scented, long-beech, and spreading wood ferns. In late summer, the backs of the fronds are freckled with *sori,* clusters of cases that hold the ferns' spores (see **#100**).

Beyond the next creek crossing, ascend some steep stone steps. In order to minimize further erosion in this area, please walk on the stones rather than the dirt next to them. As you climb higher, the hardwood forests give way to wind-pruned conifers mixed with mountain-ash. From the lookout tower at the summit (**F**), exceptional views spread around you. Moosehead Lake, the hub of a 1,200-square-mile drainage system, has seen much activity as logs fed into it from its shores and inflow streams were encircled with a boom (logs fastened together lengthwise to form an enclosure around a group of loose logs) and towed to the outlet stream. Before the coming of towboats, moving such loads across a lake the size of Moosehead was a slow and backbreaking process. A batteau (the commonly used river-driving boat, 20 or more feet long and pointed at bow and stern, which could be paddled, rowed, or poled) would carry an anchor out the distance of rope available and then drop it. Then men on a raft attached to the boom of logs would push their capstan around and around, winding up the rope, bringing the raft and boom up to the anchor spot. They would repeat this, often working 2 or 3 days and nights at a stretch, until they reached the outflow of the lake (see also **# 109** and **#111**).

Notice that the bays, headlands, and ridges of the area are arranged in roughly parallel lines trending northeast–southwest. The bedrock here is composed of numerous bands of igneous and meta-sedimentary bedrocks trending in that same northeast–southwest orientation. Differential erosion (see **#5**) of these has contributed to the lineup of landforms you see today.

From the base of the tower, a short trail leads northward to an overlook of Mirror Pond (**G**). Occupying the round basin plucked by the head of an alpine glacier during the latter stages of deglaciation, it is called a *tarn* (see **#92**). Tarns generally have small drainage basins that have been scoured down to bedrock very recently (the last glaciers melted from Maine only 10,000 to 20,000 years ago) and that, therefore, have not had time to build up much mass of organic matter. Consequently, the waters that flow into tarns tend to introduce organic sediments at a slow rate, and many of the ponds are still clear, reflecting pools, holding very little life.

As you retrace your path to the tower and then down the mountain, notice the beautifully patterned rock surface near the old wooden platform. The pale, wavy stripes that cut through the light and dark layers are formed of minerals intruded into the cracks in the sedimentary rock when it was metamorphosed some 350 million years ago. I was told I might find small garnet and tourmaline (see **#91**) crystals here. I found numerous tiny, faceted pits where garnets had once been. Perhaps you will have better luck.

Remarks: *This hike is 6½ miles long, round trip. The first half rises gently on old logging roads; the second half is a bit rockier and steeper. Camping is available at the Maine Forest Service Squaw Brook Campsite near the trailhead. For fishing, see* **#99**.

99.

Mount Kineo

Directions: **Rockwood, Maine. Follow directions in #98 to Greenville. Continue northwest on Routes 6 and 15 to Rockwood, about 20 miles more. From here, take a boat**

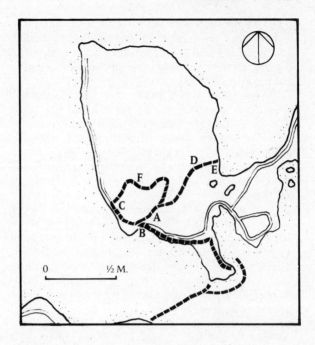

0   ½ M.

(hire one, or bring your own canoe) across the narrows to the south shore of Kineo, landing either at Kineo Cove or to the west (left) of the row of houses.

Ownership: **Private. Designated a State Game Sanctuary.**

On a narrow-necked peninsula, Mount Kineo juts into the middle of Moosehead Lake (see **Interior Maine**) as though it wanted to be able to observe all the myriad comings and goings there. Its steep southern cliff has attracted people for thousands of years. Indians who came to use its "flints" called it Koineo, or "sharp points." Thoreau wrote of its 700-foot drop, "The celebrated precipice is so high and perpendicular that you can jump from the top, many hundred feet, into the water." Visitors are not advised to test the validity of his statement.

There is no public-access road to Kineo today, so you must arrive by the traditional route over water. Be careful, as the wind can race freely down the lake, and squalls come up fast; stay alert to weather conditions and attempt small-craft crossings only if your skill is up to the day's demands.

Pick up the shore path (**A**) by climbing up the bank west of the houses or by following the dirt road past the eastern side of the old golf course and then forking left. The track is bordered thickly with wet-tolerant trees and shrubs: aspens, cottonwood, willows, alder, and red-osier dogwood.

The scree slope at **B** is a talus slope of small, angular fragments rather than the boulder-sized chunks associated with taluses in many other parts of Maine (see **#105**). This southern face of Kineo is formed of rhyolite, a felsic volcanic rock that tends to crack into smaller pieces than do most granitic rocks. This rhyolite was much sought after by Indians, who used it for making tools and weapons. Many of the talus fragments were ready-to-use blanks, making this area a prime workshop site.

Thousands of years before Europeans came here, these forests and lakes were home to Indians. The Kineo tennis courts occupy what was once a burial ground of the Red Paint People. In more recent times, Abenakis traveled the same riverine "roads" voyagers and loggers were later to use. According to one Indian myth, Mount Kineo is the body of a moose killed by the legendary hero Glooskap. Moose used to be very abundant in these woods, and Kineo had the reputation for being a watering place. Yet by 1875 all large game were becoming scarce.

Shortly beyond here, the Indian Trail takes off up the steep slope into a grove of red pines (no sign, but occasional blue blazes). As Thoreau suggested on his canoe trip through this area, "Take a pine needle in your hand. How many sides does it have? Move the needle across your lips in both directions. What do you feel? . . . [leaves] notched or serrated in minute forward-pointing bristles. . . . Why do you suppose nature designed them this way?" Botanists today still ask the same question.

During much of the summer and even well into fall, the nodding lavender flowers of harebells sprout from clefts and ledges. Bearberry manzanita also is common. At **C** an open outcrop at the edge of the cliff overlooks the old fields and empty resort of Kineo's "south shore." The first hotel on this site was built in 1848; like others in the area, it burned and was rebuilt a number of times. Lakeshore camping became another popular activity. With the completion of the first railway to Greenville in 1884, leisure travel began to boom here. The North Woods of the logger and the trapper now saw the tourist, often arriving with steamer trunks for a 2-month vacation.

Continue right at the junction, through a sheltered notch with hardwoods, ferns, and raspberries, then into spruces again, with the cloverlike, tangy leaves of wood sorrel and the nodding flowers or blue fruits of yellow clintonia or bluebead lily. About 70 feet before the next trail fork, there is a patch of one-sided pyrola on the left. Like many other members of the wintergreen family, it is a wood-land species commonly found under conifers. Although broad-leaved, it is evergreen. Its leaves are clustered near the base of the stem and are readily covered by snow. This acts as an insulating blanket against winter cold and as a protection from possible desiccation by dry breezes. The "one-sided" part of its name comes from the fact that its waxy, white flowers are arranged on just one side of the stalk, whereas other pyrolas have flowers dangling in a spiral around the stem.

Stay left at the fork and arrive shortly at the watchtower (**D**). From the top, Moosehead Lake and the North Woods spread around you. Let your eyes sweep from Blue Ridge (to the southwest, above Rockwood) to your point atop Kineo and then onward to Shaw, Little Kineo, Eagle, and Norcross mountains. They are almost in a line. All are formed of Kineo rhyolite, which, some 375 million years ago, may have burst forth along a fissure. The cone-shape of Big Spencer is also of this volcanic origin.

Opposite Kineo, the Moose River flows into Moosehead from Brassua Lake, and just south of there, the Western and Eastern Outlet streams head for Indian Pond and the Kennebec River. Until the water-level-control dams were established, Sand Bar Island (off the tip of the peninsula south of Western Outlet) was an island during high water and part of the peninsula during low water. Today it is an island at all seasons.

The waters of Moosehead are extensive, cold, and full of oxygen. The first two of these characteristics are largely responsible for the third one, because: (1) colder water can hold more oxygen dissolved in it than can warmer water; and (2) winds can mix more oxygen into water when they blow over a large surface area. Moosehead also has highly transparent water and contains a very low amount of organic material. For these reasons, it is classified as an oligo-trophic or scanty-growth lake (*oligo* from the Greek word for "few," *trophic* from the Greek word for "nourishment"). Such lakes are a good habitat for landlocked salmon, brook trout, and lake trout, or togue. Landlocked salmon, native to other lakes in Maine, were introduced to Moosehead in 1879 and are still stocked here today. They usually live in the tributary streams for their first couple of years. Feeding mainly on insects, they grow to some 6 to 8 inches in length and then take up residence in the lake itself. Here they feed on other fishes, especially smelts, which were introduced into Moosehead in 1892. The salmon spawn on gravelly areas in the streams from mid-October to late November. The discovery that the survival percentage of undersize young salmon turned back from worm-baited hooks is much less than that from fly-baited hooks and artificial lures may have been instrumental in the creation of fly-fishing-only restrictions on some of the best salmon nurseries.

Closer by, the tops of red and white spruces crowd around the tower. In many parts of their range, these species grow in separate places, the white spruces more common along the coasts, in open, younger growth and on exposed ridges, the red spruces predominantly in the more sheltered forests (see **#75**). Where these trees do not grow right next to each other, people often have a difficult time distinguishing between the two, and indeed, during the early history of the Maine woods, the two species were not separated by woodsmen. Here, the color difference between the two kinds is rather pronounced: the shiny, slightly yellowish-green of the red spruce contrasts markedly with the bluish-green of the white spruce.

From the watchtower, backtrack to the nearest junction and go left to the site of the old wooden tower (**E**). Chipped places in the rhyolite bedrock here show that the exposed surface weathers to a chalky white, while the inside remains a blue-gray. Such surface changes often disguise the identity of a rock, forcing geologists to crack it open and look inside.

Go back to the junction, turn left, and retrace the trail to the next junction. Descend right, on the Bridal Trail, through northern hardwoods and groves of eastern hemlock (**F**). This side of the mountain is formed of cyclically bedded slate (see **#29**) and sandstone, rocks a little older than the rhyolite. At the Forest Service cabin, bear left to join the shore trail and return to your craft.

Remarks: *The walk is 3 to 4 miles round trip, depending on where you join the shore trail. The footing is fairly easy, the terrain moderate, with a few steep sections on the Indian Trail. This is a good family hike, but beware of lake winds and waves. There are a number of privately run campgrounds and some river-trip outfitters and guides in the area. Big Spencer (check to see if the paper-company bridge has been replaced), Williams, Coburn, Sally, and Green mountain hikes, located between Moosehead Lake and the Maine–New Hampshire border, are described in* Fifty More Hikes in Maine.

100.

Borestone Mountain

Directions: **Monson, Maine. From Bangor, take Route 15 northwest to Dover-Foxcroft and then, joined by Route 6,** west and north to Monson, about 58 miles. At the north end of town, turn right onto Elliotsville Rd. (there is a sign for the Appalachian Trail). Cross Big Wilson Creek at about 7.5 miles, then bear left and cross the Canadian Pacific tracks. About 0.2 mile farther, the trailhead is on the right and a dirt parking space on the left.

Ownership: National Audubon Society.

In 1958, the R. T. Moore family donated their nearly 1,000-acre estate on Borestone Mountain to the National Audubon Society, to be protected as a wildlife sanctuary. A walk here today takes you through deciduous and coniferous forests that were last heavily cut in the 1890s, past clear ponds that were part of a fish hatchery and fox-breeding business during the first part of this century, and onto a rocky, windswept mountaintop.

The first half of the trail follows an old dirt road through one of the few sections of northern hardwood forest on the sanctuary. Sugar, red, and goosefoot maple, white and yellow birch, American beech, and white ash arch overhead, typical of interior Maine forests that occupy deeper, more fertile, and well-drained soils. If you are here in spring or summer, listen carefully to the birds that sing above you. You may hear the song of a robin and perhaps even find the bird sitting snugly in its nest of grasses and mud. If you are here in the fall, the nests will still be here, though the robins and other songbirds no longer occupy them. Once the young have fledged (learned to fly), the birds, young and old, abandon the nest and sleep while perched on a branch. They cannot fall off in their sleep because as soon as their weight is settled down over their feet, the tendon that shuts their toes tightens, clamping them to the branch until they raise their bodies to walk or fly away. (See **#98** for more on robins.)

As you wander up the trail, you pass through scattered groves of hemlocks, conifers of cool, moist places. They often occupy sites on the northern or eastern sides of mountains or in stream canyons, where snows lie longer and temperatures are colder (see **#23** and **#73**). Examine the top of a young hemlock. The new growth is so lax that it droops like a weeping willow, yet this floppy top will one day be a rigid tree trunk.

Quite a variety of ferns inhabit the filtered-sunlight regions of the forest floor: bracken, long-beech, oak, polypody, marginal wood, and hay-scented. In summer, the backs of the green fronds carry the spores in variously shaped sori, or spore cases. Among the clues to a fern's identity are the shape, size, and arrangement of these sori. Those of the marginal wood fern are large, round, and located along the margins of the pinnules (leaflets); those of the hay-scented fern, while also marginal, are cup-shaped and generally located in the notches of the pinnules. The bracken fern carries its spores rolled in the edges of its pinnules. In other ferns, like the cinnamon fern, the sori are attached in bunches to a separate, nonleafy frond. The basic strategy of producing spores—the asexual phase of a fern's life cycle—is the same for all, but each has evolved a slightly different structure for accomplishing the task.

Farther up the trail, you will find sheep laurel joining the ferns and herbs of the forest floor. In spring and early summer, it shows off its strategy for reproduction: bright pink flowers that attract insects. Look into some of these. They are built for sexual reproduction and have female and male parts, the female pistil in the center and ten male stamens around it. If the flower is not yet ready to pollinate, small, spurlike appendages on the petals will hold the stamens firmly against the corolla (the petals, as a group). If an insect touches them, nothing will happen. If the flower is ready to pollinate, though, the weight of an insect settling on it will act like a trigger, releasing the spurs, and the stamens will spring upward, scattering pollen on the body of the insect. That pollen will be transferred to the next flower the insect visits. Since most insects have evolved the habit of visiting only one or two kinds of flowers during any one time period, it is likely that this insect will visit another sheep laurel very soon.

Soon, you reach the ponds and the former site of the Borestone Mountain Fox Company and Fish Hatchery; the road you are on was built for the company in 1916. The capacity of the operation was some two hundred foxes, raised for pelage that was used to make fur garments and felt for hats. For more than two decades, numerous color variations were carefully propagated. Escapees during those years bred with local red foxes (see **#98**), creating a Borestone "wild" fox population that includes a high percentage of individuals with oddly colored fur. The number of foxes on the mountain is quite large today, and sightings are common.

Among the sweetgale and witherod that surround the pond are white-cedars, or arborvitae, meaning "tree of life"; it may be precisely that for the deer which feed on it in winter when food supplies are scarce. A northern species tolerant of soggy roots, white-cedar is often found along streambeds or seeps. Its fragrant wood has long been a favorite for making storage chests for woolens and linens. Because it is rot-resistant and light, it is also popular for fence posts and shingles.

From here, follow the red-blazed trail, swinging around the southern end of the pond. The cement dam you cross allowed water-level control for the fish-hatchery portion of the Borestone business. The forest on this upper flank is mostly coniferous mixed with some large yellow birches (see **#72**) and, higher up, some mountain-ash, a close relative of roses rather than of ash trees. Large, flat chunks of rock in the trail expose the insides of the mountain, a bed of dark gray slate intermixed with thin layers of lighter gray, metamorphosed siltstone. These rocks were formed in the Devonian period, some 375 million years ago, when this section of Maine was covered by a shallow sea (see **#73**). Clay and silt sediments accumulated, layer after layer, eventually becoming so compressed that the grains bonded into rock. Those sedimentary rocks were later metamorphosed by heat and pressure exerted on them by upwellings of magma and by tectonic shiftings inside the earth. Such shiftings are believed to be movements of plates of the earth's crust that underlie both continents and oceans and seem to be constantly in motion, generating such phenomena as continental drift, vulcanism, and mountain building. After being pushed up above the sea, the Borestone rocks were subjected to hundreds of thousands of years of erosion, and today they lie exposed at the surface of the earth. The parallel grooves in the chunks beneath your feet have been created by differential weathering and erosion in which some of the rock layers have decomposed more rapidly than others, forming "valleys" between ridges of more resistant rock.

As you continue upward, look for patches of clintonia or bluebead lily, named for the shiny, dark blue fruits (not edible) they produce in the fall. This northern species is able to grow as far south as Georgia, but only in the mountains there does it find cool enough conditions to survive. Throughout the warmer months, its broad, shiny, bright green leaves are conspicuous. If you look at them closely, you can see that their veins are virtually parallel, running the entire length of the leaf. This pattern of veins is typical of lilies, grasses, and other plants that have only one cotyledon, or seed leaf. Plants that have two cotyledons, such as beans, violets, and maples, have veins arranged in a netlike pattern.

In some of the steeper sections of the trail, spruce roots are exposed where soil and rock have been eroded. The sinuous roots look as though they might have flowed into liquid rock. Rather, as tiny young shoots, they probed their way into small cracks, widening them where they could by the tremendous pressure of their growth. Along with frost, running water, and foot wear, they have helped to break pieces off the bedrock mass.

The summit is long, with an east and a west peak. The curly, stunted forms of the vegetation (see **#105**) attest to the power of the winds up here. The rock-face textures are truly fascinating for the diversity of their swirls and convolutions.

Farther north in Bodfish Intervale, that winding pattern is repeated in the curves and oxbows of Long Pond Stream that flows
into Lake Onawa. As a river flows around a curve, the faster-moving
outside undercuts and erodes its bank while the slower-moving inside deposits sediments, building up its shore. Gradually, a bend
becomes more and more curved, an almost-loop or oxbow. During
floods, the water overflowing its banks may cut directly across the
narrow neck between the ends of the oxbow. An oxbow that has
been cut off will be left as a pond or marshy area with the characteristic broad curve. Long Pond Stream has wandered all over its flat
floodplain between Barren and Borestone mountains, leaving sediments and oxbows scattered in its wake. Enjoy the sound of the
wind in the trees and the deep blue of Borestone's three ponds
stringing below you, and then retrace your steps back down the
mountain.

Remarks: *This is a 4-mile hike, round trip, half on an old dirt road and
half on a steep rocky trail. It is a popular hike, especially on weekends and
holidays. There is camping at Lily Bay State Park on the eastern shore of
Moosehead Lake from ice-out to October 15; for primitive sites closer by, see
#101 and **#98**. Nearby Barren Mountain, just north of Borestone, is
described in* Fifty More Hikes in Maine.

101.

Little Wilson Falls

Directions: **Monson, Maine. Follow directions for #100 to
Elliotsville Rd. At 7.4 miles, just before the tarred road
crosses Big Wilson Creek, turn left onto a dirt road. Drive
0.7 mile to a parking space at the Little Wilson Campsite.**

Ownership: **Prentiss and Carlisle Co.**

Out West there are waterfalls that leap 1,000 feet; they roar and are
awesome. Down East, our waterfalls tumble only a few tens of feet
at most; they are lyrical and friendly. Little Wilson is one such enchanting falls. It is also one of the tallest in Maine, located at the
head of a narrow slate gorge. The walk to Little Wilson passes through
both deciduous and coniferous forests. Jack-in-the-pulpits unfurl in

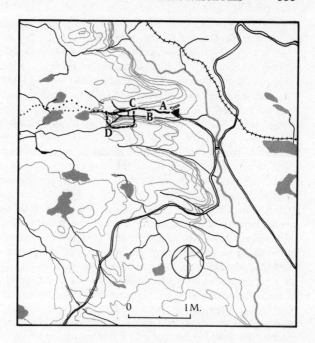

late May and, with a little probing, you may discover liverworts concealed near the falls.

The trail begins on the far side of Little Wilson Stream. Pick your way across the slate slabs and cascades, climb up to the gravel road, and go left. After 0.1 mile, turn left onto the old woods road marked with white blazes. A patch of heal-all grows along the bank at the first creek crossing. As you continue, the road runs between the brook and a rocky ridge outcrop covered with hemlock, spruce, and fir (**A**). Follow the blazes onto another dirt road where spring brings forth a superb array of wildflowers. Among them are scattered clumps of jack-in-the-pulpit. In May, look for the finger-shaped spadix of the "jack," or preacher, standing in his canopied pulpit, the flaplike spathe, often beautifully striped with green, purple, and white. Although these structures are commonly referred to as flowers, the true flowers of the jack-in-the-pulpit are tiny, hidden down at the base of the spadix. Frequently, one plant has only female flowers, while another has only male ones. Species with this separation of sexes are termed "diecious" (*di-* meaning "two," and *ecious,* coming from the same root word as *ecology,* meaning "house"). This mechanism ensures a mixing of genes through cross-pollination. Bayberry and willow plants also have this adaptation.

At **B** you skirt a wet field crowded with grasses and sedges. Although not commonly thought of as flowers, these are indeed flowering plants, as a person who is allergic to their wind-blown pollen may well tell you. Long, slender, and without conspicuous flowers, they are frequently lumped, along with rushes, under the catch-all name "grass." The three families are, in fact, readily distinguishable: sedges have edges (the central stem has a triangular cross-section); rushes are round (the stems are circular in cross-section and not jointed); and grasses have joints (the stems have joints, as in bamboo). The seeds of all these plants are eaten by a wide variety of wildlife, including mice, sparrows, and goldfinches. Sedge seeds, along with insects, were found by one researcher to be the most regular item in the diet of young ruffed grouse in the Northeast.

Just beyond this wet area, the trail swings left (the blazes are not immediately visible), entering beech and maple woods as it continues to skirt the field and then passes a couple of cut swaths. Continue through deciduous woods to the junction (**C**) where the relocation of the Appalachian Trail (AT) begins. Follow the blazes as the trail doubles back left, descends to, and crosses Little Wilson Stream where it emerges from a hemlock-fringed gorge. The clear brown color of the water, reminiscent of tea, is caused by tannins leached from the organic materials in the surrounding soil. This is a common phenomenon where stream drainages are populated with conifers or oaks, species with high tannic acid content.

Scramble *gently* up the far bank. As a site for relocation of a trail, especially one as heavily traveled as the AT, this was a poor choice. The bank is very steep, the soil very loose, and the trail was slashed almost straight up the slope—all factors that contribute to the great amount of erosion occurring here (see also **#93**). Trailing patches of creeping snowberry dot the thick duff in the coniferous forest along the top of the cliff. At the head of the gorge, you can descend on rock ledges to Little Wilson Falls (**D**). The formation of these falls and the gorge below them is a bit of an enigma, since neither the axis of the gorge nor the position of the falls corresponds to any rock structures. The bedrock is slate with nearly vertical primary cleavage. Frost- and root-wedging (see **#80** and **#100**) along these weaknesses have helped create the ledges and benches around the falls where polypody ferns (see **#100**), northern white-cedars, mosses (see **#107**), and asters find niches.

If you look in nooks near some of the clumps of sphagnum moss (see **#103** and **#76**), you may discover liverworts. Flattened, thin, and brownish-green, they resemble a flat, leafy lichen (see **#7**) combined with a moss. They are neither, but botanists believe that mosses are their closest relatives. Their evolution remains largely a matter of speculation since no one has discovered any recognizable link connecting them with other ancient plant groups, algae and pteridophytes (ferns and horsetails). The name "liverwort" comes to us from ancient and medieval pharmacopeia. The thallus (major body) of several scalelike species of liverwort has polygonal markings similar to the pattern in the cross-section of a liver. The plant was therefore believed to be good medicine for liver ailments and was dubbed "the liver wort" (*wort* meaning "plant").

For an alternate route on the return, which makes a short loop and avoids the steep bank by the creek crossing, climb back up to the trail and follow it to the top of the falls. Cross the stream on the smooth ledges and pick up a blue-blazed trail. Follow this to a junction just beyond where you cross a tributary of Little Wilson Stream and go right. This is the former route of the AT (the white blazes are now painted out with brown). It will lead you back to the current AT at junction **C**. Go left and retrace the rest of your route to Little Wilson Campsite.

Remarks: *This is a 3½-mile hike over fairly gentle terrain. There is one steep section on the new Appalachian Trail. Camping is available at the Little Wilson Campsite, maintained by the Maine Forest Service. The campsite is located at the trailhead.*

102.
Gulf Hagas

Directions: **Brownville Junction, Maine. From Bangor, take I-95 north to Exit 53, then Route 16 northwest to Milo, about 40 miles. Follow Route 11 about 7 miles north to Brownville Junction; 4.7 miles beyond the bridge there, turn left on the road to the Katahdin Ironworks (pavement quickly gives way to dirt). In another 6.4 miles you reach the ironworks and the paper-company registration booth, where maps are available and fees are collected for day use and camping. Mileages are calculated from this point, and signs point to Gulf Hagas at all the junctions. Cross the bridge, go through the gate, stay right at the**

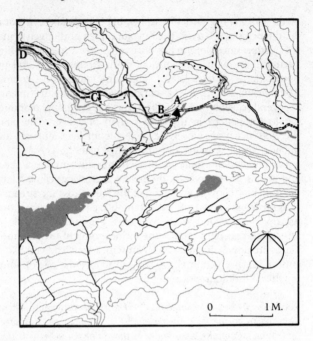

fork, and cross two more bridges. At 2.2 miles keep left, at
3.4 miles keep right, at 5.6 miles keep left and cross a bridge,
at 5.9 miles go left, at 6.2 miles keep left, and at 7.0 miles
keep right. Park in the far end of the gravel pit at 7.4 miles.

Ownership: **Diamond International Co. and St. Regis Paper
Co.**

Gulf Hagas, sometimes called Maine's miniature Grand Canyon, is a
narrow and twisting gorge, its slate walls rising up to 125 feet above
the West Branch of the Pleasant River, which churns and falls along
its floor. Tucked away in the logging country of central Maine, this
scenic treasure has been designated by the U.S. National Park Service
as a National Natural Landmark. The roiling water and precipitous
cliffs offer a vivid contrast to the quiet strength and charm of the fine
old-growth deciduous forests, the cool coniferous forests, and the
grove of old white pines through which you travel.

The trail begins as a continuation of the tote road, its lowland
sections often flooded with stream water. Pass a number of campsites
and reach Pugwash Pond (**A**) shortly after crossing on to Nature

Conservancy property. The pond is formed in a kettle hole, a depression formed when a chunk of ice became isolated from the receding glacier and was partially or completely buried in rock and sand left behind as the glacier melted. Finally, the ice chunk itself melted, creating a depression that filled with water (see **#16** and **#76**). Among the wildlife attracted to this wet spot are wood ducks (see **#14**). These lovely birds frequent woodland streams and ponds, feeding mainly on aquatic and terrestrial plant materials (including acorns) and to a smaller extent on insects, crustaceans, and mollusks. During most of the year, the colorful feathers of the males contrast markedly with the brown plumage of the females. Such a difference in appearance is called *sexual dimorphism*. In other animal species, it may take the form of a difference in size (hawks) or a difference in skeletal and muscular shape (humans). Ornithologists suspect that plumage differences between males and females of a species originally may have developed as a "badge" for quick and easy identification of sex. From these beginnings, it presumably evolved into the colorful ornamentations that many male birds use in court-ship displays.

Unlike most other ducks, wood ducks nest in tree cavities. Generally these are deep enough so that the birds are out of arms' reach of a raccoon, and sometimes they are as much as 6 to 8 feet from entrance to bottom. The ducklings leave these nests soon after they hatch. They scramble to the entrance of the cavity, using their sharp toenails, but from here they must jump because, while they are able to swim at this time, they are not yet able to fly. Fortunately, they are mostly down and air, and they seem to survive even long plunges.

At the next junction, you meet the white-blazed Appalachian Trail (AT). Go right, along the edge of the stately pine groves, to the Hermitage (**B**), named not for its large trees but for its first known human resident, a solitary Scot who built a cabin beneath the pines around 1892. In subsequent years, more cabins were constructed and the area was used intermittently as a summer camp and as a commercial sporting camp. Although the surrounding lands have a long history of use by the lumbering industry, the pines on this site were spared from the axe, presumably to preserve the aesthetics of the area around the cabins. At the time The Nature Conservancy acquired the property in 1967, the cabins were being vandalized and used for camping. Fearing fire and wanting to discourage camping on the site, the Conservancy had the cabins demolished, leaving the old pines to their forest companions.

The stand of pines occupies a moraine, or deposit of glacial sand and gravel, along the banks of the Pleasant River. White pines seem to grow readily on such well-drained, sandy and rocky sites. (For old-age stands of white pine, see **#12, #28,** and **#71.**) They also seem to favor rocky ridgetops and the steep-sided edges of water-courses. In his report for the Maine Critical Areas Program, Philip Conkling suggests that early explorers and lumbermen, traveling the woods via the waterways, may have overestimated the amount of white pine in Maine forests because they were relying on observations made in localities where white pine seems innately more abundant (as along the waterways). This illustrates one of the many kinds of factors which, if not recognized and compensated for, can bias research and give ecologists an incorrect picture of the changes that have occurred in vegetation.

Continue along the AT until you reach the junction where the Gulf Hagas Trail splits off. Stay left (straight), crossing the brook and following the blue blazes. From here on, be sure to explore all side trails left, blazed with blue and yellow stripes (the first of these, to Screw Auger Falls, is just beyond the brook). Farther along the blue-blazed trail, go left at the painted rock, onto the Gulf Hagas Rim Trail. As you descend through the next section of woods (**C**), you will pass many beech trees whose usually smooth gray bark is pock-marked with dark cankers. The combined actions of an insect and a fungus appear to be the cause, the insect creating the openings by which the infecting fungus, *Nectaria,* gains entrance. This bark disease is currently very prominent in New England, and in some localities, up to 50 percent of the beeches have died of it.

At several of the overlooks into the Gulf Hagas gorge, the bedrock is exposed. While most of the gorges in Maine are formed in granitic bedrock (see **#94**), the bedrock here is a gray slate, a metamorphic rock type. Formerly, it was shale, a sedimentary rock composed of medium-fine particles of sediment (see **#29**). In most cases, you will find that the originally horizontal bedding planes are now tilted to the vertical and that the direction of the gorge does not follow those planes of weakness. Geologists have not been able to clearly figure out the origin of Gulf Hagas. As may be seen from the vantage points of a number of the gorge overlooks, there are fluvial scour marks, potholes (see **#81** and **#110**), and sides of potholes (often with mossy seeps dripping into them) as much as 90 feet above the present level of the Pleasant River. Since such features are not apt to have survived continental glaciation, the gulf is believed to be of fairly recent origin. Dr. Thomas Brewer has suggested to Critical Areas researchers that the best explanation he has found is that the gorge was carved by a large meltwater stream that flowed under stagnant ice at the end of the glacial period. The major amounts of sand between the Hermitage and Katahdin Ironworks tend to support this theory.

As you continue discovering views into this impressive gorge, notice also the wonderful details of the woods through which you travel. Lush patches of reindeer lichen (see **#43**) are composed of myriad miniature "antlers." Violets (see **#90**) and bunchberries display conspicuous flowers near the forest floor. Rotting logs may be festooned with bright yellow-orange fruiting bodies of witches' butter, jelly fungi whose gelatinous flesh has reminded many people of rather amorphous chunks of butter. These fungi usually fruit in cool, moist weather, some in spring and early summer, others in late summer and fall. One of the more common orange species is often abundant on coniferous wood, while a common yellow one is generally found scattered on hardwood logs.

Above Billings Falls (**D**), the gorge ends and the trail, streambed, and surrounding terrain come together at one level. From here, the trail leaves the water and loops back around to the tote roads. Go right, following the woods road through older-growth deciduous forests sprinkled with cabin-sized glacial erratics (see **#78**). Forests that have been uncut as long as these are not common in Maine today. Continue straight as you pass the painted rock (right) and you are on familiar terrain for the rest of your return to your car.

Remarks: *Although the major route for this hike is about 10 miles, numerous side trails add considerably to its length. The overall rise from the Hermitage to the head of the gorge is only about 600 feet, but the terrain along the Rim Trail is very lumpy—it seems as though each step you take is either up or down. Allow plenty of time to enjoy this gorgeous area. Also give yourself plenty of time to drive the rough dirt roads. The trip from Brownville Junction to the trailhead can easily take an hour. For road conditions, contact the Katahdin Ironworks gatekeeper or the firewarden in Brownville Junction. Delorme's* Maine Atlas *is a good map for the dirt roads in the area. The campsites near the trailhead are accessible to 4-wheel-drive vehicles, rugged cars with high clearance, and to those who can carry their gear ¼ to ½ mile. Contact the Diamond Paper Co.*

103.

Orono Bog

Directions: **Orono, Maine. From Bangor, go north about 7 miles on I-95 to Exit 50. Go northwest on Kelly Rd. At the**

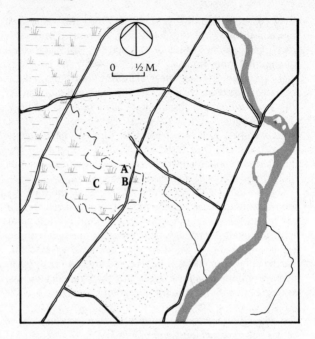

first crossroads, turn left onto Stillwater Ave. Go 0.7 mile and park on the side of the road.

Ownership: **University of Maine and private.**

The Orono Bog, some 600 acres of peatland, is a section of the much larger Caribou Bog, one of perhaps 5,000 peatlands that lie scattered across Maine. As the cost of petroleum fuel rises, the larger of these areas are drawing attention as potential sources of fuel. At the same time, scientists are realizing the wealth of information stored in these wetlands. Here you can get a better understanding of human interactions with peatlands and discover some of the special life-styles of bog dwellers such as sphagnum mosses and sundews.

As you stand on the road and look westward into the bog, the lagg, or moat section (**A**), is to your right, where maples are growing. A major forested section (**B**) is to the left of the lagg, where the spruce and tamarack are tall. The shrub heath–moss lawn section (**C**) is to the left of that, behind the thin screen of conifers that lines the wet ditch along the edge of the road. The lagg is very wet, because it is the part of the bog closest to the main water table of the area, from which it derives most of its dissolved nutrient supply. One of the plants common in the lagg and also in the roadside ditch is wild calla, or water arum, a relative of jack-in-the-pulpit (see **#101**). Also common in the lagg are red maple, alder, cinnamon fern (see **#100**) and royal fern, all more tolerant of soggy footing than most of their relatives.

There is no particular trail for this exploration. Enter the bog on the western side of Stillwater Ave., about ½ to ¾ mile south of Kelly Rd. Wend your way through the trees and into the open shrub-and-moss area (**C**). Bogs form in poorly drained areas with generally cool, moist climates (see **#76** and **Interior Maine**). Their development seems highly influenced by water-table characteristics, length of the growing season, summer temperatures, and nutrient supply. Many appear to have been marshlands or swamps at one time. During early stages of growth, a bog is connected to the local water table, and like the lagg, derives its nourishment from it. Such peatlands are called *minerotrophic*. As layers of vegetation build up, the lower ones buried in acidic, cold, oxygen-poor material where little decomposition occurs, much of the bog may develop a "perched" water table of its own, a water table above and disconnected from the ground water table. Where this occurs, the bog plants no longer receive minerals from the ground water. Rather, they derive all their nutrients from above, dissolved in rain and as dry fallout. Such peatlands are called *ombrotrophic*. In the Orono Bog, the lagg is minerotrophic, the shrub-and-moss area is ombrotrophic, and the coniferous forested area is transitional between the two.

The ombrotrophic sections of peatlands are the subject of active research in Maine today. The layers of peat (the partially decomposed organic matter of bogs) have trapped within them records of particulate fallout covering thousands of years. Carbon-dating of various bog components reveals much about the bog: plant remains convey information about the development of the bog's particular vegetation, pollen grains offer insights into past climates and environments, and concentrations of heavy metals reveal the nature of airborne particulates. One of the patterns that is showing up is a definite increase in amounts of lead and zinc beginning in the mid-1800s, or at the time of the Industrial Revolution.

Find a mossy hummock out in the middle of the open area. Sphagnum moss is one of the major bog-building plants. There are some thirty-five to forty different species of it, each adapted to its own range of acidity, moisture, and possibly tolerance of heat. Some of the open bog species are of gorgeous red and burgundy colors. Sphagnum has a remarkable capacity for absorbing and holding on to water in its casklike cells, one of the reasons it has been so valuable as an agricultural soil conditioner and, in the past, as diapers for babies. Feel the temperature on the surface of the mossy hummock and then gently burrow your hand down into the moss and peat— so cool and wet. (Please fill in the hole again.) Some of the individual moss plants are quite long. If you examine a stem, you will see that there are nodes at intervals along it, one node at the end of each year's growth.

The peat in this portion of the Orono Bog is close to 20 feet deep. Botanists studying it with a core-sampling tool have discovered that at the bottom are marine-clay sediments forming an impervious layer, which creates the poor drainage conditions in this area. These sediments were deposited some 10,000 to 12,000 years ago when the rising sea level accompanying the retreat of the continental glaciers flooded the Bangor area to what today is about 350 feet above sea level (see Northeast Coastal volume, #85). Above these marine sediments are shallow lake deposits, marsh and aquatic plants, woody plants, and then various layers of peat, sometimes composed mostly of sphagnum and other times containing lots of woody plants. All of this is now capped by the current shrub heath–moss lawn community. It was once thought that bogs were rather ephemeral features of the landscape, that they gradually became drier and drier, and eventually became covered with forest vegetation. Studies of the Orono Bog and many other bogs from Maine to Alaska indicate that bogs exist over thousands of years and that the changes that occur in them are not unidirectional to forest. Layers of peat containing woody fragments are interspersed among layers of nonwoody peat, probably resulting from drier (more woody plants) and wetter (few woody plants) periods in the life of the bog. Many bogs even invade forested areas that grow adjacent to their edges. Although there is no strict pattern, the upper layers of a bog do tend to be less decomposed and less compacted than the lower ones. Upper layers are often mined for agricultural peat, whereas the lower ones have sufficient density to be used for fuel. Current gubernatorial policy favors development of Maine's peat resources "so long as such development is not on our most outstanding peatlands and is done in an environmentally sound manner." One environmental concern is about the future of such an area. Peat, in contrast to trees, is essentially a nonrenewable resource: once it is mined from an area, it will recur there only after thousands of years, and then only if the right conditions persist. No one knows whether mined peatlands can be reclaimed in this area as shallow wetlands, forest, or future peatlands. Another major concern pertains to the effects of a new mining technique proposed by hopeful mining operations. The method involves using large quantities of water to make a slurry of the peat, which can then be piped to the processing plant. The water must then be removed. The question is how that water might affect the rivers into which it is disposed. The Caribou Bog and the Sunkhaze Heath (northeast of Old Town) are two sites being evaluated for mining potentials.

As you wander across the bog, you will encounter both tundra and tropical types of plants. Each of these environments has some characteristics that are similar to bog environments: tundra lands are cold enough so that moisture is unavailable (because it is frozen) much of the year; many tropical soils are low in nitrogen. The low pH (high acidity) of bogs makes it difficult for vegetation to absorb the abundant water and its low supply of dissolved nutrients. Northern heath plants such as labrador tea (see **#90**), bog rosemary, little cranberry, and leatherleaf (see **#74**) have waxy, hair-covered, or rolled-edged leaves that help conserve moisture. Species such as sundews and pitcher plants (see **#104**) increase their nutrient supply by taking in nitrogen in the form of insects. The shining, glandular-tipped hairs of the sundew look quite harmless but are in fact quite deadly to some creatures: they attract, trap, and absorb insects.

Notice the hummock-and-hollow topography. Some of the hollows have mud bottoms inhabited by small, greenish liverworts (see **#101**). In some cases at least, these liverworts may be the cause of the hollows they occupy. They are sometimes found growing on top of a sphagnum mound, and it is suspected that somehow they manage to kill the plants beneath them, precipitating the formation of a hollow.

As you head back to Stillwater Ave., take a side trip into the forested section (**B**). Black spruce (see **#11** and **#79**) and tamarack (see **#69**) are the major tree species. The tamarack, called hackmatack in the Maine woods, often grows supporting roots at right angles from the trunk. These thick, naturally formed angle pieces are in high demand for the construction of wooden boats, because they are much stronger than laminated and bent sections. Among the shrub species, alder, witherod, and winterberry are common. The herbs are a mixture of forest species such as starflower and bunchberry, bog species such as pitcher plant, and wetland species such as skunk cabbage (see **#62**) and hellebore. Almost certainly you will hear birds, and perhaps you will startle a wood frog in a place where you can see it. A few amphibians do inhabit bogs—wood frogs, pickerel frogs, blue-spotted salamanders, green frogs (in the pools)—but the acidity of the environment makes it difficult for their eggs to develop. Orono Bog is frequently used for research purposes, and one of the current projects is a study of its amphibian populations.

Remarks: *The Caribou Bog stretches northwest of this site for some 10 miles. A round-trip walk of 1 mile or less in the Orono section can give you a wonderful introduction to the bog environment. Although wet, the access is quite easy. The wettest section you encounter may be the roadside ditch. Knee-high boots or tennis shoes you intend to get wet are recommended. If your foot becomes embedded in the mud, be sure to pull it up toe first, so you don't lose your foot gear. Bogs are easy places in which to get disoriented. If you tie a bright red or white bandanna to a tree at the spot where you emerge onto the open bog, it can help you relocate your car. A compass may be useful. As it can be very hot and bright in the open spaces of the bog, a visored hat and some water are recommended. If you want to sit, bring something plastic and fairly tough in order to stay dry. There is camping at Villa Vaughn Campground, Bangor (year-round), and at Big Hammond St. Campground, Bangor (May 15 to October 15).*

104.
The Great Heath and
Pleasant River

Directions: **Columbia Falls, Maine. From Bangor, take U.S. 1A southeast to Ellsworth and U.S. 1 east to Harrington, where U.S. 1A rejoins U.S. 1, about 70 miles. Continue east on U.S. 1 for 2.3 miles; turn left onto Epping Rd. (opposite the road to Addison), which becomes East Base Rd. Go 1.4 miles and turn left onto the dirt road just beyond the bridge over the Pleasant River. Go almost 0.4 mile and turn left into a long, narrow dirt-and-grass parking space; a gray-and-white garage is visible about 0.1 mile down the road.**

Ownership: **Private and state of Maine.**

Until quite recently when roads were built, rivers were the highways and byways of the Maine woods. They remain the easiest access to a number of less-visited areas, among which is the Great Heath, Maine's largest peatland. Here is an invitation to explore the unique character and variety of peatland habitats and organisms, from wet and curly hummocks of sphagnum to carnivorous plants to tamaracks. The Pleasant River not only provides access to the heath but also offers its own showcase of riparian or streamside life, including spreading old maples, beaverworks, and the aerial acrobatics of dragonflies and damselflies.

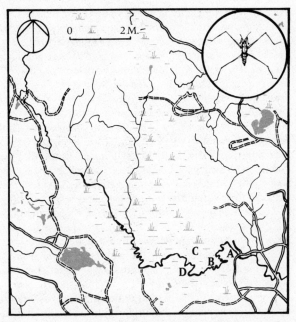

Inset: Water strider

As you head upstream from the put-in spot (**A**) yellow pond lilies, pickerelweed, and cattails emerge from the water near the banks. During most of the summer months, the fat yellow flowers of the pond lilies bloom just above the water. Although plants like cattails (see **#33**) and pickerelweed have stems stiff enough to hold them erect above and below the water, pond lilies have flexible stems and floating leaves, relying on the buoyancy of water. The stems are hollow, allowing more air passages and the capacity to float.

Water striders take advantage of the surface tension of water. It is surface tension that keeps a slightly overfull glass of water from spilling; it also keeps water striders from sinking. Although a water strider's legs are so skinny that is seems they would cut right through the surface of the water, the ends of those legs are tipped with numerous tiny hairs that repel water. If you are able to see a water strider in clear, shallow water, you may notice that the shadow it casts on the bottom has large circles at the ends of the legs, as if the insect had padlike feet. Actually the circles are shadows of the depression caused by the weight of the insect and the resistance of the surface tension around its feet. With its four striding legs splayed out around it, a water strider may appear to be four-legged. A true insect, though, it has six legs, the front two shorter and held up near its head. It uses these for grabbing its prey. The male also uses them for holding on to the female while they are mating. You may be able to see a male attracting a female to an egg-laying site he has chosen. He sits next to a stick or other submerged object and bounces the surface of the water with his middle pair of legs. You may also notice that some of the striders have red dots on their bodies. These are tiny parasitic water mites.

Two other kinds of insects common along the river during most of the warmer months are dragonflies and damselflies. The dragon-flies have very rapid wingbeats and a strong flight, often zooming, then hovering, and then darting off again. When they land, they usually hold their wings wide open. Damselflies have very slender bodies and a somewhat fluttering flight pattern. At rest, they gener-ally hold their wings above their backs. Iridescent, turquoise-green-bodied damselflies with black or half-black wings are common along the Pleasant River. These are the males. The females are brown-bodied with transparent wings with a spot, often white, near the tip. During spring and summer, the males spend much of their time defending small territories along the edge of the river. Two major ingredients in such a territory are a perching spot that overlooks the area and an aquatic-plant stem or floating debris where the female can lay eggs just beneath the surface of the water. Damselflies exhibit a number of courting behavior patterns and postures. One easily distinguishable posture a male assumes when a female enters his territory is called the cross-wing display. Standing on a perch, the male lifts his abdomen in the air and separates his two pairs of wings, spreading the rear pair downward while keeping the front pair in position above his back. Another commonly observed posture is that assumed in copulation. The male attaches the tip of his abdomen to the back of the female, just behind her head. The female then arches her abdomen down beneath her body and up to the underside of the male's second abdominal segment, where she receives the sperm. You may even see them flying around in this pretzellike position.

Just upstream from the put-in spot are two slightly rocky sections. Then, beyond two big river bends to the right, the river swings left again. The riverbank is mantled with grasses and sweetgale, and a swath of tamaracks (see **#69**) stretches away from the river to the right of a treeless area; two tall tamaracks grow together at the left edge of the open space (**B**). Pull end-in into one of the spaces be-tween the sweetgale plants and climb ashore for a terrestrial explo-ration of the Great Heath (in Maine, pronounced hāth). The section nearest the river is covered with a mosaic of almost waist-high shrubs, very wet mosses, and sedges. There is a narrow path stretching northward into the heath. Walk in a few hundred yards. The heath gently slopes up from the river. As you approach the high part of the dome, you can see another dome stretching beyond. The Great Heath is composed of a number of peat domes, each originally formed in a separate depression, which have grown upward and outward and coalesced into the large, undulating surface you see today. Each of these peat basins is underlain by impervious layers of either marine or freshwater clays, which create the poor drainage required for peatland formation (see **#103**). To the southwest of the heath is Pineo Ridge, a large emergent glaciomarine delta. Most of the Great Heath is ombrotrophic, receiving its minerals from rainwater and dry fallout (see **#103**). The strips adjacent to Pleasant River and Taylor Creek are poorly minerotrophic, receiving the bulk of their scanty nutrient supplies from groundwater systems.

As you get out into sections of the heath where the shrubs are smaller and the sphagnum hummocks are visible (**C**), look for carnivorous sundews and pitcher plants, which supplement their otherwise nitrogen-poor diets with insects. Some of the pitcher-plant leaves may be almost buried in the sphagnum. Each leaf, shaped like a pitcher, holds a pool of water. Notice also all the little white hairs on the inside, pointing downward. Imagine an ant prowling the wilds of the heath. In its explorations, it crawls down inside the pitcher leaf, the downward-pointing hairs almost aiding its progress. It discovers a "lake" at the bottom. Not interested in swimming, it tries to crawl back up the side, but now all these hairs act like a trap. The ant drowns and is absorbed into the pitcher plant's tissues. In early summer, look also for the blooming flowers of the pitchers. Bending downward from the tip of long, leafless stalks, they have fleshy, dark red sepals, reddish petals, and a broad, five-pointed stigma (the end of the female part) behind which cluster the numerous stamens. In June, you may discover the magenta, dragon-mouthed blossoms of *Arethusa* bog orchids. Each flower grows singly at the top of its stalk. This northern orchid is considered rare or declining throughout its United States range, although its populations in Maine are not thought to be threatened at this time. The major causes attributed to its decline are the drainage of peatlands and their conversion to other uses. In the Great Heath, *Arethusa* most commonly grows in wet sphagnum or sedge areas.

Wander back to the river and continue upstream (**D**). Large piles of pointed, peeled sticks on the bank edges, sometimes almost entirely surrounded by grassy vegetation, betray the presence of beavers. Look also for small dams holding water in riverbank ponds and for branches and trees, some of them 18 inches in diameter, which have been gnawed. The beavers eat the bark, cambium, and leaves from the branches and use the peeled sticks, along with sections of the trunk that they can drag, to build their lodges and dams. Although beaver are quite common in many parts of Maine today, this is one species that was virtually exterminated from the Northeast in past centuries when the animals' fur was in high demand for making coats and felt hats. Their comeback has been due to conservation efforts, which today allow limited trapping of the species.

In early summer, green frogs croak from the beaver ponds and quiet riverbanks. The voice of the male (females don't sing), as he announces his spot and calls for females to approach, sounds like a loose medium-sized rubber band being twanged, similar to a bullfrog's voice but not so deep. If you can sneak up on one, you may be able to watch its throat bulge as it sings, or see it catch an insect or other prey with its remarkable tongue. Sticky, long, and attached at the front of its mouth, a frog's tongue flicks out in deadly ambush. Notice that the frog's eyes are located on the top of its head, bulging upward so that it can sit concealed in the water with just its eyes and nostrils breaking the surface.

Beneath the surface, the Pleasant River is one of the eight rivers in Maine to host a self-sustaining though small population of Atlantic salmon, a species that at one time was common in many New England rivers (see **Connecticut River Valley** and **#57**). Major factors in its decline are man-made obstacles to migration such as dams, overfishing, water pollution, and the introduction of competitive species of fish. In this drainage, the heathlands act as aquifers that help sustain flows of water over long periods and tend to minimize high and low flows, both factors that apparently are important in the production and growth of juvenile salmon.

Continue upstream for as long as you have time, then turn around and return to your vehicle, sliding past old, leaning maples with branches sweeping out over the water. Red maples are some of the first trees to bloom in the spring and to change color in the fall. Notice that many of these riverside trees are growing in roughly circular clumps. When a red-maple trunk is cut or broken off near its base, the root crown frequently will send up a flurry of new shoots. This ability to root-sprout allows red maples to continuously colonize areas in which "disturbances" such as floods, fires, and erosion are relatively common environmental factors.

Remarks: *This is a river and walking trip of whatever length you choose to make it. There are two small rocky sections in the river, just above the put-in spot, that require a bit of maneuvering; the rest of this midriver area is generally flat and very winding. You can make a weekend trip by putting in east of Beddington and taking out at the spot described above. Check Maine canoeing guides for details. The heath is often hot and bright—*

a hat with a brim is recommended. You may also want to use a couple of bandanna markers to help keep track of your landing place and route across the heath domes. Although spring is flower time, fall is also gorgeous on the heaths. Remember that bugs love quiet rivers and heathlands, especially in the spring and early summer, so be prepared. Fishing is under state of Maine regulation; a license is required.

Nearby places
of Interest

Pineo Ridge, the emergent glaciomarine delta that forms the southwestern boundary of the Great Heath, is accessible via dirt road. Make a left turn off the Epping Road at 2.7 miles north of Route 1. The Narraguagus River, the next major drainage to the west, is another popular canoe trip. For details, check Maine canoeing guides. Petit Manan Point, south of Milbridge and Steuben, is a National Wildlife Refuge that occupies the tip of a peninsula jutting into the Gulf of Maine. It is described in the coastal volume of this guide.

Baxter
State Park

North of Bangor, the Maine woods stretch hundreds of miles, crossing the United States border and melting into Canadian forests. Amidst this sea of trees, Mount Katahdin rises massive and mystical, almost like a mirage that appears to move away as one approaches it. Around its base, particularly north of it, lie some 314 square miles of forests, ponds, and other rugged peaks protected as Baxter State Park. Rising abruptly from plain to windswept heights, untempered by the moderating influence of the sea, it is a land of extremes. A hike from the lowlands to the top of Katahdin or Traveler peaks is similar to walking from central Maine to the Arctic tundra.

Mount Katahdin looks so solid that it is difficult to imagine it has not always been there, yet geologists have pieced together a history that includes just such a scene. For some 200 million years during the early Paleozoic era, it seems that nearly all of eastern North America, including the Baxter area, was covered by a shallow sea. Sedimentary rocks were formed on this sea floor, some of them bearing fossils that helped to determine their ages. These older rocks form the bedrock of the northern quarter and the eastern edge of the park. Then, about 400 million years ago, volcanoes erupted in some parts of this sea, depositing lava and volcanic ash. These rocks are exposed today as the dark gray rhyolite of Traveler Mountain, South Branch Pond, and the north central section of the parklands. A small area along the Trout Brook drainage contains younger sedimentary rocks that were formed in part by erosion of the volcanic rocks.

Land-plant fossils within them connect them to the period when complex life forms were first emerging onto land. Then, some 350 million years ago, during roughly the same period when the granitic bedrock of Mount Desert Island and numerous other New England sites was being formed, huge chambers of magma oozed up from the bowels of the earth and cooled into granite, beneath the older rocks. A period of mountain building ensued during which the Appalachians, the New England mountains, and the mountains of England, Scotland, and Norway were uplifted, folded, and faulted. Today, millions of years of erosion later, the Katahdin granites are exposed as the bedrock of the southern half of the park, Mount Katahdin being the tallest and largest of the peaks that it forms.

The Penobscot tribe believed the mighty peak to be host to their sacred spirits, one of whom was particularly protective of the open slopes above timberline, sending all manner of harsh weather to repel those who attempted to reach the summit (see **#107**). More recently, botanists and geologists have been lured to these same windswept boulder fields and meadows, as well as to the ridges and ravines below. It was the great hardwood and softwood forests of the lower slopes that attracted loggers and lumbermen of the late 1800s and early 1900s. By 1923, almost the entire mountain had been logged. As early as the 1860s, conservation and preservation advocates proposed that the mountain be protected, but Katahdin's establishment as a park was as rocky and full of obstacles as the mountain itself. Even with Percival Proctor Baxter, longtime mayor of Portland and governor of the state of Maine, as its champion, true protection of the area came only after Baxter delved into his own pocketbook and as a citizen of Maine donated the acreage, parcel by parcel, to the state to be kept in its "natural wild state." The park is now managed by the Baxter Park Authority, an organization distinct from the Maine Department of Parks and Recreation, which administers Maine's other state parks.

Today, visitors with assorted recreational interests visit the park to enjoy not only mountaintop and forest communities but also ponds, streams, heaths, and eskers (see **#108**). The granite bulk of Mount Katahdin is by far the most famous part of the park, its slopes sweeping up from the surrounding plain and terminating in a semicircular summit ridge with six named peaks: Pamola, Chimney, South, Baxter, Hamlin, and Howe. Its upper reaches frequently shrouded in mist or clouds, Katahdin maintains an aura of mystery. Katahdin, North Traveler, and a few other peaks in Baxter State Park have treeless summits ranging from 3,300 to 5,267 feet in elevation. Scientists have long been intrigued by the fact that the New England timberline is at only about half the elevation of western timberlines of the same latitude. The discovery of small trees in sheltered areas at the summit of Mount Washington in New Hampshire (see **#84**) suggests that wind, rather than extreme cold, may be the limiting factor out here—certainly, the tops of New England mountains are known to have some of the highest winds in the country.

Below the alpine tundra of the high peaks, Baxter State Park is mantled with a variety of forests. Sunlight filters through bright green or gold deciduous forests along South Branch Pond and Howe Brook, and peaks between tightly laced, dark evergreen needles along the southeastern shore of Sandy Stream Pond. On the slopes of the Owl and the Brother mountains, spruce-fir forests grow in strange banded patterns that generally follow the contours of the slopes (see **#107**). In a great many sections of the park, the spruce-fir canopy has been opened by spruce budworm activity (see **#106**), while in other areas, wind and fire have created openings for new growth. This is particularly visible along the Perimeter Rd. between Abol and Daicey ponds. Here, in 1974, heavy snowfall combined with strong winds and saturated soils led to the blowdown of some 3,300 acres of mainly spruce-fir forest in Baxter State Park and adjacent Great Northern Paper Co. lands. In order to decrease the fire danger associated with the large amount of dead wood, a salvage operation was begun in 1976, but public protest arose over the appropriateness of the venture, since Percival Baxter had designated that the land be "forever wild." Ultimately, the court ruled that the Baxter Park Authority could proceed with the salvage, but that heavy equipment such as skidders could not be used in the woods. Effectively, this meant that salvage in the park could continue only along existing park roads.

In July 1977, the area was struck by lightning, igniting a fire that proved to be very difficult to control. After a week of intense work the blaze was extinguished, and shortly thereafter restoration steps were undertaken, such as mulching, seeding, and establishing of water bars on some of the more critical steep slopes. In the rest of the area, regrowth has proceeded on its own, creating a new set of habitats. While some erosion inevitably took place, at the same time nutrients were released for use in the soil and a new group of plants demanding a somewhat different set of nutrients was allowed the chance to grow. The first few years of new shoots and herbs provided high-quality forage for such animals as deer, moose, and snowshoe hare. Although forest fires have generally been considered "bad," studies of fires like this one are revealing that fire may be considered a regular process of the environment.

Both water and ice have eroded and sculpted the rock surfaces of Baxter, helping at once to create soil and to carry it from one place

to another. Glacial evidences are especially pronounced in the basins, tarns, and moraines on Mount Katahdin (see also **#105**) and
in the sinuous rock-and-sand ridge of the Katahdin Esker. Along
Howe Brook and at Little and Big Niagara Falls of Nesowadnehunk
Stream, more recent running-water features, such as potholes and
waterwheels, are visible. Elsewhere the waters lie in ponds where
moose and loons spend much of the summer months (see **#106**
and **#110**).

The park headquarters and visitors information desk are in Millinocket at 64 Balsam Dr. There are four points of access to the park
itself, where visitors, day and overnight, register and out-of-state
vehicles pay an entrance fee. During the summer season, these gates
are open from 6:00 a.m. to 10:00 p.m. The most commonly used
entrance is the Togue Pond gate. On the southern boundary of the
park, it is the closest access for Roaring Brook, Abol, and Katahdin
campgrounds and hiking trails on Mount Katahdin and in the rest
of the southern part of Baxter. The Matagamon gate is the northeastern entrance, closest to Trout Brook Farm and South Branch
campgrounds and to trails in the northern section of the park. To
reach it, exit I-95 at Sherman and follow Route 11 north to Patten.
Go northwest on Route 159, through Shin Pond, and in about 25
miles you will reach the Matagamon gate. Within the park, the dirt
Perimeter Rd. makes a three-quarter circle, with short spurs into
Daicey, Kidney, and South Branch ponds. Because the roads are
narrow, there is a size restriction on vehicles allowed to enter the
park; maximum dimensions are 9 feet high, 7 feet wide, and 22 feet
long (single) or 44 feet long (combined units).

Camping in Baxter has become increasingly popular. It is allowed
in designated sites only, and overnight use is limited by the number
of backcountry and drive-in campsites: when they are full, no more
overnight visitors are admitted. Reservations are highly recommended, particularly during the summer months. Mail requests and
fees to Reservations Clerk, Baxter State Park, 64 Balsam Dr., Millinocket, Maine 04462; reservation requests are accepted beginning
January 1 each year. Lean-to, tent, and camper-trailer sites are located at Roaring Brook, Abol, Katahdin Stream, Nesowadnehunk,
South Branch Pond, and Trout Brook Farm campgrounds. RVs are
permitted (within the size limitations), but toilets and sinks may not
be used while in the park. Basic facilities are provided; there is no
hot water or showers. There are cabins for rent at Daicey Pond
(park-operated) and at Kidney Pond (privately operated). Tent sites
and lean-tos are scattered throughout the backcountry. There are
also some group areas in the park. The camping season varies, depending on the weather and the specific campground; it extends

generally from about mid-May to October 15. Off-season overnight use from about December 1 to the end of snow, is by special permit; there must be at least four people in a group. Should all park sites be full, there are a number of privately operated campgrounds and sporting camps in the vicinity of the Baxter entrances. In addition, the Maine Forest Service maintains several campsites somewhat farther away in the North Woods. Groceries and gasoline are not available in the park. There is a store and gas pumps at Abol Bridge, on the Millinocket-Greenville Rd., about 4 miles west of the Baxter State Park Rd.

The park maintains over 130 miles of trails. Lowland trails are relatively flat, the footing varying from soft and muddy to quite rocky. Narrow boardwalks have been constructed in a number of more heavily used wet sections. Mountain trails are steep, rocky, and rugged. Rocks at any elevation, particularly on scree and talus slopes, may be loose, and sand, dirt, or moss on rock surfaces may make them slippery. Even in summer, weather and trail conditions can change rapidly, especially above timberline. Water, extra snacks, and some warm clothing are advised for any extended or high-elevation hiking. All hikers must register and check out at trailheads or nearby ranger stations. There are posted cutoff times after which the park asks hikers not to leave trailheads for Baxter summits.

Picnic areas with tables are located adjacent to the campgrounds and at Avalanche Field, Rum Brook, Abol Beach, Foster Field, Slide Dam, Dwelly Pond, Burnt Mountain, and the Crossing. Fires are permitted only in designated sites.

Swimming is permitted in the ponds and lakes, but there are no lifeguard services available. There are sandy beaches at Abol Pond, Daicey Pond, and South Branch Pond.

Licenses are required for all freshwater fishing in the state of Maine.

Nonmotorized boating is allowed on Baxter ponds and lakes. Canoe and boat rentals are available at South Branch, Russell, and Daicey ponds.

Pets are not allowed in the park.

Winter activities include cross-country skiing and snowshoeing. Snowmobiling is permitted only on the Perimeter Rd.

Wildlife in Baxter State Park is abundant, ranging from tiny species such as mosquitoes and wood warblers to large mammals such as moose, white-tailed deer, and black bear. Moose-watching is a popular activity. During the summer, moose spend a good deal of time in ponds, eating aquatic vegetation and getting some respite from the swarms of biting insects that plague them. They visit Sandy Stream Pond quite consistently, and Big Rock, on its southeastern shore, is a good watching spot. While you are in the area, you might also look for beavers, which are sometimes spotted near the outlet of the pond. The coyote population in Baxter is growing, and while these intelligent canines are not as visible as moose, you may be treated to a spine-tingling chorus of their beautiful voices, especially if you are in the northern parklands at night.

The Lumberman's Museum, just north of Patten, is a wonderful and fascinating window on North Woods operations. Displays include a sawmill, other equipment such as an old stream tractor, and models of camps depicting the rugged life-styles of log drivers and lumbermen.

Another place to visit is the Great Northern Paper Co. in Millinocket. During the summer, from approximately the third week in June to the third or fourth week in August, tours are led through such aspects of the operations as the wood yard and the grinder, screen, paper, and finishing rooms. Large groups should make reservations in advance. Call (207) 723-5131, extension 1274, or write to the Great Northern Paper Co., Millinocket, Maine.

If you are interested in geology or history, you might make a side trip to Ripogenus Gorge, some 15 miles west of the Baxter Park Road, on Great Northern Paper company land. The gorge is located just below Chesuncook and Ripogenus lakes, on the West Branch of the Penobscot River. A variety of rock types, including some of Maine's old sedimentary rocks, are exposed. The gorge is also famous in log-driving history.

See the **Bibliography** for useful books about Baxter State Park.

105.
South Turner
Mountain

Directions: **Baxter State Park, Maine. From Bangor take I-95 north about 60 miles to Exit 56, then Route 157 (joined by Route 11) west about 10 miles to the far side of Millinocket. From the blinking light at the bottom of the hill west of Millinocket, it is 15 miles to the Baxter State Park entrance turnoff. Follow signs as you leave town on the Millinocket Lake Rd. (Millinocket–**

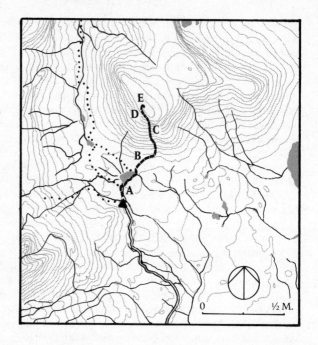

Greenville Rd.). Turn right onto Baxter State Park Rd. (dirt) and go 2 miles to the Togue Pond gate. At the fork beyond, go right 8 miles to the Roaring Brook parking area.

Ownership: **Baxter State Park, Baxter Park Authority.**

The hike up South Turner Mountain is one of the most spectacular in the Katahdin area. The first part of the trip takes you past Sandy Stream Pond (see **#106**) and through the surrounding lowlands, which are both frequented by moose. The mountain ascent is coolly wooded most of the way, and a cold spring about a mile up is a welcome refresher. From the open summit, the glacial story of Baxter State Park is spread before you like a gigantic open book. Few views of the steep-sided glacial hollows, known as *cirque basins*, on Katahdin's flanks are finer or more instructive.

From the parking area, follow the Sandy Stream Pond Trail to the far end of the pond, where the South Turner Mountain Trail begins (**A**). Keep an ear and an eye open for moose (see **#106**). In this lowland forest the pond-basin soils are poorly drained and often muddy. Red maple and white birch, which are tolerant of soggy rootings, predominate in the mixed forest. On the porous talus slopes above (**B**), sugar maple and yellow birch become more prominent.

As you ascend, you may catch a glimpse through the trees of the cliff above, which has provided the raw rock and boulder material for the talus slope (now forested) on which you walk. Most of the rocks here are fairly fine-grained, gray granitics (see **#93** and **Baxter State Park**), a type of stone that formed from molten minerals beneath the surface. That they are exposed today indicates that surficial rock, thousands of feet of it, has eroded away. The fine grain of the rocks suggests that they cooled comparatively more rapidly than, for instance, the larger-grained granitic rocks that form outcrops on Mount Katahdin (see **#107**). Since magma deeper beneath the surface and under greater pressure tends to cool more slowly, it is likely that the fine-textured South Turner rocks cooled closer to the surface than did the Katahdin outcrops.

Near the 0.9-mile point (**C**), listen for the sound of running water: a spring flows clear and cold from the rocks on the right side of the trail, another reminder that activity occurs beneath the surface of the mountain. Crack systems carry and store water underground, whereas rivers and lakes carry and store it above. A spring exists where a subsurface waterway, or *aquifer,* in this case probably a crack, meets the ground level. On dusty summer days, when soil moisture seems totally absent, one might wonder at finding this spring still flowing. Some factors that might allow it to do so are the following: (1) there may be a chamber or chambers in which water is stored; (2) the aquifer, a large underground water supply, may be so long that, like a chamber, it stores water, in this case moving water; (3) the flow may be very slow, again bridging dry times.

Notice the wonderful coolness of the water. Traveling underground, where the daily flux of sunshine has little effect, the spring waters stay consistently cold. In hot regions of the world, this coolness of underground water systems has been tapped for the air conditioning of buildings.

As you climb higher and the trees become shorter and more sparse, you can enjoy the view of the lower lands south of Katahdin. If you remain quiet long enough, some of the local inhabitants may resume their activities. Woodland mice scurry through the leaves, red squirrels forage for nuts, and white-throated sparrows ceaselessly pipe, *"Hey, Sam Peabody, Peabody, Peabody,"* over their territorial boundaries. If you can get a good view of one of these singers, look at the shape of its beak. The shape of a bird's beak makes it easier for it to eat certain kinds of foods than others. The thickened, conical shape of a white-throated sparrow's beak is well suited for cracking seeds, while the narrow, curved structure of a brown creeper's beak is ideal for picking insects out of cracks in tree-trunk bark.

Not far before the summit, the vegetation betrays the stresses of an exposed environment (**D**). Gray birch, cherry, spruce, and fir, which in other locations may grow tens of feet tall, here are short, chunky bushes stunted by desiccating winds. A patch of pearly everlasting attests to the dryness and sunniness of the site. As the name implies, the papery white flowers keep a long time when dried. The plant was used by some Indian and pioneer groups for making a tea.

At **E,** you stand above the tree line. The elevation is not particularly high here, but exposure to wind, instability of the substrate, lack of soil nutrients, and the terrain's very limited capacity to retain moisture have made it impossible for trees to grow here. *Step carefully*: some of the rocks on this slope are loose.

From the summit, enjoy the 360-degree vista of glacial topography (see **#107**): the broad, U-shaped valley of South Branch Stream to the north; the rounded cirque basins, the sharply ridged *arêtes*, high rugged ridges, and the high *tarns*, small pools or lakes in the mountains (see **#92**), of the Katahdin massif to the west. This view can be particularly fascinating because it illustrates both continental and alpine glacial features. *Continental glaciers* are huge and thick masses of ice that extend over great portions of land, frequently covering even mountaintops. *Alpine glaciers* originate near mountain summits and are often confined within a valley. Both types of glaciers form U-shaped valleys, but only alpine glaciers create cirques and arêtes.

During much of the glacial period, all of the Katahdin area was covered by continental ice so thick (from 1,000 feet to a mile or more) that the mountains and valleys beneath it affected its motion only locally, and it was able to flow over everything. Imagine, though, a time toward the end of that period when warmer conditions were melting the glacial ice faster than it was accumulating, and the tops of most of the mountains around, including the bulk of Katahdin, were exposed. Small valley glaciers lingered on the upper mountain slopes, confined by ridges. Flowing downhill, they met and merged with the thinned continental ice below. These alpine valley glaciers, through frost-wedging and plucking, eroded the steep and rounded headwalls of the cirques opposite you: Little North, North, and Great basins. Where the distance between cirques was small, glaciers in adjacent (or opposite) valleys eroded the dividing ridge into a steep and narrow arête like Hamilton Ridge, between North and Great basins.

Before you head back down the mountain, check the ponds below for signs of moose. Even if you cannot see the moose themselves, you may be able to see where they have been feeding: murky-brown swaths through bluish waters indicate where a moose has been browsing on submerged vegetation.

Remarks: *This is a 4-mile hike, round trip. It may be combined with the Sandy Stream Pond Loop Trail, making a 5-mile hike. Views into the basins on Mount Katahdin are better in morning light. Binoculars are useful for viewing the basins and for moose-watching. The first part of the trail is usually muddy. The slope just before the summit has some loose rocks, so be careful. The speed limit in Baxter State Park is 20 mph (at that speed the 8 miles from Togue Pond to Roaring Brook takes awhile). Camping may be available at Roaring Brook. During the summer months, book campsites in advance by writing: Reservations Clerk, Baxter State Park, 64 Balsam Dr., Millinocket, Maine 04462.*

106.
Sandy Stream Pond
Loop

Directions: **Baxter State Park, Maine. Follow directions for #105 to the end.**

Ownership: **Baxter State Park, Baxter Park Authority.**

The Sandy Stream Pond area is an excellent habitat for moose, and beavers, woodpeckers, herons, and spruce budworms are among their coinhabitants. If you go quietly and patiently, you *may* have the good fortune to observe some of this wildlife. Even if you do not see the creatures themselves, you are likely to discover some of the abundant signs of their activities as you prowl these fine moist woodland communities.

From the Roaring Brook ranger station, follow the Sandy Stream Pond Trail northward through mixed coniferous and deciduous woods. Watch to the right for an opening littered with downed trees (**A**). Conically pointed stumps divulge that beavers have been active here. Notice how high above ground the cuts were made. The great ancestral beavers of eons ago would have been able to chew at this height unaided, but the beavers of today cannot. These trees were cut in winter, when the beavers were raised above ground level by snow. Although beavers make an underwater food cache of bark-covered branches for use in winter, these stumps remain as evidence that they also cut some fresh growth.

Shortly after you pass the first junction of the Russell Pond Trail, the forest canopy opens, and the trail crosses a swampy brook (**B**). Approach quietly: It is possible, if you are lucky, to see beavers swimming here and moose browsing in the shrubbery. Follow either of the *blazed* shore-access trails left and emerge through dense sheep laurel, blueberry, leatherleaf, and sweetgale at the water's edge. Sandy Stream Pond (**C**) is a favorite spring, summer, and fall haunt of moose, which come here to feed on the submerged vegetation and perhaps to get a respite from the hordes of biting flies and mosquitoes. Although moose are generally most active at dawn and dusk, the ones in this area use Sandy Stream Pond at almost any time of day, and they have grown quite accustomed to park visitors spying on them from the lookout points on the shore. Elsewhere in Maine, where they are not protected from hunters, moose tend to be more elusive. A frightened moose may tear through the woods like a runaway locomotive, but a moose that does not want to be seen can move with amazing stealth. Moose have a definite advantage when

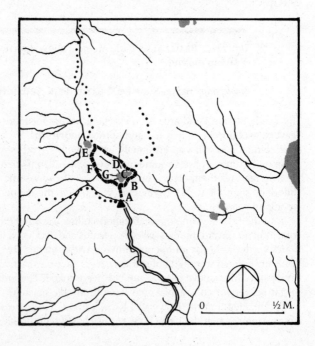

0   ½ M.

avoiding us: our eyes are much more keen than are theirs, but they can hear our footfalls *minutes* before one of us on the same spot could do so.

Continue around the end of the pond, crossing the outflow stream and passing the South Turner Mountain Trail junction. The lowlands on this side (**D**) are also moose habitat. Here they can find protection from storms and could hide from predators if necessary; however, neither wolves nor hunters are a threat in Baxter. The forest here also offers moose other kinds of food: leaves and twigs of aspen, moosewood (striped maple), and other broad-leaved trees in summer; buds, bark, and needles of balsam fir and deciduous trees in winter. You may find signs of moose-browsing 20 feet in the air, for these large animals use their weight to bend and often break slender saplings, bringing tender upper shoots into their reach.

You will find numerous blowdowns in this area. Still in evidence in the exposed root systems of the more recently fallen trees is a gray, ashlike layer of soil. Most of the minerals, except silica, have been leached from this layer. This is a common phenomenon in the humid, acidic soils of the Northeast.

At the next trail junction, go left on the Russell Pond Trail. As you descend slightly into a maple glade (**E**), look for trunks that are "kissing." Although tree trunks are quite rigid, they sway significantly in the wind, and a tree growing close to another tree or a rock can rub itself raw. Such a tree grows a "kiss," or callus, to anchor itself in the area of friction and prevent further chafing. Just beyond here, keep your nose open for the sweet smell of aspens!

At **F**, conifers are common, but almost all are now dead. Spruce budworm has been very active here during the last few years. The larva of a small moth, the budworm feeds on the buds of spruces and especially of firs. It has coevolved with the conifers of the North American boreal forests. Like all organisms, its population varies. We have become particularly aware of increases in the budworm's population because of the organism's detrimental effects on the timber industry. A peak in their populations occurred in Maine during the second decade of this century and another one recently in the late 1970s and early 1980s. Spray programs initiated to control their numbers have been reported effective or noneffective, depending on who studied which aspect of the situation.

In accordance with the strictures that former Governor Percival P. Baxter set when he deeded these lands to the people of Maine, the trees in the park have been left unsprayed. The greater portion of spruce and fir have died during the recent budworm peak. Whether or not they would have died if they had been sprayed is not known and is really immaterial here. What this situation offers is a glimpse into forest processes when not dominated by humans. Some biologists suggest that budworm killings of this kind may be part of the way in which the environment maintains diversity and long-term conditions optimal for life.

Cross a stream on rocks and look left for a wetland area (**G**). A curved "stick" protruding from the water may turn out to be a great blue heron statuesquely poised as it watches the waters for an unwary fish or frog. Long legs and long toes allow it to wade easily through shallow water and muddy bottoms, patiently and perseveringly stalking its prey.

The last part of the trail passes through a more mixed forest. Hay-scented and wood ferns are abundant (see **#100**). Luxuriant patches of shining club moss dot the ground (see **#107** and **#110**). Descend to the Sandy Stream Pond Trail junction and go right to return to Roaring Brook campground.

Remarks: *The walk is a little over 2 miles, over muddy to rocky terrain with almost no change in elevation. It is an excellent walk for a rainy day; it also makes a nice combination with the South Turner Mountain Trail. Binoculars may be useful. For camping, see* **#105**. *Some people fish in Roaring Brook, catching brook trout and occasionally landlocked salmon. Check with the rangers for regulations. A license is required.*

107.

Mount Katahdin

Directions: **Baxter State Park, Maine. Follow directions for #105 to the end.**

Ownership: **Baxter State Park, Baxter Park Authority.**

A granite monolith close to a mile high, Mount Katahdin rises imposingly above the surrounding plateau lands, its glaciated flanks sweeping outward, embracing jewellike tarns, swift mountain streams, and basins full of bilberries. Its lower slopes are mantled in protective forests; its upper reaches lie exposed to fierce sunlight, winds, rain and snow, or ice, its head often hidden in rolling mists or storm-clouds. A hike on the "greatest mountain," as its Indian name is translated, is a treat you will never forget, from the tiny details of alpine wildflowers to the vast bulk of the mountain itself to the 360-degree panorama that unfolds on sunny days from the summit—the highest in Maine.

This description is specifically for the Helon Taylor route but applies generally to features that can be seen from other trails on Katahdin. The first section of the trail has recently been relocated and is currently the same as the first tenth of a mile of the Chimney Pond Trail. Bear left onto the Helon Taylor Trail, heading away from Roaring Brook and climbing up the long flank ridge of Pamola Peak. Called Keep Ridge, it was named after the Reverend Marcus R. Keep who, in 1848, cut a trail up Katahdin, in part to facilitate the harvest of mountain cranberries which he hoped would be economically profitable in Maine, as it was in Newfoundland at that time. On this north side of the ridge (**A**), temperatures are cooler and moisture evaporates less quickly than on the southern slopes where sunlight hits the forest or the ground at a much more vertical angle. Mosses abound on this forest floor, some of the most ancient plants to venture onto land. The tough cuticle, or surface, on their leaflike scales permits them to live in air without being desiccated as seaweed would be if not submerged almost daily. Mosses are still tied

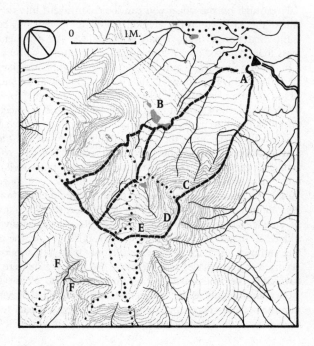

to water, however, because of the sexual part of their reproductive system. The green plant we call moss produces male and female parts at the tip of the stem. The sperm must swim to the female parts, and that requires a moist environment. Sperm are frequently scattered from one moss to another by the splashes of raindrops. From the union of sexual elements arises the filament and spore case of the asexually reproductive stage of the moss. The tiny spores fall and are blown from the capsule and, if they land in an appropriate spot, they will grow into new moss plants. Why don't they reproduce with spores only and thereby avoid a dependence on water? The answer probably lies in the fact that sexual reproduction, in combining two sets of genes, allows more rapid adaptation to environmental change. Mosses have apparently found it advantageous to retain this ability.

Also common on the forest floor in this area are club mosses, members of another branch of the family tree of plants, which have made a further step away from aquatic life. They have evolved stiff stems, roots, and internal plumbing systems that can tap water beneath the surface and send it up to their scalelike leaves. These were early steps in the ability to grow tall and gain acccess to larger, hitherto untapped spaces in which to collect sunlight.

From high on the ridge, you can look northward into the deep blue of the Basin Ponds (**B**), reminders that not so very long ago the entire Baxter area was covered with glacial ice. The continental ice mass that advanced over Maine originated in northeastern Canada, forming at a time when annual temperatures were lower than they are today and winter snowfalls did not melt entirely in the summer. Gradually, the accumulation of snow became so great that the snowflakes were compressed into ice. As the center of the ice sheet grew thicker, it began to move outward, just as cold honey poured onto a tabletop flows out from the center as you add more and more to that central point. An ice sheet in motion is called a glacier. As far as geologists can tell, the continental ice mass, sometimes well over a mile thick, advanced and receded from Maine at least four times during the last million or so years, most recently melting from this area about 12,000 years ago. In the highlands of the Katahdin massif, smaller alpine glaciers (see **#105**) lingered, flowing downward as a result of gravitational pull from their sources below the mountain summits. Such ice flows were the only form of glaciation that occurred in the Rockies and the Sierra Nevada, which were never covered by the continental ice sheet. In New England, alpine glaciers were common only as the continental ice sheet thinned, leaving the mountain flanks exposed. For this reason, alpine glacial features such as the cirque in which the Basin Ponds lie and the arête called the Knife Edge are not as common in Maine as they are in the mountains of Colorado and California. (See **#105** for discussion of alpine glacial features.) South of the Basin Ponds, a long ridge of glacially deposited stones called a moraine stretches southeast along what at one time was the zone where the alpine glaciers merged with the edge of the thinning ice sheet. Here, the concentrations of rocks plucked and carried in the edges of the glaciers joined together and, when the ice finally melted, were deposited in a long ridge.

As you continue to the summit of Pamola, you leave all trees behind. There are many tales of the Spirit of Katahdin about these areas above the timberline. The Penobscots believed that the mountain was host to a trio of spirits. Wuchowsen, the spirit of the night wind, created the harmless nighttime breezes by flapping his wings. The Stormbird, a nasty creature with a terrible beak and claws, was very powerful and easily aroused to anger, which he spent creating violent storms. The Spirit of Katahdin, of gigantic and majestic human form, with stony eyebrows and cheekbones, lived inside the mountain with his wife and children. The three spirits are combined in the white settlers' Pamola, most frequently depicted as its Storm-bird element. The Stormbird legends concern Pamola's attempts to keep men, whether Indian or white, from climbing Katahdin, particularly above the timberline where the spirit unleashed his full fury. Fog, high winds, pelting rains, and snowstorms were among his tools. They remain among the great stresses of life in this land above the trees.

Diapensia is one of the few plants that survives here (**C**). Growing in very dense tussocks, its evergreen leaves waxy, succculent, and often tinged red or purple, it is a species that is superbly adapted to arctic-alpine conditions. A hike up Katahdin is a good deal like a journey northward into the Arctic tundra. As you go to higher elevations or to higher latitudes, the growing season gets shorter and the average annual temperatures drop, as do summer highs and winter lows. In addition, exposure to ultraviolet radiation and to drying winds increases, and both soil cover and moisture-retaining capabilities drop. The environment of the higher elevations is remarkably similar to that of boreal coastlines, Arctic tundra, and even deserts. Not surprisingly, plants in all these places share a number of adaptive strategies, particularly in regard to water conservation: leaf size is often small, to cut down on surface area from which evaporation can take place; cuticles are generally thicker, frequently waxy, or covered with hairs, and leaves are thickened and succulent; photosynthetic areas are often concentrated close to the ground where winds are less strong; and leaves may have a reddish coloring, which is thought to help protect them from sunburn, the way the melanin in our skin protects us. Both tree species such as black spruce and cushionlike species such as diapensia exhibit these characteristics. (See **#35** and **#36** for more on alpine vegetation.)

From the top of Pamola Peak, follow the trail left, out along the Knife Edge (**D**). Narrowed by glacial plucking, its slopes continue to be eroded, primarily by frost-induced rockfall. Active couloirs, or gullies, are full of angular, freshly broken chunks of rock that are bare of the greenish lichens that encrust more stable surfaces.

The highest points on Katahdin are South Peak and Baxter Peak (**E**). Contrasting with the precipices of the Knife Edge are the broadly arching back and wide saddle that fall away from Baxter Peak. This rugged alpine environment is inhabited by some remarkably delicate-looking plants, among them clumps of Greenland (or mountain) sandwort. Often growing in pockets of gravel that have little resemblance to soil, it seems to be one of the few plants that can tolerate the frequently disturbed areas close to the trails. This species is considered a glacial relic in Maine, a northern plant that probably spread southward as colder climates migrated with the advance of the ice sheet. When the glaciers melted, the sandwort remained on Maine mountains, which provided islands of cool enough habitat scattered across warmer lowland environments. Alpine bilberry and dwarf birch are other arctic species that find suitable habitat in New England's alpine areas. Katahdin also has a relic insect species, the Katahdin arctic butterfly, isolated from Arctic populations long enough to be considered a subspecies. Members of this genus have a circumpolar distribution, but are rarely found in the contiguous United States. The brown and gray Katahdin arctic lives well camouflaged among the low tundra vegetation of the high tablelands that lie west of Baxter and Hamlin peaks. Like other butterflies, it has spent much of its life as an inconspicuous caterpillar, busily eating and storing energy for the fantastic metamorphosis by which it transforms itself into its winged adult form. While it is a caterpillar, only half of its cells are growing, the other half remaining small and dormant. During metamorphosis, the big larval cells die and become energy sources for the newly activated second set of cells that grow to form the adult insect. In essence, the larva consumes itself and builds a butterfly from the ashes.

Of an equally intriguing nature are the patterned spruce and fir growths, wavy horizontal stripes, that occupy the slopes of the Owl and the Brother mountains (**F**), surrounding the Klondike basin, northwest of Katahdin. An early theory was that the patterns were formed by the hurricane that swept New England in 1938 (see **#53**); this is the origin of the term "windrows," which has been applied to the phenomenon. Apparently, though, the striped pattern was observed well before 1938, and many of the dead trees are standing, not blown down. Dabney Caldwell, a geologist and naturalist who has investigated the secrets of Katahdin, has observed these patterned areas. He finds them to be composed of an edge of trees that have reached a certain age or size and then for some reason have died. Sometime thereafter, they are apparently blown over and gradually replaced by new growth. The process seems to be repeated as each new generation of trees reaches some critical stage. How the cycle got started remains a mystery. Caldwell has noted that on many of the slopes there are parallel bands of debris from rockfall and from the slower, downslope creep, or slippage of soil, that also lie along the mountain contours. He suggests that death and replacement may be initiated along such bands where trees may have only marginal moisture and rooting medium.

From the peak, descend over pink scree and among gray boulders to the Saddle, where rushes and matted plants melt leeward into low crowberry and bilberry that sweep into wind-dwarfed spruce and fir, one group sheltering the next from the full force of strong winds. The tundra areas of the Saddle and the tablelands at one time hosted eastern woodland caribou. In 1892, eighteen were counted on top of Katahdin, but the last report of the species' presence was in 1908. Presumably, hunting and the rise in human activities in the Maine woods, including roads crisscrossing the formerly large, undissected areas where the caribou roamed, have contributed to their disappearance. From the Saddle, descend to Roaring Brook either via the highly gullied Saddle Trail and the sparkling waters of Chimney Pond or via Hamlin Peak and the wide, dramatic views of Hamlin Ridge.

Remarks: *This is a 12-mile hike, round trip, over both low-angle and steep terrain, almost all of it rocky underfoot. The Knife Edge section of the trail drops awesomely on either side. There is adequate space to walk, but crossing should not be attempted if the winds are strong or the visibility poor. The hardest section is the southern end where the trail drops into and then climbs up out of the notch between Pamola and Chimney peaks, requiring careful placement of hands and feet. The Helon Taylor route up Katahdin is absolutely gorgeous, but it is exposed to the weather for most of its length. Sturdy shoes or boots, an extra pair of socks to change into before you descend, and some adhesive tape to help protect chafe spots (put some on before rubbings turn into blisters) are recommended. Also bring water, snacks, and warm clothing in case the weather is cold while you are above timberline. Because this hike is a long one and because the summit is so celebrated, hikers tend to rush to the peak, exhausting themselves and missing the details along the way that make Katahdin such a wonderful mountain. Allow yourself plenty of time, not only for walking but also for sitting or exploring as you go. A number of other trails on Katahdin could be used in conjunction with the Helon Taylor Trail or with each other. See Baxter State Park maps and the* AMC Maine Mountain Guide.

108.
The Katahdin
Esker

Directions: **Baxter State Park, Maine. Follow directions in #105, but turn left at the first fork beyond the Togue Pond gate. You are now on the esker.**

Ownership: **Baxter State Park, Baxter Park Authority.**

Winding across the countryside in many formerly glaciated parts of the world are ridges of sand and gravel called *eskers,* a term derived from the Gaelic word *eiscir,* meaning "ridge." The Katahdin Esker is part of an esker system, segments of which geologists trace south to Aurora (east of Bangor). The beautiful Katahdin Esker is highly accessible, traversed for much of its length by the Baxter State Park Perimeter Rd. This entry describes a driving tour with a few short walking forays into the surrounding woods.

About 0.2 mile beyond the fork, there is a pulloff on the right-hand side of the road (**A**). A steep path leads down the side of the esker to its base. The sand-and-rock composition of the ridge is quite apparent. Most geologists believe that eskers are deposits of streams, which flowed in channels on the surface of glaciers or in tunnels within or at the base of the ice. Over time, sediments accumulated in these streambeds, just as they do in rivers and streams. These sands, gravels, and boulders, confined by walls of ice, were left as ridges when the glaciers melted. They are generally long, narrow, and sinuous. Some eskers are only a couple of yards high, while others rise 600 or more feet. While eskers occur in many of the areas covered by the last ice sheet, they are especially numerous and finely shaped in Maine.

Study of esker formation provides data to those scientists who continue to try to unravel the most recent glacial history of the region. As is so often the case, these probings raise questions at least

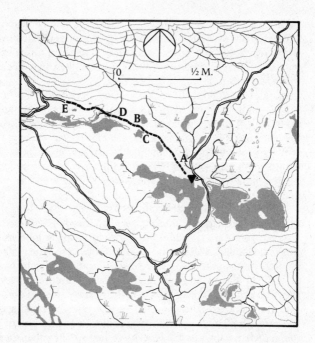

as often as they answer them. Mapping of esker segments in Maine and research into the physics of water flow at the base of the ice sheet have helped geologists deduce that the margin of the glacier at the time of the esker formation (12,000 to 13,000 years ago) was essentially parallel to the present coast of Maine and that the flow of ice was from north-northwest to south-southeast. What geologists do not yet know is why there is such an abrupt line in northern Maine beyond which esker segments are not found.

Drive a mile farther along the esker to another pulloff, also on the right (**B**), opposite to and a little beyond the bushy trail to Rocky Pond. Then walk down that trail toward the pond and go left near the shore, on the second of two side trails. The trail runs along a small esker ridge. Large red pines tower here and on the ridge on the far side of Rocky Pond. These northern trees commonly grow on well-drained, sandy sites—esker substrate suits them well. They generally thrive in soils richer than those occupied by jack pine and poorer than those colonized by white pine. This species gets established better on mineral soil than in humus or duff, and it is often used for reforestation.

On the left at **C,** there is a round depression between the two esker ridges. This is a *kettle hole* (see **#102**). These depressions are frequently less well drained than the higher ground that surrounds them. This kettle hole supports a mat of sphagnum moss, which is indicative of fairly continuous wetness and rather high acidity (see **#103** and **#76**).

Wander as far along the trail as you like (it ends in a few hundred yards) and then return to the park road. On the opposite side, next to the pulloff space, an old road heads westward along the base of the esker (**D**). Beyond the fork, where you stay left, there is a kettle hole with considerably different inhabitants than the one at **C**. Sedges, rushes, and grasses (see **#101**) crowd this wet basin, and meadow rue is common on the bank. The presence of these species suggests that conditions here are less acidic than at **C**.

You may wish to continue another half mile or so along this old road. Lush growths of bracken fern are invading sections of the roadbed. This species, with its large, triangular fronds, inhabits north-temperate forests and has a circumpolar distribution. When still curled, the fiddleheads of the fronds are tasty (if somewhat hairy), cooked or raw. As the plant grows and the fronds unfurl, however, its chemical composition changes, and the foliage can be toxic.

Covering much of the surface of the road is an outstanding growth of a gray lichen, whose pink fruiting bodies are reminiscent of British soldier lichen caps that have been washed so often that they have faded. This species of lichen is a common colonizer of disturbed sandy areas in Maine woods.

When you return to your car, drive another 1.4 miles to a pulloff space on the left (**E**). Walk away from the road, down the open-field swath, to an area of sand where esker material has been removed and the only slope stabilizers are small pines. Esker sands and gravels are in high demand as construction materials. Eskers are also valued for blueberry cultivation, for septic-system location, and as roadbeds. In Maine and other northern states where extensive bogs have developed on the relatively flat and poorly drained land, the natural pathways of eskers have been used by wildlife and humans alike. Today, many of the eskers in Maine are traversed by roads.

Follow the sandy swath as it curves around to the right and becomes an old roadbed paralleling the shore of Abol Pond. During the summer and fall, the wild and eerie call of loons may drift to you from over the water. Loons spend the winter on salt water, but they breed and raise their young on freshwater lakes. Their legs are positioned at the far rear of their bodies, which makes the birds extremely awkward on land. They nest at the very edge of the water (preferably on an islet but also in protected spots on promontories or in coves), so that they can crawl onto their nests directly from the water and can retreat to the water quickly if necessary (see also **#86**).

This old road meets the Abol Pond road in about half a mile. It is a pleasant, wooded walk with which to end your Katahdin Esker explorations. Retrace your steps in order to return to your car.

Remarks: *This entry outlines explorations along 2½ miles of an esker segment that is traversed by a dirt road. The entire trip could be walked, but you might prefer to drive the road sections and spend your walking time on the trails where vehicles are not permitted. Abol is the Baxter State Park campground nearest to the Katahdin Esker. For summr, make reservations in advance by writing to the Reservation Clerk, 64 Balsam Dr., Millinocket, Maine 04462. The season is May 15 to October 15. Day use is still permitted during the rest of the year.*

Two other segments of the Katahdin Esker system are visible to the south of the park. The Enfield Horseback is traversed by the Gould's Ridge Rd., north and east of Passadumkeag and south of Enfield. The Whalesback is traversed by Route 9, beginning a couple of miles east of Aurora. The Chesterville Esker divides two ponds south of Chesterville on Ridge Rd. Eric's Esker divides two ponds south of Oxford. De Lorme's Maine Atlas is an excellent road-map reference for these, and many other, sites. The old road at **D** *is a cross-country ski trail in the winter. A map is available from the park office.*

109.
Little and Big
Niagara Falls

Directions: **Baxter State Park, Maine. Follow directions in #105, but turn left at the first fork beyond the Togue Pond gate. Go 10.3 miles to Foster Field, turn left, and go 1.4 miles to Daicey Pond. Park in the big field on the right just before the pond (if you are staying in the cabins, you may park up there).**

Ownership: **Baxter State Park, Baxter Park Authority.**

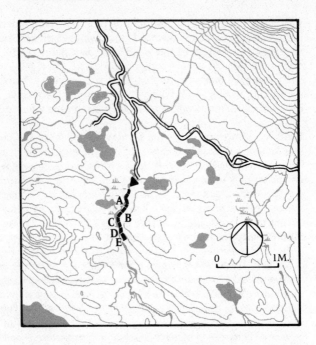

The motion of flowing water can be as captivating as the ghostly flickering of the aurora, the crashing fall of a great pine, or the dance of shadows on a forest floor. Here Nesowadnehunk Stream tumbles over a number of falls on its way to the West Branch of the Penobscot River. Little and Big Niagara are the first two of these falls. Though small, they are nonetheless alluring from aesthetic, historical, and geological perspectives. The short trail to the falls leads through a variety of forest communities and along an alder bottom bordered with raspberries.

From the big fields, walk the last hundred yards of the road to the pond. Look for the white blazes of the Appalachian Trail (AT), which you have joined. At the pond, go right on the AT (now a trail again). The forest is mixed deciduous and coniferous, with a high percentage of spruce. Gardens of lichen and "turkey tail" fungus festoon old trunks rotting on the forest floor. The small, leathery, banded, and shelflike "turkey tails" are the spore-producing (reproductive) structures of a fungus, which is busily decomposing the inside of the log. Use a hand lens to see the delicate pores (bottom side) from which its genus name *Polyporus*, or "many pores," was derived.

Just past the Daicey Pond Nature Trail junction, look for two 8-inch-diameter spruces living in the top of a big decaying stump on the right. Today, their roots grow down the stump, encasing it. When the stump is eventually rotted away, it will leave the two trees on root "stilts."

The trail drops a bit onto the wet flats of an alder bottom (**A**), where raspberries, Canada mayflower, chickweed, and a variety of ferns grow, each in its season. If you happen to be here in late July or early August when the raspberries are ripe on their vines, consider their function as well as their taste: the juicy red fruit invites passing creatures to eat it; seeds excreted in scat will most likely fall somewhere away from the parent plants, helping to avoid "family" competition for resources. Dispersal is one of the great challenges of life. (See **#96** for a discussion of seed dispersal and germination.)

The spruce woods at **B** are littered throughout with big boulders. The top of one of these is occupied by a now-dead birch with a most amazing root, 6 inches thick and covered with moss and lichens (see **#7**). Almost like a trunk, it stretches down the entire side of the boulder and finally disappears into the soil. Since roots generally grow hidden in soil and duff (decomposing organic materials on the forest floor) or in cracks between rocks, the great exposed length of this one presents a puzzle. It is hardly likely that it grew that long distance in the open. Its presence might indicate that the soil level was boulder-high when the root grew. That, too, seems improbable, because it would suggest that 5 feet of soil had eroded from here in only a few decades. While that amount of erosion is possible, the well-forested condition of these surroundings tends to contradict the idea. Another possibility is that the boulder may have been covered with a layer of moss that, with the dirt and moisture it trapped, provided enough protection and nutrients so that a long, skinny young root could burrow through it and finally reach the soil below. Again, we can only say maybe. This intriguing puzzle is as yet unsolved.

Shortly beyond the old, tumbled cabins, a side trail leads right to the remains of the Toll Dam (**C**). Some of the supports still standing were part of the original, hardwood-pegged dam built in the 1850s. The power stored here was not electric but rather water, impounded to provide enough flow to sluice logs through the narrow falls channels below. Nesowadnehunk Stream, draining quite a sizable area north of here, was a significant log-running tributary to the tumultuous "highway" of the West Branch of the Penobscot. The third and last dam on this site was constructed in 1929. The wrecked cabins you passed were part of that operation. Today, trucks and cleared roads have replaced the watercourses as log movers in the North Woods, leaving the Nesowadnehunk free to exert its own devices on the abandoned dam.

Shortly beyond the dam cutoff, another trail on the right leads to Little Niagara Falls (**D**), the first of the four major drops between the Toll Dam and the West Branch. Cedar, white birch, spruce, and fir line the bank. The stream, constricted by a large, protruding outcrop, shoots through a narrow opening over the falls. At some flow volumes, the waters hit a depression near the bottom and spin outward like a waterwheel. One can see how, over time, the constant impact of sediment-laden water deepened and smoothed old grooves and sculpted new ones into the surface of the bedrock. (The rock adjacent to both of the falls can be quite slick, even when dry, so be careful.)

Retrace your steps to the AT and continue another 0.3 mile, passing a spring (left), and descend the side trail (right) to Big Niagara Falls (**E**). As at Little Niagara, the bedrock ledges, formed of the same granite type as Mount Katahdin (see **#107**), show abundant evidence of glacial meltwater scouring: scratches, grooves, potholes. There are also a number of small round holes not of glacial origin. These used to hold iron pinnings that supported a structure from which men could "tend out," helping to keep the log stream moving through the falls area where logs were apt to jam. Were a jam to form, four possibilities existed for breaking it: (1) more water could be released from the dam upstream, floating the jam off; (2) it might be knocked loose by a well-placed blast of dynamite; (3) it might be possible to locate and free the "key" log; or (4) the crew might have to pick the jam apart log by log.

After a long gaze at the cascading waters, retrace the AT to the parking field.

Remarks: *The walk is 2.5 miles, round trip. The terrain is level, but often muddy. The falls areas offer delightful spots for picnicking. Camping may be available at Katahdin Stream or at Abol. For summer use, make reservations in advance by writing: Reservations Clerk, Baxter State Park, 64 Balsam Dr., Millinocket, Maine 04462.*

110.

Howe Brook

Directions: **Baxter State Park, Maine. From Bangor, take I-95 north about 80 miles to Sherman, then Route 11 north about 10 miles to Patten, then Route 159 (Shin Pond Rd.) about 25 miles northwest to the Matagamon gate of Baxter State Park. Continue 7 miles, then go south (left) 2.3 miles to the parking area at South Branch Pond. (Alternatively, follow directions for #105, take the left fork after Togue Pond gate, drive about 36 miles.)**

Ownership: **Baxter State Park, Baxter Park Authority.**

A day's walk alongside lovely Howe Brook will show you both depositional and erosional stream features, including pothole pools and a secluded waterfall. On both sides of the stream are hardwood forests, inhabited by deer and coyote.

Begin by following the Pogy Notch Trail from the end of the lean-to sites in the campground. Skirt the east side of South Branch Pond (**A**) through the forest of mixed-age deciduous trees with a well-developed shrub layer and a carpeting of many herbs (selfheal and large-leaved asters are prominent). This is good habitat for white-tailed deer (see also **#49**), which browse on the broad-leaved foliage. The deer population in the park is relatively low now, in part because most of the old logged areas have grown from thickets, where leaves and twigs were plentiful at accessible heights, into forests with (in many cases) sparse understory and herb layers, which provide minimal forage for deer. Look for their signs in this area, though: hoof marks in the trail; piles of cylindrical, ½-inch-long pellets (scat); living twigs with raggedly torn edges. Deer have no upper incisors, so when they browse a twig, they tear the tip away. Hares, on the other hand, having sharp lower *and* upper teeth, nip a twig off neatly.

Another animal sign you may discover is coyote scat. Often deposited right in the trail, the segments vary a great deal in size, but are frequently around 3 inches long. Although mainly a predator on small rodents and hares, the coyote is a first-rate opportunist when it comes to food, and its scat may be composed of anything from fur and bones to grasses and seeds to pieces of plastic garbage. The coyote is one of the few mammals that has managed to increase its

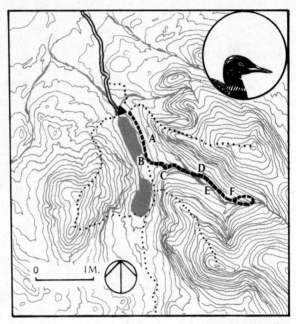

Inset: Common loon

range despite vigorous campaigns for its reduction. In the past century, it has spread from its former western range (Alaska to Central America) all the way east into New England. It began to be commonly seen in the Patten area just east of here in the 1960s. Although coyotes are often blamed for reduced deer populations, many biologists think this blame misplaced. Habitat changes such as that described above probably have a far greater effect on herd numbers than do coyotes. (See **#111** for more on coyotes.)

Pass the Traveler Mountain trailhead. At **B** alders fringe the water, and the ground is much more stony. You are walking on a *delta*, a deposit of sediments at the mouth of a river or stream. This large and fairly level area of gravel and boulders was deposited by Howe Brook where it entered what was once a single South Branch Pond. Today, the delta buildup divides that former lake into two bodies of water. Forest and massive boulders cover much of the delta, which suggests that it was formed some time ago and by a high-volume stream. Even in flood stage it is unlikely that Howe Brook could have moved the boulders; glacial meltwater is a more likely candidate.

Just before you meet Howe Brook itself, go right onto the Howe Brook Trail. A short walk takes you to a series of cascades and pools (**C**). It is easy to spend an entire day here, watching the water slide through narrow sluice grooves, bounce over drops, and become smooth and quiet in pools. Most of the pools in this section of Howe Brook are potholes, scoured into the bedrock by stones and gravel that were spun around and around in an eddy in the glacial melt-water stream. The more they whirled, the more they abraded the bedrock, eventually forming the deep and smooth-sided holes you see today (see also **#81**). On a hot day, the pools invite dipping. In the fall, yellow leaves add a delicious glow.

Above the major string of slides and pools, the brook again chatters over a broken, rocky bed. The open, white-birch woods are dotted with the rotting hulks of large, old, moss-covered stumps and recumbent trunks (**D**). Note the telltale fire scars. At least two fires are reported to have swept this area in the early 1900s. That these vestigial chunks are still recognizable attests to the relatively slow rate at which decay progresses in the coolness of this stream canyon. Scoop a handful of rotting wood from the center of one of the softer stumps. Look for decomposers: millipedes, beetles, fungi, and carpenter ants; thousands of organisms too tiny to see with the unaided eye are also aiding in this process. Combined, they do a phenomenal amount of work, which helps keep nutrients available in the canyon's soils.

Continuing upstream, you cross numerous small side streams carrying water from the mountain flanks above you. The canyon bottom is also traversed by the long depressions of dry overflow channels and former stream courses (**E**). Some of these are now vegetated, indicating infrequent use or total abandonment. Others are free even of a covering of dead leaves, suggesting that Howe Brook still uses them when its flow is high.

Where the trail climbs up and over a small, rocky ridge (**F**), enjoy some outstanding growths of club mosses: wolf's paw, shining club moss, ground cedar, and ground pine. Although these common names suggest a kinship with mosses, club moss is a discrete order in the family tree of plants. With their desiccation-resistant, needlelike or waxy foliage, club mosses are common ground-cover members of the northern woods, especially, it seems, where the concentrations of hardwoods are high.

At 1.8 miles, the trail splits into a short loop. As of this writing, the stream crossing and the south-side trail are easy to miss. Look for the fork where the opposite bank is a *vertical* bedrock outcrop and the trail on your side of the brook ascends steeply through the woods. The right-hand trail (old, bluish blazes) soon crosses the creek. If you choose to follow this route, do so on the ascent of your trip and step carefully. This trail crosses back to the north side on the smooth ledges below the falls.

Tucked away at the end of the trail, the way a special flower in a Chinese garden might be hidden from first view by a well-placed cascade of willow foliage, Howe Brook Falls roll over a ledge and into the pool at its base. These falls are receding very slowly up into the canyon, as abrasive sediments in the stream gradually erode the lip of the falls.

As you skirt South Branch Pond on your return trip, listen for the wild call of the "lonely yodeler," that great northern diver, the loon (see **#79** and **#86**). With legs attached almost at the rear end of its body, the loon can outswim any duck under water, where it hunts for fish. Even fish at depths of 200 feet may fall prey to its diving feats.

Remarks: *This is an excellent 6-mile hike for a rainy or sunny day. The terrain is generally smooth, but rocky and steep in some places. Campsites may be available at South Branch Campground. During summer, make reservations in advance through Reservations Clerk, Baxter State Park, 64 Balsam Dr., Millinocket, Maine 04462; (207) 723–5140.*

111.
Allagash
Wilderness Waterway

Directions: **Piscataquis and Aroostook counties, Maine. Follow directions for #105 onto Golden Rd. out of Milli-nocket; take it northwest about 30 miles (passing by the access road to Baxter State Park). You can begin your trip here at Ripogenus Dam at the foot of Chesuncook Lake, or you can turn north on Telos Rd. After about 20 miles, pay your camping fees and get permits at the North Maine Woods gate, and proceed to the put-in at Telos Landing. Alternatively, you can approach from the southwest; from Greenville take the road along the east shore of Moose-head Lake north 20 miles to Kokadjo, where a good log-**

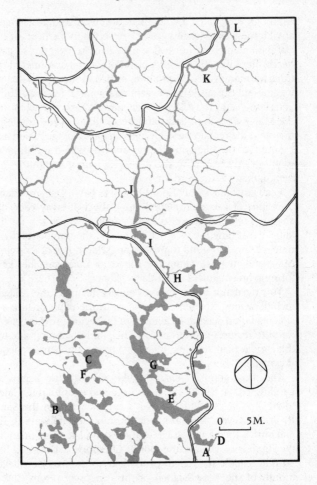

ging road takes over. Follow this 15 miles north to the junction with Golden Rd. at the foot of Caribou Lake. Bear right to reach Ripogenus Dam and take the next left onto Telos Rd. For Caucomgomoc Landing, follow Golden Rd. west from Caribou Lake, then turn right (after crossing Ragmuff Stream) and drive north 23 miles to the Caucomgomoc gate.

Ownership: Maine Bureau of Parks and Recreation.

Although designated a wilderness waterway and providing as near a wilderness experience as can be expected in the heart of commercial timberlands, the north-flowing Allagash River and its associated headwater lakes have been a blend of natural and man-altered features for many years. The route is as rich in sites associated with the logging industry as it is in exceptional natural features. The regulations imposed by the Allagash Wilderness Waterway established within the Maine Bureau of Parks and Recreation in 1966 are designed to maintain the remaining wilderness character of the region as well as ensure that the huge number of canoeists who travel the waterway each season accomplish the trip safely with a minimum of permanent damage to the corridor.

Peak season, roughly from May 20 to Labor Day, invariably finds hundreds of canoes stretched along the waterway each day, and anyone preferring more solitude should plan the trip for the early fall. At that time the weather is fine and the number of insect pests reduced. Bear in mind that lakes are seldom free of ice before early May, and new ice along the fringes of quiet stretches can begin forming on a regular basis in late October.

You need not be an expert canoeist to travel the Allagash, but include a few experienced canoeists in the party or hire a professional guide. Topographical maps of the region provide better insight into the region's features and are helpful in planning side trips, but the simple map supplied by the waterway rangers is adequate for the average visitor.

The most popular version of the Allagash trip begins at Telos Landing (**A**) at the foot of Telos Lake and ends 98 miles later at the town of Allagash and the river's confluence with the Saint John River. However, there are variations and several ways to lengthen and enrich the basic passage. A more complete route might begin at the Ripogenus Dam at the foot of Chesuncook Lake and include a 20-mile paddle the length of the lake to the historic village at the mouth of the West Branch of the Penobscot. From Chesuncook Village proceed up Umbazooksus Stream to the foot of the lake by the same name, and cross the tip of the lake to Mud Pond Carry, marked by a grove of tall white pine. Canoes and gear must be portaged the 1¾-mile length of the carry trail to Mud Pond, a shallow lake nearly filled with silt and dead and decaying vegetation. Cross the lake to the outlet at Mud Pond Stream, a narrow, twisting stream that years ago was cleared of its boulders to allow passage into Chamberlain Lake, where you join the more popular trip.

A second variation begins at the campsite and landing on the northwest corner of Caucomgomoc Lake (**B**) with a 5-mile transit of the lake to Ciss Stream. Ascend this sluggish backwater to Round

Pond, where you pick up the 3-mile carry trail into Allagash Lake (**C**). After absorbing the many sights at this lovely body of water, leave the lake by means of its outlet, Allagash Stream, and follow its 6-mile length to Chamberlain.

For a shorter trip, you can put in at Churchill Dam or at the thoroughfare at Umsaskis, thereby eliminating much of the flatwater lake travel.

The body of this text describes the basic Telos to Allagash route with mention of several side trips. If time permits, a side trip to Telos Dam (**D**) and the man-made canal below is worthwhile. The sluice was cut with minimal effort through a natural gorge in 1842. This canal, coupled with Telos Dam, built the preceding year, and another constructed at the site of the Lock Dam on Chamberlain, successfully diverted water from the Allagash headwaters into the Penobscot watershed. The ambitious project enabled Bangor lumber operators to get their Allagash-cut logs to mills and markets along the Penobscot rather than sending them down the Allagash and Saint John rivers into Canada. The dam was the scene of a confrontation and near-violence when it changed hands and the new owner insisted on charging other drivers for the privilege of sending their logs through.

The drop is steep and the current fast and strong, boiling around boulders and over ledges like any turbulent mountain stream. The work of the early engineers who cut the canal has long since been erased by the vigor of the stream, and Henry David Thoreau, traveling through the area in 1857, remarked that the stream had a natural look about it even then. "Telos Cut" can provide a thrilling 1-mile canoe ride down to Webster Lake for experts and experienced paddlers. There is also a portage trail along the right bank as an alternate route to Webster Lake. The dam is operated by the Bangor Hydroelectric Co., and the pitch of the water in the cut is determined largely by the company's generating needs.

Proceeding up Telos Lake from the landing, the traveler will notice a series of ledges topped with groves of red pine (see **#108**) on the right-hand or eastern shore. The tree is not a predominant species in the region, although it occurs sporadically. Such patches often suggest the site of an earlier forest fire, especially when the tree is found in conjunction with the short-needled jack pine. Both species have fire-resistant cones, and in a natural state the cones of the jack pine open only after the intense heat of a forest fire.

Round Pond and a short thoroughfare connect Telos with 12-mile-long Chamberlain Lake. The landing and bridge at the thoroughfare provide an alternate starting point for waterway trips. Chamberlain is the largest of the major glacial lakes within the system which together provide an immense reservoir for the river below. This reserve is regulated at Churchill Dam to ensure adequate water for canoeing the upper reaches of the river throughout the summer. Farther downstream as the river broadens, the flow is more influenced by seasonal rainfall reaching the river through its numerous tributaries.

The most direct route through the lakes is along the eastern shore of Chamberlain to Lock Dam, then through the canal below the dam into Eagle Lake. There are no campsites along this shore, but the route affords an opportunity to visit the site of the former Chamberlain Farm (**E**), a vigorous settlement during the last century established in 1846 to provision the logging industry. A single maintained building at the farm is used as a snowmobile lodge. The other buildings have fallen into disrepair, been burned, or sunk into their foundations. The boiler and associated machinery of a steamboat that once plied the lake are visible in the water at the landing, and on shore, hidden among encroaching alder and poplar, are the deteriorating frame structures of other steamboats that once served this outpost and boomed logs, along the lake.

Chamberlain, like the other headwater lakes, can become extremely rough when the wind comes up along its length. It is wise to allow a layover day in case this occurs. The strongest winds of the day generally come up late in the morning and last through late afternoon, and can be partially avoided by some early morning and early evening paddling, using the windy part of the day to swim and relax. The Lock Dam and the passage to Eagle is located 3 miles up the lake from the farm.

The route up the western shore of Chamberlain offers at its end a fine side excursion into Allagash Lake by way of Allagash Stream. There are several fine campsites along this shore, and the stream enters the lake at the extreme northwest corner. Passing through this marshy inlet section of the lake, the canoeist stands a good chance of spotting a moose. Remains of an old railroad trestle extend from either shore just before the mouth of the stream. The bridge was part of the 13-mile Eagle–Umbazooksus Railroad built in 1925–1926 to haul pulpwood into West Branch waters. Two immense oil-burning locomotives were employed for a decade, making the run first to Umbazooksus and later to Chesuncook.

The 6-mile ascent of Allagash Stream is difficult but well worth the effort. Except for the first mile or so, paddling up the stream is impossible. If the pitch of water is not too great, a setting pole may be used. This is a 10- to 13- foot pole, useful in shallow rapids and for upstream work. Although once carried by nearly everyone on the river, the poles are less prevalent today. If the current is too strong for this method, the canoes must be lined or pulled up long stretches of small rapids. Likewise, in low-water conditions it may be necessary to get out of the canoes to lift them over exposed ledges running the full width of the stream. A layover camp may be pitched at Little Round Pond above Little Allagash Falls halfway up the stream.

The lake itself provides the deepest solitude of the trip. It was carved deep by glacial action and teams with both brook trout and lake trout, the latter called togue in Maine. During the fall spawning runs the Department of Inland Fisheries and Game nets lake trout in the tributary streams to gather milt and eggs for propagation of the fish at hatcheries. Accordingly the lake enjoys special protection beyond the general regulations governing the use of the waterway. Outboard motors are strictly prohibited (elsewhere on the waterway they are restricted to 10 HP and under), snowmobiles are not allowed, and special limits are imposed on ice fishermen. Allagash Mountain (**F**) (1,500 feet) rises above the western shore, and the hike to the fire tower at the summit is rewarded with exceptional views of the headwater lakes, as well as of Mount Katahdin to the south. The well-known ice caves are located along the same shore, north of the tower trail. The buildup of ice over the winter lasts well into the summer, so that these small caves are protected. The ledges and caves are located in the woods behind Ice Cave Campsite.

An occasional visitor to campsites along the waterway is the marten, which has made a strong comeback in the region in recent years following a long period of serious decline. The marten resembles the mink, but a close look through the binoculars reveals the marten's generally lighter coat with an even lighter underbody. The large ears and facial features of this weasel give it an almost foxlike expression. The marten is also longer than the mink, averaging 2 feet including the tail. It spends a good portion of the summer high in the branches of coniferous trees, where it preys on red squirrels. Martens also eat ground-dwelling rodents and even hares, and consume quantities of raspberries in season.

Martens became so depleted in Maine during the first quarter of this century that they enjoyed full protection of the law from 1935 to 1971. Caucomgomoc was one of the few isolated areas that supported a number of the animals during the worst of the decline. The marten's revival, first documented in the 1960s, has been complete and even dramatic north of the Appalachian Trail.

Like other members of the weasel family, the female marten undergoes a curious biological function in its reproductive cycle known as delayed implantation. Eggs fertilized during the July and August mating season divide only partially, then go into a hormone-induced dormancy for up to 6 months before real embryonic and fetal development begins. This results in an extremely long gestation period for such a small creature. The young are born in March or April.

The descent of the stream back to Chamberlain Lake is easy compared to the trip up. Again, a setting pole can be used to good advantage. Upon reaching the lake, paddle along the east shore of Chamberlain to Lock Dam. The dam was built in 1841 as a means of lifting logs with a lock from Eagle up into Chamberlain for the East Branch drive. Carry around the right side of the dam and put in at the small stream to the left of the campsite. Water is released by the park ranger at the dam, enabling a party to negotiate the short section of the former lock to Eagle's Martin Cove. Two miles up the lake lies Pillsbury Island (**G**), boasting a campsite once used by Thoreau and his Penobscot Indian guide, Joe Polis. The island represents the Concord author-naturalist's deepest penetration into the Allagash region; his three trips into the Maine wilds concentrated mostly on the Penobscot watershed.

Two massive locomotives used in the Eagle-Umbazooksus Railroad as well as the remains of an ingenious tramway may be found another 2 miles up the lake on the western shore. The landing is marked by a white post a few hundred yards below an old pier. For years the locomotives were sheltered by a large shed that has since burned, but the engines appear to be in surprisingly good condition. The tramway built in 1901–1903 used over a mile of cable and an innovative system of clamps and wheels to move millions of feet of logs from Eagle into Chamberlain over a period of 6 years.

Follow another thoroughfare at the north end of Eagle into yet another Round Pond. A bridge crosses the waterway at the north end of this small lake, and a second thoroughfare leads into 4-mile-long Churchill Lake and eventually to Churchill Dam (**H**) at the end of Heron Lake (1 mile long). A logging community once occupied the site and several buildings remain along with a ranger station on the right-hand bank. Water is released at the dam to maintain suitable levels for running 4-mile Chase Rapids below. Here, in the toughest stretch of the entire trip, you will get your first taste of fast water. The ranger at the dam will tote gear around the pitch in his truck for a reasonable fee, and will portage the canoes as well should a party decide to avoid the whitewater. Most canoeists elect to run the rapids empty, since the canoes are more maneuverable without heavy loads, and the risk of losing gear in the event of an upset is eliminated. The type of run to expect depends largely upon water conditions. Large volumes released from the dam will result in rapids that are fast and powerful but which require little maneuvering. Slowing the canoes' progress by backpaddling in the standing waves helps prevent water from sloshing aboard. In lower conditions more precise control is required to avoid the greater number of exposed rocks and ledges. Whatever the conditions, expect the more challenging paddling in the lower half of the rapids. An old carry trail on the right bank is still in evidence. A bridge crosses the river at the rapids' end, and most travelers take a breather here before repacking the gear left at the spot by the ranger.

The 3-mile easy paddle to the meadows above Umsaskis Lake consisting of quickwater and gentle rapids provides a further chance to relax after the exertion of Chase Rapids. The bottomland preceding Umsaskis Lake (**I**) is an interesting combination of marsh and meadow. The river braids around a number of low islands providing various possible routes, and the mountains beyond Umsaskis Lake stand out strikingly above the trees lining the bank. Keep a sharp lookout here for gaggles of Canada geese. The birds were introduced into the area in 1965, and the original stocking was supplemented until 1974, by which time the geese had established a resident breeding population. The meadows provide a good combination of submerged and emergent vegetation on which the birds like to graze. Those originally introduced into the Umsaskis region were nonmigratory "nuisance" geese from states farther south. They had become used to living in the proximity of man, had forsaken their natural migratory patterns, and were often considered pests around farms and golf courses. In their new habitat they have been forced to fend for themselves and to migrate according to the seasons like other wild geese.

Umsaskis is a rock-rimmed lake whose shoreline harbors a variety of deciduous and coniferous species including stands of red pine. The waterway headquarters building on the west shore burned to the ground in the fall of 1982. It had originally been built as a lodge for paper company officials and guests, and was purchased by the state when the waterway was established. The plush structure was manned by a ranger during the canoeing season, and was used for certain waterway functions. Water from an excellent spring on a nearby slope is piped to the site, providing cold, fresh drinking water for travelers. There is a ranger station on the left of the passage between Umsaskis and Long lakes. The American Realty Rd., a major logging artery, crosses the river nearby, a reminder that the corridor provides only the illusion of wilderness in a region of intensive and even excessive timber harvesting. The growl of skidders, logging trucks, and tree harvesters is constantly audible along many stretches. The corridor itself is composed of two overlapping zones. The inner zone extending 500 feet back from the high-water mark is owned by the state, and all timber harvesting and construction within the zone is strictly prohibited. The outer zone of 1 mile is a joint-management area where a great deal of commercial tree harvesting takes place on the private lands in accordance with plans approved by the state. Although this seems like minimal protection for the river, it is much more of a buffer than is found elsewhere in the northern part of the state, where extensive clear-cutting is often noticeable behind a thin screen of trees left standing on the banks.

The waterway maintains 66 fire-safe campsites throughout the length of the corridor, complete with fireplaces and grates. Outhouses discreetly set well back from the more popular sites help eliminate the problems associated with unburied human waste. The campsites are well maintained by the rangers, who do a commendable job preserving a sense of wilderness for up to 15,000 canoeists annually.

Camping fees are collected by the rangers, and registration is required at the party's first opportunity. This is usually taken care of at the North Maine Woods gates upon entering the commercial woodland owners' road system. This agency represents the major landowners in the region, providing access into the region for recreationalists who will interfere little with the owners' primary interest—timber harvesting.

Follow Long Lake (**J**) to the narrow neck at the north end, and enter Harvey Pond. The remains of Long Lake Dam stand at the northern tip of Harvey, 8 miles north of Umsaskis Lake. The route through these smaller lakes is enhanced by the proximity of Grey Brook Mountain and a shoreline attractive to both moose (see **#106**) and white-tailed deer (see **#49**). Chemquasabamticook Stream winds around the mountain after leaving Clayton Lake, and enters Long Lake on the western shore just before the thoroughfare into Harvey. The stream can be ascended without great difficulty for a distance of about 3 miles, offering another side trip. The rapids at Long Lake Dam can usually be run through one of the two right-hand channels, but debris from the old structure, including long protruding spikes, may make the short portage on the right a safer choice in certain conditions.

The river continues at a pleasant clip below the dam all the way to Round Pond, the canoeist passing through a combination of flat quickwater and gentle rapids. Common mergansers as well as Canada geese frequent this stretch. The trees lining the bank are again a mix—predominantly fir, varieties of spruce, poplar, and birch with an occasional white pine towering above the rest. Up to three separate harvestings of the region's timber have taken their toll on the quality of the trees now growing in the region. Gone forever are the massive white pines reaching 170 feet into the sky, 6 feet across at the butt (see **#12**, **#28**, and **#71**). Ironically some of the largest logs proved too heavy and cumbersome to float downstream once spring came, and the tree and the loggers' efforts were wasted as the huge trunk rotted into the forest floor.

Round Pond is the last opening in the river, its approach marked by two large islands and an extensive marsh area just below another logging bridge. Take any of the three resulting channels. An exploration of these lowlands should afford glimpses of muskrat (see **#70**), mink, and moose, and a profusion of birdlife predominated by the red-winged blackbird and common shorebirds. At Round Pond the river completes a 4-mile eastward leg, so resume a northerly course the length of the pond to locate the outlet at Turk Island.

When darkness descends upon the waterway it is not unusual to hear the howls of the eastern coyote. There are wide variations in the pitch, tone, and frequency of the howls, and certain refrains can be somewhat unsettling to anyone not familiar with this canine's dextrous vocal cords. The coyote is a relative newcomer to the state, and the Allagash corridor is one of the regions where the first established populations of the animal were recognized. Reports of half-wolf, half-dog animals date back to the 1930s, but it was not until the 1960s that the coyote populations really took hold and began appearing throughout the state.

Mature eastern coyotes weigh an average of 30 to 35 pounds, the males slightly larger than the females, making them larger than their western counterparts. They live and hunt mainly as a family group, adult pairs establishing set boundaries. Dispersal of the pups occurs as early as October and as late as the following April, and older pups often join the parents in their search for food. Juveniles will wander great distances, which may account for the rapidly increasing range of the animal. The increased incidence of howling in late summer and early autumn is often attributed to wandering youngsters making contact with the family group.

The coyote is not selective about diet and can fairly be termed opportunistic. Snowshoe hares are the most important species in the diet, with white-tailed deer running a close second. It is now generally accepted that coyotes can and will make their own kills upon deer when the opportunity presents itself, but as yet no studies have been completed with conclusive information on the overall effect of this predation on a healthy deer herd. Blueberries and raspberries are important to the coyote's diet in late summer.

Coyotes are not frequently sighted by canoeists, but their presence is readily suggested by tracks as well as by their nighttime serenades. A traveler along the waterway in the winter would stand a much better chance of viewing the grayish-brown animals as they traveled the wind-packed snow along the surface of the river.

Below Round Pond there are about 2 miles of brisk current before it is checked by the 2-mile-long Musquacook Deadwater. An old tornado path crossing the river just above the deadwater offers a chance to observe the tree-succession pattern in the region. The scar is visible as a band of hardwoods, principally poplar and birch, amidst a sea of dark green fir and spruce.

Below the deadwater a series of easy rapids makes for brisk canoeing the remaining 8 miles to Michaud Farm. Although now a ranger station, accessible by car, the site once boasted a farming settlement established by Michael Michaud shortly after the Civil War. A mile downstream, abreast of a series of sizable islands, are the sites of two additional former farms—Finley Bogan on the left bank and the Moores Farm on the right. Three private cabins on the high bank above the river mark the Moores Farm, all destined to be destroyed by the state when the lifetime easement granted to the former owners expires.

Be alert for the carry trail around Allagash Falls (**K**) a bit over a mile downstream. The trail is well marked, and the roar of the falls unmistakable. The trail, which is on the right-hand bank, is obviously well used, and a pair of campsites along it will generally be filled to capacity during the peak season. Here the river plunges 40 feet, and for many this is the scenic highlight of the trip. Good photographs of the main falls may be taken from several points along the carry trail. The smaller branch of the falls is best viewed by crossing the pool below and climbing the ledges directly facing the outcrop that divides the flow into two branches.

Eight miles of quickwater and rapids—all relatively easy—bring the canoeist to the official end of the waterway at Twin Brook Rapids (**L**). Use caution when running the latter, which may be rough although only half a mile long. This spot 6 miles above the confluence of the Saint John was chosen as the end of the waterway because water from the proposed Dickey-Lincoln Hydro-electric Project (now de-authorized) would have flooded back to this spot.

Nearly continuous gentle rapids aid the paddler the final 6 miles to Allagash Village, where there are a number of convenient take-out spots. Professional outfitters are available to shuttle parties back to their cars at Telos. To ensure prompt service, arrangements should be made in advance. Many canoeists prefer to drive directly to Allagash Village before starting the trip, hiring an outfitter to bring them to the starting point. Lengthy shuttling in the woods is thus eliminated at the trip's end, and the weary traveler can simply load up his car and head home.

Remarks: *The 98-mile canoe trip from Telos Landing to Allagash Village takes about 6 days to complete at a leisurely pace. Plan a layover day for wind on the lakes, heavy rain, or just for relaxing and exploring. Also, 2 or 3 additional days should be set aside if you wish to ascend the Allagash Stream into Allagash Lake. The trip beginning at the foot of Chesuncook Lake requires 3 days beyond the time allotted for the Telos–Allagash route.*

Permits and fees for waterway camping and for use of the private roads are required and may be taken care of at the North Maine Woods gates at Telos or Caucomgomoc. Separate permits for open fires are not required so long as you use the numerous official fire-safe campsites. There is plenty of standing dead spruce and fir throughout the region to provide ample firewood; living trees should never be taken for this purpose. The paper company roads providing access into the region are kept in good condition but can be dusty and rough, and sections can be flooded in periods of heavy rain. Logging vehicles naturally have the right of way and should never be challenged.

Gasoline and provisions are not available along these private roads or along the Allagash corridor, and the canoeing party should come fully prepared to be self-sufficient the duration of the trip. An adequate map and a list of the special regulations enforced along the waterway are essential in planning a trip and may be obtained by writing the Bureau of Parks and Recreation, Maine Department of Conservation, State House Station 19, Augusta, Maine 04333. Animals do not present a problem along the waterway as long as food is properly protected and kept away from tents. Biting insects, including black flies, midges, mosquitoes, and deer and moose flies, can be fierce in late spring and summer. Bring a tent with fine bug mesh and a supply of an effective insect repellent. Some people find headnets essential while doing camp chores during the worst of the season in June and early July.

Glossary

acidic: Containing an abundance of hydrogen ions. Very acidic soils are poor in nutrients.

alga: Any of a large group of primitive and mostly aquatic plants, ranging from tiny one-celled to large multicelled organisms.

basalt: A dark, fine-grained igneous rock formed of solidified lava.

basic: Containing any one substance or a combination of substances that combine with acids to form salts. Slightly basic soils are rich in nutrients and are generally very fertile. Highly basic soils are toxic.

bird of prey: One of the carnivorous birds, such as hawks, owls, and eagles.

bog: A wet, soggy area with little or no drainage.

bottomland: Low-lying ground that may be flooded from time to time.

boulder train: A glacial deposit of large boulders, usually scattered in a fan-shaped pattern; an important indicator of glacial movement.

calcite: A mineral made up of calcium, carbon, and oxygen; also known as *calcium carbonate.*

canopy: An umbrella of trees formed by the tallest trees in a stand.

carnivore: A flesh-eating animal.

cirque: A deep, steep-sided hollow formed on mountainsides by glacial erosion.

climax forest: A forest in which the mix of species is relatively stable over time.

competition: Rivalry of plants or animals for the same resources or habitat.

coniferous: Evergreen and cone-bearing.

deciduous: Shedding leaves annually.

dike: A body of igneous rock imbedded in the structure of surrounding rocks when molten material was forced through cracks to the surface.

disjunct: Set apart from the main distribution of the species.

drumlin: An elongated or oval hill composed of glacial till, lying on an axis parallel to the direction of the ice flow.

ecosystem: The interaction of plants, animals, and their environment.

erosion: The process by which the earth's surface is worn away by water, wind, or waves.

esker: A long, narrow ridge of sand, gravel, and boulders deposited by a stream flowing in a tunnel beneath a stagnant, melting glacier.

fault: A crack in the earth's surface where movement has taken place.

glacial drift: Debris deposited by a glacier without being reworked by glacial meltwaters; usually found in jumbled piles in irregular patterns.

glacial erratic: A boulder that has been carried from its point of origin by glacial ice and deposited elsewhere when the ice melted.

glacial scouring: The erosion of rock and soil by moving ice, usually identified by surface polishing and scrape marks.

gneiss: A metamorphic rock with a banded structure due to the separation of dark and light minerals by heat and pressure.

granite: A very common New England rock composed of quartz, feldspar, and other minerals. It is a very durable and coarse igneous rock with the individual mineral grains clearly distinguishable.

habitat: The natural environment of an animal or plant.

herbivore: A plant-eating animal.

humus: Decomposed animal and plant matter that forms the organic portion of soil.

Ice Age: A period from about 10,000 to 2 million years ago during which a large portion of the earth was covered by glaciers; also called the *glacial epoch.*

igneous rock: Rock, such as basalt and granite, that has solidified from a molten state.

impoundment: An artificial pond or lake.

interglacial: Warm periods that occurred between glacial advances when the ice sheets withdrew toward the poles.

kame: A short ridge or hill of stratified glacial drift deposited by meltwaters.

kame terrace: A narrow, level plain of sand and gravel deposited by glacial meltwaters running between a valley wall and a deposit of ice. A kame terrace usually borders a river, stream or lake.

kettle hole: A bowl-shaped depression formed by a mass of glacial ice that has broken off from a melting glacier and become buried in gravel. When the ice melts, a hole is created. Many bogs are in kettle holes.

larva: The immature, wingless stage of certain insects.

litter: The layer of slightly decomposed plant material on the surface of a forest floor.

magma: Molten material within the earth's crust.

mantle rock: The loose rock and soil lying on top of bedrock, usually deposited by melting glaciers.

marsh: Low, wet land covered by grassy vegetation.

meander: A bend in a river.

metamorphic rock: Sedimentary and igneous rock that has been changed in appearance and composition by heat and pressure.

migration: The rhythmic seasonal movement of certain birds and other animals.

moraine: A deposit of glacial debris. A *terminal moraine* is the deposit of glacial material at the point at which a glacier ceased its advance.

old field: A stage in the succession of cleared land to forest characterized by grasses, flowering plants, and shrubs.

omnivore: A flesh- and plant-eating animal.

outwash plain: A sandy or gravelly plain of glacial debris formed by streams from a melting glacier.

peat: Partially decomposed plant material common to wet areas with poor drainage.

peneplain: A land surface either worn down by erosion or built up by deposits or by upward thrusting of the earth's surface.

photosynthesis: The process by which green plants convert water and carbon dioxide into carbohydrates.

pioneer: One of a number of plants that appear early in the process of succession.

Pleistocene epoch: The geological epoch during which the Ice Age occurred.

runoff: Rainwater, melting snow, or groundwater that drains away across the surface of the ground.

schist: A coarse-grained metamorphic rock with a mostly parallel structure of minerals.

secondary growth: The forest that appears after land has been cleared.

sedimentary rock: Layered rocks formed by sediments of different materials building upon each other.

shrub: A woody perennial plant that usually has several stems and is generally smaller than a tree.

species: A group of related plants or animals that interbreed to produce fertile offspring.

sphagnum: A coarse but soft moss found on bog surfaces; also known as *peat moss*.

succession: The process by which the vegetation of an ecosystem changes over time.

swamp: Low, wet forest that is regularly flooded and poorly drained.

talus: A pile of broken rocks and boulders at the bottom of a cliff.

tannin: Any one of a variety of large, complex molecules contained in most woody plants.

tarn: A small mountain pool or lake.

till: Unstratified glacial drift, consisting mostly of clay, sand, and boulders.

understory: The trees found growing beneath the canopy species and above the shrub layer.

waterfowl: Aquatic birds, including geese, ducks, and swans.

Bibliography

AMC Guide to Mount Washington and the Presidential Range. 1982. Boston: Appalachian Mountain Club.

AMC Field Guide to Mountain Flowers of New England. 1977. Boston: Appalachian Mountain Club.

AMC Maine Mountain Guide. 1976. Boston: Appalachian Mountain Club.

AMC Massachusetts and Rhode Island Trail Guide. 1982. 5th ed. Boston: Appalachian Mountain Club.

AMC New England Canoeing Guide. 1971. 3rd ed. Boston: Appalachian Mountain Club.

AMC River Guide. Vol. 1, Maine. 1980 Boston: Appalachian Mountain Club.

AMC Trail Guide to Mount Desert Island and Acadia National Park. 1975. Boston: Appalachian Mountain Club.

AMC White Mountain Guide. 1979. 22nd ed. Boston: Appalachian Mountain Club.

Appalachian Trail Guide to Maine. 1983. 10th ed. Harpers Ferry, W. Va.: Appalachian Trail Conference.

Appalachian Trail Guide to Massachusetts and Connecticut. 1983. 6th ed. Harpers Ferry, W. Va.: Appalachian Trail Conference.

Appalachian Trail Guide to New Hampshire and Vermont. 1983. 4th ed. Harpers Ferry, W. Va.: Appalachian Trail Conference.

Audubon Society Field Guide to Butterflies. 1981. New York: Alfred A. Knopf.

Audubon Society Field Guide to Fishes, Whales, and Dolphins. 1983. New York: Alfred A. Knopf.

Audubon Society Field Guide to North American Birds: Eastern Region. 1977. New York: Alfred A. Knopf.

Audubon Society Field Guide to North American Mammals. 1980. New York: Alfred A. Knopf

Audubon Society Field Guide to North American Rocks and Minerals. 1978. New York: Alfred A. Knopf.

Audubon Society Field Guide to Reptiles and Amphibians. 1979. New York: Alfred A. Knopf.

Audubon Society Field Guide to Seashells. 1981. New York: Alfred A. Knopf.

Baldwin, Henry I. 1980. *Monadnock Guide.* 3rd ed. Concord: Society for the Protection of New Hampshire Forests.

Berrill, Michael and Deborah. 1981. *A Sierra Club Naturalist's Guide: The North Atlantic Coast.* San Francisco: Sierra Club Books.

Brady, John, and Brian White. 1983. *Fifty Hikes in Massachusetts.* Woodstock, Vt.: Backcountry Publications.

Brockman, C. Frank. 1979. *Trees of North America.* New York: Golden Press.

Butcher, Russell D. 1977. *Guide to Acadia National Park.* New York: Reader's Digest Press.

Caldwell, Dabney. 1972. *The Geology of Baxter State Park.* Augusta: Maine Geologic Survey.

Carson, Rachel. 1962. *Silent Spring.* New York: Fawcett Books.

Carson, Rachel. 1965. *A Sense of Wonder.* New York: Harper & Row.

Catlett, Cloe. 1980. *Fifty More Hikes in Maine.* Woodstock, Vt.: Backcountry Publications.

Chamberlain, Barbara B. 1964. *These Fragile Outposts.* Garden City, N.Y.: Natural History Press.

Chapman, Carleton A. 1970. *The Geology of Acadia National Park.* Old Greenwich, Conn.: Chatham Press.

Conklin, Philip. 1981. *Islands in Time.* Camden, Maine: Down East Books.

Detels, Pamela, and Janet Harris. 1977. *Canoeing Trips in Connecticut.* Chester, Conn.: Globe Pequot Press.

Doane, Daniel. 1983. *Fifty Hikes in the White Mountains.* 3rd rev. ed. Woodstock, Vt.: Backcountry Publications.

Doane, Daniel. 1983. *Fifty More Hikes in New Hampshire.* 2nd ed. Woodstock, Vt.: Backcountry Publications.

Dwilley, Marilyn. 1973. *Spring Wildflowers of New England.* Camden, Maine: Down East Publishing Co.

Eppee, Anne Orth. 1983. *The Amphibians of New England.* Camden, Maine: Down East Books.

Federal Writers Project. 1983. *WPA Guide to Massachusetts.* Reprint ed. New York: Pantheon Books.

Gabler, Ray. 1981. *New England White Water River Guide.* Boston: Appalachian Mountain Club.

Gibson, John. 1983. *Fifty Hikes in Maine*. 2nd ed. Woodstock, Vt.: Backcountry Publications.

Godin, Alfred J. 1977. *Wild Mammals of New England*. Baltimore: Johns Hopkins University Press.

Guide Book of the Long Trail. 1977. 21st ed. Montpelier, Vt.: Green Mountain Club.

Hardy, Gerry and Sue. 1978. *Fifty Hikes in Connecticut*. Woodstock, Vt.: Backcountry Publications.

Harlow, William M. 1957. *Trees of the Eastern and Central United States and Canada*. New York: Dover Publications.

Harper and Row's Complete Field Guide to North American Wildlife: Eastern Edition. 1981. New York: Harper & Row.

Hildebrandt, Barry and Susan. 1979. *Coastal Connecticut: Eastern Region*. Old Saybrook, Conn.: Peregrine Press.

Irland, Lloyd C. 1982. *Wildlands and Woodlots: The Story of New England's Forests*. Hanover, N.H.: University of New England Press.

Johnson, Charles W. 1980. *The Nature of Vermont*. Hanover, N.H.,: University of New England Press.

Jorgensen, Neil. 1977. *A Guide to New England's Landscape*. Chester, Conn.: Globe Pequot Press.

Jorgensen, Neil. 1978. *A Sierra Club Naturalist's Guide: Southern New England*. San Francisco: Sierra Club Books.

Kingsbury, John M. 1970. *The Rocky Shore*. Old Greenwich, Conn.: Chatham Press.

Kostecke, Diana M., ed. 1975. *Franconia Notch: An In-Depth Guide*. Concord: Society for the Protection of New Hampshire Forests.

Leopold, Aldo. 1966. *A Sand County Almanac*. New York: Oxford University Press.

Mallett, Sandy. 1978. *A Year with New England's Birds: 25 Field Trips*. Somersworth, N.H.: New Hampshire Publishing Co.

Matthews, L. Harrison. 1978. *The Natural History of the Whale*. New York: Columbia University Press.

Michelin Green Guide to New England. 1982. New Hyde Park, N.Y.: Michelin Guides & Maps.

Miller, Dorcas. 1979. *The Maine Coast: A Nature Lovers Guide*. Charlotte, N.C.: East Woods Press.

Moore, Patrick. 1980. *The Pocket Guide to Astronomy*. New York: Simon & Schuster.

Morrison, Samuel Eliot. 1960. *The Story of Mount Desert Island, Maine*. Boston: Little, Brown & Co.

Murie, Claus J. 1975. *A Field Guide to Animal Tracks*. Boston: Houghton Mifflin Co.

Perry, John and Jane Greverus. 1980. *The Random House Guide to Natural Areas of the Eastern United States*. New York: Random House.

Peterson, Roger Tory. 1980. *A Field Guide to The Birds of Eastern and Central North America.* 4th ed. Boston: Houghton Mifflin Co.

Pierson, Elizabeth and Jan. 1981. *A Birder's Guide to the Coast of Maine.* Camden, Maine: Down East Books.

Preston, Philip, and Jonathan Kannau. 1979. *White Mountains West.* Ashland, N.H.: Waumbek Books.

Proctor, Noble S. 1978. *Twenty-Five Birding Areas in Connecticut.* Chester, Conn.: Globe Pequot Press.

Rand McNally Campground and Trailer Park Guide: Eastern Edition. 1983. New York: Rand McNally & Co.

Randall, Peter E. 1983. *Mount Washington: A Guide and Short History.* Camden, Maine: Down East Books.

Riley, Laura and William. 1979. *Guide to the National Wildlife Refuges.* Garden City, N.Y.: Doubleday & Co., Anchor Press.

Robbins, Braun and Zim. 1966. *Birds of North America.* New York: Western Publishing Co.

Roberts, Mervin F. 1977. *The Tidemarsh Guide.* New York: E. P. Dutton.

Roth, Charles E. 1982. *The Wildlife Observer Guidebook.* Englewood Cliffs, N.J.: Prentice-Hall.

Sandlier, Hugh and Heather. 1983. *Short Walks on Cape Cod and the Vineyard.* Chester, Conn.: Globe Pequot Press.

Steele, Frederick L. 1982. *At Timberline: A Nature Guide to the Mountains of the Northeast.* Boston: Appalachian Mountain Club.

Stokes, Donald W. 1976. *A Guide to Nature in Winter: Northeast and North Central America.* Boston: Little, Brown & Co.

Stokes, Donald W. 1979. *A Guide to the Behavior of Common Birds.* Boston: Little, Brown & Co.

Stokes, Donald W. 1983. *A Guide to Observing Insect Lives.* Boston: Little, Brown & Co.

Strabler, Arthur N. 1966. *A Geologist's View of Cape Cod.* Garden City, N.Y.: Natural History Press.

Thompson, Betty Flanders. 1977. *The Changing Face of New England.* Boston: Houghton Mifflin Co.

Weber, Ken. 1978. *25 Walks in Rhode Island.* Somersworth, N.H.: New Hampshire Publishing Co.

Maps

Delorme's Map and Guide of Baxter State Park and Katahdin. 1982. Freeport, Maine: Delorme Publishing Co.

Illustrated Map of the Maine Coast. 1982. Freeport, Maine: Delorme Publishing Co.

Maine Atlas and Gazetteer. 1982. Freeport, Maine: Delorme Publishing Co.

New Hampshire Atlas and Gazetteer. 1982. Freeport, Maine: Delorme Publishing Co.

Rand McNally Road Atlas: United States/Canada/Mexico. 1982. New York: Rand McNally Co.

Trail Map and Guide to the White Mountain National Forest. 1982. Freeport, Maine: Delorme Publishing Co.

Vermont Atlas and Gazetteer. 1982. Freeport, Maine: Delorme Publishing Co.

Index

Except for bird species, of which every citation is included, the index lists only those plant and animal species that are significantly mentioned or described in detail. *Italic* figures refer to major discussions; **boldface** figures refer to site numbers.

A Note
About the Authors

Stephen Kulik is a writer living in rural Massachusetts who works in the energy and environmental fields.

Pete Salmansohn is a naturalist at the National Audubon Society Camp in Maine, and has taught in Rhode Island, Connecticut, New York, and Oregon.

Matthew Schmidt is a free-lance writer from Massachusetts who has written about travel and history in New England for several regional publications.

Heidi Welch is a naturalist and environmental educator living in Maine who has worked for both the National Park Service and the National Audubon Society in Maine, and at the Yosemite Institute in California.

Notes

Notes